AF605254

Pearson Australia
(a division of Pearson Australia Group Pty Ltd)
707 Collins Street, Melbourne, Victoria 3008
PO Box 23360, Melbourne, Victoria 8012
www.pearson.com.au

First published 2013 by Pearson Australia
2020 2019 2018 2017
10 9 8 7 6 5 4 3 2 1

Publishers: Amanda Marasco and Tanya Smith
Project Manager: Jennifer Boyce
Editor: Liz Waud
Designer: Anne Donald
Typsetter: Nikki M Group Pty Ltd
Copyright & Pictures Editor: Julia Weaver
Mac Operator: Rob Currulli
Cover design: Glen McClay
Illustrator: Nikki M Group Pty Ltd
Printed in Australia by the SOS Print + Media Group

ISBN 978 1 4425 6616 3

Pearson Australia Group Pty Ltd ABN 40 004 245 943

Acknowledgements
We would like to thank the following for permission to reproduce copyright material.
Dreamstime: p. 65.
Every effort has been made to trace and acknowledge copyright. However, if any infringement has occurred, the publishers tender their apologies and invite the copyright holders to contact them.

Contents

How to use this book vi

Chapter 1 Integers and indices

1.1 Integers review 2
1.2 Integer multiplication 4
1.3 Integer division 6
1.4 Combined operations with integers 8
1.5 Multiplying and dividing numbers in index form 10
1.6 Powers of powers, products and quotients 12

Chapter 2 Fractions, decimals and percentages

2.1 Working with fractions and decimals A 14
2.1 Working with fractions and decimals B 16
2.2 Types of decimals 18
2.3 Negative fractions and decimals A 20
2.3 Negative fractions and decimals B 22
2.4 Estimating percentages 24
2.5 Writing fractions and decimals as percentages 26
2.6 Writing percentages as fractions and decimals 28
2.7 Writing one amount as a percentage of another 30
2.8 Finding a percentage of an amount 32
2.9 Increasing or decreasing by a given percentage 34
2.10 Financial applications of percentages A 36
2.10 Financial applications of percentages B 38

Chapter 3 Algebra

3.1 Variables and expressions 40
3.2 Substitution for variables 42
3.3 Using formulas 44
3.4 Simplifying expressions 46
3.5 Multiplying and dividing algebraic terms 48
3.6 Expanding brackets A 50
3.6 Expanding brackets B 52
3.7 Factorising 54

Chapter 4 Ratio and rate

4.1 Writing ratios 56
4.2 Simplifying ratios 58
4.3 Unit ratios and scale factors 60
4.4 Using ratios to find amounts 62
4.5 Scale drawings 64
4.6 Sharing an amount in a given ratio 66
4.7 Rates A 68
4.7 Rates B 70

Chapter 5 Measurement

5.1	Perimeter	72
5.2	Circle relationships	74
5.3	Circumference	76
5.4	Area A	78
5.4	Area B	80
5.5	Area of a circle	82
5.6	Finding the area of composite shapes	84
5.7	Volume and capacity A	86
5.7	Volume and capacity B	88
5.8	Time	90

Chapter 6 Linear graphs

6.1	Interpreting linear graphs	92
6.2	Linear relationships A	94
6.2	Linear relationships B	96
6.3	Finding the rule	98
6.4	Using linear relationships	100

Chapter 7 Linear equations

7.1	The language of equations	102
7.2	Solving linear equations A	104
7.2	Solving linear equations B	106
7.3	Solving more complex equations	108
7.4	Solving equations where the unknown appears on both sides A	110
7.4	Solving equations where the unknown appears on both sides B	112
7.5	Solving problems using equations	114

Chapter 8 Geometry

8.1	Angles review	116
8.2	Shapes review	118
8.3	Congruence and transformation	120
8.4	Congruent triangles	122
8.5	Congruence and quadrilaterals	124

Chapter 9 Statistics and probability

9.1	Population sampling	126
9.2	Using sample measures of centre and spread	128
9.3	Frequency tables and graphs	130
9.4	Statistics from grouped data	132
9.5	Understanding probability	134
9.6	Theoretical probability for single-step experiments	136
9.7	Venn diagrams and two-way tables A	138
9.7	Venn diagrams and two-way tables B	140

Answers 142

Summary of important rules and formulas 160

How to use this book

The *Pearson Mathematics 8 Bridging Workbook* is designed to support less confident students through the Year 8 curriculum using simplified support material and questions.

It revises necessary prerequisite skills taught in Year 7 and below, and also scaffolds skills covered in the *Pearson Mathematics 8 Student Book.*

Double-page sections that correspond to each section in the *Pearson Mathematics 8 Student Book.*

4.1 Writing ratios

Comparing amounts using a ratio

Ari has \$50 and Bill has \$70.

Ari has 5 lots of \$10 and Bill has 7 lots of \$10.

So the ratio of the amounts is 5 : 7.

Simplifying ratios is the same process as simplifying fractions: divide all parts in the ratio by the highest common factor.

$$\div 10 \; \begin{matrix} 50 : 70 \\ 5 : 7 \end{matrix} \; \div 10$$

Comparing parts to a whole

Altogether, Ari and Bill have \$120 (12 lots of \$10).

Ari : total
= 50 : 120
= 5 : 12

Bill : total
= 70 : 120
= 7 : 12

Ratios as fractions and percentages

If Phil had \$15 and Hilary had \$20, then the ratio of their amounts would be 3 : 4.

Phil : Hilary
15 : 20
= 3 : 4

We could say:

Phil has $\frac{3}{4}$ of Hilary's amount

or Phil has 75% of Hilary's amount.

$3:4 = \frac{3}{4} = 75\%$

If Leo had \$12 and Sophie had \$28, the total would be \$40.

We could write a ratio to compare Leo's amount with the total amount.

Leo : total
= 12 : 40
= 3 : 10

Leo has $\frac{3}{10}$ of the total amount

or Leo has 30% of the total amount.

Language scaffolding for low-literacy and EAL/D students.

Word Bank

Equivalent ratios

→ Multiplying or dividing each part of a ratio by the same number produces equivalent ratios; the result is equivalent to the original ratio.

1 Write as ratios in simplest form.

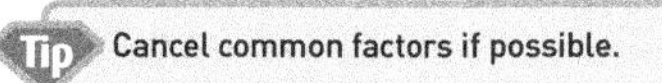

a Number of buttons to number of bows.

[:]

b Number of dots to number of dashes.

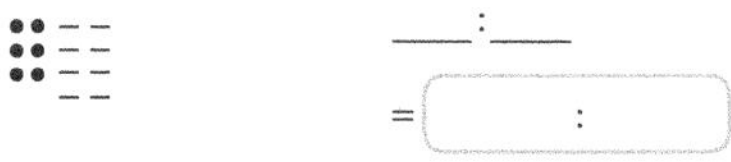

___ : ___

= [:]

c Number of kittens to number of puppies.

___ : ___

= [:]

Scaffolded questions to support weaker or less confident students in revising skills necessary for success in Year 8.

2 Write each of the following ratios in simplest form.

Tip Divide each part in the ratio by the same number.

a 45:40
÷5↓ ↓÷5
= [:]

b 22:330
÷22↓ ↓÷22
= [ ]

c 9:63
÷___↓ ↓÷___
= [ ]

d 84:28:104
↓ ↓ ↓
= [ ]

3 Find the ratios.

a Number of apples to the total number of fruit.

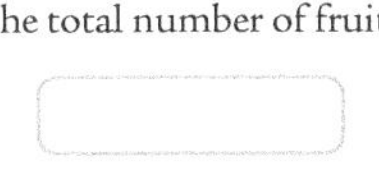

[ ]

b Number of oranges to the total number of fruit.

[ ]

c Number of apples to the number of oranges.

[ ]

d Number of oranges to the number of apples.

4 Out of the total number of birds find the following ratios.

Tip Write the part : whole ratio as a fraction first.

a The percentage of birds that are pigeons.

pigeons : total — Percentage pigeons

= ___:___ — = $\frac{\_\_}{\_\_}$ × 100%

= [ ]

b The percentage of birds that are crows.

crows : total — Percentage crows

= ___:___ — = $\frac{\_\_}{\_\_}$ × 100%

= [ ]

Write-in exercises to bridge students from primary workbooks to textbook usage.

5 Circle the letter next to the correct response.

In a box of coloured pencils 6 are blue, 5 are green and 3 are red.

a The ratio of green to blue is:

A 6:5 B 5:11 C 5:14 D 5:6

b The number of red as a fraction of the number of blue is:

A $\frac{1}{2}$ B $\frac{9}{14}$ C $\frac{3}{14}$ D $\frac{3}{11}$

c The number of blue as a fraction of the total is:

A $\frac{6}{11}$ B $\frac{3}{4}$ C $\frac{3}{14}$ D $\frac{3}{7}$

NAPLAN-ready

Shade the box beneath the correct answer.

The Australian Tic Tac Toe team for the World Games has 1 member of the team from each of Tasmania, Queensland and Western Australia, and 2 members each from New South Wales and Victoria.

The percentage of members that are from New South Wales is closest to:

20%	30%	40%	50%
▭	▭	▭	▭

Tip Write the ratio of the members from New South Wales to the total as a fraction first.

Extra NAPLAN support.

Chapter 4 Ratio and rate 57

1.1 Integers review

Simplifying the signs

- We can write a positive number *without* a sign.

  +7 is just 7

- Adding a negative term is the same as *subtracting* the amount.

  +6 + (-2) = 6 − 2

- Subtracting a negative term is the same as *adding* the amount.

  -5 − (-1) = -5 + 1

Same sign, same direction

- If the **integers** have the *same* sign after simplifying, find the *total* amount in *that direction*. On a number line, the positive direction is to the right and the negative direction is to the left.

Positive direction
3 + 2 = 5

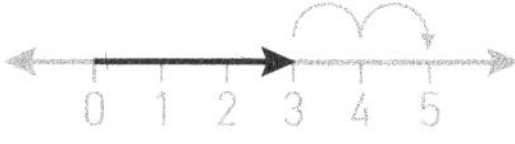

Negative direction
-3 − 2 = -5

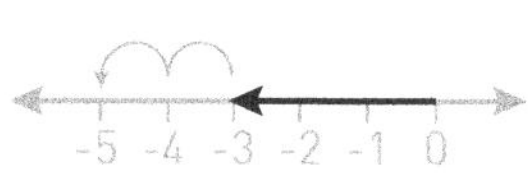

Opposite signs, opposite directions

- If the integers have *different* signs after simplifying, find the *difference* between the amounts.
- The sign in front of the *larger amount* will be the *sign* of the answer.

6 − 2 = 4

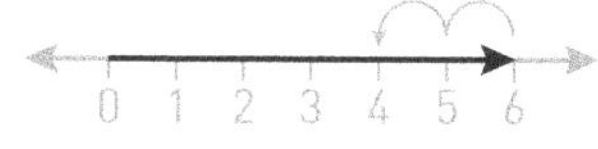

-6 + 2 = -4

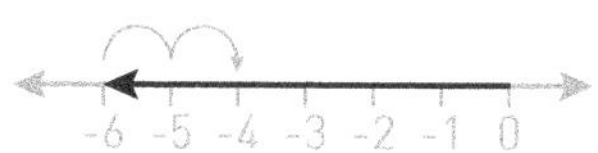

Word Bank

Integer

➜ An integer is a whole number that is either positive (+) or negative (-).

+6 means an amount of 6 to the right of zero.

-6 means an amount of 6 to the left of zero.

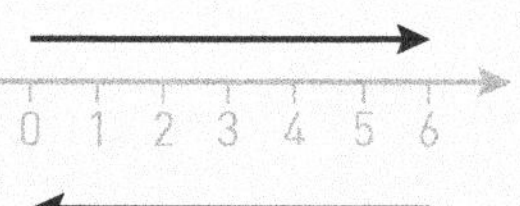

Ascending order

➜ Numbers in ascending order increase from smallest to largest.

As we move to the right on a number line, the numbers become greater in value.

Descending order

➜ Numbers in descending order decrease from largest to smallest.

As we move to the left on a number line, the numbers become smaller in value.

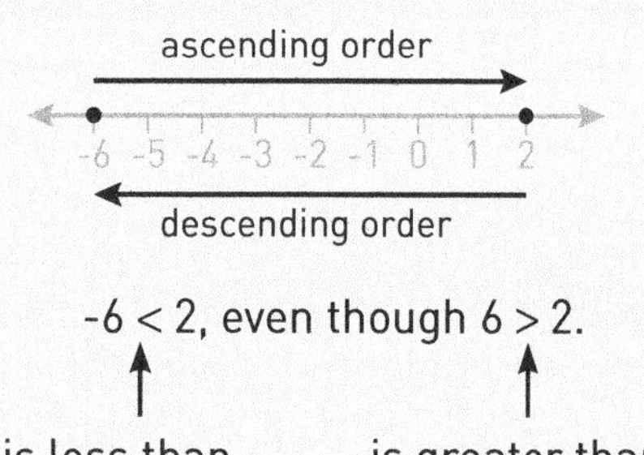

1 For each **integer** addition, remove the brackets and simplify the signs by writing one sign between the two numbers.

a +6 + (+2) simplifies to 6 ________

b -5 + (-3) simplifies to -5 ________

c +4 + (-6) simplifies to ________

2 For each subtraction, simplify the signs.

a +2 − (+4) simplifies to ________

b -2 − (-6) simplifies to ________

c +7 − (-8) simplifies to ________

3 Calculate:

Tip For integers with the same sign, find the total amount in that direction.

a 4 + 3

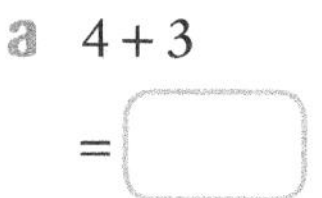

b 1 + 9

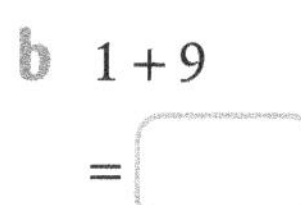

c -4 − 5

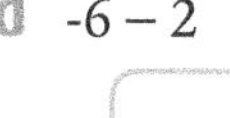

d -6 − 2

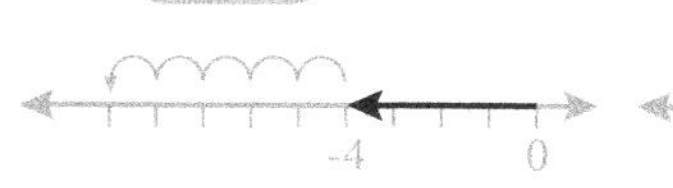

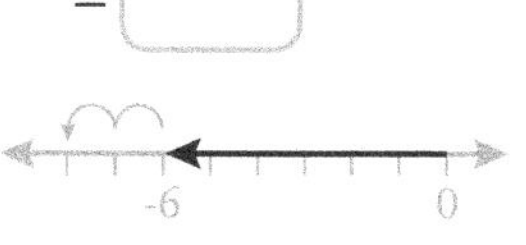

e 8 + 3

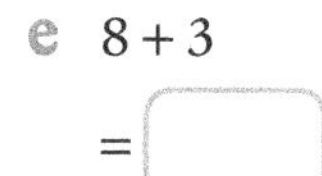

f -8 − 3

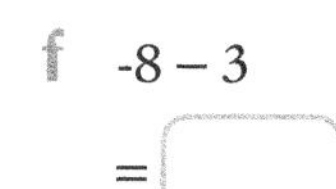

4 Calculate:

Tip For integers with opposite signs, find the difference between the amounts. The sign of the larger amount gives the sign of the answer.

a -2 + 9

= 

b -5 + 3

= ____

c 1 − 4

= 

d 8 − 5

= 

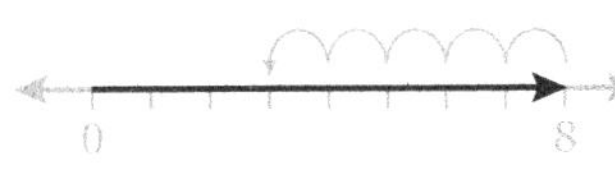

5 Simplify the signs and then calculate the answer.

a +6 + (-3)
= 6 − 3
= ____

b -2 − (+8)
= ________
= ____

c -5 − (-2)
= ________
= ____

d -1 + (+4)
= ________
= ____

6 Circle the letter next to the correct answer.

a +2 − (-6) − (-8) simplifies to:

A 2 − 6 + 8 B 2 + 6 − 8

C 2 − 6 − 8 D 2 + 6 + 8

b -6 − 3 + 4 is equal to:

A -13 B -5 C 1 D 7

7 Calculate each of the following and then mark the answers with an arrow on the number line below.

a -7 + 5
= ____

b -7 − 5
= ____

c 7 + 5
= ____

d 7 − 5
= ____

-13 -12 -11 -10 -9 -8 -7 -6 -5 -4 -3 -2 -1 0 1 2 3 4 5 6 7 8 9 10 11 12 13

8 Mark the following numbers on the below number line and then write them in **ascending** order.

Tip Ascending means getting larger, from left to right on the number line. < means is less than.

-3, -8, +5, -10

____ < ____ < ____ < ____

9 For each of the following, write in any three whole-number amounts so that the answer is zero.

e.g. 3 + 5 − 8 = 0

a - 12 + ____ + ____ = 0

b ____ − ____ − ____ = 0

c - ____ + ____ − ____ = 0

NAPLAN-ready

Shade the box beneath the correct answer.

An island in the Pacific Ocean rises 5350 m from the ocean floor. The ocean is 4860 m deep in this locality.

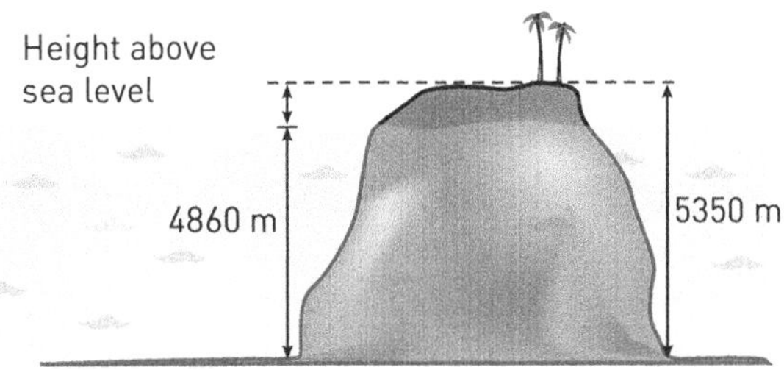

How far above sea level is the highest point on the island?

490 m ☐ 510 m ☐

9510 m ☐ 10 210 m ☐

Tip Decide whether you are finding the total of, or the difference between, the given amounts.

1.2 Integer multiplication

Changing direction

- When an integer has no written sign, we assume it is positive (e.g. $6 = +6$).
- When multiplying a positive integer by a *negative* integer, the *negative* integer changes the sign of the answer to negative.

$2 \times -4 = -2 \times 4 = -8$

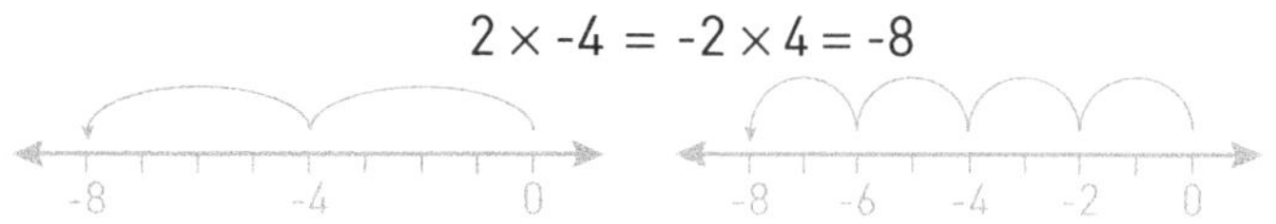

- A *second negative* factor in a product changes the direction *back to positive*.

$-2 \times -4 = +8$ (the opposite direction of -8)

Multiplying two numbers with the same sign will give a positive answer.

Summary for multiplication

$+ \times + = +$	$- \times + = -$
$+ \times - = -$	$- \times - = +$

More than two factors

In any product the *amount* (the size of the number) and *direction* (the sign) can be calculated separately.

Step 1: Multiply in any order.

$3 \times 2 \times 4 = 24$

Step 2: Decide on the sign.

$3 \times -2 \times 4$ $= -24$	$-3 \times 2 \times -4$ $= 24$ (i.e. +24)	$-3 \times -2 \times -4$ $= -24$
A single negative gives a single change of direction, so negative.	Two negatives give two changes of direction, so positive.	Three negatives give three changes of direction, so negative.

Powers

- To raise a negative number to a power, use brackets around the number amount and its sign.

$(-5)^2$ means -5×-5

$(-5)^3$ means $-5 \times -5 \times -5$

-5^2 means $-(5 \times 5)$, which is equal to -25.

Therefore, $(-5)^2$ is not the same as -5^2.

Word Bank

Product

➔ A product has two or more *factors* multiplied together.

factor ⟶ 6×3 ⟵ factor (product)

Power

➔ A power (or index) is the number of times a repeated factor (or base) is multiplied by itself when written in index form.

$-7 \times -7 = (-7)^2$

base ⟶ $(-7)^2$ ⟵ power or index

1 The number line below shows $4 \times -3 = -12$ (i.e. four lots of -3).

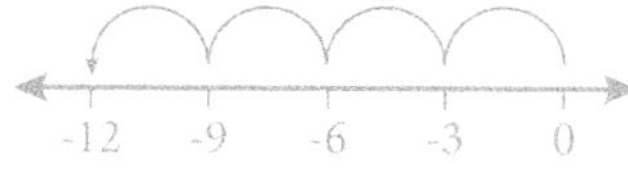

Complete of the following calculations, showing each on a number line.

a $2 \times -7 =$ ☐

b $-2 \times 5 =$ ☐

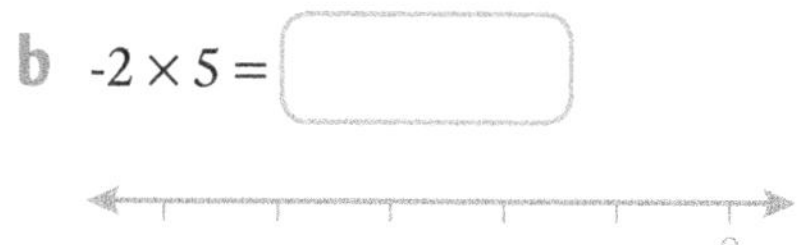

2 Fill in the box to make the equation true.

a $-3 \times \square = -15$

b $4 \times \square = -24$

c $\square \times -6 = 12$

d $-8 \times \square = 32$

e $-12 \times \square = -84$

f $\square \times -7 = 56$

3 Calculate the following products.

Tip Ignore the signs and multiply the amounts. Then look at the signs to find the sign of the product.

a $-8 \times 7 = \square$ b $3 \times -6 = \square$

c $-2 \times -20 = \square$ d $-9 \times -4 = \square$

4 State whether each number sentence is true (**T**) or false (**F**), by circling the correct answer.

Tip Consider the amount and sign of each answer.

a $-6 \times -2 = 4 \times 3$ **T or F**

b $5 \times -6 = -2 \times 15$ **T or F**

c $-9 \times 4 = -12 \times -3$ **T or F**

d $8 \times 3 = -6 \times -4$ **T or F**

5 Circle the multiplication with the negative product.

a A 4×-10 B -6×-2

C -8×-8 D -1×-15

b A $4 \times -1 \times -5$ B $-10 \times 7 \times -2$

C $-3 \times -3 \times -4$ D $-6 \times -5 \times 9$

6 Circle the multiplication with the positive product.

a A -7×2 B 8×-6

C -3×-3 D -4×4

b A $-2 \times -8 \times -7$ B $-4 \times 1 \times 5$

C $3 \times 10 \times -8$ D $6 \times -4 \times -9$

7 Calculate the following products.

Tip Use mental maths strategies to find the product (e.g. $2 \times 5 = 10$).

a $-2 \times 5 \times 4 = \square$ b $3 \times -6 \times -1 = \square$

c $-4 \times 2 \times -5 = \square$ d $-10 \times -3 \times -7 = \square$

8 Calculate the value of each number in index form.

Tip Write the powers as products first.

a $(-6)^2$

$= -6 \times -6$

$= \square$

b $(-3)^2$

$=$ ______ $\times$ ______

$= \square$

c -9^2

$=$ ____________

$= \square$

d -1^2

$=$ ____________

$= \square$

9 Calculate the value of each number in index form.

a $2 \times (-5)^2$

$= 2 \times (-5 \times -5)$

$= 2 \times$ ______

$= \square$

b $-4^2 \times 10$

$= -(4 \times 4) \times 10$

$= -$ ______ $\times 10$

$= \square$

c 3×-10^2

$= 3 \times$ ____________

$= 3 \times$ ____________

$= \square$

d $(-2)^2 \times 3^2$

$=$ ______ $\times$ ______

$=$ ______ $\times$ ______

$= \square$

NAPLAN-ready

Shade the box beneath the correct answer.

Ned multiplied three integers together to get -800. Two of the integers were the same.

The third integer could not have been:

-2	-4	-8	-100
☐	☐	☐	☐

Tip Consider the amounts and signs separately.

1.3 Integer division

Division is connected to multiplication

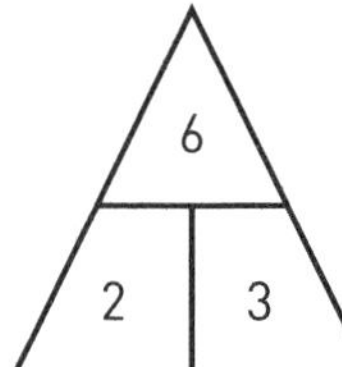

The triangle diagram shows three number sentences.

$2 \times 3 = 6$ $\qquad$ $6 \div 2 = 3$ or $\frac{6}{2} = 3$ $\qquad$ $6 \div 3 = 2$ or $\frac{6}{3} = 2$

Sign rules for multiplication and division

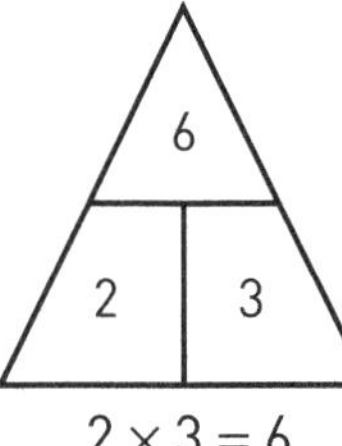

$2 \times 3 = 6$ $\qquad$ $-2 \times 3 = -6$ $\qquad$ $2 \times -3 = -6$ $\qquad$ $-2 \times -3 = 6$

From the same diagrams we can see that:

$\frac{6}{2} = 3$ and $\frac{6}{3} = 2$ $\qquad$ $\frac{-6}{-2} = 3$ and $\frac{-6}{3} = -2$ $\qquad$ $\frac{-6}{2} = -3$ and $\frac{-6}{-3} = 2$ $\qquad$ $\frac{6}{-2} = -3$ and $\frac{6}{-3} = -2$

Summary for division

$+ \div + = +$ $\qquad$ $- \div + = -$ $\qquad$ $+ \div - = -$ $\qquad$ $- \div - = +$

The sign rules for division are the same as for multiplication.

- A single negative in a division gives a negative result (e.g. $6 \div -3 = -2$ or $-6 \div 3 = -2$).
- Two negatives in a division give a positive result (e.g. $-6 \div -3 = 2$).

Word Bank

Quotient

→ A quotient is the result of a division.

$6 \div 2 = 3$

The quotient is 3.

1 Place the numbers -2, -9 and 18 below to make four true number sentences.

___ × ___ = ___ $\qquad$ ___ × ___ = ___

___ ÷ ___ = ___ $\qquad$ ___ ÷ ___ = ___

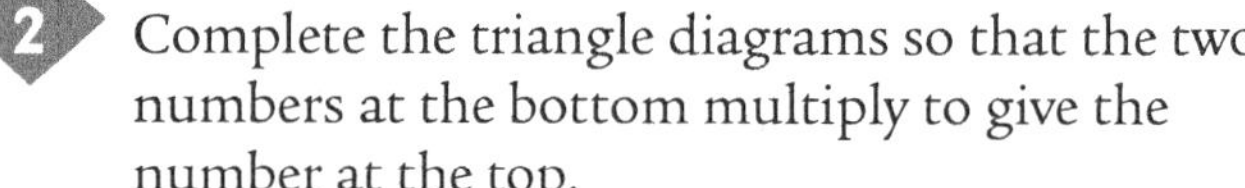

2 Complete the triangle diagrams so that the two numbers at the bottom multiply to give the number at the top.

a

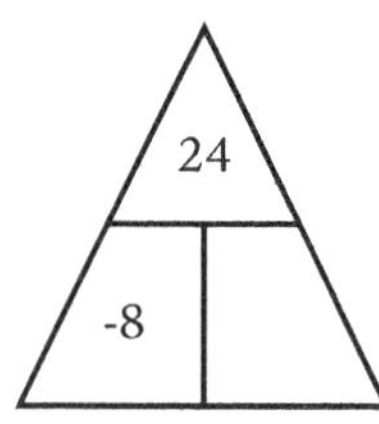

b

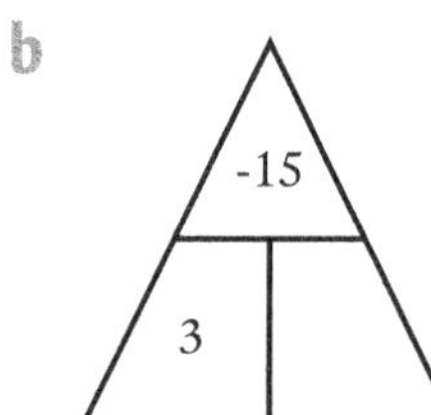

c

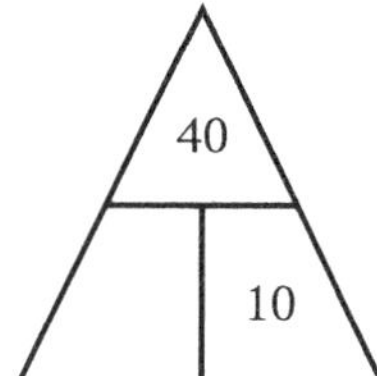

d

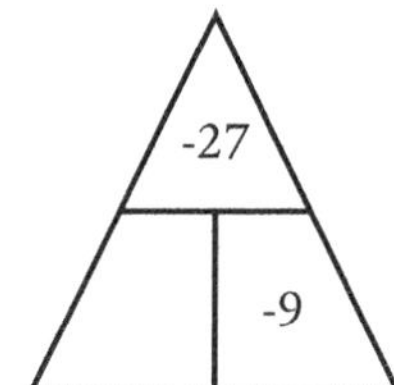

3 State whether each number sentence is true (T) or false (F) by circling the correct answer.

Tip Calculate the amount and sign of each side of the equal sign and then compare the answers.

a $-20 \div -4 = 30 \div -6$ **T or F**

b $42 \div -7 = -60 \div 10$ **T or F**

c $-80 \div 4 = 100 \div -5$ **T or F**

d $25 \div 5 = -30 \div -6$ **T or F**

4 Circle the calculation that gives a different **quotient**.

a A $15 \div -3$ B $-20 \div 4$

C $-50 \div -10$ D $-45 \div 9$

b A $21 \div 3$ B $-42 \div -6$

C $14 \div -2$ D $-35 \div -5$

5 Circle the calculation that gives a negative quotient.

A $-24 \div -6$ B $-18 \div -9$

C $50 \div -2$ D $-3 \div -1$

6 Circle the calculation that gives a positive quotient.

A $-44 \div 11$ B $-56 \div 8$

C $-28 \div -7$ D $63 \div -9$

7 Complete the diagrams so that each factor at the bottom is the same as its partner. Two diagrams have been given because there are two possible answers for each.

Tip Think positive! Think negative!

a

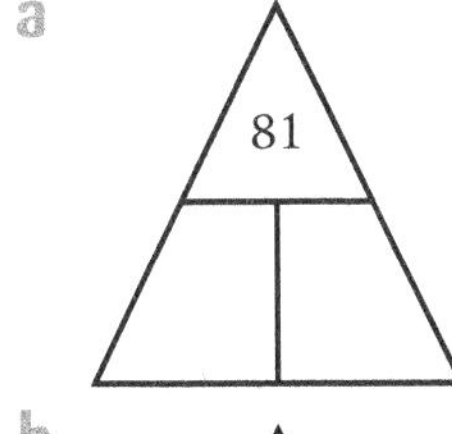

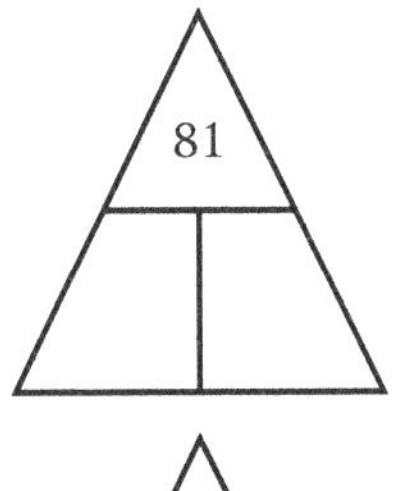

b

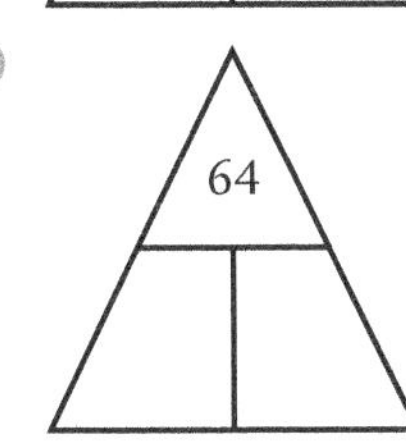

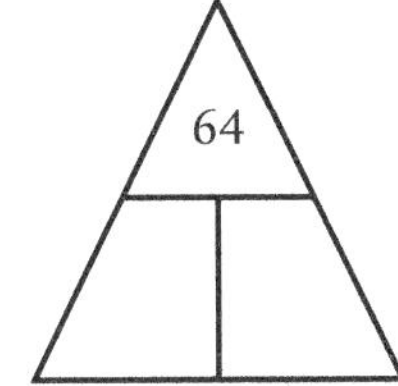

8 Calculate each of the following quotients.

Tip Determine the amount and then the sign.

a $-72 \div -8 =$ ☐ b $55 \div -11 =$ ☐

c $-60 \div 10 =$ ☐ d $88 \div 22 =$ ☐

9 Calculate each of the following quotients.

a $\frac{16}{2} =$ ☐ b $\frac{-48}{8} =$ ☐

c $\frac{-55}{5} =$ ☐ d $\frac{-20}{-5} =$ ☐

10 Suri places a new $360 netbook on lay-by. Each month she pays $30 off her debt.

a What is the lay-by balance after one month?

- ☐

b How long will it take Suri to pay for the netbook?

= __________

= ☐

c If she paid an extra $10 per month, how long would it take for Suri to pay for the netbook?

= __________

= ☐

NAPLAN-ready

Shade the box beneath the correct answer.

Three of these calculations have the answer -6.

The calculation that does not give -6 as the answer is:

$\frac{-3\times-14}{-7}$	$\frac{-36}{2\times3}$
☐	☐
$4 \times -12 \div 8$	$360 \div 10 \times -6$
☐	☐

Tip Calculate the top and bottom of each fraction first, or work from left to right to find each answer.

1.4 Combined operations with integers

The order of operations

The four operations are +, –, × and ÷. When there is more than one operation we use an agreed order so that we all get the same answer.

1 Brackets

- Brackets are used when we want a particular order.

$3 \times (2-7)$ ← (brackets first)
$= 3 \times -5$
$= -15$

2 Powers and square roots

- Calculate powers and square roots before multiplication or division.

-2×4^2
$= -2 \times 16$
$= -32$

$24 \div \sqrt{64}$
$= 24 \div 8$
$= 3$

3 Multiplication and division—working left to right

$-20 \div 2 \times 10$
$= -10 \times 10$
$= -100$

4 Addition and subtraction—working left to right

$5 \times -2 - 30 \div -3$ (× and ÷ first)
$= -10 - -10$ (+ and –)
$= -10 + 10$ (simplifying the signs)
$= 0$

Operations within fractions

A division can be written as a fraction. The line in a fraction acts as a bracket around the top and bottom parts.

$$\frac{2+3}{12-7} = (2+3) \div (12-7)$$

$$\frac{20}{2 \times 5} = 20 \div (2 \times 5)$$

1 Calculate each of the following, using the correct order of operations.

 For × and ÷ only, work left to right.

a $-20 \div 5 \times 2$

= ______

= [ ]

b $36 \div -6 \div -2$

= ______

= [ ]

2 Calculate:

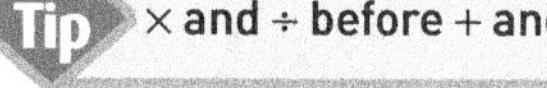

a $3 \times -8 - 6 \times 2$

= ______

= [ ]

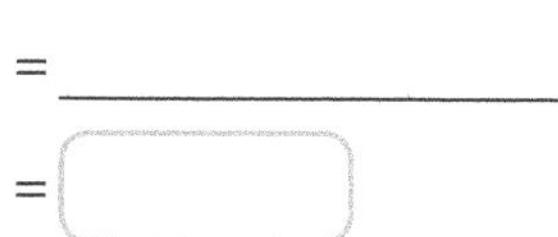

b $1 + 15 \div -3$

= ______

= [ ]

3 State whether each number sentence is true (T) or false (F) by circling the correct answer.

a $5 \times 8^2 = 40^2$ **T or F**

b $-6^2 = -36$ **T or F**

c $(-5)^2 = -25$ **T or F**

4 Underline the calculation/s to be performed first and then evaluate the answer.

e.g. $40 \div (\underline{6 - 16})$
$= 40 \div -10$
$= -4$

a $(-6 + 4) \times (4^2 - 1)$
= ____ × ____
= ☐

b $7 \times -5 - 8 \times -1$
= ____________
= ☐

c $6^2 \div -6 \times 2$
= ____ × 2
= ☐

d $\frac{-18}{-2} \div 3$
= ____________
= ☐

e $(-5)^2 - 4 \times 9$
= ____________
= ☐

f $\sqrt{81} - 6 \times 32$
= ____ − 6 × ____
= ____ − ____
= ☐

5 Show the working out for each of the following, using the correct order of operations.

a $(2 - 3) \times (-3 + 7)$
= ☐ × ☐
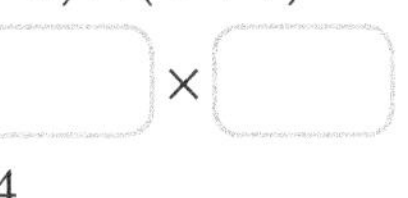
$= -4$

b $\frac{20-2}{-1+10}$
$= \frac{☐}{☐}$
$= 2$

c $-6^2 + (-7)^2 - \sqrt{25}$
= ☐ + ☐ − ☐
$= 8$

6 Calculate:

a $2^2 - 3 \times 6 + 4 \times -5$
= ____________
= ____________
= ☐

b $-2 \times 5 \times 3 - 4^2$
= ____________
= ☐

c $-20 \div 2 \times 5 + 9 \div 3 \div -3$
= ____________
= ____________
= ☐

7 Three numbers are written on cards as shown below.

2	4	12

Place the cards in the correct positions to make the answers correct.

a ☐ − ☐ ÷ ☐ = -2

b -5 × ☐ + ☐ × ☐ = 4

c -☐ × (☐ − ☐) = 24

NAPLAN-ready

Shade the box beneath the correct answer.

One expression below has the same value as $-8 + \frac{10}{-2\times5}$.

The expression is:

$-8 - 10 \div 2 \times 5$ ☐	$-8 + 10 \div (-2 \times 5)$ ☐
$-8 + (10 \div -2) \times 5$ ☐	$\frac{10}{-2\times5} - (-8)$ ☐

Tip The line in the fraction acts as a bracket around the product.

1.5 Multiplying and dividing numbers in index form

Index form

The **index,** or **power** in a number in index form tells you *how many* factors are multiplied together.

base → $3^4 = 3 \times 3 \times 3 \times 3$ (4: index or power)

index form   expanded form

Multiplying index numbers with the same base

$6^3 \times 6^4 = \underbrace{6 \times 6 \times 6}\times\underbrace{6 \times 6 \times 6 \times 6}$
$= 6^7$

We are multiplying the total number of factors of the base (six), so *add* the **indices**.

$6^3 \times 6^4 = 6^{3+4}$ ← add
$= 6^7$

Dividing index numbers with the same base

$\frac{8^6}{8^2} = \frac{\cancel{8} \times \cancel{8} \times 8 \times 8 \times 8 \times 8}{\cancel{8} \times \cancel{8}}$
$= 8^4$

We are finding how many factors are left after cancelling, so *subtract* the indices.

$8^6 \div 8^2 = 8^{6-2}$ ← subtract

Index numbers with a negative base

$\frac{(-3)^9}{(-3)^5} = (-3)^4 = 3^4$ ← even ← positive

A negative number raised to an even power gives a positive answer.

$(-3)^4 \times (-3)^3 = (-3)^7 = -3^7$ ← odd ← negative

A negative number raised to an odd power gives a negative answer.

Word Bank

Index form
→ A number written as a base and an index (power) is in index form (e.g. 5^4).

Expanded form
→ A number written as repeated multiplications is in expanded form (e.g. $5 \times 5 \times 5 \times 5$).

Base
→ When written in index form, the base is the number that is multiplied repeatedly (e.g. in 5^4, the base is 5).

Index (power)
→ When written in index form, the index or power tells you how many times the base is multiplied (e.g. in 5^4, the index is 4).

Indices
→ The plural of index is indices.

1 Write in expanded form.

a 10^3

$= \_\_\_ \times \_\_\_ \times \_\_\_$

b $4^5 \times 3^2$

$= \_\_\_ \times \_\_\_ \times \_\_\_ \times \_\_\_ \times \_\_\_ \times \_\_\_ \times \_\_\_$

2 $6 \times 6 \times 5 \times 5 \times 5 \times 5$ written in index form is:

A $6^2 \times 5^4$ B 30^6
C $(6 \times 5)^8$ D 6×5^6

3 The expressions have been simplified below. Write each expression in expanded form.

a $11^3 \times 11^4$

$= \_\_\_ \times \_\_\_ \times \_\_\_ \times \_\_\_ \times \_\_\_ \times \_\_\_ \times \_\_\_$

$= 11^7$

b $\frac{5^2 \times 5^5}{5^4}$

$= \frac{\_\_\_ \times \_\_\_ \times \_\_\_ \times \_\_\_ \times \_\_\_ \times \_\_\_ \times \_\_\_}{\_\_\_ \times \_\_\_ \times \_\_\_ \times \_\_\_}$

$= 5^3$

4 Simplify each of the following.

a $2^4 \times 2^2 = 2^{\square}$

b $3^6 \div 3^4 = 3^{\square}$

c $\dfrac{7^6 \times 7^2}{7^5} = 7^{\square}$

5 State whether each number sentence is true (T) or false (F) by circling the correct answer.

a $(-6)^4 = -6^4$ **T or F**

b $(-5)^3 = -5^3$ **T or F**

c $(-4)^2 = 4^2$ **T or F**

6 Simplify and then evaluate.

a $(-2)^2 \times (-2)^2$

$= \square^{\square}$

= ______________

$= \square$

b $(-3)^7 \div (-3)^4$

$= \square^{\square}$

= ______________

$= \square$

7 Simplify each of the following.

Tip You can only add the indices for powers that have the same base.

a $3^2 \times 5^3 \times 3^3 = 3^{\square} \times 5^{\square}$

b $10^2 \times 8^3 \times 10 \times 8 = 10^{\square} \times 8^{\square}$

8 Simplify each of the following.

Tip Write divisions in fraction form first.

a $5^6 \times 4^3 \div (5^2 \times 4)$

$= \dfrac{\_\_\_ \times \_\_\_}{\_\_\_ \times \_\_\_}$

$= 5^{\square} \times 4^{\square}$

b $7^5 \times 3^3 \div (7^3 \times 3^2)$

$= \dfrac{\_\_\_ \times \_\_\_}{\_\_\_ \times \_\_\_}$

$= 7^{\square} \times 3$

9 Simplify and then evaluate.

Tip Use the correct order of operations.

a $\dfrac{7^4 \times 7^3}{7^5}$

$= \dfrac{\square^{\square}}{\square^{\square}}$

$= 7^{\square}$

$= \square$

b $4^8 \div (4^2 \times 4^3)$

$= \square \div \square$

$= 4^{\square}$

$= \square$

c $5^2 \times 5^2 \div 5$

$= \square \div \square$

$= 5^{\square}$

$= \square$

NAPLAN-ready

Shade the box beneath the correct answer.

A single bacterium in a ham sandwich divides into two after $\frac{1}{2}$ hour out of the fridge. The number of bacteria doubles every $\frac{1}{2}$ hour after that.

The number of bacteria after 5 hours is:

10	32	100	1024
☐	☐	☐	☐

Tip How many bacteria after 1 hour? $1\frac{1}{2}$ hours? 2 hours? Find a pattern.

1.6 Powers of powers, products and quotients

Prime factors

Composite numbers can be broken down to a product of prime numbers using a factor tree. The prime factors of 100 can be simplified using rules to do with powers, known more commonly as index laws.

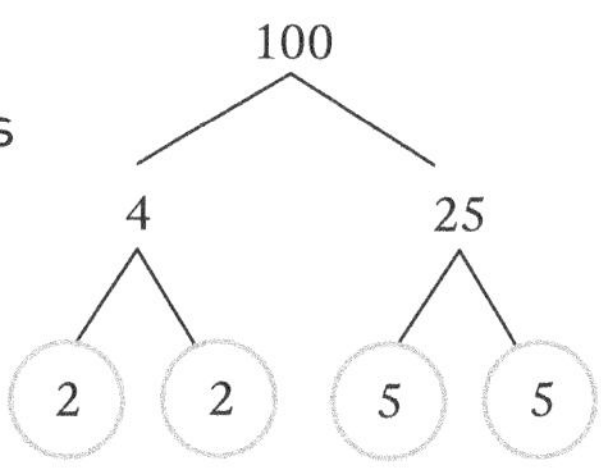

$100 = 2 \times 2 \times 5 \times 5$
$= 2^2 \times 5^2$
$= (2 \times 5)^2$

$100 = 10^2$
$= (2 \times 5)^2$

Index laws

- **Power of a power**

$(8^2)^3 = 8^2 \times 8^2 \times 8^2$
$= \underbrace{8 \times 8} \times \underbrace{8 \times 8} \times \underbrace{8 \times 8}$
$= 8^6$

When raising a power to a second power, we *multiply* the indices.

$(8^2)^3 = 8^{2 \times 3}$

- **Power of a product**

$10^3 = (2 \times 5)^3$
$= 2^3 \times 5^3$

When a product is raised to a power, raise *each factor* to the same power.

- **Power of a quotient**

$\left(\frac{3}{5}\right)^2 = \frac{3}{5} \times \frac{3}{5}$
$= \frac{3 \times 3}{5 \times 5}$
$= \frac{3^2}{5^2}$

When a quotient is raised to a power, raise the *numerator and denominator* to the same power.

1 Express each number as a product of prime factors in index form.

Tip Draw a factor tree to find the prime factors.

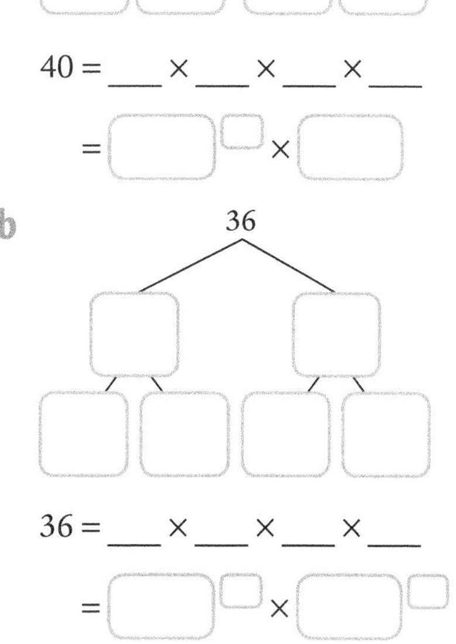

a $40 = \_\_\_ \times \_\_\_ \times \_\_\_ \times \_\_\_$
$= \square^{\square} \times \square$

b $36 = \_\_\_ \times \_\_\_ \times \_\_\_ \times \_\_\_$
$= \square^{\square} \times \square^{\square}$

2 Expand and simplify.

a $(6^2)^4 = \_\_\_ \times \_\_\_ \times \_\_\_ \times \_\_\_$
$= \square^{\square}$

b $(6^4)^2 = \_\_\_ \times \_\_\_$
$= \square^{\square}$

3 Expand and simplify.

$(3 \times 8)^3$
$= 3 \times 8 \times 3 \times \_\_\_ \times \_\_\_ \times \_\_\_$ (pairs of factors)
$= 3 \times 3 \times \_\_\_ \times 8 \times \_\_\_ \times \_\_\_$ (rearrange)
$= \square^{\square} \times \square^{\square}$

4 Expand and simplify.

$\left(\frac{4}{7}\right)^3 = \square \times \square \times \square$
$= \frac{\_\_\_ \times \_\_\_ \times \_\_\_}{\_\_\_ \times \_\_\_ \times \_\_\_}$
$= \frac{\square^{\square}}{\square^{\square}}$

5 State whether each number sentence is true (T) or false (F).

Tip Any number raised to a power of zero is equal to 1.

a $\frac{5^6}{5^6} = 1$ **T or F**

b $3 \times 4^0 = 12^0$ **T or F**

c $(3 \times 4)^0 = 1$ **T or F**

6 Fill in the shapes with any three different whole numbers to make a true number sentence.

$\square^5 = \bigcirc^5 \times \diamond^5$

7 Complete:

Tip $1 \times 1 = 1$

$\left(\frac{1}{6}\right)^2 = \frac{1}{\_\_}$

8 Use a rule to complete the first line and then evaluate the answer.

a $4^3 \times 5^3 = (\quad)^3$

$= (\quad)^3$

$= \quad$

b $\left(\frac{6}{7}\right)^2 = \frac{\_\_^2}{\_\_^2}$

$= \frac{\_\_}{\_\_}$

9 Simplify the fraction below using prime factors and index laws.

$\frac{36}{100} = \frac{\_\_^2}{\_\_^2}$

$= \frac{(\_\_ \times \_\_)^2}{(\_\_ \times \_\_)^2}$

$= \frac{\_\_ \times \_\_^2}{\_\_ \times \_\_^2}$

$= \frac{\_\_^2}{\_\_^2}$

10 Simplify each of the following.

a $\frac{(5 \times 3^2)^4}{(2 \times 5)^2}$ (power of products and power of power)

$= \frac{5^4 \times 3^{2 \times 4}}{2^{-} \times 5^{-}}$ (simplify powers)

$= \frac{5^{-} \times 3^{-}}{2^{-} \times 5^{-}}$ (to divide powers with the same base, subtract the indices)

$= \frac{5^{-} \times 3^{-}}{2^{-}}$

b $\left(\frac{1}{4^2}\right)^2 \times \frac{3}{4} = \frac{1}{4^{-}} \times \frac{3}{4}$

$= \frac{\_\_}{4^{-}}$

NAPLAN-ready

Shade the box beneath the correct answer.

The strength of an earthquake is measured on a Richter scale, a system that compares the strength of earthquakes using the powers of 10.

Richter scale	1	2	3	4	5	6	7	8
Comparative strength	10^1	10^2	10^3	10^4	10^5	10^6	10^7	10^8

How much stronger is an earthquake with a magnitude of 7 than an earthquake with a magnitude of 3?

100 ☐ 1000 ☐ 10 000 ☐ 10 000 000 ☐

Tip Divide the strongest magnitude by the smaller magnitude.

2.1 Working with fractions and decimals A

Fractions and **decimals** are used to represent *parts* of a number.

The decimal 0.3 means '3 tenths', which can be written as the fraction $\frac{3}{10}$, therefore $0.3 = \frac{3}{10}$.

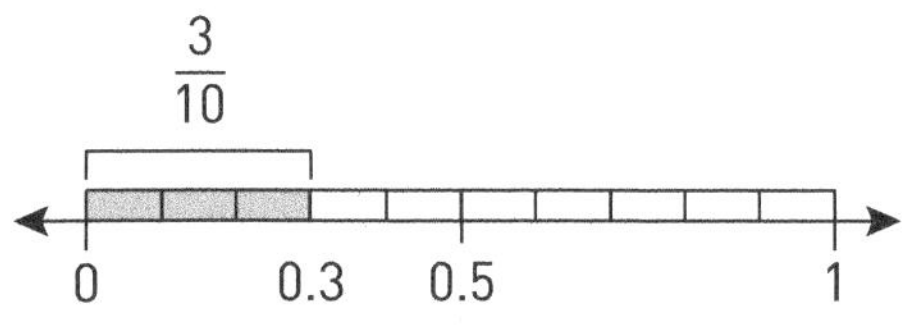

Converting fractions to decimals

Here are two ways to convert a fraction to a decimal.

- Divide the numerator by the denominator.

$$\frac{5}{8} = 5 \div 8 = 0.625$$

$$8\,\overline{)\,5.0^{2}0^{4}0} = 0.625$$

A calculator can be used to perform this division.

- Change the denominator to a power of 10 by multiplying or dividing.

$$\frac{3}{4} \underset{\times 25}{\overset{\times 25}{=}} \frac{75}{100} = 0.75$$

power of 10 ($100 = 10^2$)

Converting decimals to fractions

The decimal system is based on powers of 10. This can be shown in a place value chart.

tens 10	ones 1	.	tenths	hundredths	thousandths
1	2	.	1	2	5

$12.125 = 12 + \frac{1}{10} + \frac{2}{100} + \frac{5}{1000}$ ← (expanded fraction form)

$= 12\frac{125}{1000}$

$= 12\frac{1}{8}$ (divide by a common factor to simplify)

A calculator can simplify a fraction. Use the [fraction] button and press [=].

Word Bank

Improper fraction

→ The numerator (the top number) of an improper fraction is bigger than, or equal to, the denominator.

Mixed number

→ A mixed number has a whole number part and a fraction.

improper fraction → $\frac{7}{6} = 1\frac{1}{6}$ ← mixed number

1 Simplify these fractions.

Tip Divide the top and bottom by the biggest number (highest common factor) possible.

a $\frac{20}{35} = \square$ b $\frac{24}{32} = \square$

2 Write as improper fractions.

a $3\frac{4}{7} = \frac{3\times\_\_\_+4}{7} = \frac{\_\_\_}{7}$

b $6\frac{1}{2} = \frac{6\times\_\_\_+1}{2} = \frac{\_\_\_}{2}$

3 Write as mixed numbers.

a $\frac{16}{3}$

[16 ÷ 3 = ___ rem ___]

$\frac{16}{3} = \square \frac{\ \ }{3}$

b $\frac{8}{7} =$

[8 ÷ 7 = ___ rem ___]

$\frac{8}{7} = \square$

4 a 1.023 × 100 is equal to:

A 0.01023 B 0.1023

C 10.23 D 102.3

b 25.3 ÷ 1000 is equal to:

A 0.0253 B 0.253

C 2530 D 25 300

5 Shade in the fractional amount and then state its decimal equivalent.

a $\frac{8}{10} = \square$

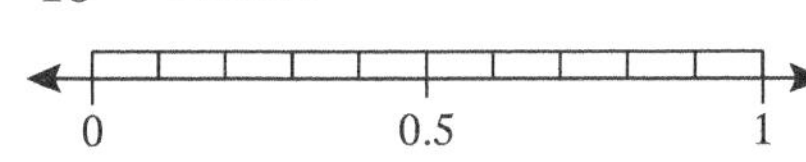

b $\frac{13}{10} = \square$

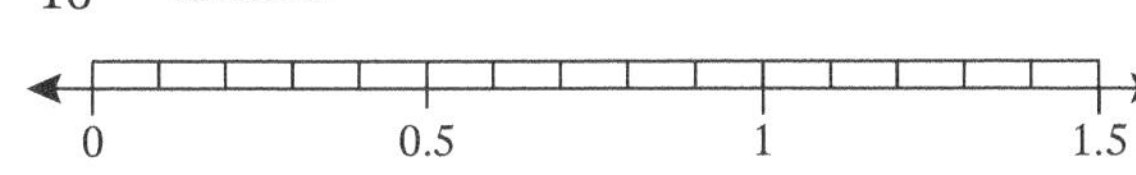

6 State the fraction and decimal values of the shaded area below.

Tip **Write an equivalent fraction whose denominator is a power of 10.**

a

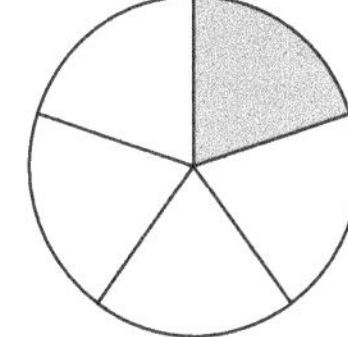

$\_\_\_ = \frac{\ \ }{10}$

$= \square$

b

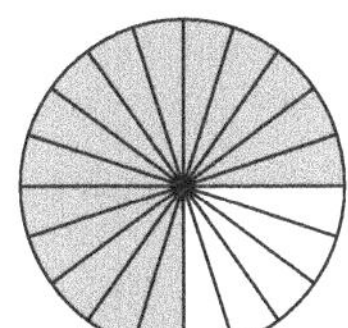

$\_\_\_ = \frac{\ \ }{100}$

$= \square$

7 Write the following fractions as decimals.

a $\frac{3}{5} = \frac{\ \ }{10}$

= 0.____

b $\frac{17}{20} = \frac{\ \ }{100}$

= 0.____

8 What is the place value of the 2 in each of the following decimals?

a 1.0526

A 200 B $\frac{2}{10}$ C $\frac{2}{100}$ D $\frac{2}{1000}$

b 70.321

A 20 B $\frac{2}{10}$ C $\frac{2}{100}$ D $\frac{2}{1000}$

9 Write 8.45 in expanded fraction form and then as a mixed number in simplest form.

$8.45 = 8 + \square + \square$

$= 8 \square$

10 Write the decimals as fractions.

Tip **Write as a fraction with 10, 100 or 1000 as the denominator and then simplify if possible.**

a $0.05 = \frac{5}{100}$

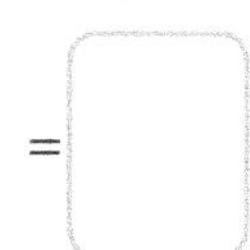

$= \square$

(÷ 5 top and bottom)

b $0.12 = \frac{12}{\ \ }$

$= \square$

(÷ 4 top and bottom)

c $1.25 = \frac{125}{\ \ }$

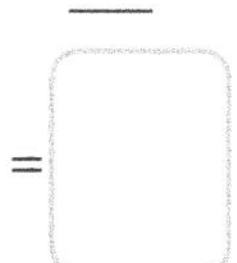

$= \square$

d $2.2 = \frac{22}{\ \ }$

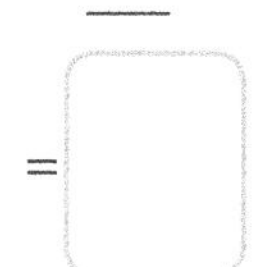

$= \square$

e 0.006 =

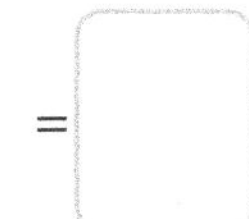

$= \square$

f 0.015 =

$= \square$

2.1 Working with fractions and decimals B

Ascending order: fractions and decimals

An easy way to compare numbers is to use a calculator to convert fractions to decimals.

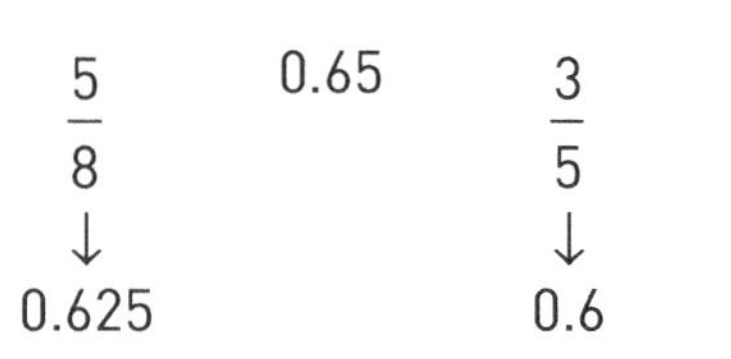

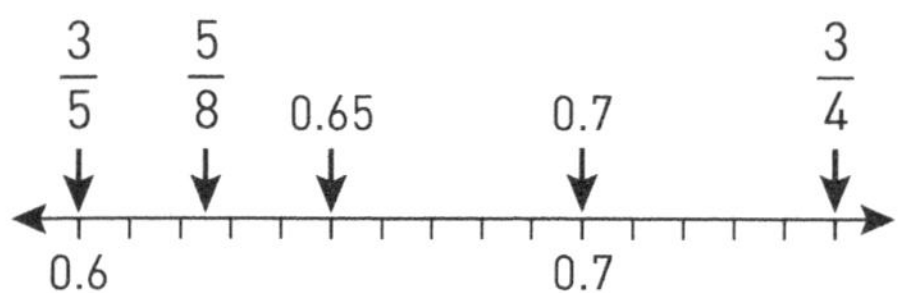

In ascending order: $\frac{3}{5} < \frac{5}{8} < 0.65 < 0.7 < \frac{3}{4}$

(< means 'is less than' and > means 'is greater than')

Working with remainders

How many 6 cm long pieces can be cut from a 20 cm rod?

Step 1:

How many lots of 6 in 20?

$20 \div 6 = 3.333...$

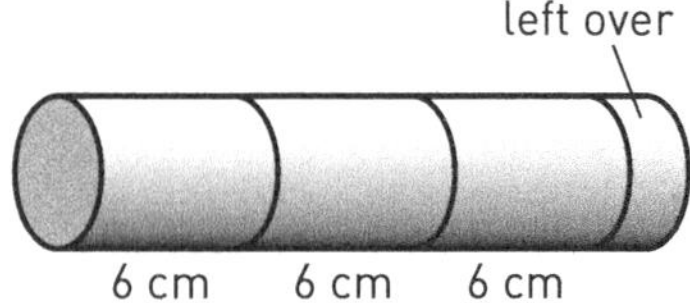

Number of whole pieces: 3

Amount used: $6 \text{ cm} \times 3 = 18 \text{ cm}$

Step 2:

How much remains?

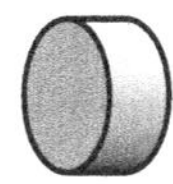

Original amount − amount used
$= 20 \text{ cm} - 18 \text{ cm}$
$= 2 \text{ cm}$

Check:

$6 \times 3 + 2 = 20$

Writing one amount as a fraction of another

How does 3 cm compare with 4 cm?

$3 \div 4 = \frac{3}{4}$ or 0.75

So 3 cm is $\frac{3}{4}$ of 4 cm or 3 cm is 0.75 of 4 cm.

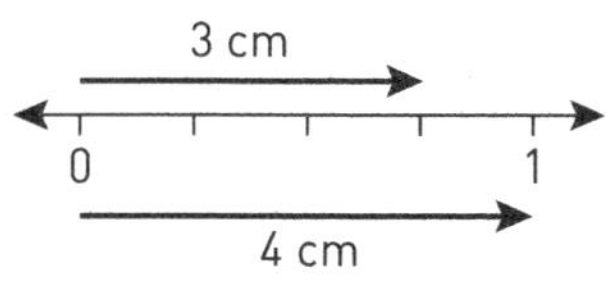

Word Bank

Remainder

→ When a quantity is divided into equal-sized parts, the remainder is any part left over.

$14 \div 3 = 4$ rem 2

Check: $3 \times 4 + 2 = 14$

1 Write the numbers in ascending order, first showing their positions on the number line.

Tip Change fractions to decimals using your calculator.

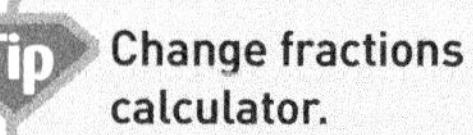

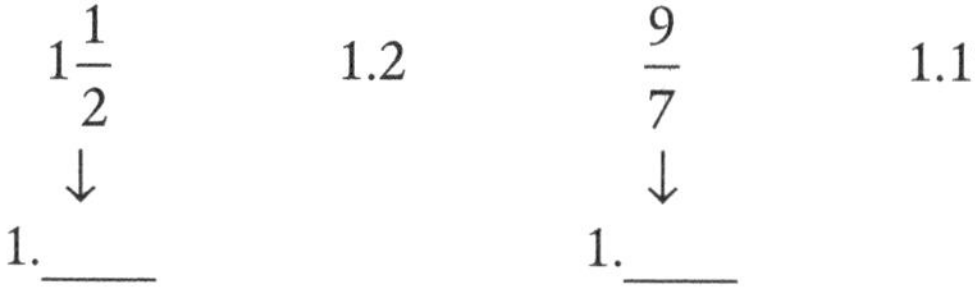

2 A 4 m ribbon is cut into pieces each 90 cm long.

a How many pieces can be cut?

Draw a diagram to show this.

[ ] pieces can be cut.

b How much is left over?

[ ] cm is left over.

3 8.5 L of juice is poured into glasses each holding 150 mL.

a How many glasses can be filled?

8.5 L = ______ mL

$\frac{\_\_\_}{150}$ = ______ . ____ ... (calculator)

[ ] glasses can be filled.

b How much juice is used?

150 × ____ = ____ mL

c How much juice is left over?

____ − ____

[ ] mL

4 Circle the remainder when:

a 40 is divided by 6

A 2 B 3 C 4 D 5

b 14.9 is divided by 3.5

A 4.26 B 1.9 C 0.4 D 0.9

5 Write 800 mL as a fraction of 2L.

Tip 1L = 1000 mL

800 mL is [ ] of 2 L.

6 Circle the numbers that are greater than 3.208.

You may use your calculator.

$\frac{3199}{1000}$ 3.082 $\frac{16}{5}$ 10.001 $\frac{13}{4}$

↓ ↓ ↓

[ ] [ ] [ ]

7 How much will a tradesperson charge for $3\frac{1}{2}$ hours work at $45 per hour?

Tip Decide whether to multiply or divide.

45 [ ] $3\frac{1}{2}$

= ________

= [ ]

The tradesperson will charge $__________.

NAPLAN-ready

Shade the box beneath the correct answer.

A 40 m length of timber is cut into 7 m pieces.

The length of unused timber is:

1 m	3 m	5 m	7 m
▭	▭	▭	▭

Tip Find how much timber has been used.

2.2 Types of decimals

Terminating decimals

'Terminating' means stopping. Terminating decimals have a definite number of decimal places.

$\frac{3}{4} = \frac{75}{100} = 0.75$ (2 d.p.)

$\frac{5}{8} = \frac{625}{1000} = 0.625$ (3 d.p.)

Check on your calculator if there is some doubt about whether a decimal terminates or not.

Irrational numbers

Surds are square roots of numbers that are not perfect squares. The decimal form of a surd has *no repeating pattern* in the *infinite decimal places*.

$\sqrt{7} \rightarrow 2.645751311$ $\sqrt{18.5} \rightarrow 4.301162634$

You *cannot* write a surd as an exact decimal.

$\sqrt{7} \approx 2.65$ (2 d.p.) $\sqrt{18.5} \approx 4.30$ (2 d.p.)

Remember, to find the square root of a number is to find what number is multiplied by itself. Approximating surds is easier if you know the following square roots.

$\sqrt{1}$	$\sqrt{4}$	$\sqrt{9}$	$\sqrt{16}$	$\sqrt{25}$	$\sqrt{36}$	$\sqrt{49}$	$\sqrt{64}$	$\sqrt{81}$	$\sqrt{100}$	$\sqrt{121}$	$\sqrt{144}$
1	2	3	4	5	6	7	8	9	10	11	12

Recurring decimals

A recurring decimal has decimal places that go on forever, but there is always a pattern.

$\frac{1}{3} = 0.333\,333...$

$\frac{9}{14} = 0.642\,857\,142\,857\,142...$

The above fractions can be written in exact decimal form by placing a dot above the first and last digit in the pattern, or a bar across the repeating section.

$\frac{1}{3} = 0.\dot{3}$ or $0.\overline{3}$

$\frac{9}{14} = 0.6\dot{4}2\,857\,\dot{1}$ or $0.6\overline{42\,857\,1}$

- **Approximating**

We use the symbol $\approx$ which means 'is approximately equal to' when we need to round values.

$\frac{1}{3} \approx 0.33$ (2 d.p.)

$\frac{9}{14} \approx 0.64$ (2 d.p.)

Word Bank

Non-terminating decimal

→ Non-terminating decimals are numbers whose decimal places go on forever (recurring decimals or irrational numbers).

Exact value

→ The exact value of a number has not been rounded off. This includes fractions, surds (written in square root form), terminating decimals and recurring decimals that have been written with the 'dot' or 'bar' notation.

1 Place the surds on the number line.

Tip Find approximate values using a calculator, correct to one decimal place.

$\sqrt{80}$ ↓ ____ $\sqrt{43}$ ↓ ____ $\sqrt{67}$ ↓ ____ $\sqrt{12}$ ↓ ____

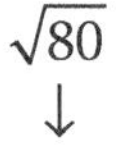

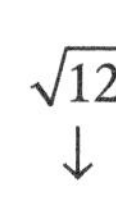

2 Write the surds in Question **1** in ascending order.

$\sqrt{\_\_\_\_} < \sqrt{\_\_\_\_} < \sqrt{\_\_\_\_} < \sqrt{\_\_\_\_}$

3 Without using a calculator, circle the number closest to:

a $\sqrt{48}$

A 7   B 8   C 9   D 10

b $\sqrt{10}$

A 2   B 3   C 4   D 5

4 Circle the irrational numbers.

Tip Check on your calculator for *non-terminating* decimals with *no pattern* in the digits.

$\sqrt{8.6}$	$\frac{6}{11}$	$\sqrt{31.36}$	$14 \div 6$
↓	↓	↓	↓
____	____	____	____

5 Circle the letter next to the exact value for each fraction.

a $\frac{7}{90}$

A 0.0777 777 778   B $0.0\dot{7}$

C $0.0\dot{7}8$ D 0.08

b $\frac{10}{11}$

A 0.909 090 9091   B $0.\dot{9}$

C 0.91   D $0.\overline{90}$

6 Use your calculator to write each fraction in exact decimal form.

a $\frac{2}{3} =$ ☐

b $\frac{8}{11} =$ ☐

c $\frac{5}{18} =$ ☐

d $\frac{7}{6} =$ ☐

e $\frac{200}{7} =$ ☐

7 State whether each recurring decimal has been written correctly by circling Y (yes) or N (no).

a $6.053\,143\,1... = 6.05\overline{3\,14}$ **Y or N**

b $\frac{9}{7} = 1.\overline{285\,714}$ **Y or N**

8 Write approximations to each of the following surds, rounded to two decimal places.

Tip Show the third place before rounding.

a $\sqrt{12} = 3.$___ ___ ___...

$\approx 3.$___ ___ (2 d.p)

b $\sqrt{56.1} =$ ________

$\approx$ ________ (2 d.p)

9 Use your calculator to write each fraction as a decimal, rounded to two decimal places.

a $5\frac{3}{8} = 5.$___ ___ ___...

$\approx$ ☐ (2 d.p)

b $16\frac{2}{3} = 16.$___ ___ ___...

$\approx$ ☐ (2 d.p)

c $1\frac{2}{7} =$ ________

$\approx$ ☐ (2 d.p)

NAPLAN-ready

Shade the box beneath the correct answer.

The four expressions have similar values. Which expression is marked on the number line?

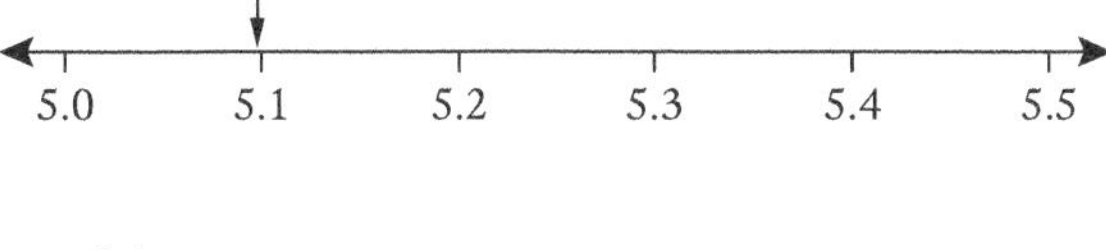

$\frac{36}{7}$	$\sqrt{26.2}$	$20.5 \div 4$	$5 \times \sqrt{1.04}$
☐	☐	☐	☐

Tip Write decimal values for each expression.

2.3 Negative fractions and decimals A

Number lines

A negative fraction or decimal is the same distance to the left of zero as the positive amount is to the right.

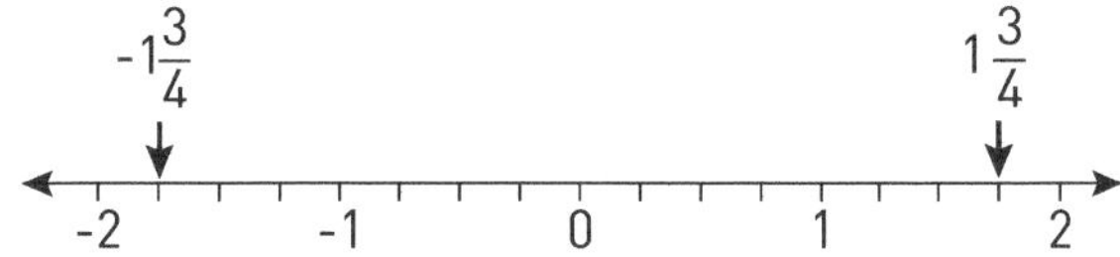

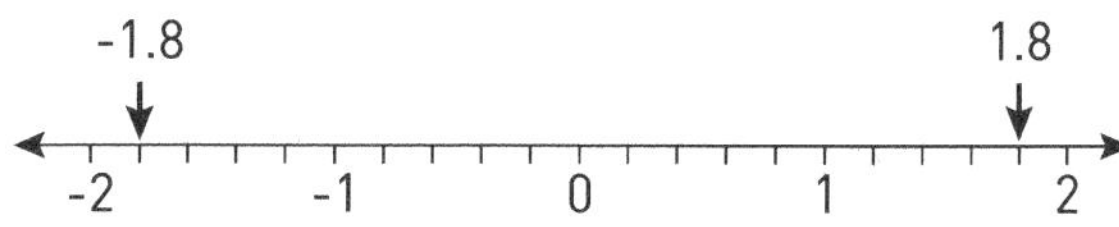

Adding and subtracting negative fractions

When working with fractions with negatives, place the negative sign with the numerator. To add or subtract fractions, remember that the denominators must be the same.

$-\frac{5}{8} + \frac{1}{6}$

$= \frac{-15}{24} + \frac{4}{24}$ (LCD is 24)

$= \frac{(-15+4)}{24}$ (add or subtract the numerators)

$= -\frac{11}{24}$ (place the negative sign in front of the fraction)

Adding and subtracting negative decimals

When calculating answers to questions that involve negative decimals, estimate the answer first by rounding to the closest whole number.

$-2.16 + 4.5 - 7.2$
$\approx -2 + 5 - 7$
≈ -4

To calculate the exact value, follow these steps.

Step 1: Add the numbers that have the same direction (all the positive numbers or all the negative numbers).

$-\underline{2.16} + 4.5 - \underline{7.2}$
$= -9.36 + 4.5$

$$\begin{array}{r} 2.16 \\ +\ 7.20 \\ \hline 9.36 \end{array}$$

Step 2: Find the difference of the two amounts (this can be done by swapping the signs).

$9.36 + 4.5$
$\rightarrow -9.36 - 4.5$

$$\begin{array}{r} 9.36 \\ -\ 4.50 \\ \hline 4.86 \end{array}$$

Step 3: Place the correct sign with the answer.

$= -4.86$

Word Bank

Lowest common denominator (LCD)

→ The LCD is the smallest number that is a common multiple of each of the denominators being considered.

e.g. The LCD of $\frac{1}{2}$ and $\frac{1}{3}$ is 6.

2: 2, 4, <u>6</u>, 8
3: 3, <u>6</u>, 9, 12

1 **a** Place these numbers on the number line.

$-1\frac{1}{4}$, $-2\frac{3}{4}$

b What is the difference between the two numbers in part **a**?

____

____

2 Circle the decimal number shown on the number line.

a 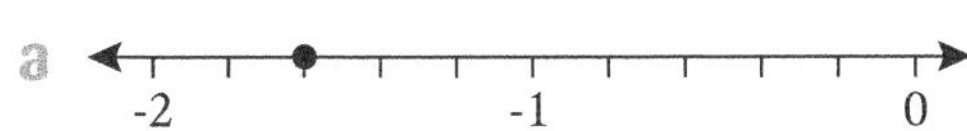

A -1.2 B -1.3 C -1.6 D -2.4

b

A -0.9 B -1.1 C -0.95 D -0.45

3 Calculate the following. The number lines may help.

a $\frac{1}{2} - \frac{3}{4}$

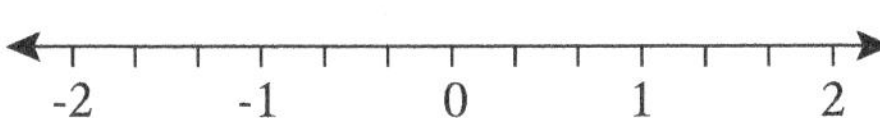

a $-\frac{1}{5} + \frac{4}{5}$

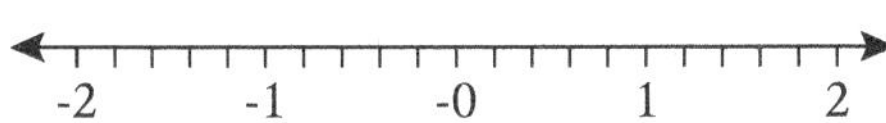

a $-\frac{3}{8} + \frac{3}{4}$

4 Calculate:

Tip Find common denominators.

a $\frac{-2}{3} - \frac{1}{6}$

$= \frac{-\_\_}{6} - \frac{1}{6}$

$= \frac{\_\_}{6}$ (simplify)

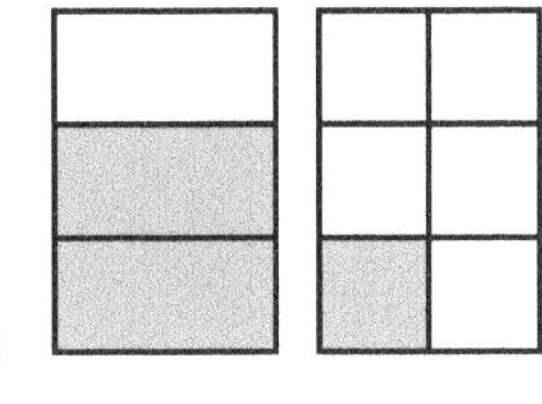

b $\frac{1}{8} + \left(-\frac{5}{6}\right)$ LCD is ______

$= \frac{\_\_}{\_\_} + \frac{\_\_}{\_\_}$

$= \frac{\_\_}{\_\_} + \frac{\_\_}{\_\_}$

= ☐

c $-\frac{4}{5} + \frac{3}{7}$

$= \frac{-\_\_ \times \_\_}{35} + \frac{\_\_ \times \_\_}{35}$

$= \frac{-\_\_ + \_\_}{35}$

$= \frac{\_\_}{35}$

$= -\frac{\_\_}{35}$ (move the negative sign to the front)

5 Calculate:

Tip Line up decimal points, fill empty place values with zeroes and borrow where necessary.

10.3 − 2.17

= ☐

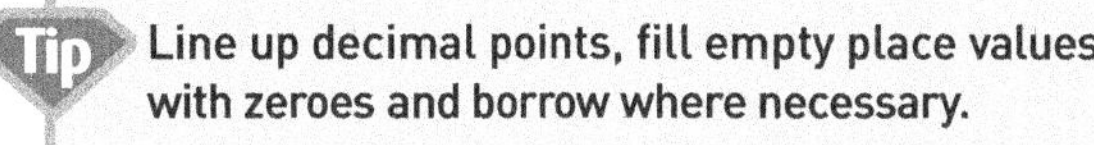

6 a Estimate -6.5 + 8.7 − 4.3

____

____

b Calculate: -6.5 + 8.7 − 4.3

Tip Add the amounts in the same direction. Subtract amounts in opposite directions.

-6.5 + 8.7 − 4.3 (add the negative amounts)

= ______ + 8.7 (find the difference)

− 8.7

= ☐ (decide on the sign)

2.3 Negative fractions and decimals B

Fractions and decimals involving negatives are performed by:

- ignoring the signs
- calculate the amount
- decide on the sign of the answer

Rules for × and ÷

Two 'like signs' give a positive answer.
e.g. $-4 \times -7 = 28$
Two different signs give a negative answer.
e.g. $+5 \times -8 = -40$

Multiplication of fractions

When multiplying fractions the numerators and denominators are multiplied separately.

e.g. $-\frac{2}{7} \times \frac{3}{5}$

- Ignore the signs. $\frac{2}{7} \times \frac{3}{5}$
- Calculate the amount. $\frac{2 \times 3}{7 \times 5} = \frac{6}{35}$
- Decide on the sign (two different signs equal a negative). $-\frac{2}{7} \times \frac{3}{5} = -\frac{6}{35}$

Division of fractions

Change the divide sign to a multiplication and 'flip' the second fraction.

e.g. $-\frac{3}{4} \div -6$

- Ignore the signs. $\frac{3}{4} \div 6$
- Calculate the amount. $\frac{3}{4} \times \frac{1}{6} = \frac{3}{24} = \frac{1}{8}$
- Decide on the sign (two negatives makes a positive). $-\frac{3}{4} \div -6 = \frac{3}{24} = \frac{1}{8}$

Multiplication of decimals

-6.34×1.7

Leave out the decimal point, complete the multiplication, then place it in the answer at the end.

$$\begin{array}{r} 634 \\ \times \quad 17 \\ \hline 4438 \\ 6340 \\ \hline 10778 \end{array}$$

-6.34×1.7
$= 10.778$

The question has three decimal places so the answer will have three decimal places.

Division of decimals

Change the divisor to a whole number by multiplying by 10, 100 or 1000. Change the other number in the same way.

$-2.81 \div -0.5$
$= 28.1 \div 5$
$= 5.62$

$$5 \overline{)\, 28.{}^{3}1{}^{1}0} \quad = 5.62$$

Word Bank

Reciprocal

→ A reciprocal is the inverted ('flipped-over') version of a fraction.

e.g. The reciprocal of $\frac{3}{5}$ is $\frac{5}{3}$.

The reciprocal of 7 or $\frac{7}{1}$ is $\frac{1}{7}$.

Cancelling

→ Cancelling fractions simplifies them by dividing numerators and denominators by common factors.

e.g. $\frac{3}{\not{5}_1} \times \frac{\not{60}^{12}}{7} = \frac{3}{1} \times \frac{12}{7}$ (cancelling a common factor of 5)

1 The multiplication of two fractions is shown. Circle the letter next to the correct multiplication.

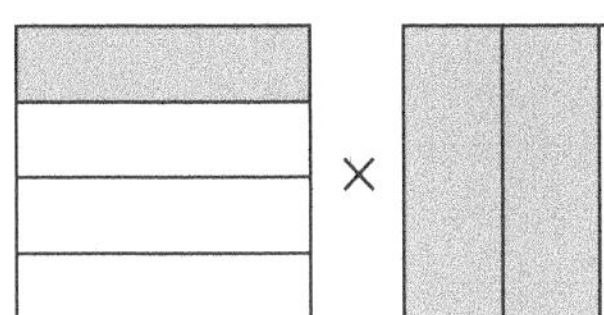

A $\frac{2}{4} \times \frac{1}{3}$ B $\frac{3}{4} \times \frac{1}{3}$

C $\frac{1}{4} \times \frac{2}{3}$ D $\frac{2}{3} \times \frac{1}{3}$

2 Calculate:

Tip Cancel common factors first, if possible.

a $\frac{-5}{6} \times \frac{5}{7}$

= ☐

b $-1\frac{1}{2} \times \frac{-4}{5}$

= ☐ $\times \frac{4}{5}$

=

= ☐ as a mixed number

3 Calculate the following divisions.

Tip Multiply by the reciprocal.

a $\frac{5}{9} \div -2$

$= \frac{5}{9} \times \frac{1}{\_\_}$

= ☐

b $\frac{-7}{8} \div \frac{3}{5}$

= ☐ × ☐

= ☐

= ☐

4 Calculate:

Tip Place the decimal point as the last step.

a 4.62 × -7.3

= __ __ . __ __ __

```
   4 6 2
×    7 3
________
________
________
```

b -5200 × -1.2

= ______ 0.0

= ______

```
   5 2
×  1 2
______
______
______
```

5 Calculate, rounding the answer to two decimal places.

Tip Change the divisor to a single digit whole number and then change the other number in the same way.

a 1.62 ÷ 0.6

= ______ ÷ 6

= ______

6) __ __ . __

b -5 ÷ 70

= ____ ÷ 7

= ______ (2 d.p.)

7) __ . __ __ __

6 Calculate:

Tip Ignore the signs when you complete the multiplication or division. Then use the rules of negative numbers to find the sign of the answer.

$-\frac{2}{5} \div -6$

=

☐

NAPLAN-ready

Shade the box beneath the correct answer.

Three of the calculations have the same answer. The calculation with a different answer is:

$\frac{4}{5} \times -\frac{2}{3}$ ☐

$-\frac{4}{5} \div \frac{3}{2}$ ☐

$\frac{5}{4} \div -\frac{2}{3}$ ☐

$\frac{2}{3} \times -\frac{4}{5}$ ☐

Tip Calculate the amount, and then the sign, in separate steps.

2.4 Estimating percentages

Halves, quarters and eighths

One whole is said to be 100%.

$\frac{1}{2} = \frac{50}{100} = 50\%$	$\frac{1}{4} = \frac{25}{100} = 25\%$	$\frac{1}{8} = \frac{1}{2}$ of 25% = 12.5%
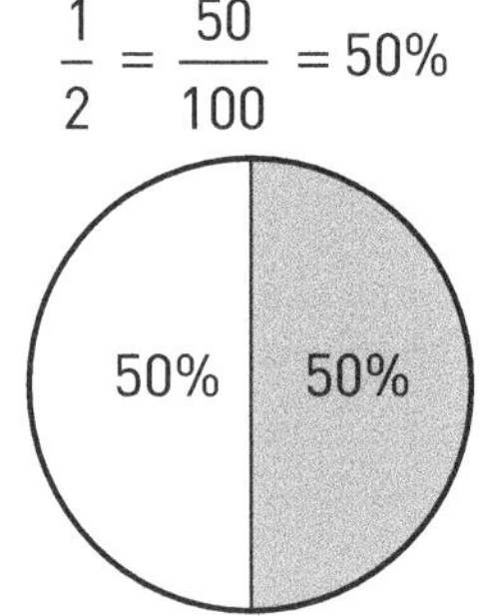	25% 25% 25% 25%	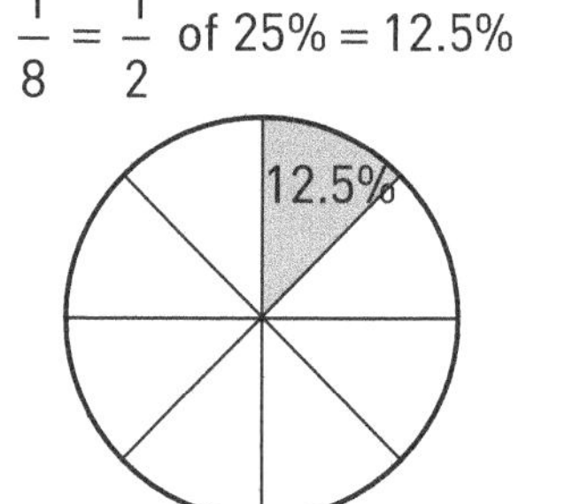

When estimating the percentage of a circle in a sector, cut the circle into halves, quarters or eighths, and then compare.

The sector is between 12.5% and 25%. It is closer to 12.5%. A good estimate is 15%.

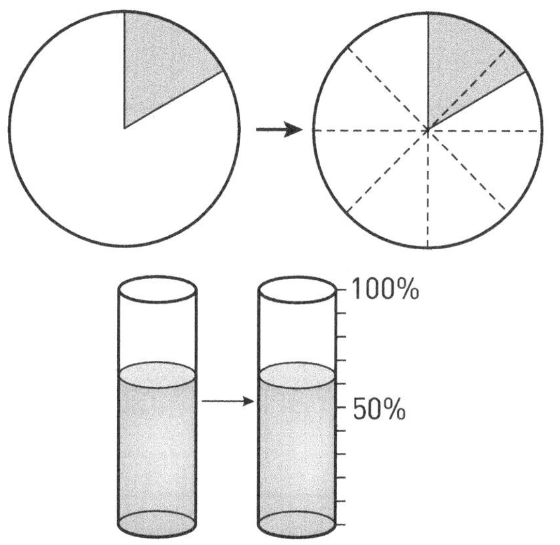

Tenths

When estimating a percentage of a certain length or height, break the distance into 10 equal sections, each worth 10%.

The cylinder is between 60% and 70% full. It is a little less than half way, so a good estimate is 63%.

Word Bank

Per cent

→ Per cent means 'for every hundred', e.g. 27% is 27 out of 100 or $\frac{27}{100}$.

1 Estimate the percentage shaded.

Tip Break the whole amount into halves, quarters or tenths.

a

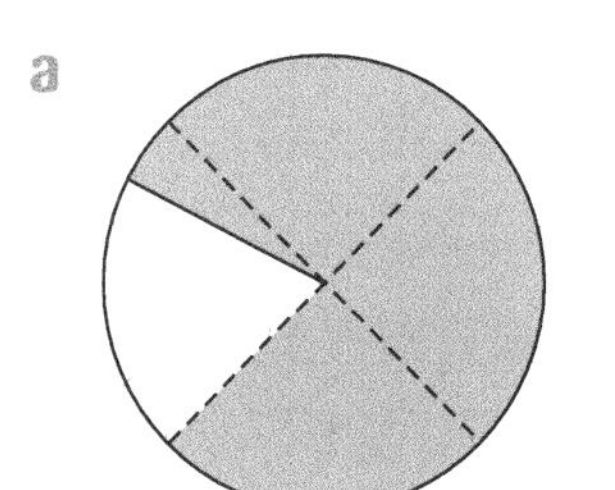

A 30% B 60%
C 70% D 80%

b

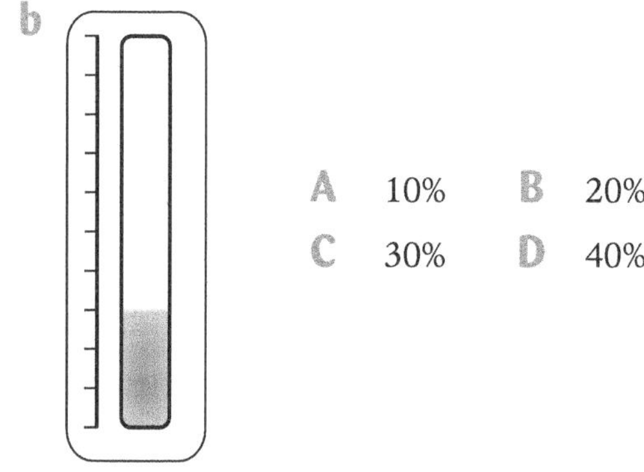

A 10% B 20%
C 30% D 40%

c

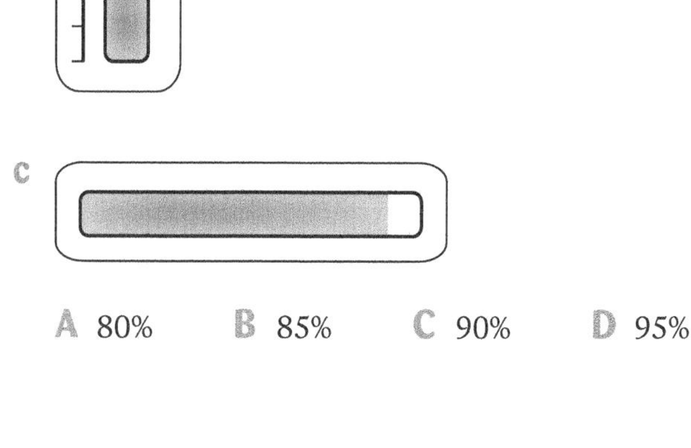

A 80% B 85% C 90% D 95%

2 Draw and shade a sector of each circle to show an estimate of the given percentage.

Tip Start with half and quarter circles.

a 20%

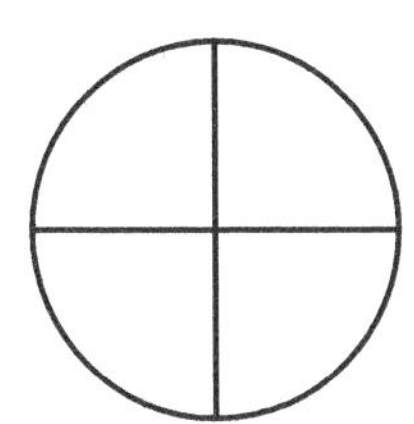

b 40%

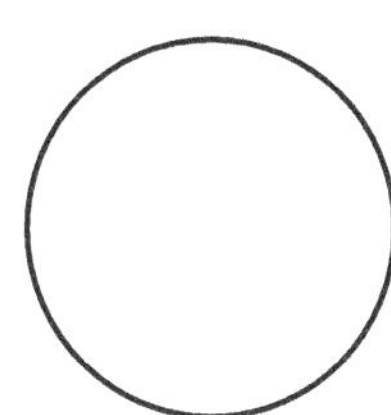

c 60%

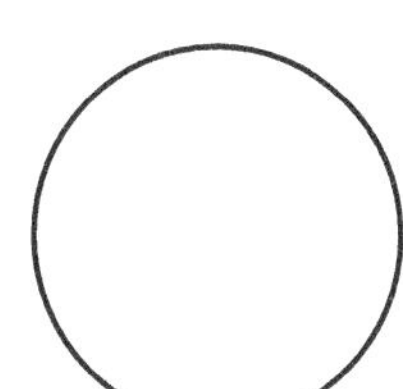

d 15%

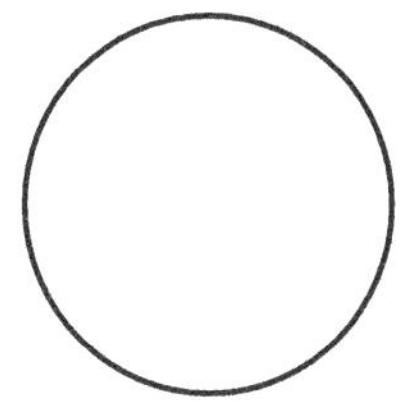

3 On the beaker, mark a level of 35% full.

Tip Divide the height into 10 equal amounts.

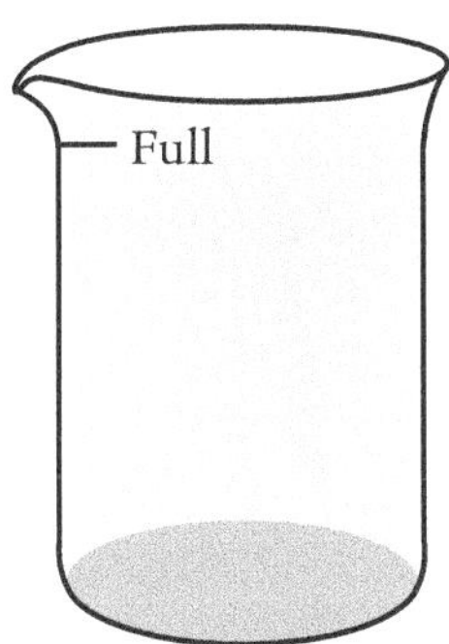

4 Shade the following percentages.

a 43%

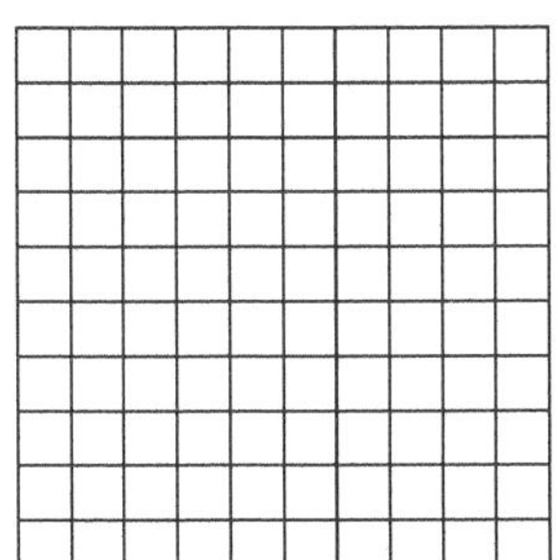

b 86%

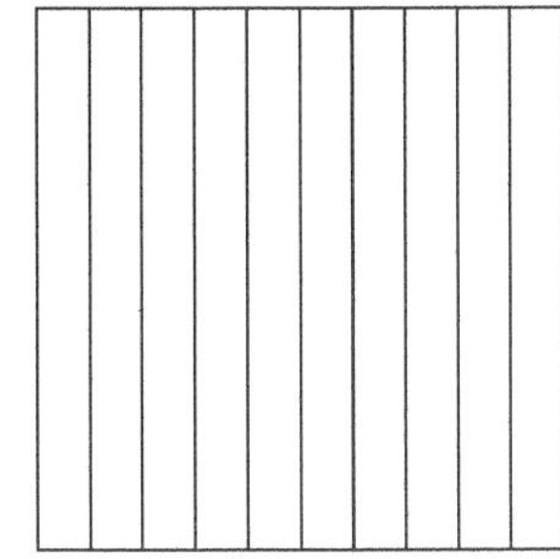

5 Estimate the equivalent percentage by representing the given fraction with shading.

a $\frac{5}{7}$

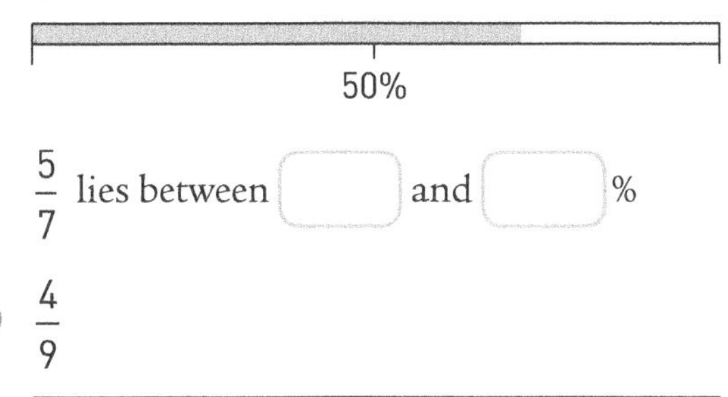

$\frac{5}{7}$ lies between ☐ and ☐ %

b $\frac{4}{9}$

50%

$\frac{4}{9}$ lies between ☐ and ☐ %

c $\frac{3}{8}$

50%

$\frac{3}{8}$ lies between ☐ and ☐ %

NAPLAN-ready

Shade the box beneath the correct answer.

Most of the area of Australia is taken up by the six states and the Northern Territory (NT).

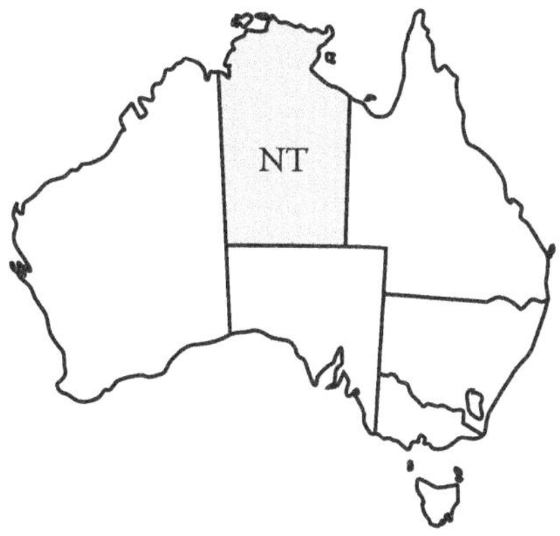

The approximate percentage of Australia taken up by the Northern Territory is:

5%	15%	25%	35%
☐	☐	☐	☐

Tip Shade areas equal to the size of the Northern Territory.

2.5 Writing fractions and decimals as percentages

Fractions, decimals and percentages are all ways of writing part of a number. We can convert fractions and decimals to percentages by multiplying by 100 and then writing a % sign.

Fractions to percentages

When the denominator of a fraction is 100, the conversion is easy.

$$\frac{43}{100} = 43\%$$

If the denominator of the fraction is a factor of 100 (2, 4, 5, 10, 20, 25, 50), it can be converted to an equivalent fraction with a denominator of 100.

$$\frac{4}{5} = \frac{80}{100} = 80\% \quad (\times 20 \text{ top and bottom})$$

0	$\frac{1}{5}$	$\frac{2}{5}$	$\frac{3}{5}$	$\frac{4}{5}$	1
0%	20%	40%	60%	80%	100%

For fractions with denominators that are not 100—use fraction multiplication.

$$\frac{3}{8} = \frac{3}{8} \times 100\%$$

$$= \frac{3}{\cancel{8}_2} \times \frac{\cancel{100}^{25}}{1}\% \quad \text{(cancel common factors)}$$

$$= \frac{75}{2}\% \quad \text{(divide the top number by the bottom number)}$$

$$= 37\frac{1}{2}\% \quad \text{(write the remainder as a fraction of the denominator)}$$

or 37.5%

If the fraction is an improper fraction write as a mixed number first and then multiply by 100%.

Decimals to percentages

Multiply the decimal by 100%. We show this by shifting the decimal point two places to the right.

$$0.09 = 9\% \ \left(\frac{9}{100} = 9\%\right)$$

↑ hundredths place

0	0.1	0.2	0.3	0.4	0.5	0.6	0.7	0.8	0.9	1
0%	10%	20%	30%	40%	50%	60%	70%	80%	90%	100%

Fractions to decimals to percentages

Fractions can be changed to percentages by writing the equivalent decimal.

Step 1: Convert the fraction to a decimal by dividing the numerator by the denominator.

$$\frac{5}{8} = 5 \div 8$$
$$= 0.625$$

Step 2: Convert the decimal to a percentage by multiplying by 100.

$$0.625 = 0.625 \times 100\%$$
$$= 62.5\%$$

$$1\frac{1}{4} = 1.25$$
$$= 125\%$$

1 Convert each decimal to a percentage.

Tip To multiply by 100, move the decimal point two places to the right.

a $0.06 = \square\ \%$ b $0.5901 = \square\ \%$

c $1.8 = \square\ \%$ d $0.004 = \square\ \%$

2 Use equivalent fractions to convert each fraction to a percentage.

Tip Multiply to change the denominator to 100 and then multiply the numerator by the same number.

a $\frac{3}{20} = \frac{\quad}{100} = \square\ \%$

b $\frac{23}{50} = \frac{\quad}{\quad} = \square\ \%$

3 Which circle has the greatest percentage shaded?

Tip Convert the fraction shaded to a percentage for each circle.

A
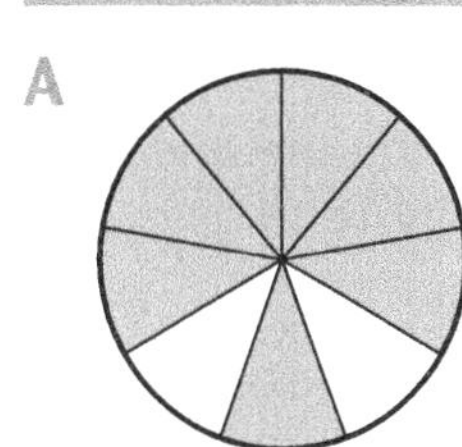

B
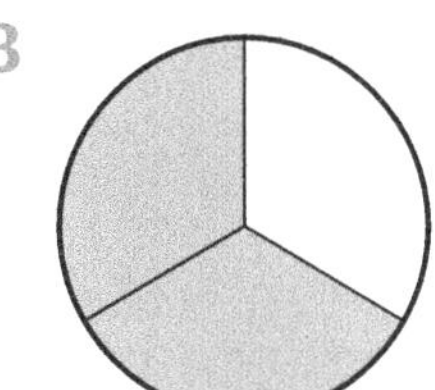

C
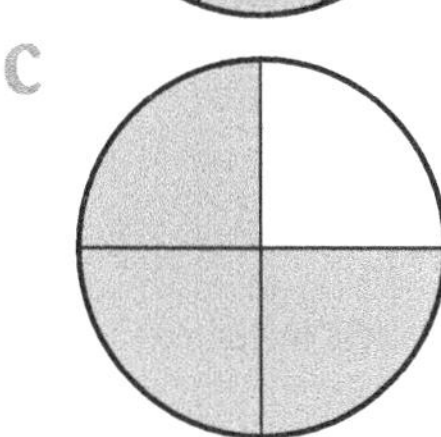

D
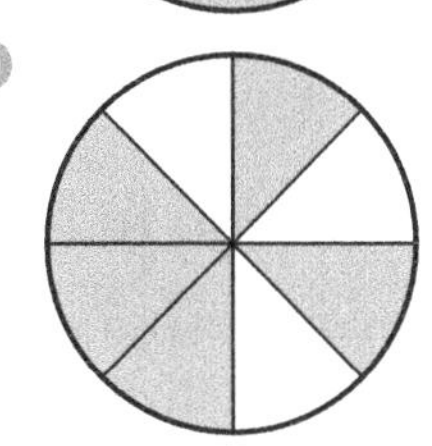

4 Convert to percentages.

Tip Convert to decimals first.

a $1\frac{1}{2} = 1.$____

$= \square\%$

b $2\frac{7}{10} = 2.$____

$= \square\%$

5 Convert to percentages. Round your answer correct to one decimal place.

Tip Use your calculator to convert the fraction to a decimal and then convert to a percentage.

a $\frac{2}{3} = 0.$____...

= ____.____...%

≈ $\square$% (1 d.p.)

b $1\frac{1}{6} = 1.$____...

= ____.____...%

≈ $\square$% (1 d.p.)

6 Convert the fractions and mixed numbers to percentages.

Tip Multiply by 100% using fraction multiplication.

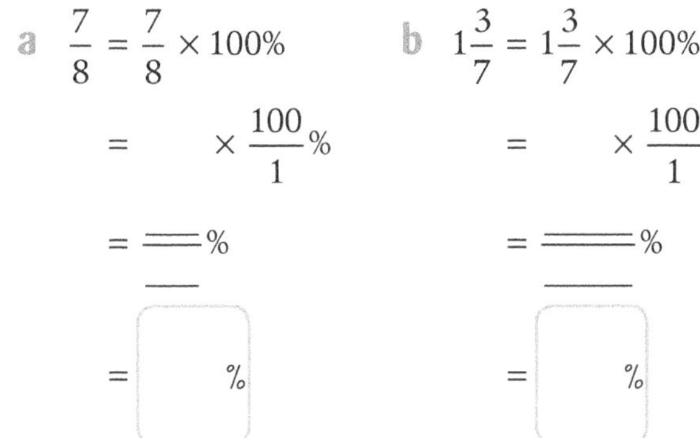

a $\frac{7}{8} = \frac{7}{8} \times 100\%$

$= \quad \times \frac{100}{1}\%$

$= \frac{\quad}{\quad}\%$

$= \square\%$

b $1\frac{3}{7} = 1\frac{3}{7} \times 100\%$

$= \quad \times \frac{100}{1}\%$

$= \frac{\quad}{\quad}\%$

$= \square\%$

7 Convert each fraction and decimal to a percentage, then mark the original values with an arrow on the number line.

45%   0.13 $\frac{1}{4}$ $\frac{7}{10}$

↓   ↓   ↓

$\square$ $\square$ $\square$

0% 10% 20% 30% 40% 50% 60% 70% 80% 90% 100%

8 State whether each number sentence is true (T) or false (F).

a $0.45 = 4.5\%$ **T or F** $\square$

b $\frac{3}{7} > 40\%$ **T or F** $\square$

c $\frac{1}{5} < 25\%$ **T or F** $\square$

9 a What percentage of the balls are white?

____ = $\square$ (2 d.p.)

b What percentage of the balls are not white?

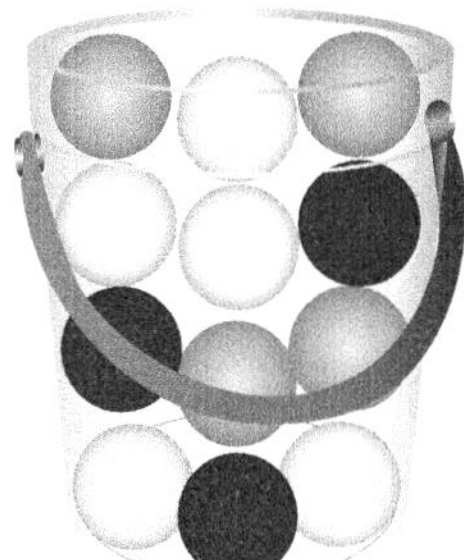

______

= $\square$

NAPLAN-ready

Shade the box beneath the correct answer.

Natalie is comparing her test results for English, German, Geography and Science.

Which test score gives the highest percentage?

English 14 out of 20	German 41 out of 50
▭	▭
Geography 8 out of 10	**Science** 30 out of 40
▭	▭

Tip Write the scores as fractions first.

2.6 Writing percentages as fractions and decimals

Per cent means per hundred, so replace % with ÷ 100.

Percentage to fraction

We can write the percentage as a fraction of 100.

$18\% = \frac{18}{100}$ (simplify by cancelling a common factor of 2)

$= \frac{9}{50}$

Number line: 0 (0%), $\frac{1}{4}$ (25%), $\frac{1}{2}$ (50%), $\frac{3}{4}$ (75%), 1 (100%)

A percentage greater than 100% will give a number bigger than 1.

$125\% = \frac{125}{100}$ (simplify by cancelling a common factor of 25)

$= \frac{5}{4}$

$= 1\frac{1}{4}$ (a mixed number)

For fractional percentages, use fraction calculation methods.

$12\frac{1}{2}\% = 12\frac{1}{2} \div 100$ i.e. $\div \frac{100}{1}$

$= \frac{\cancel{25}^{1}}{2} \times \frac{1}{\cancel{100}_{4}}$ (cancel a common factor of 25)

$= \frac{1}{8}$

Decimal percentages need to be written as $\frac{\text{whole number}}{\text{whole number}}$.

$6.5\% = \frac{6.5}{100}$ (Multiplying top and bottom by 10 to give whole numbers)

$= \frac{65}{1000}$ (cancel a common factor of 5)

$= \frac{13}{200}$

Percentage to decimal

To convert a whole number or decimal percentage, divide by 100.

The digits move two places to the right. More simply, move the decimal point two places to the left.

$35\% = 35 \div 100$
$= 0.35$

$6.3\% = 6.3 \div 100$
$= 0.063$

For a fractional percentage, change to a decimal percentage before dividing by 100.

$2\frac{1}{2}\% = 2.5\%$
$= 2.5 \div 100$
$= 0.025$

1 Convert each percentage to a decimal.

Tip Move the decimal point two places to the left.

a $15\% = 15 \div 100$
= ______

b $24.7\% =$ ______
= ______

c $187\% =$ ______
= ______

d $0.4\% =$ ______
= ______

2 Convert each fractional percentage to a decimal.

Tip Use a calculator, if necessary, to change the fraction to a decimal first.

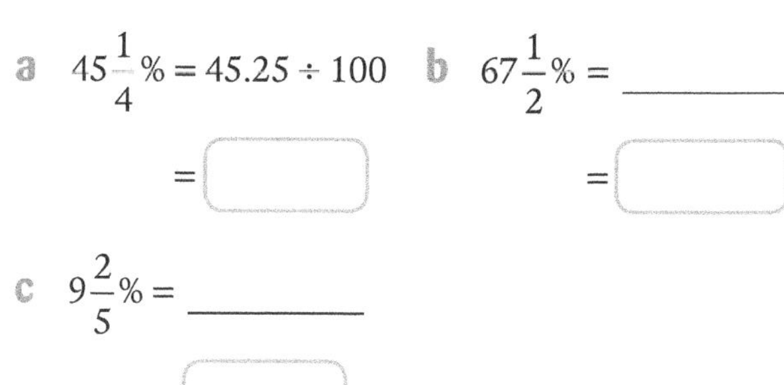

a $45\frac{1}{4}\% = 45.25 \div 100$
= ______

b $67\frac{1}{2}\% =$ ______
= ______

c $9\frac{2}{5}\% =$ ______
= ______

3 Convert each of the percentages to fractions.

Tip If the numerator is a multiple of 2 or 5, you must cancel down.

a $15\% = \frac{15}{100}$

$= \square$

b $24\% = \underline{\hspace{2cm}}$

$= \square$

c $80\% = \underline{\hspace{2cm}}$

$= \square$

4 Convert each of the mixed number percentages to fractions.

Tip You must use fraction calculation methods.

a $6\frac{1}{2}\% = \frac{13}{2} \div 100$

$= \frac{13}{2} \times \frac{1}{100}$

$= \square$

b $8\frac{1}{4}\% = \underline{\hspace{2cm}}$

$= \square$

c $22\frac{1}{3}\% = \underline{\hspace{2cm}}$

$= \square$

5 Convert each fraction and percentage to a decimal, then mark the original values with an arrow on the number line.

54% ↓ □ 0.7 $\frac{3}{4}$ ↓ □ $\frac{1}{10}$ ↓ □

Number line: 0, 0.5, 1

6 Write the original values in Question **5** in ascending order (smallest to largest).

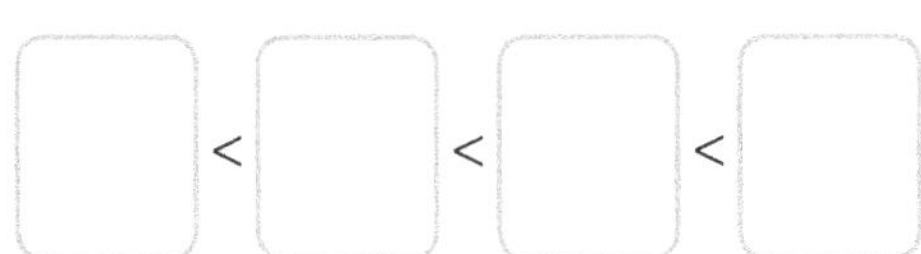

□ < □ < □ < □

7 State whether each number sentence is true (T) or false (F) by circling the correct answer.

Tip Convert the fractions and percentages to decimals first.

a $\frac{1}{8} < 8\%$ **T or F** □

b $\frac{1}{20} < 20\%$ **T or F** □

c $\frac{1}{10} = 10\%$ **T or F** □

8 Each of the following values is less than 1%. Convert each percentage to a fraction.

Tip To divide by 100, multiply by $\frac{1}{100}$.

a $\frac{1}{4}\% = \frac{1}{4} \div 100$

$= \frac{1}{4} \times \frac{1}{100}$

$= \square$

b $\frac{2}{5}\% =$

$=$

$= \square$

NAPLAN-ready

Shade the box beneath the correct answer.

In a game, Abbey rolled two dice. A 2 followed by a 4 meant she had to write down 24% and then convert to a fraction in simplest form.

When Thomas rolled the dice, he ended up with the fraction $\frac{14}{25}$.

The numbers on Thomas' dice were:

4 and 5	2 and 4
□	□
3 and 2	5 and 6
□	□

Tip Remember $24\% = \frac{24}{100} = \frac{6}{25}$.

2.7 Writing one amount as a percentage of another

Comparing numbers

If 3 girls and 2 boys are in a group, the total number of children is 5.

The number of girls compared to the total number is 3 to 5.

To write the comparison as a percentage:

- write the fraction

$\frac{3}{5}$

- multiply by 100%

$\frac{3}{{}_{1}\cancel{5}} \times \frac{\cancel{100}^{20}}{1}\% = 60\%$

The percentage of girls in the group is 60%.

The percentage of boys would be 40%.

Check: 60% + 40% = 100%

Comparing amounts with units

To compare two quantities, the units for the amounts must be the same (e.g. both measured in centimetres).

1.5 m = 150 cm

$\frac{93}{{}_{3}\cancel{150}} \times \frac{{}^{2}\cancel{100}}{1}\%$

$= \frac{{}^{31}\cancel{93}}{{}_{1}\cancel{3}} \times \frac{2}{1} = 62\%$

Noah's height as a percentage of his sister Amy's height is 62%.

 Find the percentage of flowers that have bees on them. Round your answer to one decimal place.

$\frac{\square}{\square} \times 100\% =$

$\approx \square$ % (1 d.p.)

 Write the first number as a percentage of the second. Round your answers to one decimal place, where necessary.

a 14, 20

$\frac{\square}{\square} \times \frac{100}{1}\%$

$= \square$ %

b 10, 7

$\frac{\square}{\square} \times 100\%$

= ______...%

$\approx \square$ % (1 d.p.)

c 8, 50

$\frac{\square}{\square} \times \frac{100}{1}\%$

$= \square$ %

3 Write the first quantity as a percentage of the second.

Tip Convert to the smaller unit before forming the fraction.

a 70 cents, \$1.40

\$1.40 = ____ cents

$\frac{\_\_}{\_\_} \times \frac{100}{1}\%$

= ☐ %

b 200 mL, 5 L

5 L = ______ mL

$\frac{\_\_}{\_\_} \times \frac{100}{1}\%$

= ☐ %

c 50 minutes, 1 hour (correct to one decimal place)

1 hour = ____ minutes

$\frac{\_\_}{\_\_} \times \frac{100}{1}\%$

= ____...%

≈ ☐ % (1 d.p.)

d 6 mm, 3 cm

3 cm = ____ mm

$\frac{\_\_}{\_\_} \times \frac{100}{1}\%$

= ☐ %

e 400 kg, 2 tonne

2 tonne = _____ kg

$\frac{\_\_}{\_\_} \times \frac{100}{1}\%$

= ☐ %

4 Which of the following gives 30 seconds as a percentage of 5 minutes?

A $\frac{30}{5} \times \frac{100}{1}\%$

B $\frac{30}{50} \times \frac{100}{1}\%$

C $\frac{5}{30} \times \frac{100}{1}\%$

D $\frac{30}{300} \times \frac{100}{1}\%$

5 Which is a better mark: 30 out of 40 for English or 50 out of 65 for Science?

Tip Convert each mark to a percentage.

English:

$\frac{\_\_}{\_\_} \times \frac{100}{1}\% =$ ☐ %

Science:

$\frac{\_\_}{\_\_} \times 100\% =$ ________...%

≈ ☐ %

So ____ out of ____ for ☐ is the better mark.

6 The cost of petrol increased from 153 c/L to 165 c/L. What was the percentage increase, rounded to one decimal place?

Tip Calculate the amount of increase first.

Increase: ____ − ____ = ____ c/L

% increase = $\frac{\_\_}{153} \times 100\%$

= ________...%

≈ ☐ % (1 d.p.)

NAPLAN-ready

Shade the box beneath the correct answer.

One glass of juice has been poured from the jug.

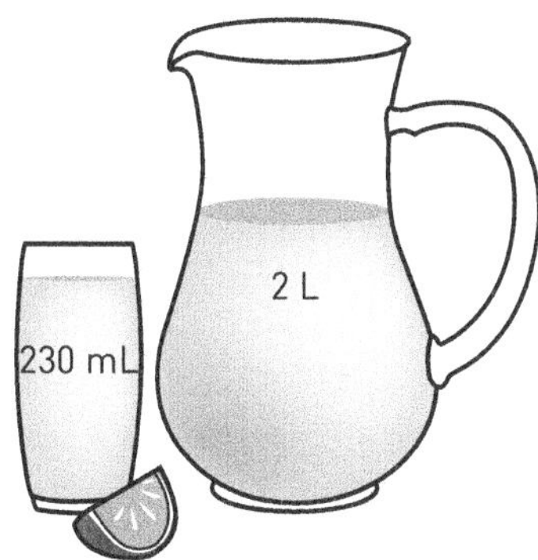

The percentage of juice remaining in the jug is closest to:

12%	13%	89%	112%
☐	☐	☐	☐

Tip Convert to the same units. Subtract to see how much juice remains.

2.8 Finding a percentage of an amount

Fraction of an amount

To find the fraction of an amount, multiply the fraction by the amount.

$\frac{1}{3}$ of \$21 $= \frac{1}{\cancel{3}_1} \times \frac{\cancel{21}^7}{1}$
$= \$7$

$\frac{1}{3}$ of \$21 $= 21 \div 3$
$= \$7$

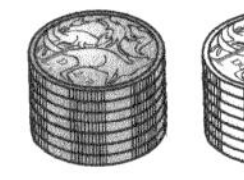 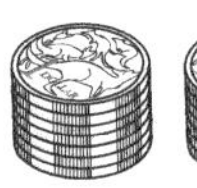 

\$7	\$7	\$7

Sometimes it is easier to find a fraction of an amount by dividing the amount by the denominator (to find one part), and then multiplying the answer by the numerator.

$\frac{1}{8}$ of \$32 $= 32 \div 8$
$= \$4$

$\frac{5}{8}$ of \$32 $= \$4 \times 5$
$= \$20$

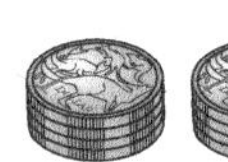  

\$4	\$4	\$4	\$4	\$4	\$4	\$4	\$4

Percentage of an amount

Each of the three methods listed below can be used to find the percentage of an amount.

e.g. Find 6% of \$70

Method 1: A mental strategy

Finding 6% of \$70 is the same as finding 1% and then multiplying that amount by 6.

1% of \$70
$= 70 \div 100$
$= \$0.70$

6% of \$70
$= \$0.70 \times 6$
$= \$4.20$

Method 2: Fractional method

6% of \$70
$= \frac{6}{100} \times \frac{70}{1}$
$= \frac{420}{100}$
$= \$4.20$

Method 3: Decimal method

6% of \$70 (6% is the same as 0.06)
$= 0.06 \times 70$
$= 4.2$

Therefore, 6% of \$70 is \$4.20.

1 Calculate, showing individual amounts in each box.

Tip Finding $\frac{1}{3}$ of an amount is the same as dividing by 3.

a $\frac{1}{4}$ of \$36 = ____ ÷ ____
= [ ]

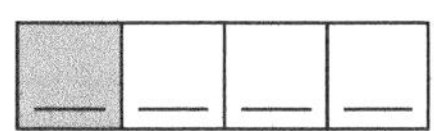

b $\frac{1}{2}$ of 44 kg = ____ ÷ ____
= [ ]

c $\frac{1}{5}$ of 55 mL = ____ ÷ ____
= [ ]

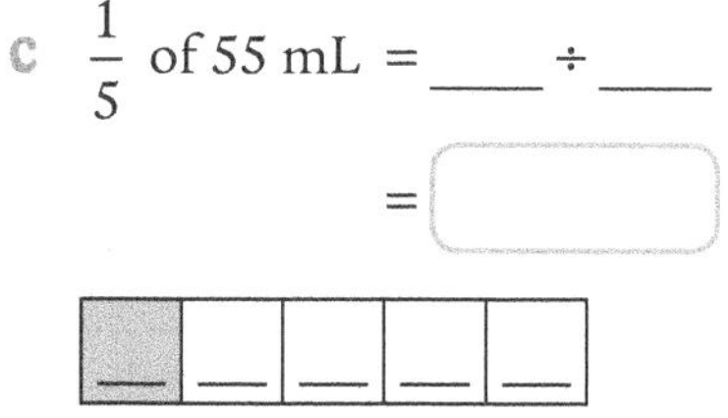

2 Calculate the following amounts.

Tip First divide to find one part.

a $\frac{3}{5}$ of 65 L

$\frac{1}{5}$ of 65 L = ____ ÷ ____
= ____ L

$\frac{3}{5}$ of 65 L = ____ L × 3
= [ ]

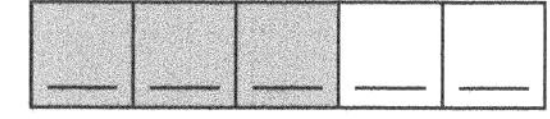

b $\frac{2}{9}$ of 45 cm

$\frac{1}{9}$ of 45 cm = _____ ÷ _____

= ______ cm

$\frac{2}{9}$ of 45 cm = ______ cm × 2

= ☐

___	___	___	___	___	___	___	___	___

3 State whether each statement is true (T) or false (F) by circling the correct answer.

a Finding $\frac{4}{7}$ of an amount is the same as dividing the amount by 4 and then multiplying the result by 7. **T or F**

b Finding 78% of an amount is the same as dividing the amount by 100 and then multiplying the result by 78. **T or F**

4 Complete the table by finding 1% of each amount.

Tip Divide each amount by 100.

Amount	$400	$70	$3
1% of amount			

5 Calculate:

Tip Find 1% first.

a 12% of $80

1% of $80 = ______

12% of $80 = $______ × 12

= ☐

b 2.5% of $300

1% of $300 = ______

2.5% of $300 = $______ × 2.5

= ☐

6 Use fraction methods to calculate:

a 5% of 60 L

$\frac{\_\_}{100} \times \frac{\_\_}{1}$

= ☐

b 40% of 85 m

$\frac{\_\_}{100} \times \frac{\_\_}{1}$

= ☐

7 Use decimal methods to calculate:

Tip To change a percentage to a decimal, divide by 100.

a 27% of $97

= 0.____ × ____

= ☐

b 4% of 500 mL

= 0.____ × ____

= ☐

8 Use fraction methods to calculate:

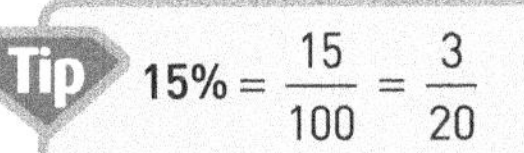

a 35% of 220

$= \frac{\_\_}{100} \times \frac{\_\_}{1}$

= ☐

b 60% of 45

$= \frac{\_\_}{100} \times \frac{\_\_}{1}$

= ☐

c 75% of 84

$= \frac{\_\_}{100} \times \frac{\_\_}{1}$

= ☐

d 45% of 160

$= \frac{\_\_}{100} \times \frac{\_\_}{1}$

= ☐

NAPLAN-ready

Shade the box beneath the correct answer.

Three of the calculations below correctly finds 25% of 82.

The incorrect calculation is:

$82 \div 4$	$\frac{25}{100} \times 82$
☐	☐
$(100 \div 25) \times 82$	0.25×82
☐	☐

Tip Write 25% as a simple fraction and as a decimal.

2.9 Increasing or decreasing by a given percentage

Increasing

A total amount is 100%.

To increase an amount by a percentage, add the percentage onto 100% and then multiply the amount by this percentage.

e.g. Increase $60 by 25%

$100\% + 25\% = 125\%$

125% of $60
$= 1.25 \times 60$ (125% = 1.25)
$= \$75$

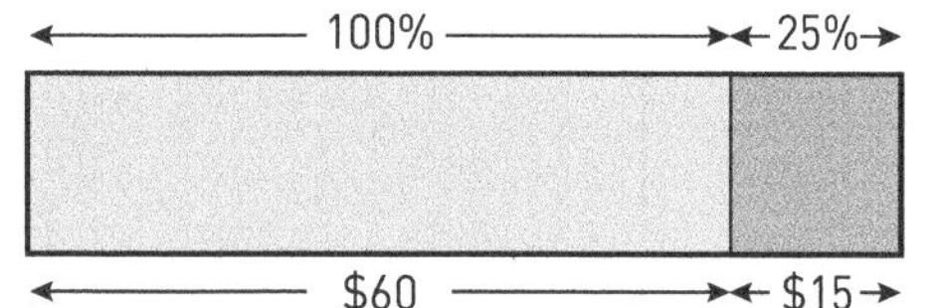

Decreasing

To decrease an amount by a percentage, subtract the percentage decrease from 100% and then multiply this percentage by the amount.

e.g. Decrease $60 by 25%

$100\% - 25\% = 75\%$

75% of $60
$= 0.75 \times 60$ (75% = 0.75)
$= \$45$

Finding the percentage increase or decrease

Percentages can be used to compare the amount of increase (or decrease) with the original amount.

If $60 increases to $75, the increase is $15.

$$\% \text{ increase} = \frac{\text{increase}}{\text{original}} \times 100\%$$
$$= \frac{15}{60} \times 100\%$$
$$= 25\%$$

1 Calculate each of the following.

Tip Find the amount of increase and then the new amount for each.

a Increase $70 by 10%.

Amount of increase 100% + ____ = ____%

____% of $70 = $\frac{\_\_}{100}$ × ____

= ☐

New amount: $____

b Increase $250 by 40%.

Amount of increase 100% + ____ = ____%

____% of $250 = $\frac{\_\_}{100}$ × ____

= ☐

New amount: $____

2 Calculate each of the following.

Tip Find the amount of decrease, then the new amount for each.

a Decrease $90 by 25%.

Decrease = 100% − ____ = ____%

= $\frac{\_\_}{100}$ × ____

= ☐

New amount: $____

b Decrease $360 by 15%.

Decrease = 100% − ____ = ____%

= $\frac{\_\_}{100}$ × ____

= ☐

New amount: $____

3 Find the percentage increase to the nearest whole per cent when Sarah's wage goes up from \$630 to \$650.

Increase = ____ − ____

= \$____

% increase = $\frac{\quad}{630}$ × 100%

≈ ☐ %

4 Choose the correct calculation.

a When \$80 goes up to \$85, the % increase is:

A $\frac{5}{85}$ × 100% B $\frac{80}{85}$ × 100%

C $\frac{5}{80}$ × 100% D $\frac{85}{80}$ × 100%

b When \$450 goes down to \$300, the % decrease is:

A $\frac{150}{450}$ × 100% B $\frac{150}{300}$ × 100%

C $\frac{450}{750}$ × 100% D $\frac{300}{450}$ × 100%

5 Calculate the increased amount.

Tip **Add the percentage to 100% then convert to a decimal.**

a Increase \$280 by 32%.

Total %: 100% + 32% = ______%

132% = 1.____

132% of \$280 = ____ × 1.____

= ☐

b Increase \$83 by 6%.

Total %: ____ + ____ = ______%

_____% = 1.____

____% of \$83 = ____ × 1.____

= ☐

6 Calculate the decreased amount.

Tip **Subtract the percentage from 100% then convert to a decimal.**

a Decrease \$420 by 8%.

Reduced %: 100% − 8% = ____%

92% = 0.____

92% of \$420 = ____ × 0.____

= ☐

b Decrease \$65 by 40%.

Reduced % ____ − ____ = ____%

____% = 0.____

____% of \$65 = ____ × 0.____

= ☐

7 State whether each statement is true (T) or false (F) by circling the correct answer.

Tip **Convert the fractions and percentages to decimals first.**

a \$3400 increased by 80% is \$3400 × 1.08 **T or F**

b \$275 decreased by 5% is \$275 × 1.05 **T or F**

8 The cost of a haircut goes up by 3.5%. How much will Dana pay now if she used to pay \$63.20?

NAPLAN-ready

Shade the box beneath the correct answer.

The cost of a bucket of chicken went up from \$5.60 to \$6.50.

The percentage increase is closest to:

10%	15%	20%	25%
☐	☐	☐	☐

Tip **Find the amount of increase and compare it with the original.**

2.10 Financial applications of percentages A

Mark up

When retailers sell goods, they add a percentage of the cost of the goods to cover their expenses and make a **profit**. The amount that is added is called the **mark up**.

If an item cost \$60, the **selling price** after a 50% mark up is:

$$\begin{aligned}\text{Mark up} &= 50\% \text{ of } \$60\\ &= 0.5 \times \$60\\ &= \$30\end{aligned}$$

Selling price

$= \text{cost price} + \text{mark up}$
$= \$60 + \$30$
$= \$90$

More directly:

$100\% + 50\% = 150\%$ or 1.5

So selling price
$= \text{cost price} \times 1.5$
$= \$60 \times 1.5$
$= \$90$

Discount

A discount reduces the original selling price by a given percentage.

If an item is marked at \$150, to find the **sale price** after a 20% discount:

$$\begin{aligned}\text{Discount} &= 20\% \text{ of } \$150\\ &= 0.2 \times \$150\\ &= \$30\end{aligned}$$

Sale price

$= \text{marked price} - \text{discount}$
$= \$150 - \$30$
$= \$120$

More directly:

$100\% - 20\% = 80\%$ or 0.8

So sale price
$= \text{marked price} \times 0.8$
$= \$150 \times 0.8$
$= \$120$

Profit and loss

When a person buys an item and then sells it at a different price, they make either a **profit** or **loss**.

If an item is bought for \$820 and then sold for \$1000, the profit as a percentage of the cost price is:

Profit

$= \text{selling price} - \text{cost price}$
$= \$1000 - \$820$
$= \$180$

% profit

$= \dfrac{\text{profit}}{\text{cost price}} \times 100\%$

$= \dfrac{180}{820} \times 100\%$

$\approx 22\%$ (correct to the nearest whole percentage)

Word Bank

Cost price (CP)
→ The cost price is the cost of making or buying goods.

Selling price (SP)
→ The selling price is the price of goods after the storeowner has added the mark up to the cost price.

SP = CP + mark up

Profit
→ A profit is made if SP is greater than CP.

Profit = SP − CP

Loss
→ A loss is made if SP is less than CP.

Loss = CP − SP.

1 A shop buys apples for \$1.40 per kg. They place them in 2 kg bags and sell each bag for \$5. State the following amounts for each kilogram of apples.

a The cost price ______

b The selling price ______

c The mark up ______

2 State whether each of the following shows a profit or loss, by circling the correct answer, and then calculate the amount of the profit or loss.

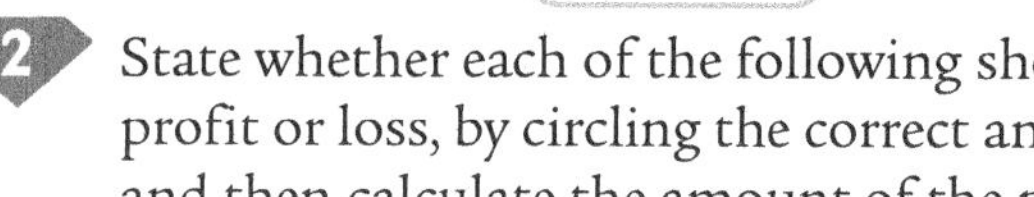

	Cost price	Selling price		Amount
a	\$885	\$700	profit/loss	
b	\$71.20	\$85	profit/loss	
c	\$30	\$41.50	profit/loss	

3 For each part of Question **1**, calculate the percentage profit or percentage loss, based on the cost price. Write your answers correct to the nearest whole percentage.

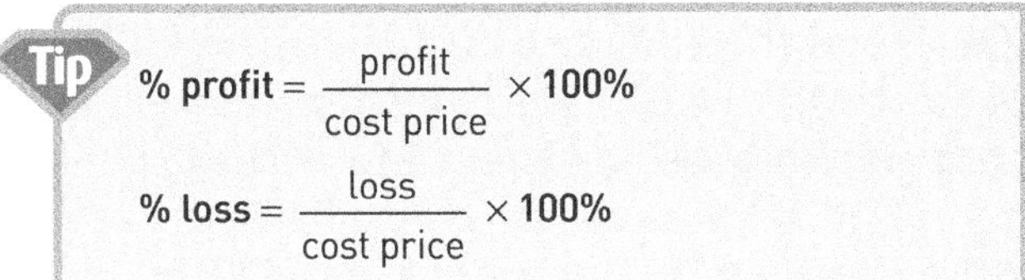
Tip $\% \text{ profit} = \dfrac{\text{profit}}{\text{cost price}} \times 100\%$

$\% \text{ loss} = \dfrac{\text{loss}}{\text{cost price}} \times 100\%$

a $\% \text{ loss} = \dfrac{\_\_\_\_}{\text{cost price}} \times 100\%$

$= \dfrac{\_\_\_\_}{\_\_\_\_} \times 100\%$

$\approx$ ☐ (nearest whole percentage)

b % ______ $= \dfrac{\_\_\_\_}{\text{cost price}} \times 100\%$

$= \dfrac{\_\_\_\_}{\_\_\_\_} \times$ ______

$\approx$ ☐ (nearest whole percentage)

c % ______ =

=

$\approx$ ☐ (nearest whole percentage)

4 Find the selling price of a $350 jacket after a mark up of 65%.

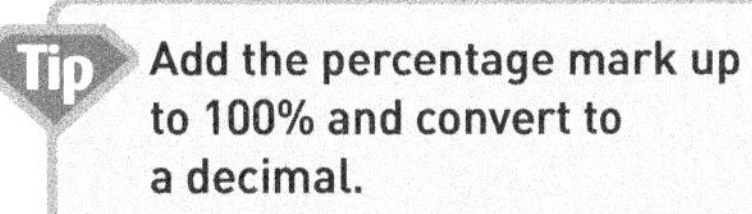
Tip Add the percentage mark up to 100% and convert to a decimal.

100% + 65% = ______%

= 1.65 (as a decimal)

Selling price = cost price × 1.65

= ________ × 1.65

= ____________

5 Find the sale price of a $35 vase after a discount of 25%.

Tip Subtract the percentage discount from 100% and then convert to a decimal.

100% − ____% = ____%

= ____ (as a decimal)

Sale price = marked price × ____

= ____ × ____

= ________

6 An item cost a store $40. To find the selling price of the item after a mark up of 64% we would:

A find 64% of $40, then add this to $40

B multiply $40 by 1.64

C divide $40 by 1.64

D either **A** or **B**

7 An item is marked at $120. To find the sale price of the item after a discount of 5% we would:

A find 5% of $120, then add this to $120

B multiply $120 by 0.95

C divide $120 by 0.95

D either **A** or **B**

8 A person buys an item for $600 and then sells it for $630. The calculation to find the percentage profit is:

A $\dfrac{30}{100} \times 600\%$

B $\dfrac{600}{630} \times 100\%$

C $\dfrac{30}{630} \times 100\%$

D $\dfrac{30}{600} \times 100\%$

2.10 Financial applications of percentages B

GST

Most goods sold and services provided in Australia are required to have 10% tax added to the selling price.

To find how much a customer must be charged for an item so that the store receives $80:

GST = 10% of $80
= 0.1×80
= $8 ← (sent to the government)

So the customer pays:

$80 + $8 = $88

More directly:

100% + 10% = 110% or 1.1

The amount the customer pays be can calculated as:

$80 × 1.1 = $88

| $80 | + GST = | $88 |

Determining the original price

• GST

If we know the amount a customer paid for goods after 10% GST was added, we can work backwards to see how much the price was before the tax was added (this is how much the store keeps). If the customer paid $71.50:

Before tax price × 1.1 = $71.50

Before tax price = $71.50 ÷ 1.1 ← (÷ 1.1 is the opposite of × 1.1)
= $65

• Mark ups

If we know the selling price (SP) of an item after a 70% mark up, we can work backwards to find the cost price (CP). For an item sold for $734.40:

CP × 1.7 = $734.40

So CP = $734.40 ÷ 1.7 ← (the opposite of × 1.7 is ÷ 1.7)
= $432

• Discounts

If we know the sale price of an item after a 15% discount, we can work backwards to find the marked price (MP). For an item on sale for $35.70:

MP × 0.85 = $35.70

So MP = $35.70 ÷ 0.85 ← (the opposite of × 0.85 is ÷ 0.85)
= $42

Word Bank

GST
→ The Goods and Services Tax is 10% of the 'before tax' price, which is paid to the federal government on goods and services.

1 Write the operation that would undo each of the following.

Tip To undo multiplication we divide.

a × 1.1 is undone by ______

b × 1.52 is undone by ______

c × 0.75 is undone by ______

2 Find the amount paid by the customer for each of the goods and services, given the 'before tax' price.

Tip Adding 10% to a price is the same as multiplying the price by 1.1.

		Before tax price	Price paid by the customer
a	TV	$3200	$3200 × 1.1 =
b	paint job	$15 500	
c	shoes	$49	
d	hair cut	$25	

3 Find the before tax price of an item that sold for $423.50 after 10% GST was added.

> **Tip** Adding 10% is the same as multiplying by 1.1. To undo multiplication, we divide.

Before tax price × 1.1 = $423.50

Before tax price = $423.50 ÷ ____

= ________

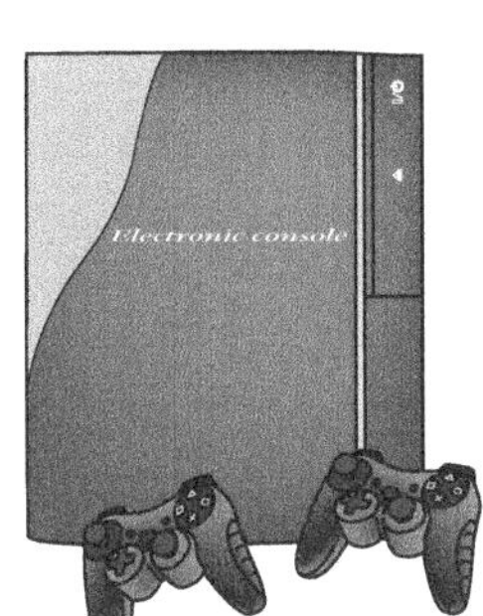

4 Find the before tax price of fixing the gutters and drain pipes if Nick had to pay $495 after 10% GST had been added.

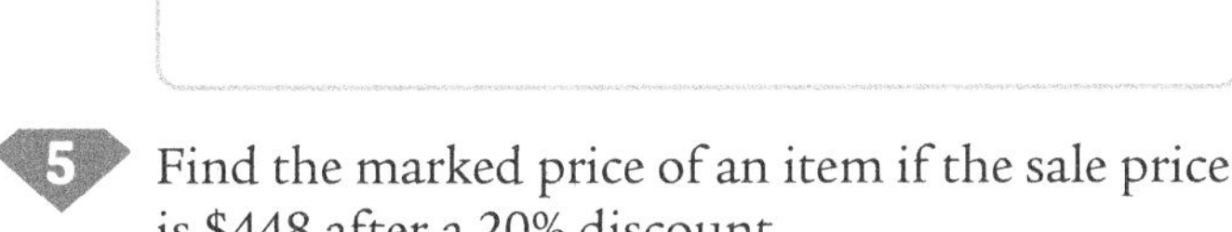

5 Find the marked price of an item if the sale price is $448 after a 20% discount.

100% − 20% = 80% = 0.____

MP × 0.____ = $448

MP = $448 ÷ ____

= ____

6 Find the marked price of a rug if it is on sale for $140 after a 60% discount has been given.

7 Find the cost price (CP) of an item that sells for $59.94 after a 62% mark up.

CP × 1.62 = $59.94

CP = $59.94 ÷ ____

= ____

8 Find the cost price of an outdoor setting that sells for $420 after a 75% mark up had been added

9 If an item is on sale for $135 after a discount of 15%, we can backtrack to find the marked price by:

A multiplying by 1.15

B dividing by 1.15

C multiplying by 0.85

D dividing by 0.85

10 If a mobile phone sells for $84 after a 55% mark up we can backtrack to find the cost price by:

A multiplying by 1.55

B dividing by 1.55

C multiplying by 0.45

D dividing by 0.45

NAPLAN-ready

Shade the box beneath the correct answer.

A store pays $520 for a tennis racquet then marks up the price by 65%. When the racquet doesn't sell a discount of 15% is given. The final sale price, to the nearest dollar is:

$312	$780	$729	$936
☐	☐	☐	☐

> **Tip** This calculation requires two steps. Increasing by 65% is the same as multiplying by ____. Decreasing by 15% is the same as multiplying by ____.

3.1 Variables and expressions

The language of algebra

- An **expression** is made up of one or more **terms**. The expression $2x + 7$ is made up of two terms, $2x$ and 7.
- An **equation** links two expressions with an equal sign

  $2x + 7 = 25$ ← equation

  expressions

- The **coefficient** in an algebraic term is the number at the front.

  $5x$ means 5 lots of x

  $2ab^2$ means 2 lots of ab^2

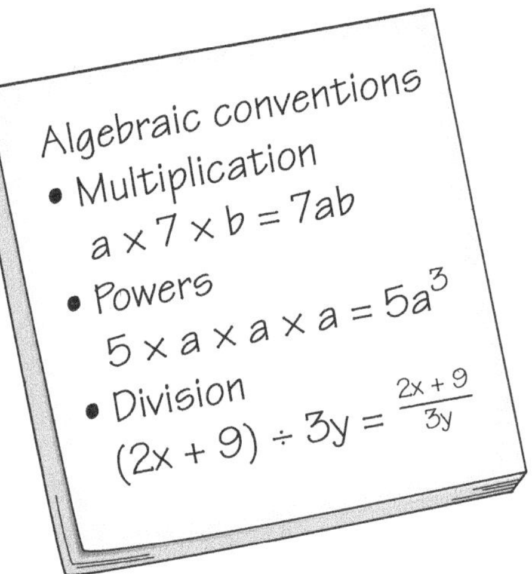

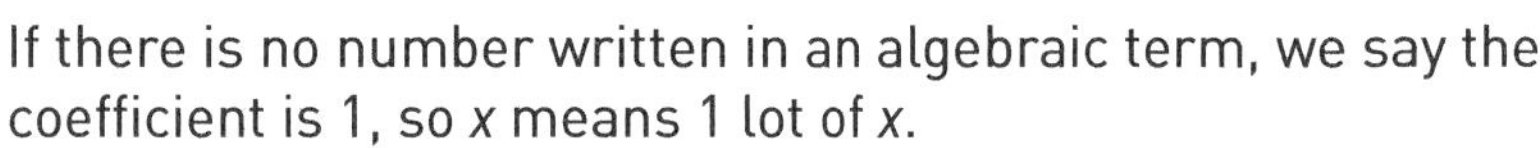

If there is no number written in an algebraic term, we say the coefficient is 1, so x means 1 lot of x.

- **Variables** are unknown amounts (or amounts that can change, or vary) represented by symbols, usually letters.

  $5xy^2 + ax$: The variables are x, y and a.

- A **constant** term has no variables, so its value cannot change.

  $2a - b - 4$: The constant term is -4.

Writing words as algebraic expressions

In changing from words to algebraic expressions:

- define your variables (e.g. 'Let x be the number of jellybeans that Bill has')
- look for key words to decide which operation to use.

Sara has three times as many jellybeans as Bill. →	Sara's number of jellybeans: $x \times 3 = 3x$
Harry has 8 fewer than Bill →	Harry's number of jellybeans: $x - 8$
Bill shared his jellybeans between 6 people →	Each person's share: $\frac{x}{6}$

1 State whether each statement is true (**T**) or false (**F**) by circling the correct answer.

a $2x + 3y = 8$ is an expression. **T or F**

b The number of terms in $5x^2 - 3x + 4$ is 3. **T or F**

c The coefficient of x^2 in $3x^2 + 5x - 1$ is 5 **T or F**

d The constant term in $8x - 9$ is -9. **T or F**

2 The variables in $6a^2b^2 + 5ab + 3$ are:

A a^2b^2 and ab

B a^2b^2, ab and 3

C a^2, b^2 and ab

D a and b

3 a Write down the coefficient of each variable term in the expression: $2x^2 + xy - 5x + 3$

Tip Where a term is subtracted, the coefficient is negative.

x^2: ☐ xy: ☐ x: ☐

b The constant term in $2x^2 + xy - 5x + 3$ is:

☐

4 Write the number of terms in each expression.

Tip Terms are separated by plus or minus symbols.

a $2 + b$ ☐

b $4x^2 - xy + a$ ☐

c $3x^2yz^5$ ☐

5 Rewrite each expression using algebraic conventions.

a $9 \times p =$ ☐ b $k \div 10 =$ ☐

c $4 \times d \div 7 =$ ☐ d $4 \div (b \times a) =$ ☐

e $x \times 5 \times x =$ ☐ f $(3y + x) \div 5 =$ ☐

6 Write an algebraic expression for each of the following given that k is the number of kites flying in the park on Saturday.

a On Sunday there were twice as many kites as Saturday.

☐

b On Friday there were six fewer kites than Saturday.

☐

c On Monday there were half as many kites as Saturday.

☐

d The following Saturday there were five more than double the kites as the first Saturday.

☐

7 If m is the number of chips in a packet, write a meaning for each expression.

a $6m$

☐

b $m - 30$

☐

c $\frac{m}{2}$

☐

NAPLAN-ready

Shade the box beneath the correct answer.

If a number is represented by x, an expression for 5 fewer than double the number is:

$2x - 5$	$x - 10$
☐	☐
$\frac{x-5}{2}$	$2(x-5)$
☐	☐

Tip Double means multiply by 2. 5 fewer means subtract 5.

3.2 Substitution for variables

Replacing variables with numbers

When we 'substitute' a variable, we replace it with an actual number value in an expression.

If $a = -3$ and $b = 4$: $a + b = -3 + 4$

Evaluating: $-3 + 4 = -1$

- Replacing the multiplication symbol

  For terms such as $2x$ or xy, when we replace the variables with numbers we must insert the multiplication symbols.

  If we substitute $x = 3$ into the expression $2x$:

  $2x = 2 \times 3$
  $= 6$

If we substitute $x = 4$ and $y = -5$ into the expression xy:

$xy = 4 \times -5$
$= -20$

- Powers of negative numbers

  When a negative number replaces a variable in a power, brackets are needed so that the power applies to the entire value.

  When $x = -5$, $x^2 = (-5)^2$
  $= -5 \times -5$
  $= 25$

Substitution using a rule

For $y = 2x - 6$, substitute each value of x in the table into the expression $2x - 6$, and then evaluate. The result is the corresponding value for y.

$y = 2x - 6$

x	-4	0	3
y	-14	-6	0

$2x - 6$	$2x - 6$	$2x - 6$
$= 2 \times -4 - 6$	$= 2 \times 0 - 6$	$= 2 \times 3 - 6$
$= -8 - 6$	$= 0 - 6$	$= 6 - 6$
$= -14$	$= -6$	$= 0$

Word Bank

Substitute
→ To substitute means to replace a variable with an actual value.

Evaluate
→ To evaluate means to find the answer, i.e. a single value for the expression.

1 What are the values of the following expressions if $x = 10$?

a $x - 25$

$= \_\_\_\_ - 25$

$= \square$

b $3x$

$= 3 \times \_\_\_\_$

$= \square$

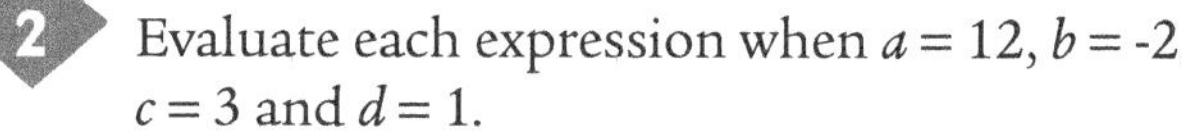

2 Evaluate each expression when $a = 12$, $b = -2$, $c = 3$ and $d = 1$.

a $a + d$

$= \_\_\_\_ + \_\_\_\_$

$= \square$

b $3a$

$= 3 \times \_\_\_\_$

$= \square$

c bc

$= \_\_\_\_ \times \_\_\_\_$

$= \square$

d $\frac{a}{4}$

$= \frac{\_\_}{4}$

$= \square$

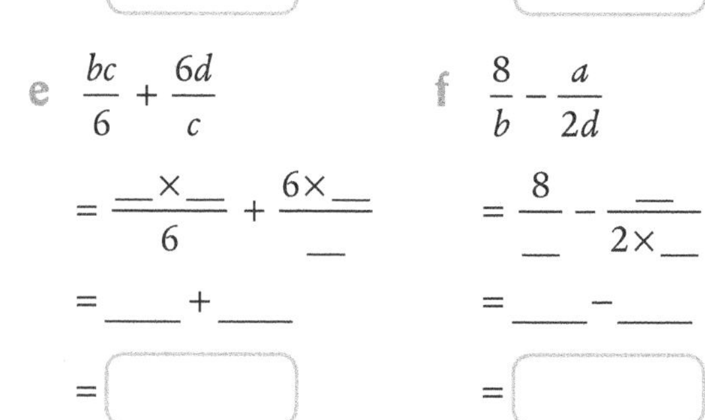

e $\frac{bc}{6} + \frac{6d}{c}$

$= \frac{\_\_ \times \_\_}{6} + \frac{6 \times \_\_}{\_\_}$

$= \_\_\_\_ + \_\_\_\_$

$= \square$

f $\frac{8}{b} - \frac{a}{2d}$

$= \frac{8}{\_\_} - \frac{\_\_}{2 \times \_\_}$

$= \_\_\_\_ - \_\_\_\_$

$= \square$

3 Evaluate each expression when $x = 2$ and $y = -3$.

Tip When substituting a negative number into a power, place brackets around the number including the negative sign.

a x^2
$= 2^2$
$= 2 \times 2$
$=$ ☐

b y^2
$= (-3)^2$
$= -3 \times -3$
$=$ ☐

c x^2y
$= (\_\_\_\_)^2 \times \_\_\_\_$
$= \_\_\_\_ \times \_\_\_\_ \times \_\_\_\_$
$=$ ☐

d $\frac{x^3}{4}$
$= \frac{\_\_\_^3}{4}$
$= \frac{\_\_ \times \_\_ \times \_\_}{4}$
$=$ ☐

e $2x^3 + y^2$
$= 2 \times \_\_\_\_^3 + (\_\_\_\_)^2$
$= 2 \times \_\_\_\_ \times \_\_\_\_ \times \_\_\_\_ + \_\_\_\_ \times \_\_\_\_$
$= \_\_\_\_ + \_\_\_\_$
$=$ ☐

4 One of the following shows correct substitution. For each incorrect substitution, write the correct expression. For the correct one, write 'correct'.

a If $x = 3$ and $y = -5$:
$xy = 3 - 5$

☐

b If $a = 9$:
$2a^3 = 29^3$

☐

c If $p = 6$:
$3p + \frac{p}{2} = 3 \times 6 + \frac{6}{2}$

☐

d If $t = -7$:
$t^2 = -7^2$

☐

5 Complete the table of values for each rule.

Tip Substitute each value in the x-row into the expression and evaluate. Write the answer in the y-row below the matching x-value.

a $y = x + 7$

x	-4	0	3
y	3		

$y = x + 7$	$y = x + 7$	$y = x + 7$
$= \_\_\_ + 7$	$= \_\_\_ + 7$	$= \_\_\_\_\_\_$
$= 3$	$= \_\_\_$	$= \_\_\_$

b $y = -2x$

x	-2	0	5
y			

c $y = 3x - 5$

x	0	2	4
y			

NAPLAN-ready

Shade the box beneath the correct answer.

$$L = \frac{a+b}{a-b}$$

Which values of a and b give $L = 5$?

$a = 12, b = 8$ ☐ $a = 22, b = 18$ ☐

$a = 17, b = 3$ ☐ $a = 37, b = 23$ ☐

Tip Find the values for the numerator and denominator first.

3.3 Using formulas

A formula is an equation that is used in a practical situation.

The **formula** for converting temperature in degrees Celsius, c (°C), to degrees Fahrenheit, f (°F), is:

$$f = \frac{9c}{5} + 32$$

To find a temperature of 25°C in °F:

1 Write the given information in symbols.

$c = 25$

2 Substitute into the expression and evaluate.

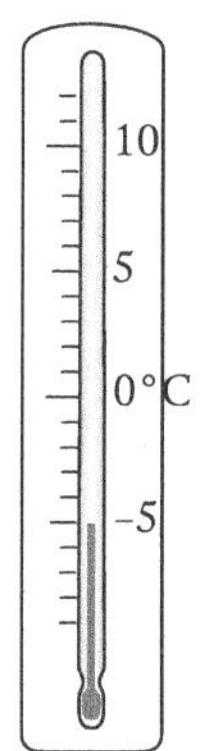

$$f = \frac{9c}{5} + 32$$
$$= \frac{9 \times 25}{5} + 32$$
$$= 45 + 32$$
$$= 77$$

3 Write the answer in a sentence, including any units.

A temperature of 25°C is the same as 77°F.

1 If $a = 3$ and $b = 7$, what is the value of y in the following equations?

a $y = 2b - a$

$= 2 \times$ ____ $-$ ____

$=$ ________

$y =$ ▭

b $y = ab$

$=$ ________________

$y =$ ▭

2 Mia charges \$12 to mow lawns in her neighbourhood. The money she earns could be described using the formula: $m = 12n$, where:

m = money earned in dollars
n = number of lawns

a Complete the table of values to show how much Mia could earn.

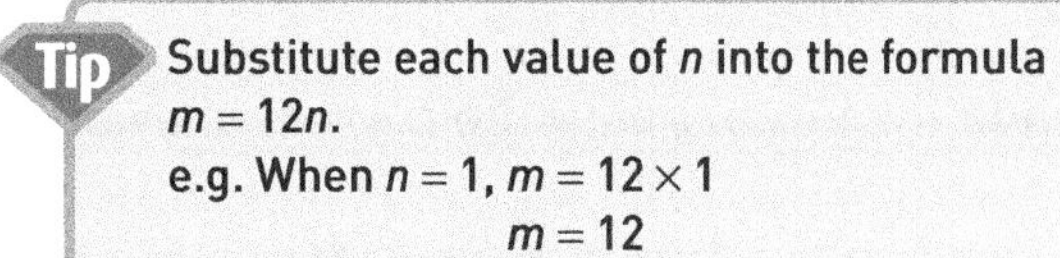

Tip Substitute each value of n into the formula $m = 12n$.
e.g. When $n = 1$, $m = 12 \times 1$
$m = 12$

Number of lawns mowed (n)	1	2	3	4	5
Money earned in dollars (m)					

b One week Mia mowed 8 lawns. How much money did she make?

c What is the minimum number of lawns she would need to mow to earn over \$100?

3 The formula for the distance travelled, d (km), for a car after a certain amount of time, t (hours), when travelling at an average speed of s (km/h) is $d = st$.

a Find the distance covered in 3 hours, if a car is travelling at an average speed of 80 km/h.

$d = st$

$=$ ____ $\times$ ____ (substitute in the values for s and t)

$=$ ▭ km

b Find the distance covered in 2 hours, if a car is travelling at an average speed of 50 km/h.

$d =$ ________________

$=$ ____ $\times$ ____

$=$ ▭ km

4 The cost of a taxi fare (F), in dollars, can be calculated using the formula $F = 1.2d + 3.30$, where d is the distance travelled in kilometres.

a What is the cost of a taxi fare if you travel 5 km?

b What is the cost of a taxi fare if you travel 20 km?

5 The formula used to calculate Annette's bonus (in dollars) at the end of the month is $b = 5(e - a)$, where e is the number of days she put in extra effort and a is the number of days she was absent. Find the amount of Annette's bonus if she put in extra effort on 10 days and was absent twice.

$e =$ ____, $a =$ ____

$b = 5(e - a)$

$=$ ________

$=$ ________

$=$ ____

Annette's bonus is ☐

6 The formula for finding the total area (in cm^2) of the faces of a square-based prism is:

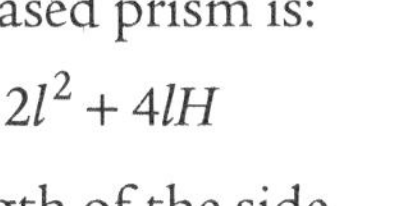

$$T = 2l^2 + 4lH$$

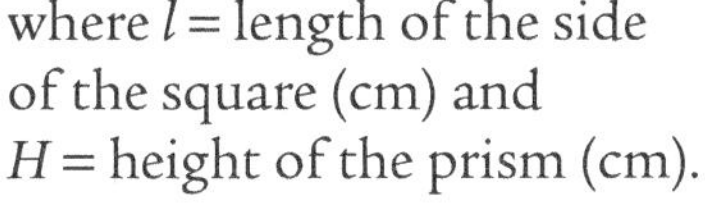

where l = length of the side of the square (cm) and H = height of the prism (cm).

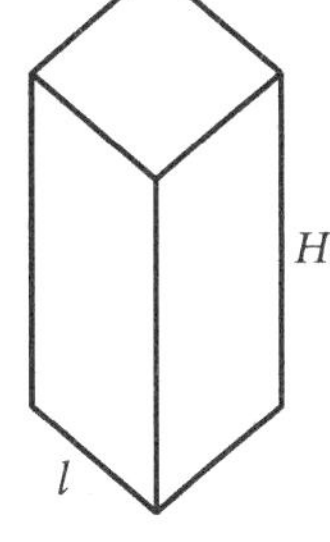

Find T when $l = 15$ cm and $H = 5$ cm.

$T = 2l^2 + 4lH$

7 The number of edges, E, on a 3D shape can be found using the formula $E = V + F - 2$, where V is the number of vertices (corners) and F is the number of faces. This formula is known as Euler's formula.

Use Euler's formula to find the number of edges on the following shapes.

Tip Check that your calculations are correct by counting the number of edges on each shape.

a

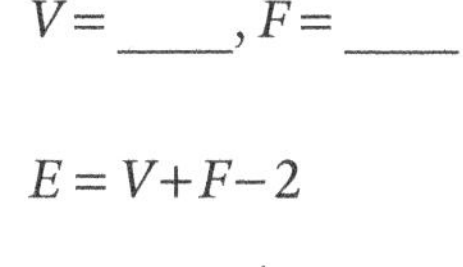

$V =$ ____, $F =$ ____

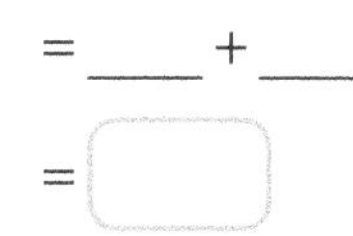

$E = V + F - 2$

$=$ ____ $+$ ____

$=$ ☐

b

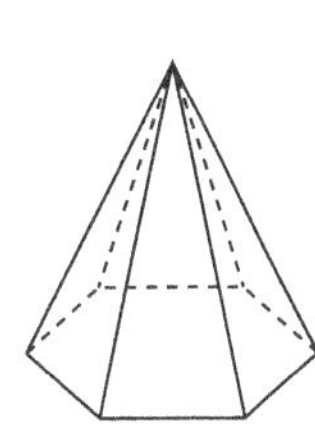

$V =$ ____, $F =$ ____

$E = V + F - 2$

$=$ ____ $+$ ____ $- 2$

$=$ ☐

8 Convert the following temperatures to degrees Fahrenheit.

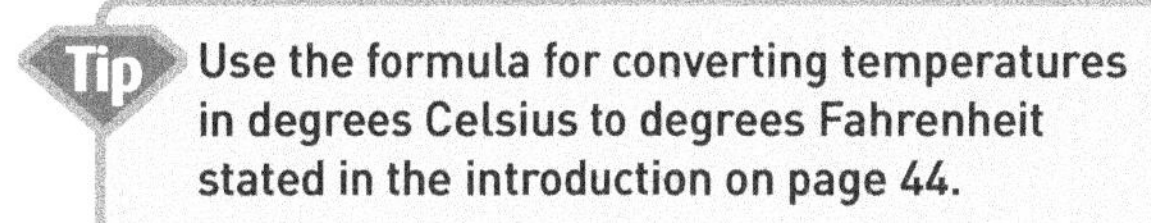

Tip Use the formula for converting temperatures in degrees Celsius to degrees Fahrenheit stated in the introduction on page 44.

a 10°C

b 35°C

NAPLAN-ready

Shade the box beneath the correct answer.

The formula for converting length, c in cm, to length i, length in inches, is $i = \dfrac{c}{2.54}$.

The length, in inches, of a 30 cm ruler is approximately:

11.8 inches ☐	12.2 inches ☐
75.8 inches ☐	76.2 inches ☐

Tip Substitute for c in the formula.

3.4 Simplifying expressions

Like terms

Like terms have algebraic factors that are *identical* in type and number. Only the coefficient can be different:

- **Like terms**
  - $2x$ and $3x$
  - $5ab$ and ab
  - $8x^2$ and $-6x^2$

- **Not like terms**
  - $3x$ and $3y$
  - x and $5x^2$
  - xy^2 and x^2

Collecting like terms

- **Addition and subtraction**

Like terms can be added and subtracted.

$3x + 5x = 8x$ ← (add the coefficients: $3 + 5 = 8$)

This is true for any variable or product of variables:

$3ab + 5ab = 8ab$

Terms must be 'like' to be subtracted.

$9h^2 - 5h^2 = 4h^2$

This process of combining groups is called 'collecting like terms'.

Unlike terms

$3x + 4y$ cannot be simplified.

Neither can $2x + 6x^2$ because $2x$ and $6x^2$ are not like terms.

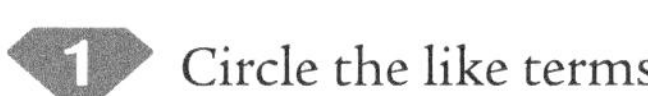

1 Circle the like terms.

a $2x$ $2y$ $3x$ x

b $5ab$ $2bc$ $6ab$ $3a$

2 a Which of the following is a pair of like terms?

A $3x^2, 3y^2$

B $5xy, 2yx$

C $3ab, 9ab^2$

D $x^4, 4x$

b Which of the following is a pair of unlike terms?

A $3a, -a$

B $-3cd, 2cd$

C $4ab^2, ab^2$

D $2pn, 4pm$

3 Which of the following expressions can be simplified?

A $4r + r$

B $-3mn - nm$

C $5w^2 + w$

D $8de + de - 5de$

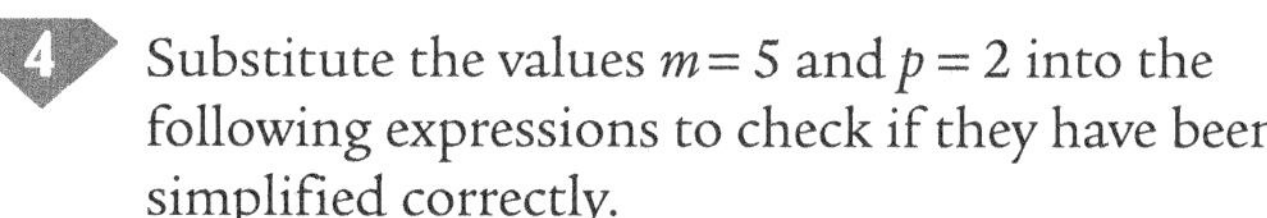

4 Substitute the values $m = 5$ and $p = 2$ into the following expressions to check if they have been simplified correctly.

a $m + m = m^2$

________ = ________ ✓ ✗

b $3mp + mp = 4mp$

________ = ________ ✓ ✗

c $5p - p = 5$

________ = ________ ✓ ✗

d $4m + 7p = 11mp$

________ = ________ ✓ ✗

5 State the perimeter of of the triangle below using algebra.

Tip The perimeter is found by finding the sum of all side lengths.

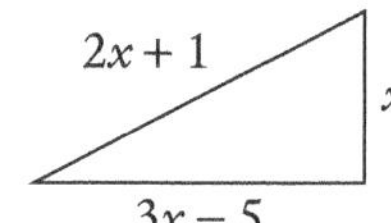

6 Simplify, if possible, by collecting like terms.

Tip Add (or subtract) the coefficients. Remember x means $1x$.

a $4e + 6e$

= ____

b $-6f + 8f$

= ____

c $15y - 12y$

= ____

d $-2s - s$

= ____

e $5t^2 + 9t^2$

= ____

f $t^3 + 8t$

= ____

g $9mn + mn$

= ____

h $5a^2b - a^2b$

= ____

7 Simplify by collecting like terms.

Tip Place like terms side by side first.

a $6e + 9xy + xy + 9e$
$= 6e + 9e + 9xy + xy$
$= 15e +$ ____

b $-8f + p + 2f + 8p$
$= -8f +$ ____ $+ p +$ ____
$= -6f +$ ____

c $11y - 5x + 2x - 10y$
= ____ − ____ $- 5x +$ ____
= ____

d $-3s - 5s^2t - s - 3s^2t$
= ____ − ____ − ____ − ____
= ____

e $4t^2 - 5t^2u - 5t^2u + 9t^2$
= ____ + ____ − ____ − ____
= ____

8 Check that collecting like terms has 'worked' by substituting $x = 3$ and $y = 5$ to find a value for each term, and then add the values in the last column.

e.g. $7x - 5x = 2x$
If $x = 3$, $7x - 5x$
$= 21 - 15$
$= 6$
$2x = 6$ ✓

a $3xy$
$= 3 \times 3 \times 5$
= ____

$4xy$
$= 4 \times 3 \times 5$
= ____

$7xy$
$= 7 \times 3 \times 5$
= ____

$3xy + 4xy = 7xy$
Check:
____ + ____ = ____

b x^2y
$= 3^2 \times 5$
=
=

$-6x^2y$
=
=
=

$-5x^2y$
=
=
=

$x^2y - 6x^2y = -5x^2y$
Check:
____ − ____ = ____

9 State whether each statement is true (T) or false (F) by circling the correct answer.

a $x^2y = xy^2$ **T** or **F**

b $5x - x = 5$ **T** or **F**

c $3mn = 3nm$ **T** or **F**

d $4a^2b^2 = 2ab^2$ **T** or **F**

NAPLAN-ready

Shade the box beneath the correct answer.

Poppy has x 20-cent coins and $3x$ 50-cent coins.

The amount of money Poppy has in cents is:

$70x$	$170x$	$17x$	$300x$
☐	☐	☐	☐

Tip Find how much she would have with one 20-cent coin and three 50-cent coins first.

3.5 Multiplying and dividing algebraic terms

Multiplication with algebra

When multiplying, we can rearrange the calculation without changing the result.

$2 \times 5 = 5 \times 2$

We can also regroup factors. This may make the calculation easier to do, or help us to see common factors.

$(3 \times 10) \times 2 = 3 \times (10 \times 2)$

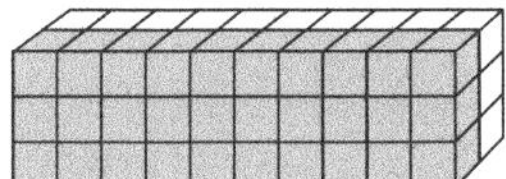

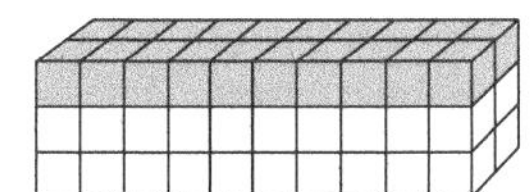

We can use this in algebra to simplify expressions. We multiply all coefficients together and then multiply all the variables.

$5 \times 6a = (5 \times 6) \times a$
$= 30a$

$e \times 4f \times 2p = (4 \times 2) \times (e \times f \times p)$
$= 8efp$

Don't forget to write variables in alphabetical order.

Division with algebra

Division is the reverse process of multiplication.

We use fraction rules to cancel out common factors of the numerator and denominator.

$8ab \div 4bc = \frac{\overset{2}{\cancel{8}}ab}{{}_{1}\cancel{4}bc}$ ← (writing the division as a fraction, dividing top and bottom by 4)

$= \frac{2a\overset{1}{\cancel{b}}}{{}_{1}\cancel{b}c}$ ← (dividing top and bottom by b)

$= \frac{2a}{c}$

We could have done the two divisions above in one step, by dividing by $4b$, which is the highest common factor (HCF) of the two expressions.

$\frac{8ab}{4bc} = \frac{\overset{2}{\cancel{8}}a\cancel{b}}{{}_{1}\cancel{4}\cancel{b}c}$

$= \frac{2a}{c}$

Word Bank

Highest common factor (HCF)

→ For two numbers, the HCF is the largest number and/or letter that divides into both. e.g. the HCF of $6ef$ and $8et$ is $2e$.

1 Simplify each of the following.

Tip Rearrange and group the factors as needed.

a $5 \times 2a$
= ______

b $8b \times 4$
= ______

c $3 \times 7c$
= ______

d $6e \times 10a$
= ______

e $2t \times 11s$
= ______

f $9p \times 5m$
= ______

2 Simplify each of the following.

Tip Ignore the negative signs until the end. A single negative gives a negative answer. Two negatives multiplied together give a positive answer.

a $4 \times -9q$
= ______

b $-3m \times 5$
= ______

c $-5n \times -6d$
= ______

d $-6d \times -11h$
= ______

e $-7r \times 4g$
= ______

f $-y \times -z$
= ______

g $15a \div 3$
= ______

h $28f \div 4f$
= ______

3 Simplify each of the following.

Tip Cancel HCF of the numbers and then any common algebraic factors.

a $\frac{20f}{5}$

$= \frac{{}^{4}\cancel{20}f}{{}_{1}\cancel{5}}$

= ☐

b $\frac{14ch}{2}$

= ☐

c $\frac{6bc}{c}$

= ☐

d $\frac{8mx}{2m}$

$= \frac{\quad}{m}$ (cancelling a common factor of 2)

= ☐ (cancelling a common factor of m)

e $\frac{-6bj}{3j}$

$= \frac{\quad}{\quad}$ (cancelling a common factor of 3)

= ☐ (cancelling a common factor of j)

f $\frac{-4jk}{-2j}$

$= \frac{\quad}{\quad}$

= ☐

4 Simplify each of the following.

Tip Write as fractions first.

a $40by \div 8y$

$= \frac{{}^{5}\cancel{40}b\cancel{y}}{{}_{1}\cancel{8}\cancel{y}}$

= ☐

b $-24pq \div -6p$

$= \frac{\quad}{\quad}$

= ☐

c $90cw \div -3cw$

$= \frac{\quad}{\quad}$

= ☐

5 Circle the letter next to the correct answer.

a $4ac \div 16c$ simplifies to:

A $\frac{4}{a}$ B $\frac{a}{4}$ C $4ac$ D $4a$

b $-5g \div -50gh$ simplifies to:

A $10h$ B $-10h$ C $-\frac{1}{10h}$ D $\frac{1}{10h}$

c $42kl \div -30dl$ simplifies to:

A $-\frac{7k}{5d}$ B $-\frac{7d}{5k}$ C $2k$ D $-35kd$

6 Two rectangles are shown.

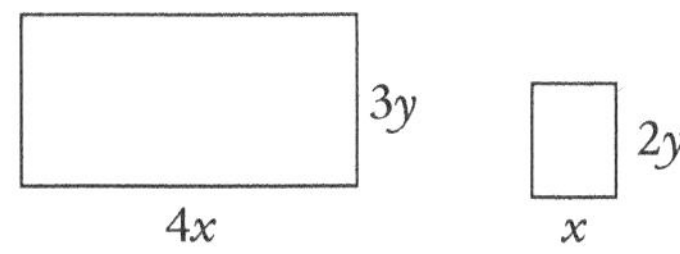

The area of a rectangle can be found using the formula $A = l \times w$.

a What is the area of the larger rectangle?

b What is the area of smaller rectangle?

c How many small rectangles can fit inside the large rectangle?

Tip Write as a fraction. Cancel common factors

NAPLAN-ready

Shade the box beneath the correct answer.

The expression $(ab \times 7cd \times 5e) \div 10def$ simplifies to:

$\frac{14abc}{f}$	$7cd$	$\frac{7abc}{2def}$	$\frac{7abc}{2f}$
☐	☐	☐	☐

Tip Write as a fraction then cancel out common factors.

3.6 Expanding brackets A

The Distributive Law

The 3×7 rectangle has the side of 7 split into $5 + 2$.

The total area can be written as
$3 \times 5 + 3 \times 2$ or $3 \times (5 + 2)$ or $3(5 + 2)$

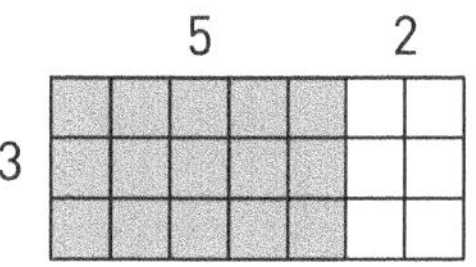

This rectangle has a length of $b + 2$ and a width of 3.

Its area can be written as $3 \times b + 3 \times 2$ or $3(b + 2)$.

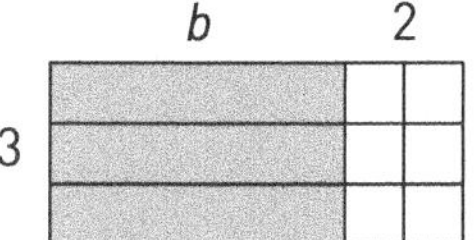

This rectangle has a length of $b + 2$ and a width of a.

Its area can be written as $a \times b + a \times 2$ or $a(b + 2)$.

So $a(b + 2) = a \times b + a \times 2$
$= ab + 2a$

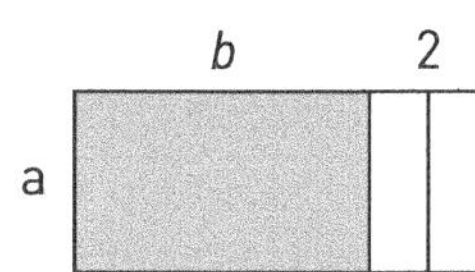

As a general rule: $a(b + c) = ab + ac$

This rule is known as the **Distributive Law**. We use it to multiply the terms inside a set of brackets by the term in front. This is called 'expanding the brackets'.

b c — a | $a(b + c)$; b c — a | ab | ac | a

It is helpful to use the 'crab claws'.

$a(b + c) = ab + ac$

- **Mental maths**

We can use the Distributive Law to help multiply large numbers, using addition to break up the number.

Examples

$5 \times 23 = 5(20 + 3)$
$= 100 + 15$
$= 115$

$4 \times 102 = 4(100 + 2)$
$= 400 + 8$
$= 408$

1 Use the Distributive Law to calculate:

e.g. $5 \times 47 = 5(40 + 7)$
$= 200 + 35$
$= 235$

a 8×34

$8 \times 34 = 8(\_\_\_\_\_\_ + \_\_\_\_\_\_)$

$= \_\_\_\_\_\_ + \_\_\_\_\_\_$

$=$ ☐

b 7×603

$7 \times 603 = 7(600 + \_\_\_\_\_\_)$

$= 4200 + \_\_\_\_\_\_$

$=$ ☐

c 43×1001

$43 \times 1001 = 43(1000 + \_\_\_\_\_\_)$

$= \_\_\_\_\_\_ + \_\_\_\_\_\_$

$=$ ☐

2 Complete the following grids by multiplying the numbers. Add the columns to calculate the total.

a 9×15

	10	5	Total
9			

b $4(x + 10)$

	x	10	Total
4			

3 Use the Distributive Law to expand the brackets.

a $6(x+3) = 6 \times$ ______ $+ 6 \times$ ______

$=$ ______

b $7(2x+10) = 7 \times$ ______ $+ 7 \times$ ______

$=$ ______

c $6(2x-1) = 6 \times$ ______ $- 6 \times$ ______

$=$ ______

4 Use the Distributive Law to expand the brackets.

Tip Group the numbers and variables separately. Remember $x \times x = x^2$.

a $9b(2c+5)$

$= 9b \times$ ______ $+ 9b \times$ ______

$=$ ______

b $2b(8+b)$

$=$ ______ $\times$ ______ $+$ ______ $\times$ ______

$=$ ______

5 Simplify the following expressions.

Tip Expand the brackets first then collect like terms

a $3(x+5) - 2x$

$=$ ____ $+$ ____ $- 2x$

$=$ __ $- 2x +$ __

$=$ ______

b $5m(p+4) + m$

$=$ ____ $+$ ____ $+$ ____

$=$ ______

c $2a(6+a) + 3(a+4)$

$=$ ____ $+$ ____ $+$ ____

$=$ ____ $+ 12a + 3a +$ ____

$=$ ______

6 Demonstrate expanding brackets using the rectangle as an example.

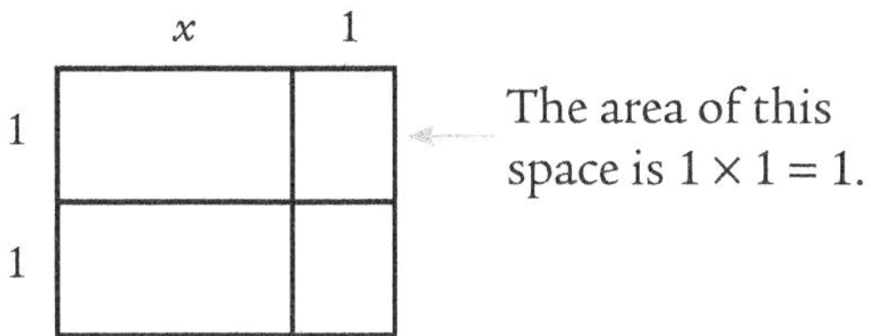

a The four individual areas are:

x, __, 1, __

Total area = __ + __

b Length of rectangle: __ + 1

Width of rectangle: __

Area = length × width

= (__ + 1) × __

= __(__ + 1)

i.e. 2(__ + __) = __ + __

7 A rectangle is $(3x+5)$ cm long and $2x$ cm wide.

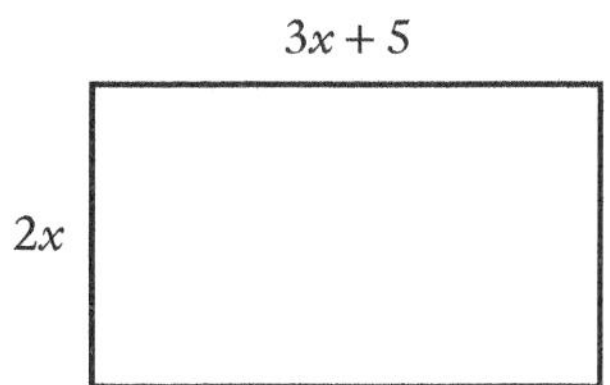

a Write an expression for the area of the rectangle in cm^2.

______

b Expand your answer in **a**.

______

c Write an expression for the perimeter of the rectangle in cm.

______

d Expand and simplify your answer from **c**.

______

3.6 Expanding brackets B

The Distributive Law and subtraction

If the bracket contains a subtraction, we apply the Distributive Law in the same way.

$a(b-c) = ab-ac$

$4(x-5) = 3x-15$

So $-a(b+c) = -ab-ac$ ← (each positive term changes to negative)

and $-a(b-c) = -ab+ac$ ← (each term changes to the opposite sign)

- **Mental maths**

We can use the Distributive Law to help multiply large numbers, using subtraction to break down the number.

$5 \times 29 = 5(30-1)$
$= 150-5$
$= 145$

$4 \times 98 = 4(100-2)$
$= 400-8$
$= 392$

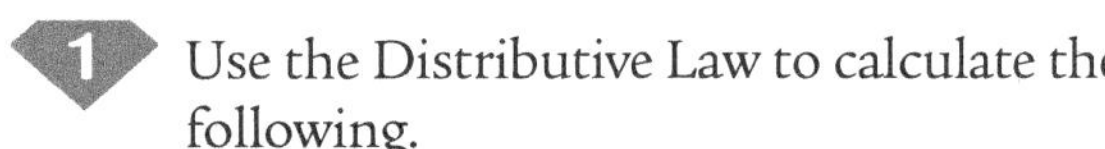

1 Use the Distributive Law to calculate the following.

Tip The Distributive Law can be used to perform multiplications, making it easier to do calculations in our head.
e.g. $3 \times 76 = 3 \times (80-4)$
$= 240-12$
$= 228$

a $4 \times 58 = 4(60-2)$

$=$ ____ $-$ ____

$=$ ☐

b $7 \times 106 =$ ____ $(110-$ ____ $)$

$=$ ____ $-$ ____

$=$ ☐

c $8 \times 199 = 8(200-$ ____ $)$

$= 1600-$ ____

$=$ ☐

d $21 \times 97 = 21(100-$ ____ $)$

$=$ ____ $-$ ____

$=$ ☐

2 Use the Distributive Law to expand the following.

a $3(a-2) = 3 \times$ ___ $- 3 \times$ ___

$=$ ☐

b $4(2x-y) = 4 \times$ ___ $- 4 \times$ ___

$=$ ☐

c $m(m-7) = m \times$ ____ $- m \times$ ____

$=$ ☐

d $h(4a-h) = h \times$ ____ $- h \times$ ____

$=$ ☐

3 Expand the brackets.

Tip Group the numbers and variables separately. Remember $x \times x = x^2$.

a $7m(3n-r)$

$= 7m \times$ ____ $- 7m \times$ ____

$=$ ☐

b $3f(4f-5c)$

$=$ ____ $\times$ ____ $-$ ____ $\times$ ____

$=$ ☐

4 Expand the brackets and then collect like terms.

Tip Multiply each term in a bracket by the number in front of that bracket.

a $5(m+1)+4(3m-2)$

$= 5 \times$ ____ $+ 5 \times$ ____ $+ 4 \times$ ____ $- 4 \times$ ____

$=$ ____ $+$ ____ $+$ ____ $-$ ____

$=$ ____ $+$ ____ $+$ ____ $-$ ____ (collect like terms)

$=$ ______

b $5s(3p-2)+7(4sp-6s)$

$= 5s \times$ ____ $- 5s \times$ ____ $+ 7 \times$ ____ $- 7 \times$ ____

$=$ ____ $-$ ____ $+$ ____ $-$ ____

$=$ ______

c $8ab+3a(2b-7)$

$= 8ab + 3a \times$ ____ $- 3a \times$ ____

$=$ ____ $+$ ____ $-$ ____

$=$ ________ $-$ ________

d $2gh(4-3a)-8gh$

$=$ ____ $\times$ ____ $-$ ____ $\times$ ____ $- 8gh$

$=$ ______ $-$ ______ $- 8gh$

$=$ ______

5 Expand $6(p-2)+5(2p+4)$ and collect like terms.

6 Expand and collect like terms.

Tip When multiplying by a negative factor outside the brackets, the sign of each term in the bracket changes to the opposite sign.

a $2(a+4)-5(a-6)$

$= 2 \times$ ____ $+ 2 \times$ ____ $- 5 \times$ ____ $+ 5 \times$ ____

$=$ ____ $+$ ____ $-$ ____ $+$ ____

$=$ ____ $-$ ____ $+$ ____ $+$ ____ (collecting like terms)

$=$ ______

b $3(b-7)-2(b+8)$

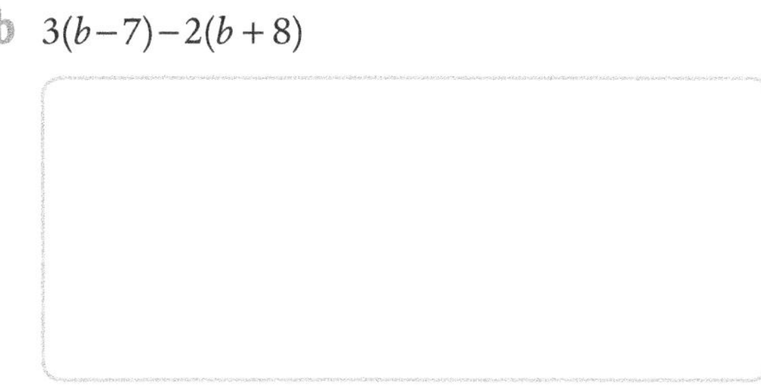

c $2p(m-6)-3(2mp+3n)$

$= 2p \times$ ____ $- 2p \times$ ____ $-3 \times$ ____ $-3 \times$ ____

$=$ ____ $-$ ____ $-$ ____ $-$ ____

$=$ ____ $-$ ____ $-$ ____ $-$ ____

$=$ ______

d $4hk-9k(6h-1)$

$= 4hk -$ ____ $\times$ ____ $+$ ____ $\times 1$

$=$ ________________

$=$ ______

NAPLAN-ready

Shade the box beneath the correct answer.

The illustration shows some cups, each of which contains the *same number* of counters, and some loose counters.

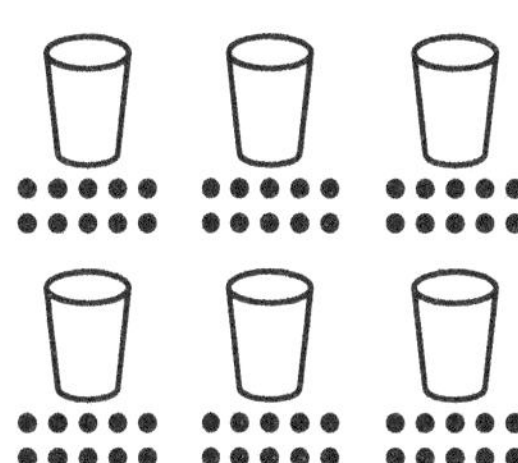

If x stands for the number of counters in each cup, the expression that does *not* match the diagram is:

$2(3x+30)$	$6x+10$
☐	☐
$6(x+10)$	$6x+60$
☐	☐

Tip Group the cups and counters to match each expression.

3.7 Factorising

Factorising algebraic expressions using the Distributive Law is the reverse of expanding.

When factorising an expression we need to:

1 Identify the highest common factor (HCF) of the terms in the expression. The HCF could consist of numbers, variables or both.

2 Write the HCF in front of a set of brackets and write the remaining factors inside the brackets.

e.g. Factorise $6x + 10xy$

$= 2 \times 3 \times x + 2 \times 5 \times x \times y$ ← (write each term as a product of individual factors)

$= \boxed{2} \times 3 \times \boxed{x} + \boxed{2} \times 5 \times \boxed{x} \times y$ ← (highlight the factors common to each term, HCF = $2x$)

$= 2 \times x(3 + 5 \times y)$ ← (place the common factors at the front of the brackets and the 'left over' factors inside)

$= 2x(3 + 5y)$ ← (remove multiplication symbols)

Always *check* factorising by expanding your answer.

$2x(3 + 5y) = 2x \times 3 + 2x \times 5y$

$= 6x + 10xy$

- **Powers**

When a term contains a power, write the power in expanded form so you can 'see' the individual factors.

$x^2 + 7xy$

$= \boxed{x} \times x + 7 \times \boxed{x} \times y$

$= x(x + 7y)$

- **Negative common factors**

When the first term is negative, write a negative sign to the factor in front of the brackets so that the first term in the brackets is positive. Each term will need to change to the opposite sign from its original sign.

$-6x + 5xy$

$= -6 \times \boxed{x} + 5 \times \boxed{x} \times y$

$= -x(6 - 5y)$ (the + in front of the second term becomes minus)

Word Bank

Highest common factor (HCF)

→ The HCF of an algebraic expression is the highest factor of any numbers and common pronumerals (letters).

e.g. The HCF of $4ab$ and $6bc$ is $2b$

Therefore, the expression $4ab + 6bc$ would factorise to $2b(2a + 3c)$.

1 Find the HCF of each pairs of terms by stating each term as a product of its factors.

a $24a$ and 20

$24a =$ ____ × ____ × a

$20 =$ ____ × ____

HCF of $24a$ and 20 is ____

b $6p$ and $18pq$

$6p =$ ____ × ____ × ____

$18pq =$ ____ × ____ × ____ × ____

HCF of $6p$ and $18pq$ is ____

2 Factorise:

Tip Write the numbers as products, if necessary, so you can 'see' the HCF.

a $9 + 3b$

$= 3 \times 3 + 3 \times b$

$= 3(\_\_\_\_ + \_\_\_\_)$

Check:

b $10m - 8n$

$= \_\_\_\_ \times 5 \times m - 2 \times \_\_\_\_ \times \_\_\_\_$

$= 2(\_\_\_\_ - \_\_\_\_)$

Check:

c $14d + 7$

$= \_\_\_\_ \times \_\_\_\_ \times d + 7 \times 1$

$= \_\_\_\_(\_\_\_\_ + 1)$

Check:

3 Factorise:

Tip Remember to circle common factors for the numbers *and* the variables.

a $20g + 30gh$

$= 10 \times \_\_\_\_ \times \_\_\_\_ + \_\_\_\_ \times 3 \times \_\_\_\_ \times \_\_\_\_$

$= 10g(\_\_\_\_ + \_\_\_\_)$

Check:

b $15p^2 - 18pr$

$= 3 \times \_\_\_\_ \times \_\_\_\_ \times p - \_\_\_\_ \times \_\_\_\_ \times \_\_\_\_ \times r$

$= \_\_\_\_(\_\_\_\_ - \_\_\_\_)$

Check:

4 Factorise:

Tip If the first term is negative, take a negative factor outside the brackets. The terms inside will now have the opposites of their original signs.

$-16k + 12kn$

$= -\_\_\_\_ \times \_\_\_\_ \times k + \_\_\_\_ \times \_\_\_\_ \times k \times \_\_\_\_$

$= \_\_\_\_(\_\_\_\_ - \_\_\_\_)$

Check:

5 Use factorising to write the formula in another way.

Perimeter of a rectangle:

$P = 2l + 2w$

NAPLAN-ready

Shade the box beneath the correct answer.

Which of the expressions has a highest common factor of 1:

$2xy + 15z^2$ ☐	$3x - 5ax$ ☐
$8ab + 50cd$ ☐	$xy - ay$ ☐

Tip Check the numbers and the variables in each pair of terms.

4.1 Writing ratios

Comparing amounts using a ratio

Ari has \$50 and Bill has \$70.

Ari has 5 lots of \$10 and Bill has 7 lots of \$10.

So the ratio of the amounts is 5 : 7.

Simplifying ratios is the same process as simplifying fractions: divide all parts in the ratio by the highest common factor.

$$\div 10 \left(\begin{array}{c} 50 : 70 \\ 5 : 7 \end{array} \right) \div 10$$

Comparing parts to a whole

Altogether, Ari and Bill have \$120 (12 lots of \$10).

Ari : total
= 50 : 120
= 5 : 12

Bill : total
= 70 : 120
= 7 : 12

Ratios as fractions and percentages

If Phil had \$15 and Hilary had \$20, then the ratio of their amounts would be 3 : 4.

Phil : Hilary
15 : 20
= 3 : 4

We could say:

Phil has $\frac{3}{4}$ of Hilary's amount

or Phil has 75% of Hilary's amount.

$3:4 = \frac{3}{4} = 75\%$

If Leo had \$12 and Sophie had \$28, the total would be \$40.

We could write a ratio to compare Leo's amount with the total amount.

Leo : total
= 12 : 40
= 3 : 10

Leo has $\frac{3}{10}$ of the total amount

or Leo has 30% of the total amount.

Word Bank

Equivalent ratios

→ Multiplying or dividing each part of a ratio by the same number produces an equivalent ratio. The result is equivalent to the original ratio.

1 Write as ratios in simplest form.

Tip Cancel common factors if possible.

a Number of buttons to number of bows.

= ____ : ____

b Number of dots to number of dashes.

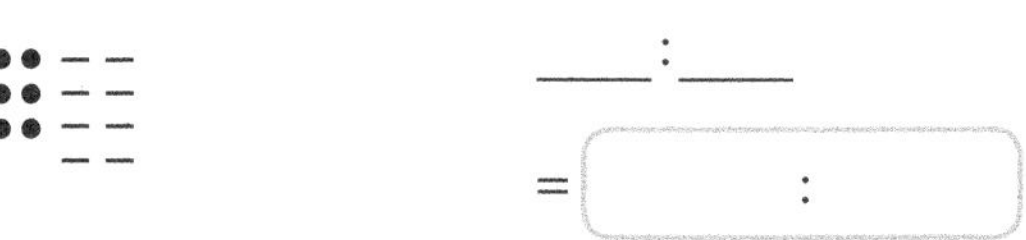

____ : ____

= ____ : ____

c Number of kittens to number of puppies.

____ : ____

= ____ : ____

2 Write each of the following ratios in simplest form.

Tip Divide each part in the ratio by the same number.

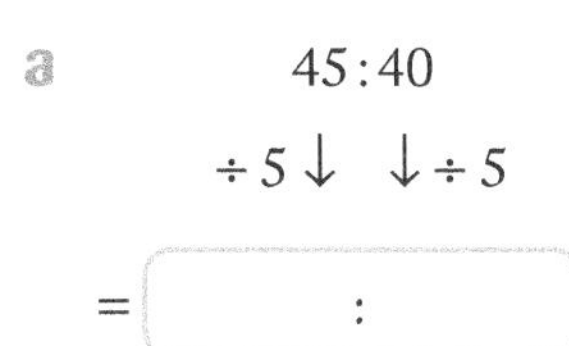

a $45:40$

$\div 5 \downarrow \quad \downarrow \div 5$

$= \boxed{\quad : \quad}$

b $22:330$

$\div 22 \downarrow \quad \downarrow \div 22$

$= \boxed{\quad}$

c $9:63$

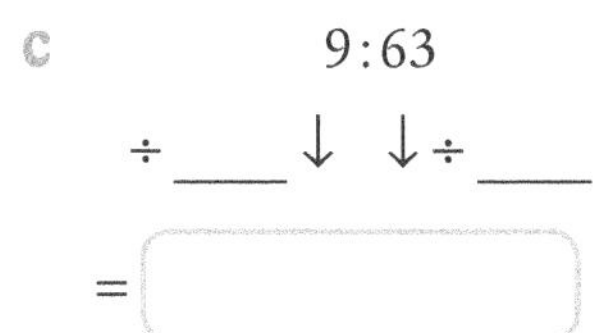

$\div \_\_\_ \downarrow \quad \downarrow \div \_\_\_$

$= \boxed{\quad}$

d $84:28:104$

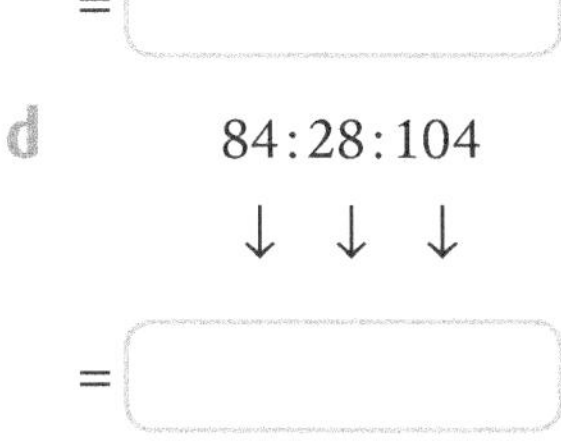

$\downarrow \quad \downarrow \quad \downarrow$

$= \boxed{\quad}$

3 Find the ratios.

a Number of apples to the total number of fruit.

b Number of oranges to the total number of fruit.

c Number of apples to the number of oranges.

d Number of oranges to the number of apples.

4 Out of the total number of birds find the following.

Tip Write the part : whole ratio as a fraction first.

a The percentage of birds that are pigeons.

pigeons : total $= \_\_\_ : \_\_\_$

Percentage pigeons $= \frac{\_\_\_}{\_\_\_} \times 100\%$

$= \boxed{\quad}$

b The percentage of birds that are crows.

crows : total $= \_\_\_ : \_\_\_$

Percentage crows $= \frac{\_\_\_}{\_\_\_} \times 100\%$

$= \boxed{\quad}$

5 Circle the letter next to the correct response.

In a box of coloured pencils 6 are blue, 5 are green and 3 are red.

a The ratio of green to blue is:

A $6:5$ B $5:11$ C $5:14$ D $5:6$

b The number of red as a fraction of the number of blue is:

A $\frac{1}{2}$ B $\frac{9}{14}$ C $\frac{3}{14}$ D $\frac{3}{11}$

c The number of blue as a fraction of the total is:

A $\frac{6}{11}$ B $\frac{3}{4}$ C $\frac{3}{14}$ D $\frac{3}{7}$

NAPLAN-ready

Shade the box beneath the correct answer.

The Australian Tic Tac Toe team for the World Games has 1 member of the team from each of Tasmania, Queensland and Western Australia, and 2 members each from New South Wales and Victoria.

The percentage of members that are from New South Wales is closest to:

20%	30%	40%	50%
☐	☐	☐	☐

Tip Write the ratio of the members from New South Wales to the total as a fraction first.

4.2 Simplifying ratios

Units

Ratios can be used to compare amounts such as length, money, time and weight. To write amounts using ratios, first change one or both amounts to the same unit.

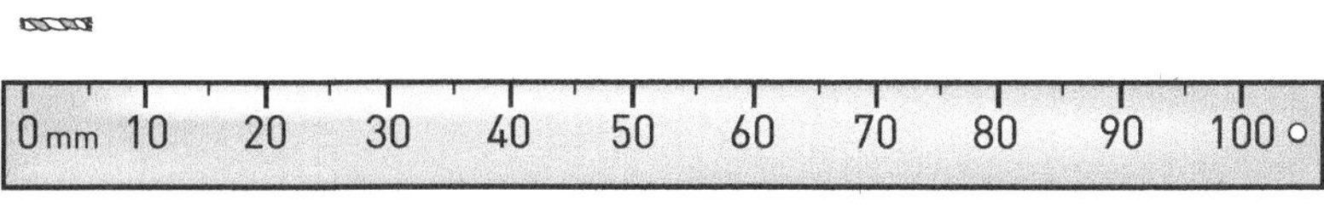

To write the lengths of string as a simplified ratio:

$5\text{ mm} : 10\text{ cm}$ (change to smaller unit)

$= 5\text{ mm} : 100\text{ mm}$

$= 5 : 100$ (divide both parts by 5, the HCF of 5 and 100)

$= 1 : 20$

Ratios should always be written in **simplest form** in whole numbers.

Simplifying ratios involving fractions

When any part of a ratio is a fraction (or mixed number) we use a common denominator.

$2 : 1\frac{1}{3}$

$= \frac{2}{1} : \frac{4}{3}$ (convert one or both fractions so they have the same denominator) $\frac{2}{1} = \frac{6}{3}$

$= \frac{6}{3} : \frac{4}{3}$

$= 6 : 4$

$\div 2$ $\div 2$

$= 3 : 2$

Simplifying ratios involving decimals

If parts of a ratio are in decimal form, multiply each part by the same power of 10 (i.e. 10, 100, ...) to make all parts whole numbers.

$4.1 : 6$

$= 4.1 \times 10 : 6 \times 10$

$= 41 : 60$

Word Bank

Simplest form (of a ratio)

→ In simplest form, each part of the ratio must be a whole number, with no common factors and no units.

1 Write each of the following ratios in simplest form.

Tip Write each quantity in the same units first.

a 36 cents : \$3

= ____ cents : ____ cents (divide by the highest common factor of 12 to simplify)

= ____ : ____

b 5 days : 5 weeks

= ____ : ____ (simplify)

= ____ : ____

c 2 L : 250 mL

= _____ mL : 250 mL

= [   ]

d 500 g : 3.5 kg : 2 kg

= _____ : _____ : _____

= _____ : _____ : _____

= _____ : _____ : _____

2 Write each of the following ratios in simplest form.

Tip Write each part of the ratio as an improper fraction first.

a $5:7\frac{1}{2}$

$= \frac{5}{1}:\frac{\_\_}{2}$

$= \frac{10}{2}:\frac{\_\_}{2}$

$= 10:15$

$=$ ______

b $2\frac{2}{3}:2$

$= \frac{\_\_}{3}:\frac{2}{1}$

$= \frac{\_\_}{3}:\frac{\_\_}{3}$

$= 8:6$

$=$ ______

c $3:1\frac{3}{4}$

$= \frac{\_\_}{4}:\frac{\_\_}{4}$

$=$ ____ : ____

d $3\frac{1}{5}:6$

$=$

$=$

3 Simplify each of the following.

Tip Multiply the parts of the ratio by the same power of 10 (i.e. 10 or 100) first, so that each part is a whole number.

a $2.4:4$

$= 24:$____ $(\times 10)$

$=$ ______ (simplify)

b $1.64:2.4$

$=$ ____ : ____ $(\times 100)$

$=$ ____ : ____ (simplify)

c $3.5:4.75$

$=$ ____ : ____ $(\times$ ____$)$

$=$ ____ : ____ (simplify)

4 Circle the letter next to the correct response.

a $3\frac{1}{2}:4\frac{1}{5}$ simplifies to:

A 35:42 **B** 32:45

C 3:4 **D** 5:6

b $6:5\frac{3}{4}$ is the same as:

A 60:58 **B** 600:534

C 60:53 **D** 600:575

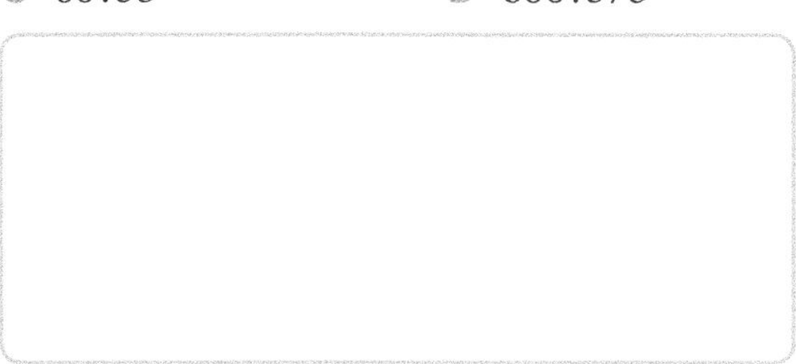

5 Circle the letter next to the correct answer.

a The ratio shown in the diagram is the same as:

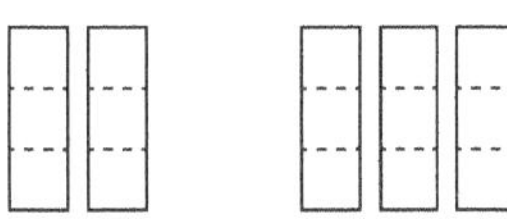

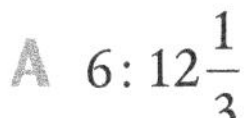

A $6:12\frac{1}{3}$ **B** $2:13$

C $2:4\frac{1}{3}$ **D** $6:\frac{13}{3}$

b The ratio shown in the diagram is the same as:

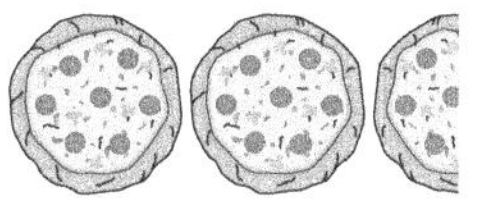

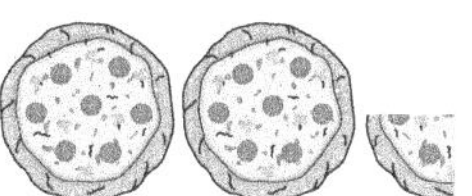

A $2\frac{1}{2}:2\frac{1}{3}$ **B** $\frac{10}{4}:\frac{9}{4}$

C $3\frac{2}{4}:1\frac{3}{4}$ **D** $\frac{5}{4}:\frac{10}{4}$

NAPLAN-ready

Shade the box beneath the correct answer.

Gemma runs around the oval in 1 min 40 sec, whereas Danny takes 2 min 10 sec.

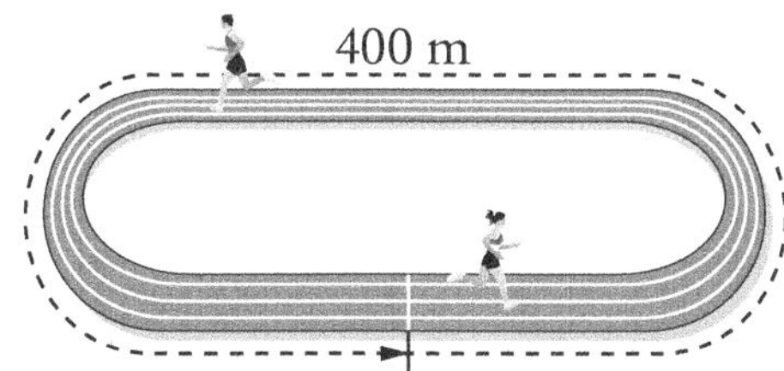

The ratio of Gemma's time to Danny's time is:

2:3	10:13	3:4	1:2
☐	☐	☐	☐

Tip Convert each time to seconds first.

4.3 Unit ratios and scale factors

The simple ratio of 3 : 1 is equivalent to:

\$30 : \$10	14.4 kg : 4.8 kg

In each case, the first part of the ratio is 3 times the second part.

The ratio of 0.7 : 1 is equivalent to:

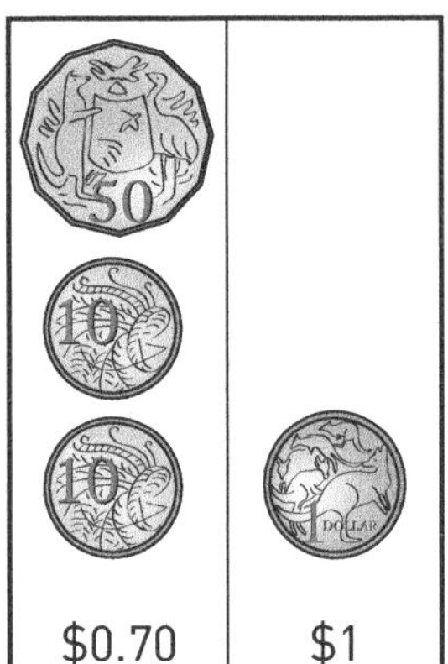

In each case, the first part of the ratio is 0.7 times the second part.

Unit ratio

A unit ratio is a ratio where the second part is 1.

3 : 1, 2.5 : 1 and 0.7 : 1 are examples of **unit ratios**.

To change a ratio to a unit ratio, divide both parts by the second part.

2 cm : 5 cm

$$2:5$$
$$= \frac{2}{5} : \frac{5}{5}$$
$$= 0.4:1$$

2 cm is 0.4 of 5 cm.

\$3 : \$2

$$3:2$$
$$= \frac{3}{2} : \frac{2}{2}$$
$$= 1.5:1$$

\$3 is 1.5 of \$2

Using scale factor to find amounts

The first part of each unit ratio is the **scale factor**.

0.4 : 1 ← 0.4 is the scale factor

1.5 : 1 ← 1.5 is the scale factor

The scale factor can be used to find an unkown amount in a ratio.

e.g.

$$3.6:1 \quad (\times 3.6)$$
$$x:25 \quad (\times 3.6)$$
$$x = 25 \times 3.6 = 90$$

$$3.6:1 \quad (\div 3.6)$$
$$72:y \quad (\div 3.6)$$
$$y = 72 \div 3.6 = 20$$

The first part is 3.6 times as big as the second.

Word Bank

Unit ratio

→ A unit ratio has two parts and the second part is 1 (e.g. 4 : 1).

Scale factor

→ The scale factor is the first part of a unit ratio (e.g. in 4.5 : 1 the scale factor is 4.5).

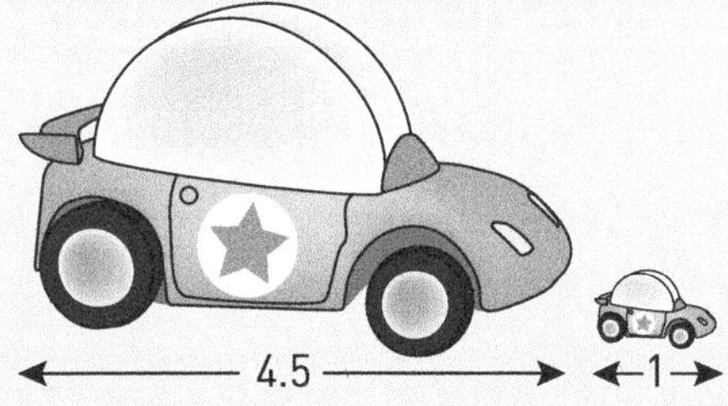

Scale factor is 4.5.

1 Write each of the following as a unit ratio.

Tip Divide each part in the ratio by the second part.

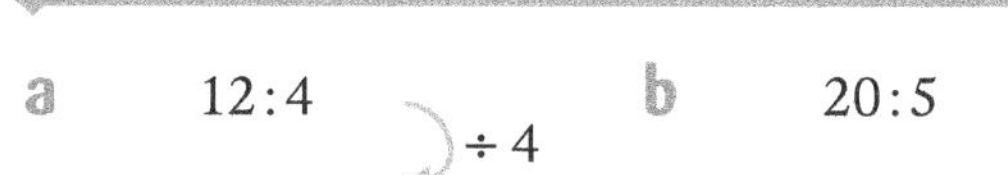

a 12 : 4 (÷ 4)
= ____ : ____

b 20 : 5
= ____ : ____

2 For each part of Question **1**, write the scale factor.

Tip The scale factor is the first part of the unit ratio.

a scale factor = ☐

b scale factor = ☐

3 The ratio of Isabella's height to her little brother's height is 1.13 : 1. Find the following heights, to the nearest cm.

Tip Decide whether to multiply or divide by the scale factor.

a Isabella's height, if her little brother is 125 cm tall.

_____ × 1.13 (Isabella is the taller one)

= _____ cm (nearest cm)

b Her little brother's height, if Isabella is 165 cm tall.

_____ ÷ 1.13 (Isabella's brother is the shorter one)

= _____ cm

4 The ratio of Gail's swim times to Martin's times is 0.85 : 1. Find the following times, to the nearest second.

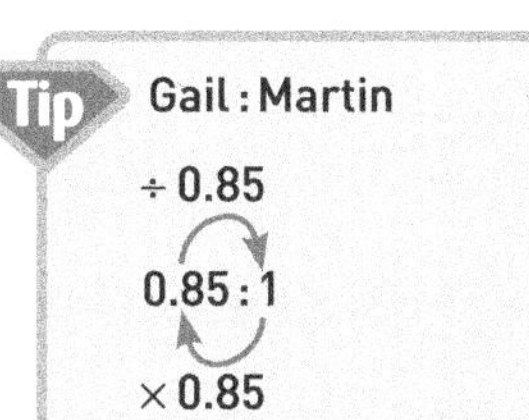

a Gail's swim time, if Martin's time is 50 seconds.

Gail : Martin

0.85 : 1

____ : 50

× 0.85

Gail's swim time is [seconds]

b Martin's swim time, if Gail's time is 90 seconds.

Gail : Martin

0.85 : 1

÷ 0.85

90 : ____

Martin's swim time is [seconds]

5 Calculate the amounts, given that the mass ratio of sultanas to peanuts in a recipe is 1.4 : 1.

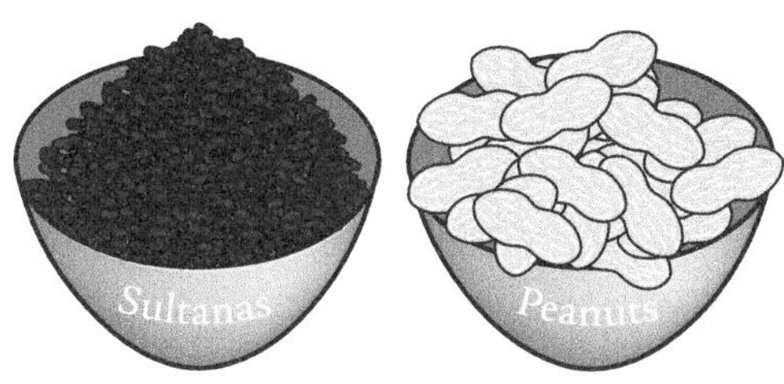

a How many grams of peanuts are needed, if 350 grams of sultanas are used?

sultanas : peanuts

1.4 : 1

÷ 1.4

350 : ____

[grams] of peanuts are needed.

b How many grams of sultanas are needed, if 500g peanuts are used?

sultanas : peanuts

1.4 : 1

____ : 500

× 0.1.4

[grams] of sultanas are needed.

6 Complete the table.

Tip Divide the first number by the second and then round to two decimal places.

Ratio of two quantities	Unit ratio	Scale factor	What it means
5 : 6	____ : 1		The first quantity is 0.83 of the second.
19 : 15			The first quantity is ____ of the second.
20 : 3			The first quantity is ____ of the second.

NAPLAN-ready

Shade the box beneath the correct answer.

100 points of rainfall is the same as an inch of rain. 1 inch = 25 mm

A downpour of 340 points overnight is the same as:

13.6 mm	27.2 mm	85 mm	315 mm
☐	☐	☐	☐

Tip There are two steps: points to inches and inches to mm. Find and use the scale factor for each step.

4.4 Using ratios to find amounts

Equivalent ratios

To find an equivalent ratio, we multiply or divide each part by the same number.

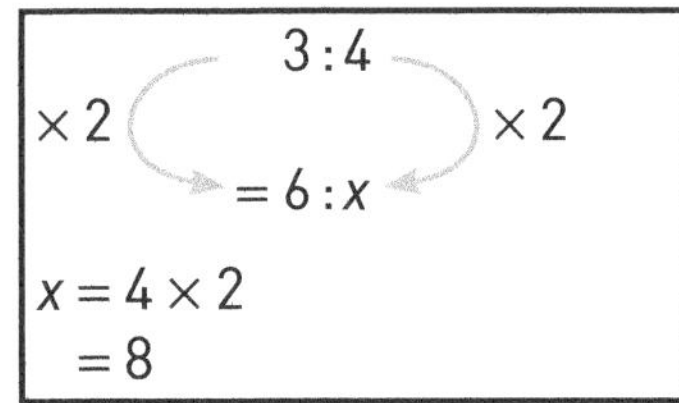

Calculating unknown amounts

If flour and sugar are mixed in the ratio 4:3, find the amount of flour used with 120 g of sugar.

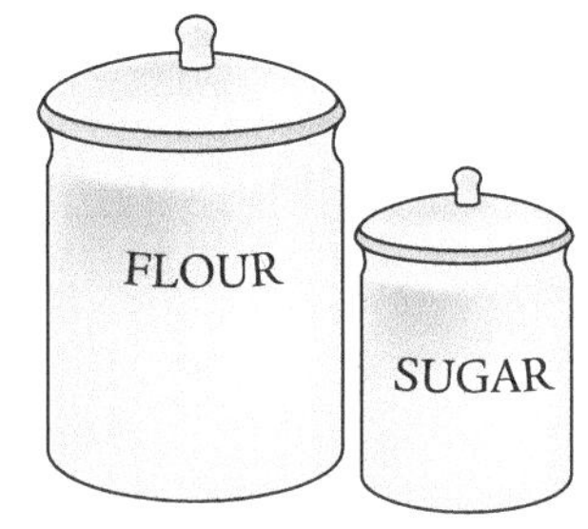

It is often useful to write the ratio in words first, to make sure the amounts are in the right order.

flour : sugar

$4:3$, ×40 on both sides, gives $x:120$

$x = 4 \times 40$

$= 160$

So 120 g of sugar and 160 g of flour is needed for the recipe.

Finding an unknown part

Sometimes there is not a whole number factor connecting the given parts of the equivalent ratios. In these cases, it is useful to work in two steps, changing one of the parts of the ratio to 1.

Step 1: change the given part to 1 by dividing, $3 \div 3 = 1$

$3:5 = 8:x$

$3:5$, ÷3 on both sides, gives $1:\frac{5}{3}$

Step 2: change to the required value by multiplying, $1 \times 8 = 8$

$1:\frac{5}{3}$, ×8 on both sides, gives $8:x$

$x = 5 \div 3 \times 8$

$\therefore x \approx 13.33$ (2 d.p.)

Finding an unknown part using algebra

To solve using algebraic methods, change the ratios to fractions:

$3:5 = 8:x$ becomes $\frac{3}{5} = \frac{8}{x}$

If the variable is on the denominator, invert (flip) both fractions. $\frac{5}{3} = \frac{x}{8}$

To solve, undo the division by multiplying:

$x = \frac{5}{3} \times 8$

$= \frac{40}{3}$

≈ 13.33 (2 d.p.)

1 Find the value of the unknown in each ratio.

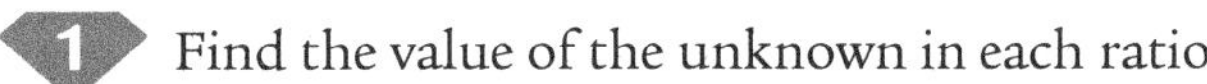

a $a:55 = 2:5$

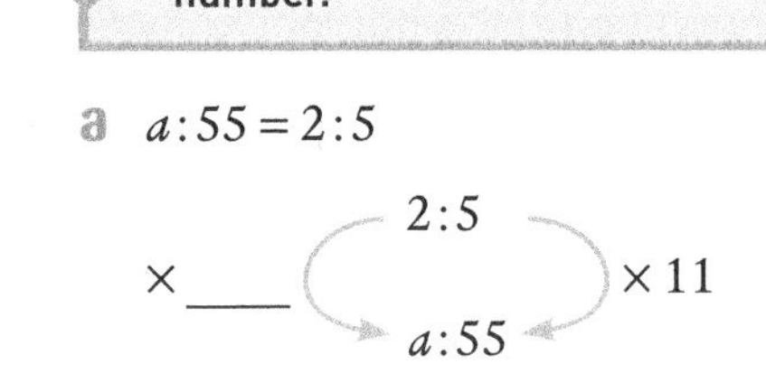

$a = 2 \times$ ____

= ______

b $4:7 = b:28$

4:____ , × ____ on both sides, gives b:____

$b =$ ____ × ____

= ______

c $6:15 = 18:c$

____:____ , × ____ on both sides, gives ____:____

$c =$ ____ × ____

= ______

2 Solve the following.

Tip Use headings and let the unknown be x.

a Weed killer is made by blending ingredients A and B in the ratio 3 : 8. How much of ingredient B is used with 48 drops of ingredient A?

Ingredient A : Ingredient B

3 : 8

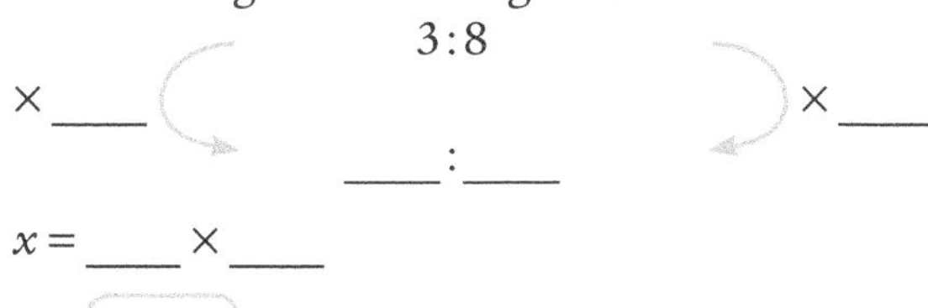

× ___ ___ : ___ × ___

$x =$ ___ × ___

= ☐ drops of ingredient B

b The number of Maths and IT lessons for 8C are in the ratio 5 : 2. How many IT lessons will 8C have had when they have had 100 Maths lessons?

________ : ________ (in words first)

____ : ____

____ : ____

$x =$ ____ × ____

= ☐ lessons of IT

3 Find the value of the unknown, rounded to two decimal places where necessary.

Tip Convert the known part to 1 first.

a $5:6 = a:8$

5 : 6

÷ 6 ÷ 6

$\frac{\;}{\;}$: 1

× ___ × 8

$a:8$

$a =$

≈ ☐ (2 d.p.)

b $9:b = 5:4$

5 : 4

÷ ___ ÷ ___

1 : $\frac{\;}{\;}$

× ___ × ___

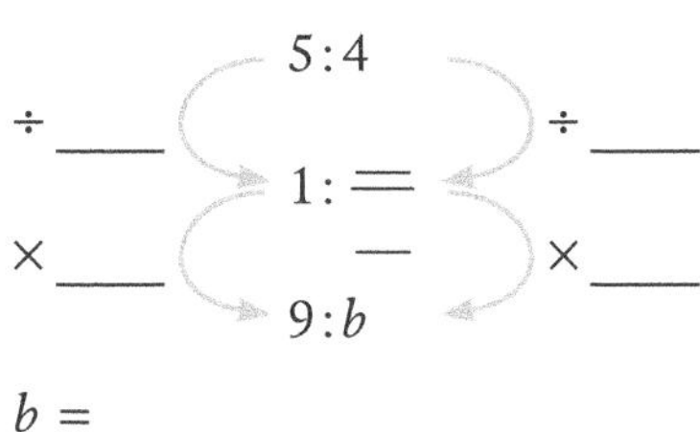

$9:b$

$b =$

= ☐

4 The mass of a dog is 12.6 kg. Calculate the mass of her pup, rounded to one decimal place, if the ratio of the pup's mass to his mother's mass is 2 : 19.

Tip Use headings, write as fractions and then use algebraic solving techniques.

Let the pup's mass be x.

pup : mother

2 : 19

= ____ : ____

$\frac{2}{19} = \frac{\;}{\;}$ (write each ratio as a fraction)

$\frac{x}{\;} = \frac{\;}{\;}$ (rewrite with x on the LHS)

$x = \frac{\;}{\;} \times$ ____

≈ ____ (1 d.p.)

The pup's mass is approximately ☐.

5 State whether each statement is true (T) or false (F) by circling the correct answer.

a If $a:30 = 5:3$ then $a = 18$. **T or F**

b If $25:4 = 200:b$ then $b = 32$. **T or F**

c If $c:4 = 10:3$ then $c = \frac{10}{3} \times 4$. **T or F**

d If $17:d = 3:5$ then $d = \frac{3}{5} \times 17$. **T or F**

NAPLAN-ready

Shade the box beneath the correct answer.

A girl's height and her brother's height are in the ratio 9 : 8.

The heights could *not* be:

1.26 m, 1.12 m	1.35 m, 1.21 m
☐	☐
1.44 m, 1.28 m	1.53 m, 1.36 m
☐	☐

Tip Use unit ratios to compare each pair of values.

4.5 Scale drawings

Scale ratio

When we use diagrams or maps to represent objects or distances in the real world, the **scale ratio** is diagram length : real length.

When the diagram is smaller than the real version, we divide both parts by the diagram length so the ratio becomes $1 : \frac{\text{real length}}{\text{diagram length}}$.

The Komodo dragon below shows a scale drawing where 1 cm represents 0.5 m.

This can be written as a simplified ratio.

  1 cm : 50 cm
= 1 : 50

Scale factor

In the ratio 1 : 100, 100 is the scale factor.

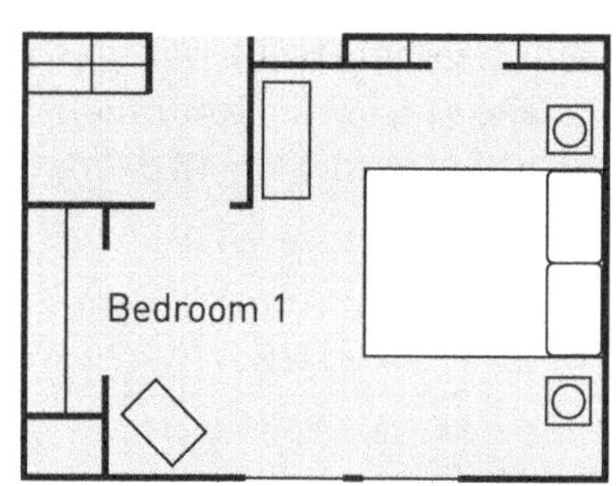

The bed in the house plan above is about 2 cm long.

Its real length is 2 cm × 100 = 200 cm (or 2 m).

Queen-size beds are 153 cm wide.

The diagram width should be 153 cm ÷ 100 = 1.53 cm

diagram length → × scale factor → real length
real length → ÷ scale factor → diagram length

1 Convert the following to scale ratios and highlight the scale factor for each.

Tip Convert to the smaller unit, then leave out units and divide both parts by the first part.

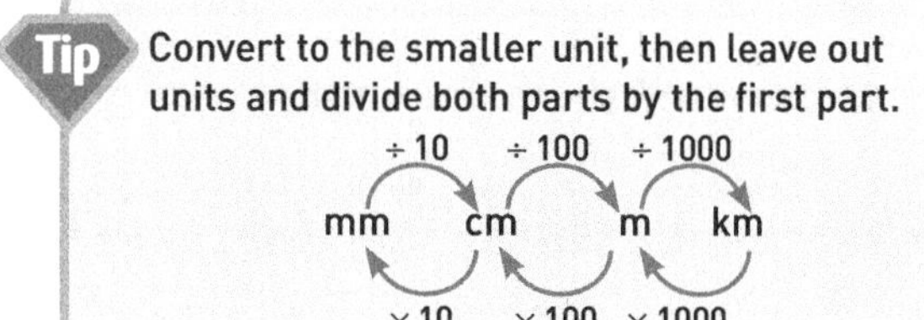

a 5 mm : 1 m

= 5 mm : _____ mm (convert to smaller unit)

= _____ : _____ (leave out units)

= 1 : _____

b 1 cm : 10 m

= 1 cm : ______ cm (convert to smaller unit)

= _____ : ______ (leave out units)

c 2 cm : 1 km

= _____ : _____

= _____ : _____

2 For a scale ratio of 1 : 5, find the real length if the diagram length is:

Tip Multiply the diagram length by the scale factor.

a 12 cm

Real length = diagram length × scale factor

= ________ × 5

= ________ cm

b 2.7 m

Real length = ________ × scale factor

= 2.7 × _____

= ________ m

3 For a scale ratio of 1 : 500, find the real length in metres if the diagram length is:

Tip Multiply the diagram length by the scale factor and then convert to metres.

a 5 mm

Real length = diagram length × scale factor

= _____ mm × _____

= ______ mm

= [   ] m

b 3.4 cm

Real length = ________ × scale factor

= ____ cm × ____

= ______ cm

= [   ] m

4 For a scale ratio of 1 : 10, find the diagram length in mm if the real length is:

Tip Divide the real length by the scale factor.

a 48 cm

= ______ mm

Diagram length:

______ mm ÷ 10

= ____ mm

b 7 m

= ______ mm

Diagram length:

______ mm ÷ 10

= ____ mm

5 For a scale ratio of 1 : 1000, find the diagram length in millimetres, if the real length is:

Tip First convert the units to mm and then divide the real length by the scale factor.

a 7 m

7 m = ______ mm

Diagram length = ______ mm ÷ ______

= [   ] mm

b 150 m

150 m = ________ mm

Diagram length = ______ ÷ ______

= [   ] mm

6 The scale on a map is 1 : 5000. Find the real distances in metres, if the map distance is:

a 7 cm

Real length = ____ cm × ______

= ______ cm

= [   ] m

b 11.5 cm

Real length = ____ × ________

= ________ cm

= [   ] m

7 Calculate the scale factor for the image of the tree, given that its actual height is 10 m.

[   ]

8 Complete the table.

	Scale ratio	Scale factor	Diagram distance	Real distance
a	1 : 4000	4000	20 000 m ÷ 4000 = ______	20 km
b		500	12 cm	
c	1 : 1 000 000			150 km
d			4.2 cm	2.1 km

NAPLAN-ready

Shade the box next to the correct answer.

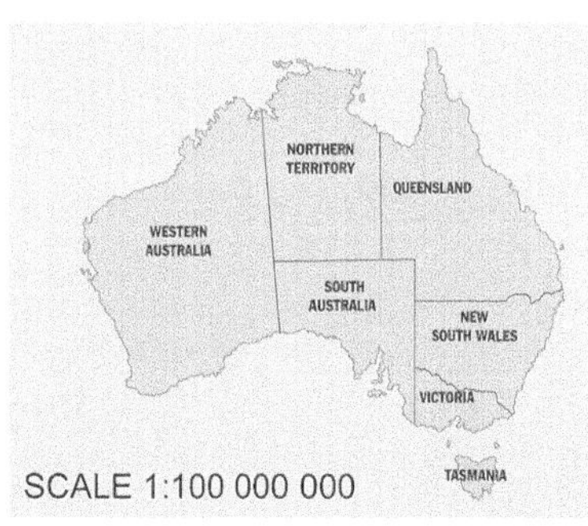

The distance across Australia from east to west is approximately:

- 425 km ☐
- 475 km ☐
- 4150 km ☐
- 4750 km ☐

Tip Measure the map distance in centimetres.

4.6 Sharing an amount in a given ratio

Sharing the total amount

If Victor and Zelda share \$104 in the ratio 3:5, how much will each get?

- The first step in calculating the amount of each part is to find the total number of parts:

  $3 + 5 = 8$ parts

- Next, write each part as a fraction of the total, then use fractions to calculate the amount in each person's part:

  Victor's share: $\frac{3}{8}$ of \$104

  $\frac{3}{8} \times 104 = \$39$

  Zelda's share: $\frac{5}{8}$ of \$104

  $\frac{5}{8} \times 104 = \$65$

- Check that the amounts you have found add up to the total:

  $\$39 + \$65 = \$104$

Proportion table

A proportion table can help us to visualise the situation.

	Victor	Zelda	Total	Unit amount
Parts	3	5		1
Amount			\$104	

Step 1: Add the parts to get the total parts.

$3 + 5 = 8$

Step 2: Divide the total amount by the total parts to get the amount for 1 part (the unit amount).

$\$104 \div 8 = \$13$

Step 3: Multiply the amount in 1 part by the number of parts for each person.

	Victor	Zelda	Total	Unit amount
Parts	3	5	8	1
Amount	\$39	\$65	\$104	\$13

Step 3

Check that the parts add up to the total (\$39 + \$65 = \$104) and that \$39 : \$65 simplifies to 3:5.

1 Share the amounts in the given ratio.

 **Find the total number of parts first.**

a \$24 in the ratio 1:5

Total parts: ____ + ____ = 6

First share: $\frac{1}{{}_{1}\not{6}} \times \frac{{}^{4}\not{24}}{1} = \$$____

Second share: $\frac{5}{{}_{1}\not{6}} \times \frac{{}^{4}\not{24}}{1} = \$$____

b \$36 in the ratio 7:2

Total parts: ____ + ____ = ____

First share: $\frac{7}{9} \times \frac{36}{1} = \$$____

Second share: $\frac{__}{__} \times \frac{__}{1} = \$$____

c Share \$72 is the ratio 5:4.

d Share \$65 in the ratio 4:1.

2 Find the total number of parts in the following ratios.

a 6:9:4

A 3 B 8 C 10 D 19

b 1:1:1

A 1 B 3 C 6 D 9

3 After 20 basketball games, the Tigers had a win:loss ratio of 3:2.

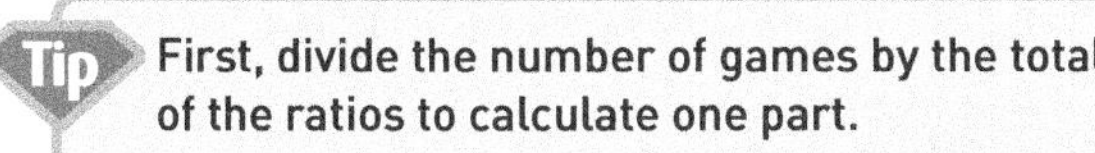

Tip First, divide the number of games by the total of the ratios to calculate one part.

a How many games have they won?

b How many games have they lost?

4 a Share \$45 in the ratio 5:4:6.

Total parts: ____________

First share: $\frac{__}{__} \times \frac{__}{1} = \$$____

Second share: $\frac{__}{__} \times \frac{__}{1} = \$$____

Third share: $\frac{__}{__} \times \frac{__}{1} = \$$____

b Share \$120 in the ratio 2:1:5.

c Share \$56 in the ratio 3:3:4.

5 Complete the table to show how \$81 would be shared among 4 people in the ratio 2:2:1:4.

					Total
Parts	2	2	1	4	
Amount					\$81

6 In a game of Paintball, Leah, Lacie and Libby made paint ball hits in the ratio 3:7:2.
If 72 paint balls hit the girls in total, calculate:

a how many times each girl made a hit

Total parts: ______

Leah: ______

Lacie: ______

Libby: ______

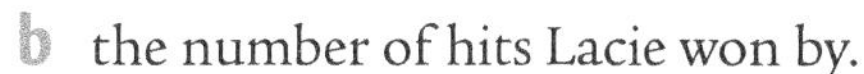

b the number of hits Lacie won by. ______

7 Harriet shares this box of chocolates with her sister and brother in the ratio 3:5:4.

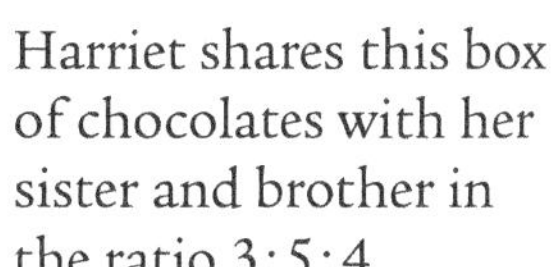

How many chocolates will Harriet have, if hers is the smallest share?

Tip Find the total number of parts in the ratio first.

NAPLAN-ready

Shade the box beneath the correct answer.

Tori gives away her sticker collection to three of her friends in the ratio 5:8:1.

The fraction of stickers given to the first person is:

$\frac{1}{5}$ ☐ $\frac{5}{14}$ ☐ $\frac{5}{13}$ ☐ $\frac{5}{8}$ ☐

Tip Find the total number of parts first.

4.7 Rates A

A **rate** compares two amounts that have different units. They are written as the amount of one quantity per unit amount of another. They are calculated by dividing the first quantity by the second. Unlike ratios, we write rates with their units.

Speed

- The rate of distance travelled in time taken is called **speed**.

$$\text{speed} = \frac{\text{distance}}{\text{time}}$$

If 150 km is travelled in 3 hours, the average speed is:

$$\frac{150\text{ km}}{3\text{ h}} = 50\text{ km per hour or } 50\text{ km/h}$$

An average of 50 km is travelled each hour.

If 40 m is travelled in 8 seconds, the average speed is:

$$\frac{40\text{ m}}{8\text{ s}} = 5\text{ m/s}$$

An average of 5 m is travelled each second.

The word 'per' means 'for each'. Sometimes the symbol '/' is used instead.

Comparing prices

We are able to compare prices by calculating the cost per unit amount, or **unit price**.

If we paid \$6.20 for 400 g of burgers, the cost per kilogram $= \frac{\text{cost (\$)}}{\text{mass (kg)}}$

$$\frac{\$6.20}{0.4\text{ kg}} = \$15.50 \text{ per kg or } \$15.50\text{/kg}$$

Finding amounts using a unit price

Calculating a unit price first, allows us to calculate the cost for any amount.

If 5 kg of apples cost \$8.60, what will you pay for 6.5 kg?

	Amount	Cost		
	5 kg	\$8.60		
÷ 5	1 kg	\$1.72	÷ 5	← unit price is 1.72 \$/kg
× 6.5	6.5 kg	\$11.18	× 6.5	← cost of 6.5 kg is \$11.18

Word Bank

Rate

➜ A rate is the amount of a quantity per unit amount of another. A rate is calculated by dividing the first quantity by the second quantity, then writing units (e.g. \$/kg).

Unit price

➜ The cost of a unit amount such as 1 litre of petrol or 1 kg of apples, or 100 g of jam.

1 Find the average speed for the following.

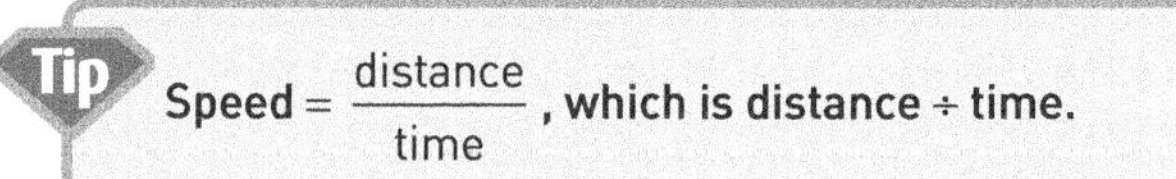

a A car travelled 400 km in 5 hours.

Average speed $= \frac{\_\_\_\text{ km}}{\_\_\_\text{ h}}$

$=$ ☐ km/h

b A bicycle travelled 30 m in 6 seconds.

Average speed $= \frac{\_\_\_\text{ m}}{\_\_\_\text{ s}}$

$=$ ☐ m/s

c An aeroplane flew 18 000 km in 20 hours.

Average speed = ________

=

d A tortoise crawled 20 m in 5 hours.

Average speed = ________

= 

2 Find the rate at which each customer has been charged, in \$/kg.

Tip Divide cost in \$ by mass in kg.

a Potatoes cost \$4.20 for 3 kg.

÷ 3 ______ for 1 kg ÷ 3

Potatoes cost \$______/kg

b Raspberries cost \$16 for 250 g.

× 4 ______ for 1 kg × 4

Raspberries cost \$______/kg

3 Use the proportion tables to calculate the amounts, given that the rate does not change.

Tip Multiply or divide by the same number for each quantity in the row.

a same speed

Distance	Time
240 km	4 h
	1 h
	7 h

÷ ____
× ____

b same value for money

Cost	Mass
\$48	1.5 kg
	1 kg
	3.2 kg

÷ ____
× ____

c same heartbeat

Beats	Time
20	15 seconds
	1 minute
	1 hour

× ____
× ____

d same rate of water loss from a leaky tap (1000 mL = 1 L, 1000 L = 1 kL)

Amount	Time
12 mL	5 minutes
L	1 day
kL	1 year (365 days)

× ____
× ____

4 State whether each statement is true (T) or false (F) by circling the correct answer.

Tip Change quantities of the same type to the same units.

a 8 kg for \$5 is the same as 800 g for 50 cents.

T or F

b 4 km in 20 minutes is faster than 100 km/h.

T or F

c 300 g for \$1 is more expensive than 3 kg for \$19.

T or F

5 Which is the better buy?

A

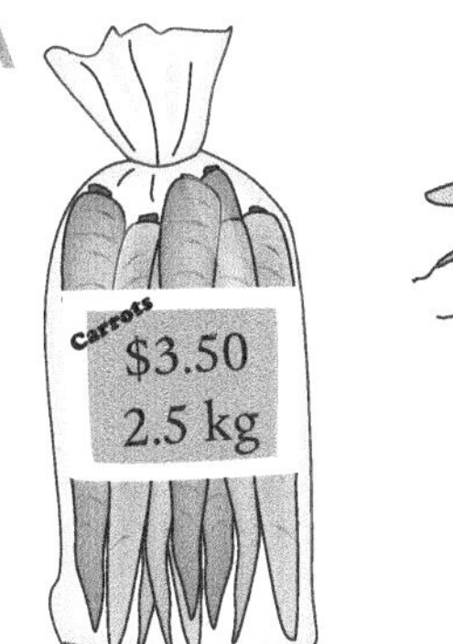

B

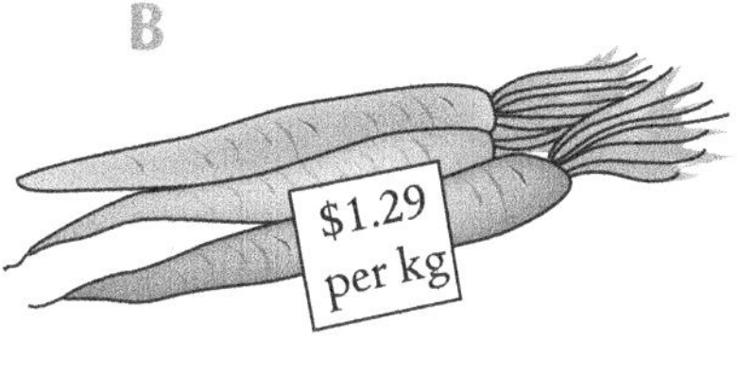

4.7 Rates B

We use the rate at which quantities have grown in the past to estimate amounts for the future.

Growth rate is the amount of increase per unit of time.

Jamie's bank balance went from \$200 to \$280 over 4 weeks.

$$\text{Growth rate} = \frac{\text{increase}}{\text{time}} = \frac{280-200}{4} = \frac{\$80}{4\text{ weeks}} = \$20/\text{week}$$

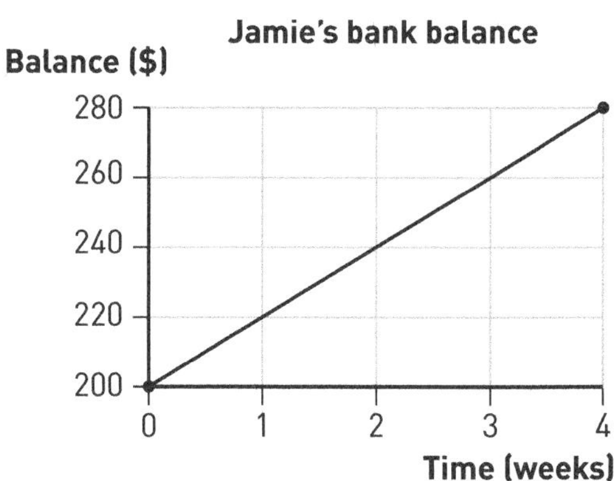

The growth rate can be expressed as a **percentage**.

$$\text{Percentage increase} = \frac{\text{increase}}{\text{original}} \times 100\% = \frac{80}{200} \times 100\% = 40\%$$

$$\text{Average percentage increase} = \frac{\text{percentage increase}}{\text{time}} = \frac{40\%}{4\text{ weeks}} = 10\% \text{ per week}$$

Growth factor

The population of a town increased from 5000 to 6500 in one year.

$$\text{Increase} = 6500 - 5000 = 1500 \text{ people}$$

$$\text{Percentage increase} = \frac{1500}{5000} \times 100\% = 30\%$$

The new amount is 130% of the original amount.

130% = 1.3, so 1.3 is the **growth factor**.

We can predict the population for the next year, if we assume the same percentage rate of increase.

$6500 \times 1.3 = 8450$ people

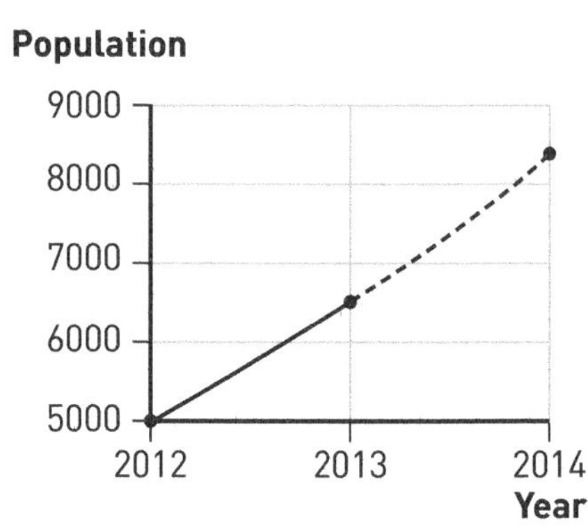

1 Find the amount of increase in each of the following.

a 20 cm to 28 cm

Increase:

____ − ____

= ____ cm

b \$180 to \$200

Increase:

____ − ____

= \$____

2 If the increases in Question **1** occurred over 4 weeks, find the growth rate for each.

Tip Divide each the increase by the number of weeks.

a Growth rate

$= \frac{\text{increase}}{\text{time}}$

$= \frac{\_\_\text{ cm}}{4\text{ weeks}}$

= ____ cm/week

b Growth rate

$= \frac{\text{increase}}{\text{time}}$

$= \frac{\$\_\_}{4\text{ weeks}}$

= \$____/week

3 Mark has grown from 120 cm at the start of Year 4 to 170 cm at the start of Year 8. Find his average growth rate in cm/year.

Increase:

____ − ____ = ____ cm

____ cm in ____ years ÷ 4

= ______ cm per year

4 Barrack was doing 40 minutes of homework every night until he worked out a study plan.

After 3 weeks, he found he was studying 70 minutes every night.

a Find the increase in nightly study.

Increase = ____ − ____

= ____ minutes

b Find the percentage increase in nightly study.

$$\text{Percentage increase} = \frac{\text{increase}}{\text{original}} \times 100\%$$

$$= \frac{\_\_}{\_\_} \times 100\%$$

= ____%

c Find his **average percentage increase** over the 3 weeks in % per week.

$$\frac{\text{percentage increase}}{\text{time}} = \frac{\_\_\_\%}{\_\_\text{ weeks}}$$

= ____% per week

5 The largest colony of Australian fur seals is at Seal Rock in Victoria. The graph below shows an estimate of the seal population on Seal Rock, Victoria.

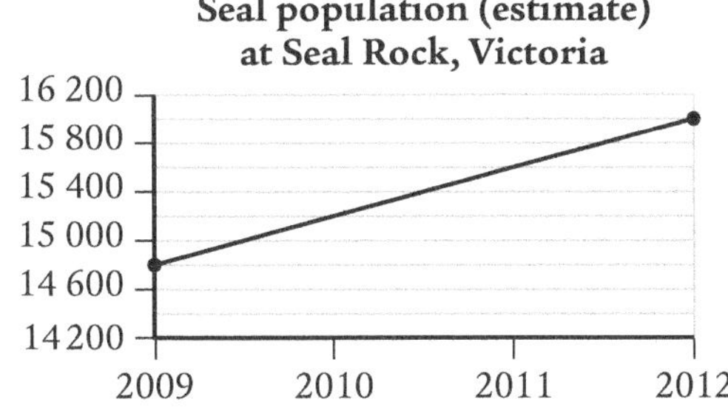

a What is the increase in seal population from 2009–2012?

b What is the average percentage increase over the 3 years (to 1 decimal place)?

6 The number of students using mobiles phones in a school increased from 400 to 420 in a month.

a What is the **growth factor** for the month?

$$\text{Growth factor} = \frac{\text{new amount}}{\text{original amount}}$$

$$= \frac{\_\_}{\_\_}$$

= 1.____

b What percentage increase is this?

1.05 × 100% = ____%

The increase is ____% − 100% = ____%

c If the growth factor remained the same, how many students had mobiles after another month?

New amount

= starting amount × growth factor

= 420 × ____

= ____

NAPLAN-ready

Shade the box beneath the correct answer.

The number of seals appearing at an island near Tasmania increase from 6500 to 8500 in a year.

If the same percentage increase continues each year, what will the population be after two more years, to the nearest 100 seals?

11 100	12 500	14 500	19 000
☐	☐	☐	☐

Tip Find the growth factor first and then multiply by the growth factor for each of the two years.

5.1 Perimeter

Perimeter is the length around the boundary of a shape. To find the perimeter of a shape, the lengths of all sides are added together.

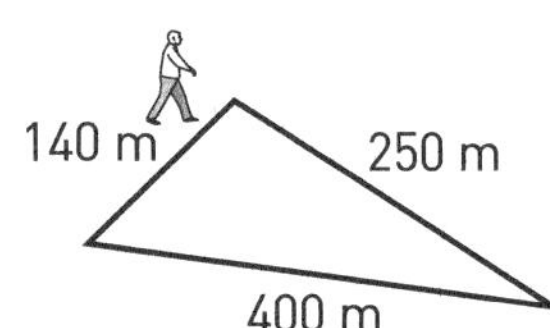

P = sum of all side lengths
= 140 m + 250 m + 400 m
= 790 m

The perimeter of the triangle is 790 m.

Perimeter formulas

A formula can make it easier to find the perimeter of some shapes.

Square	Rhombus	Rectangle	Parallelogram
$P = 4 \times$ length	$P = 4 \times$ length	$P = 2 \times$ (length + width)	$P = 2(a + b)$
9 mm	1.5 cm	3 m, 7 m	a = 2.5 km, b = 8 km
$P = 4 \times 9$ mm = 36 mm	$P = 4 \times 1.5$ cm = 6 cm	$P = 2 \times (7$ m + 3 m) = 2×10 m = 20 m	$P = 2 \times (a + b)$ = $2 \times (8$ km + 2.5 km) = 2×10.5 km = 21 km

Note: Sides with the same number of dashes are the same length.

Word Bank

Rhombus

→ A rhombus is a shape with four equal side lengths. The opposite sides of a rhombus are parallel.

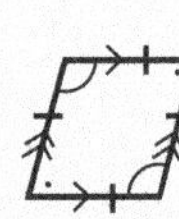

Parallelogram

→ A parallelogram is a four-sided shape with two pairs of parallel sides of equal length.

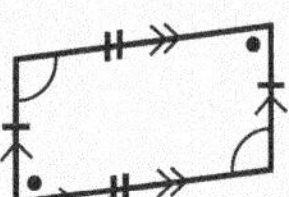

1 What is the perimeter?

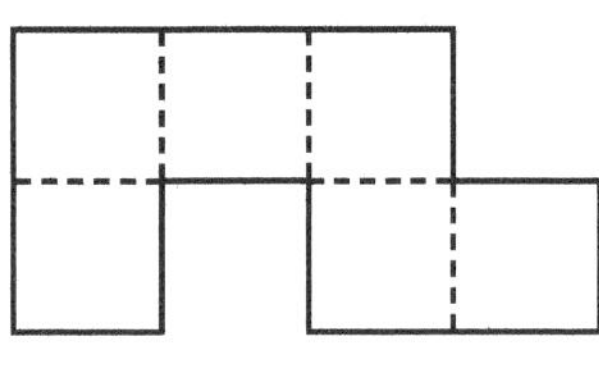

P = ______ cm

2 Add the side lengths together (starting at the ✗) to find the perimeter.

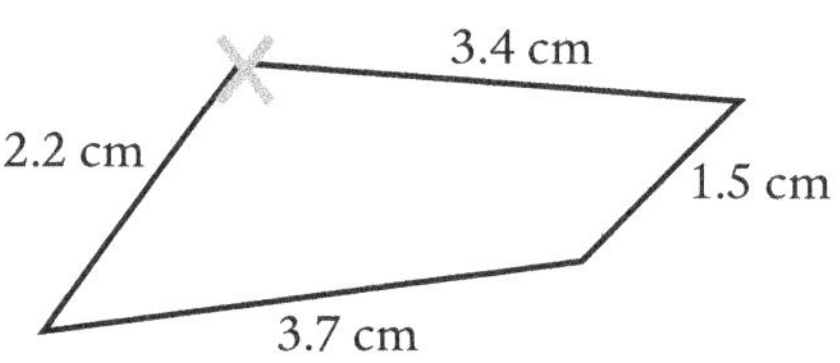

P = ____ + ____ + ____ + ____

= ______ cm

3 Calculate the perimeter using the formula $P = 4 \times$ length.

a

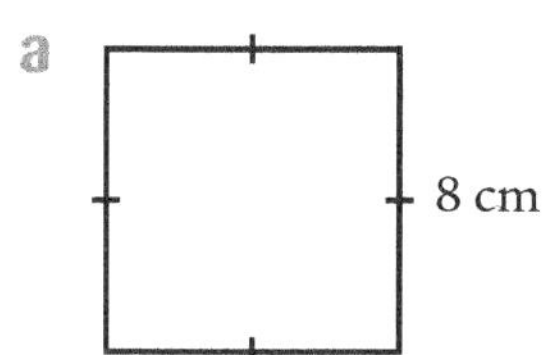

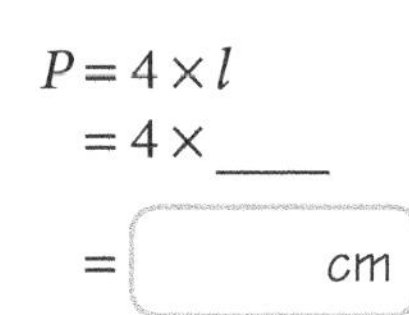

$P = 4 \times l$
$= 4 \times$ ____
= ______ cm

b

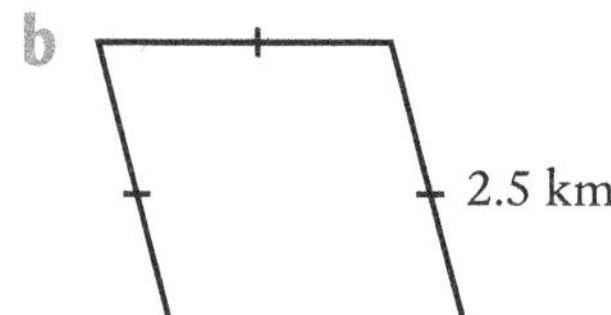

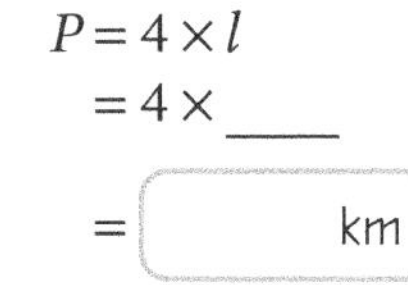

$P = 4 \times l$
$= 4 \times$ ____
= ______ km

4 Use a formula to calculate the perimeter of the regular hexagon below.

Tip The side lengths of a regular polygon are equal. The perimeter can be calculated using the formula *P* = *number of sides* × *length of side*.

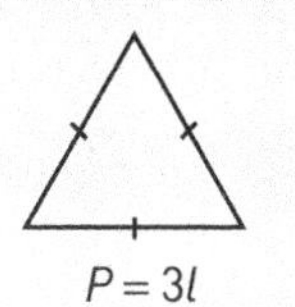

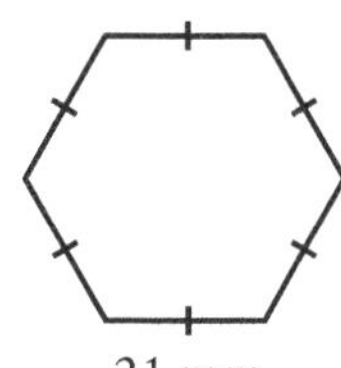

$P =$ ______

$=$ ___ × ___

$=$ [ ] mm

5 The perimeter of the rectangle is stated. Show the workings.

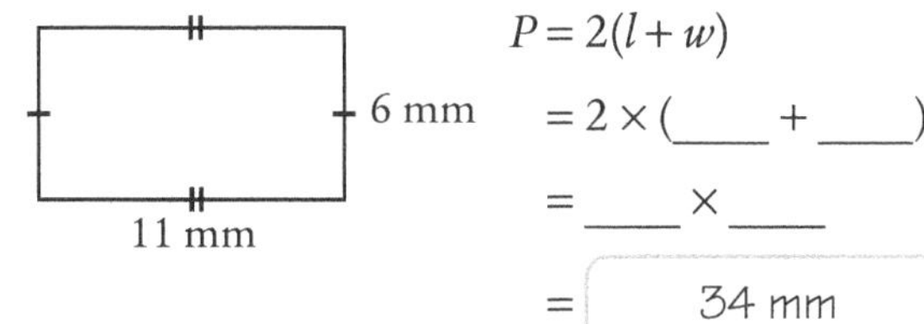

$P = 2(l + w)$

$= 2 \times ($___ + ___$)$

$=$ ___ × ___

$=$ 34 mm

6 Calculate the perimeter of the parallelogram using the formula $P = 2(a + b)$

Tip Lengths *a* and *b* are the two different side lengths of a parallelogram. *b* usually stands for the *base* of a shape.

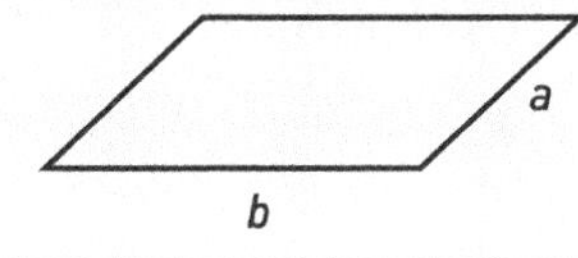

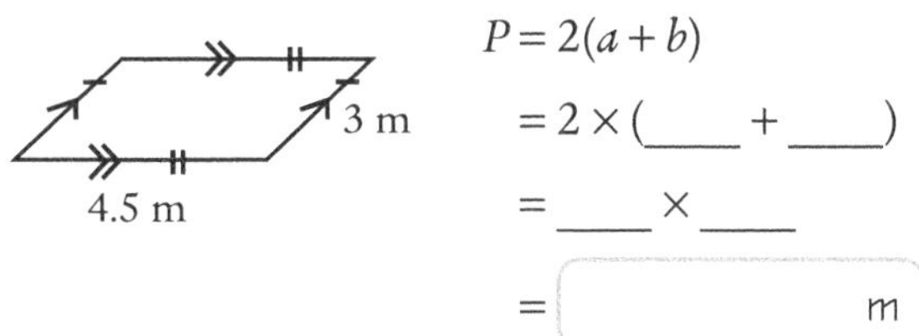

$P = 2(a + b)$

$= 2 \times ($___ + ___$)$

$=$ ___ × ___

$=$ [ ] m

7 Convert the following lengths.

Tip This chart will help to convert measurements.

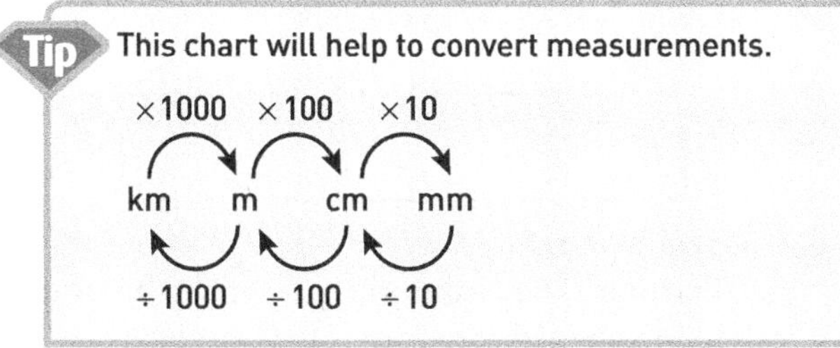

a 24 mm = ___.___ cm (÷ 10)

b 300 cm = ___ m (÷ 100)

c 5 cm = ______ mm

d 1.5 m = ________ cm

e 1200 m = ______ km

f 2.5 km = __________ m

8 Calculate the perimeter in centimetres.

Tip The lengths of each side must be in the same unit of measurement before calculating the perimeter.

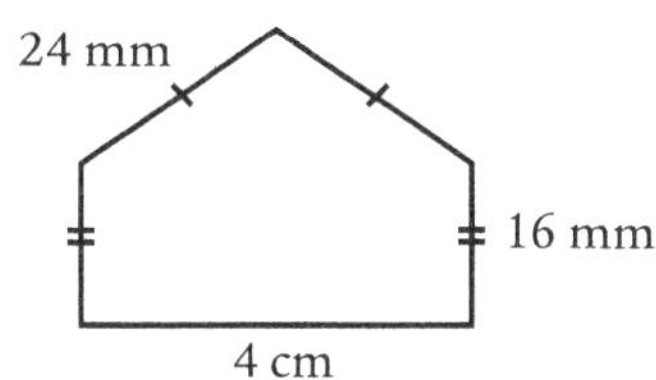

24 mm = ____ cm

16 mm = ____ cm

$P =$ ___ + ___ + ___ + ___ + ___

$=$ [ ] cm

NAPLAN-ready

Shade the correct answer.

Twelve pavers are arranged to make a small patio.

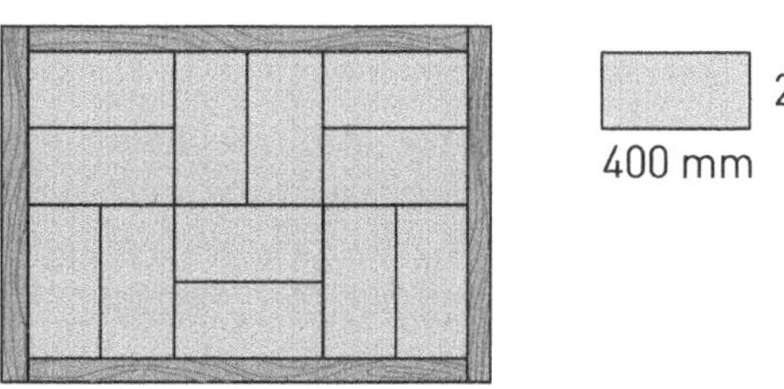

What length of timber is required to go around the patio?

2000 mm	2800 mm	3200 mm	4000 mm
☐	☐	☐	☐

Tip Find the perimeter of the shape by adding all side lengths together, or use the formula $P = 2(l + w)$.

5.2 Circle relationships

The **circumference** is the length around the outside of a circle. It is measured in mm, cm, m or km.

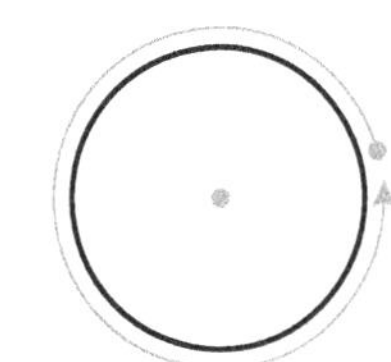

An approximate length for the circumference of a circle can be found by placing a piece of string around the circle's edge. The string can then be straightened and measured with a ruler.

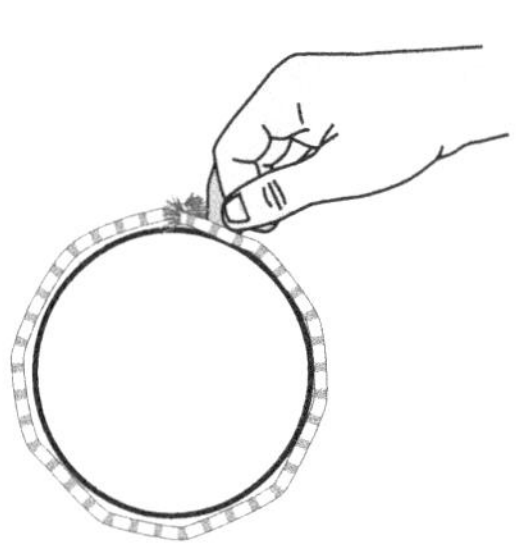

The **diameter** of a circle is the length from one side to the other, passing through the centre.

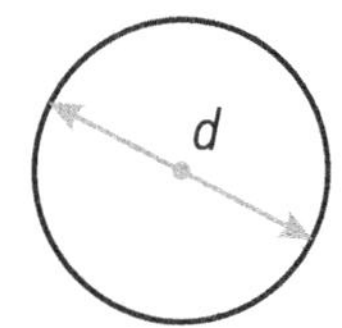

The **radius** is the length from the centre of a circle to its edge.

The radius is half the length of the diameter.

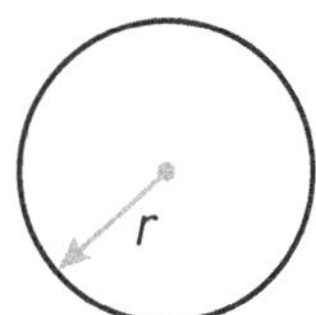

1 The circle below is drawn on centimetre square paper.

a Mark in the centre of the circle.

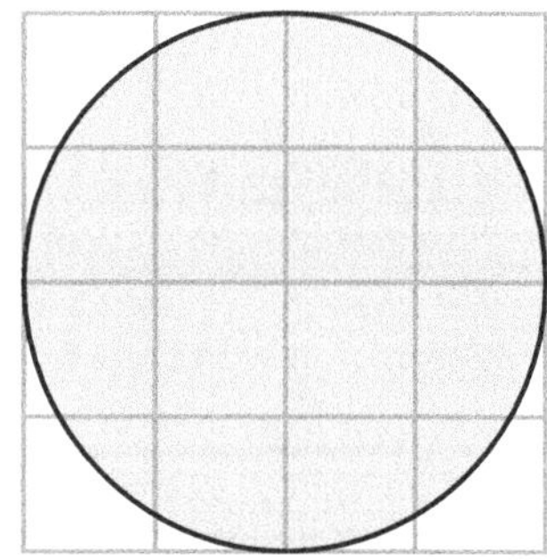

b Draw a line to show the diameter of the circle. What is the length of the diameter?

cm

c Draw a line to show the radius of the circle. What is the length of the radius?

cm

2 a What is the radius of a circle with a diameter of 22 mm?

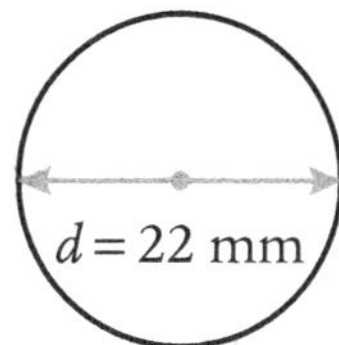

$r =$

b A circle has a radius of 1.6 cm. What is its diameter?

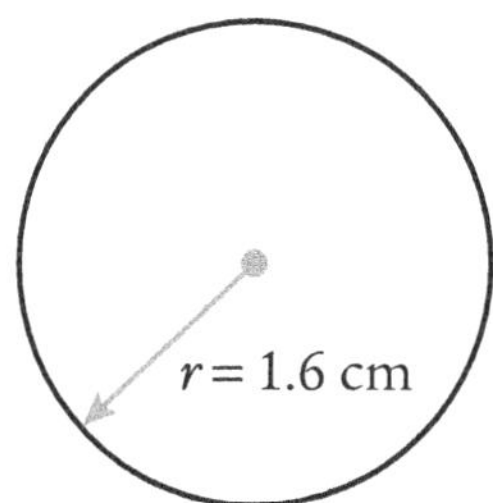

$d =$

3 a Measure the lengths of the radius and diameter of the button.

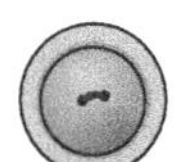

$r =$ $d =$

b The button has been rolled along a ruler for one full turn.

Tip The circumference of a circle can be estimated by rolling a circular object in a straight line along a tape measure, starting and ending at the same point on the circle.

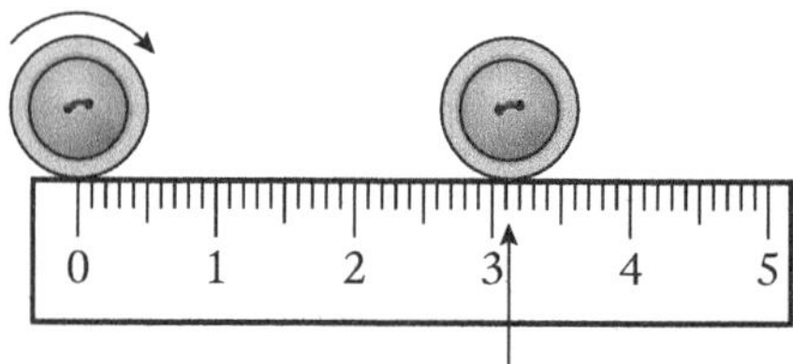

Estimate the circumference of the button using the ruler.

$C =$ cm

4 a What is the radius and diameter of an Australian \$2 coin?

$r =$

$d =$

b A \$2 coin has been rolled along a ruler for one full turn.

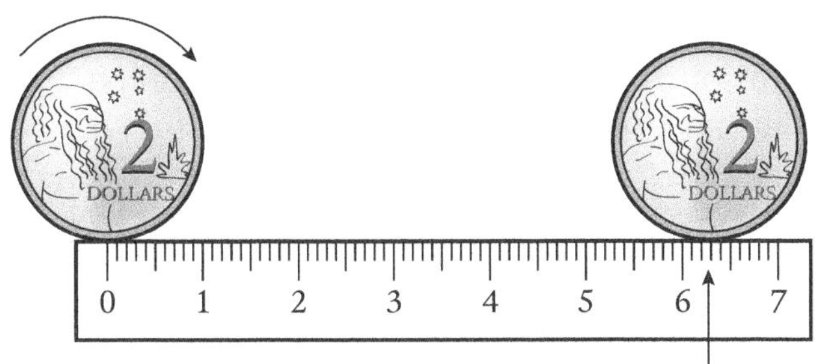

Estimate the circumference of the coin using the ruler.

$C =$ cm

5 a Write the answers from Question **3** and Question **4** in the table below.

	Radius	Diameter	Estimation of circumference
Button			
\$2 coin			

× 2 × ______

b What is the relationship between the diameter and circumference?

______

______

6 Use a ruler to measure the diameter of the following circles. Estimate the length of the circumference.

Tip The circumference of a circle is 3 and a bit times longer than its diameter.

a

Diameter =

Circumference ≈

× 3 and a bit

b

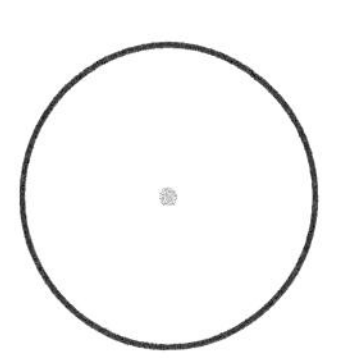

Diameter =

Circumference ≈

c

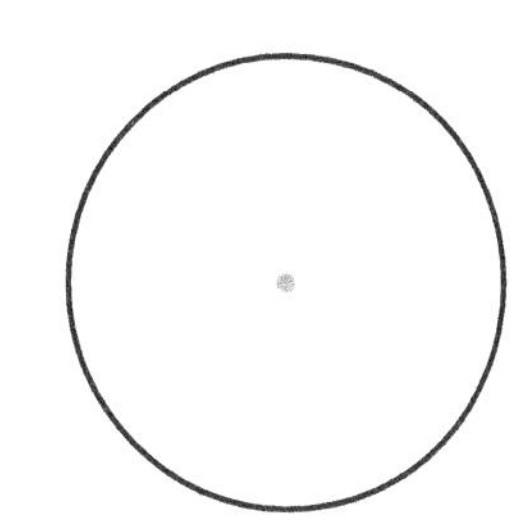

Diameter =

Circumference ≈

NAPLAN-ready

Shade the box beneath the correct answer.

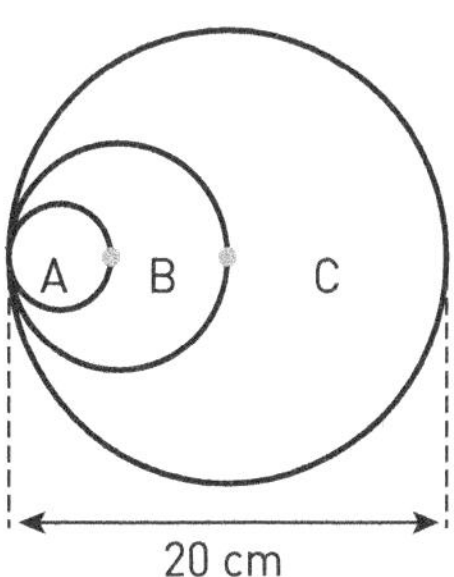

What is the radius of Circle A?

2 cm	2.5 cm	4 cm	5 cm
▭	▭	▭	▭

Tip To find the radius of each circle, half the diameter.

5.3 Circumference

The **circumference** of a circle is the perimeter of a circle. It is the length around the edge of the circle. The circumference can be calculated by multiplying the diameter by a special number known as π (Pi).

π is a number a little larger than 3.

- To calculate the circumference, multiply the diameter by π.

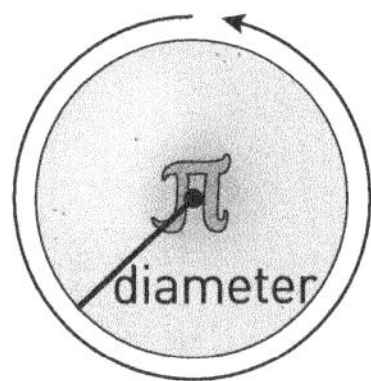

$C = \pi \times \text{diameter}$

Scientific calculators have a π button. Use this button to calculate the circumference of a circle.

Circumference formulas

To calculate the circumference, multiply the diameter by π.

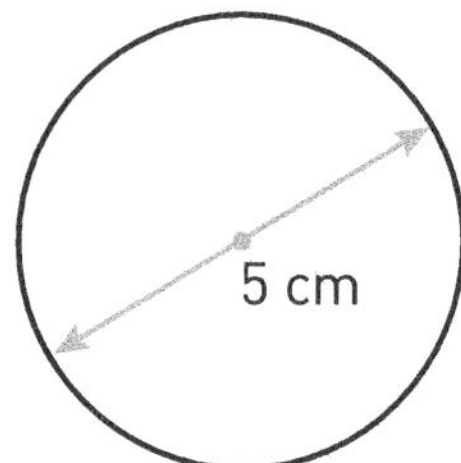

$C = \pi \times diameter$
$C = \pi d$
$C = \pi \times 5$ cm
≈ 15.71 cm (2 d.p.)

OR to calculate the circumference, double the radius and then multiply by π.

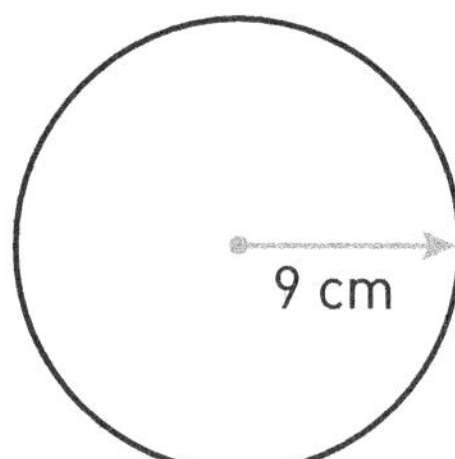

$C = 2 \times \pi \times radius$
$C = 2\pi r$
$C = 2 \times \pi \times 9$ cm
≈ 56.55 cm (2 d.p.)

Word Bank

π
→ The symbol π (pronounced *pie*) represents an irrational number (a number with infinite decimal places) a little larger than 3. It is used to find the circumference and area of a circle.

$\pi = 3.141\,592\,6...$

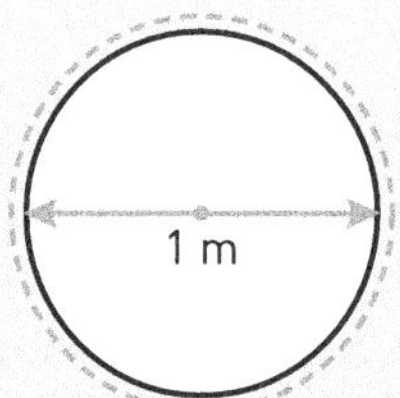

$d = 1$ m $\quad C \approx 3.14$ m

The circumference of a circle is approximately 3.14 times larger than its diameter.

You will need a compass for Question **1**.

1 Place one point of the compass on the dot and open the compass arms to the middle of one of the sides of the square. Draw a circle inside the square.

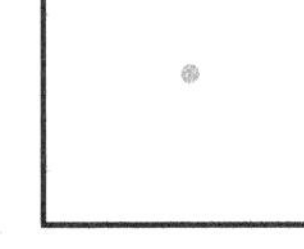

a What is the diameter of the circle?

b Estimate the circumference of the circle you drew.

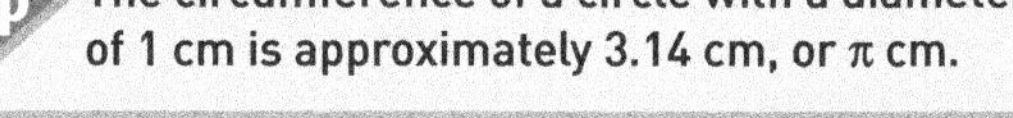

2 Find π on your calculator.

Push (π) and then (=).

(You may have to push (SHIFT) or (2ndF) first)

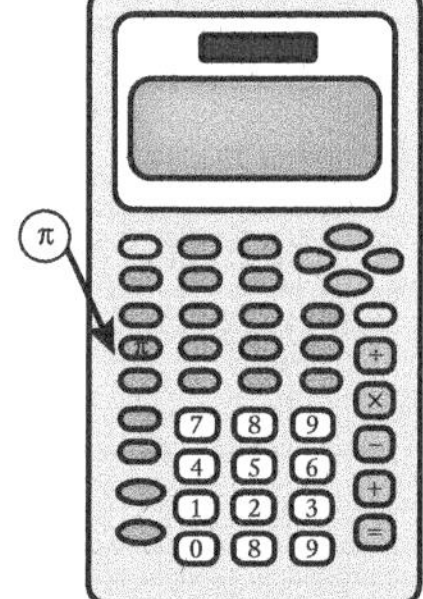

a What is the value of π given by a calculator?

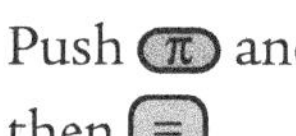

b What is an approximate value of π, rounded to two decimal places?

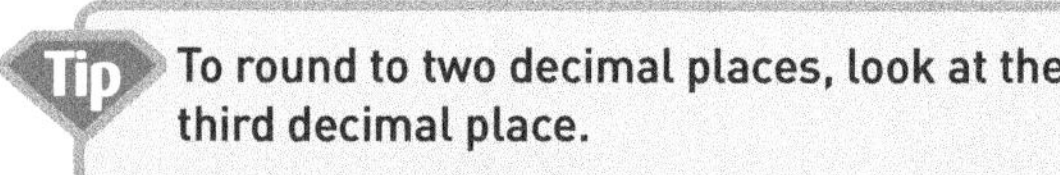

π ≈ (2 d.p.)

3 Calculate the circumference of the circle below.

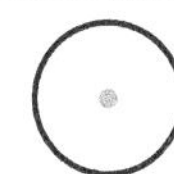

$C = \pi \times d$

$= \pi \times$ ____

$=$ ______ (2 d.p.)

4 Calculate the circumference of the following circles, using a ruler and calculator. Round to two decimal places.

> **Tip** Estimate the circumference before using a calculator. It should be just over three times as long as the diameter.

a

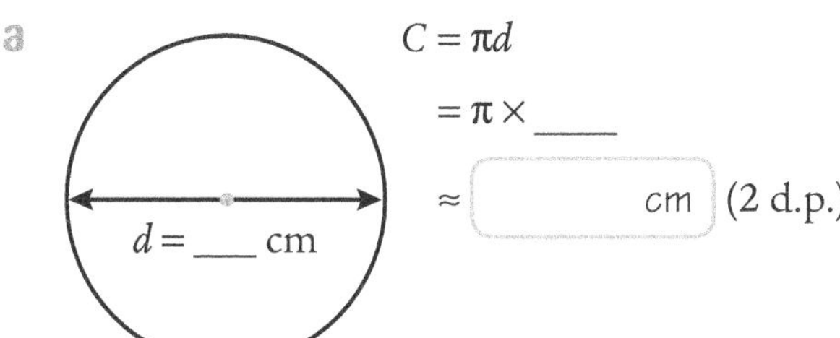

$C = \pi d$

$= \pi \times$ ____

$\approx$ ______ cm (2 d.p.)

b

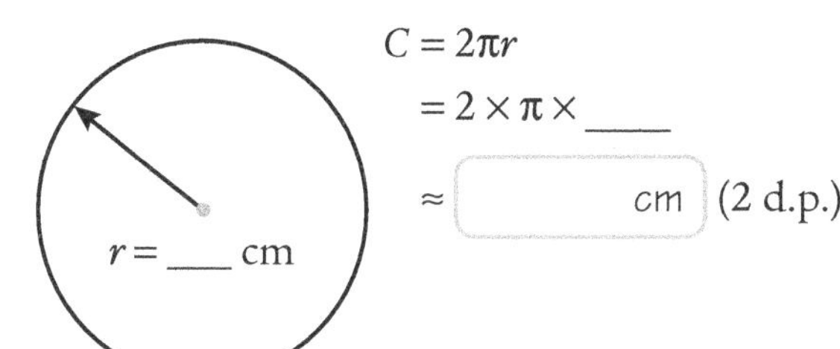

$C = 2\pi r$

$= 2 \times \pi \times$ ____

$\approx$ ______ cm (2 d.p.)

5 **a** What is the circumference of the circle below?

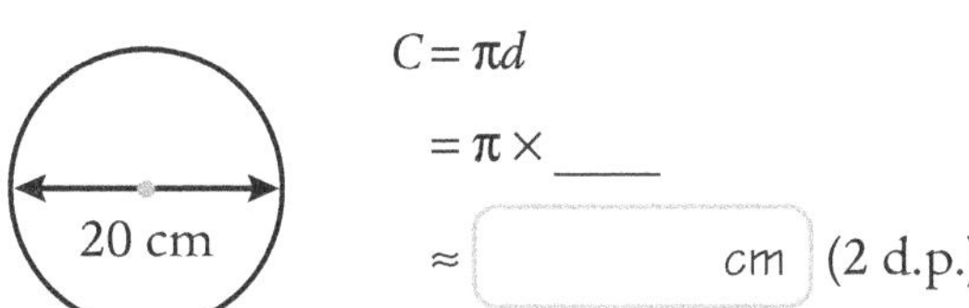

$C = \pi d$

$= \pi \times$ ____

$\approx$ ______ cm (2 d.p.)

b The above circle is cut in half. What is the perimeter of half the circle?

> **Tip** To calculate the perimeter of a semicircle.

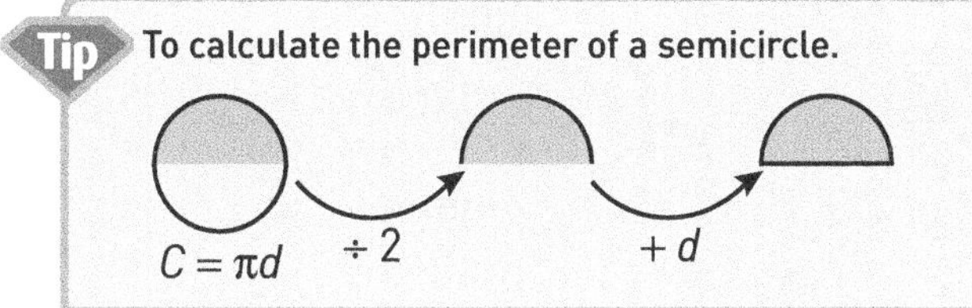

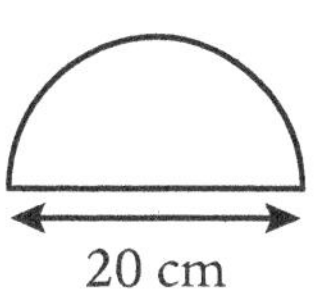

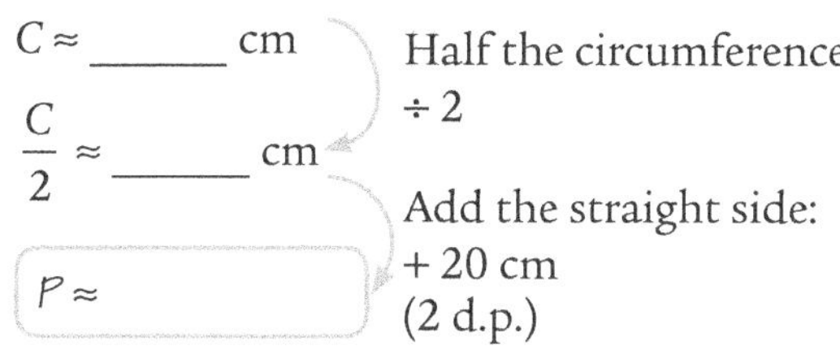

$C \approx$ ______ cm — Half the circumference: ÷ 2

$\frac{C}{2} \approx$ ______ cm — Add the straight side: + 20 cm

$P \approx$ ______ (2 d.p.)

6 Calculate the perimeter of the shaded shape.

> **Tip** Perimeter is the total distance *around* a shape. Don't forget to add together the curved sides and the straight sides.

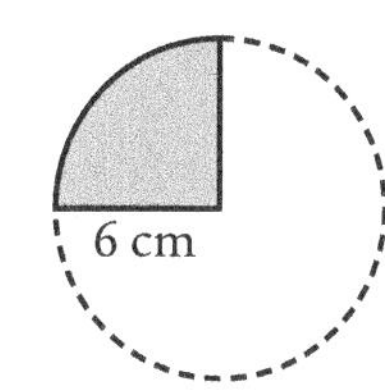

$C = 2\pi r$

$= 2 \times \pi \times$ ____

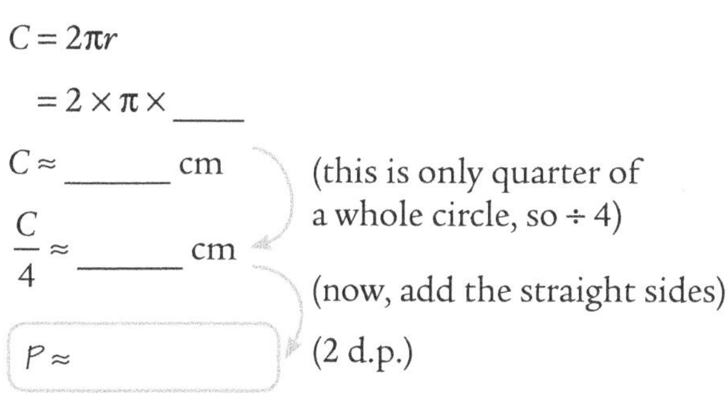

$C \approx$ ______ cm (this is only quarter of a whole circle, so ÷ 4)

$\frac{C}{4} \approx$ ______ cm (now, add the straight sides)

$P \approx$ ______ (2 d.p.)

NAPLAN-ready

Shade the box beneath the correct answer.

A paper circle with a diameter of 6 cm was cut into quarters and then rearranged as shown.

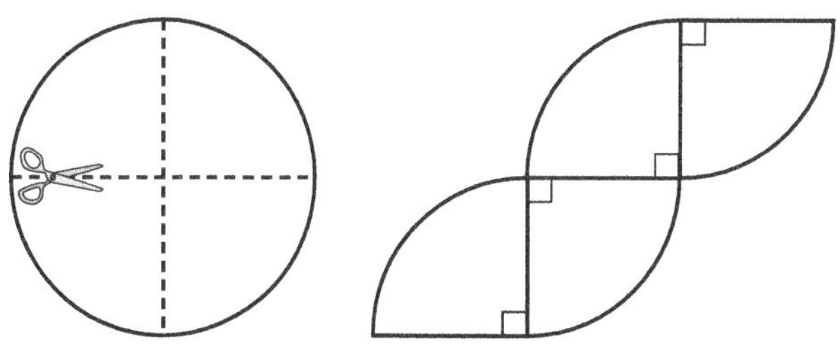

The circumference of the paper circle was approximately 18.85 cm. What is the perimeter of the new shape, rounded to two decimal places?

18.85 cm	24.85 cm	27.85 cm	30.85 cm
☐	☐	☐	☐

> **Tip** How much larger is the perimeter of the new shape? Look for straight sides.

5.4 Area A

Area is the amount of surface inside a 2D shape. Area is measured in squares, such as mm^2, cm^2, m^2 and km^2.

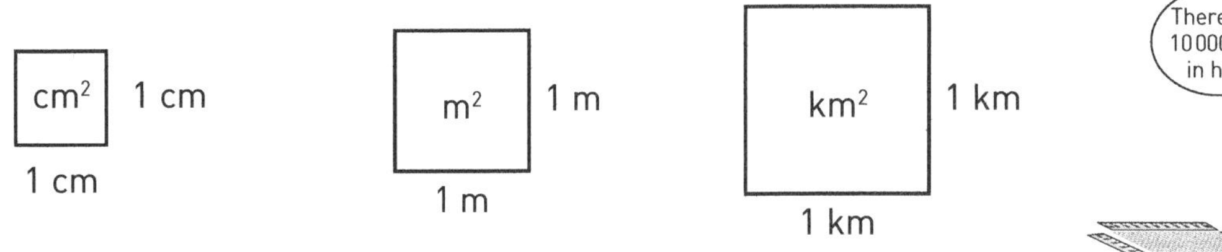

If a square were made with four metre rulers on graph paper, there would be ten thousand centimetre squares inside the square!

Area formulas

Square $A = l^2$	Rectangle $A = lw$	Parallelogram $A = bh$
Area = length × length	Area = length × width	Area = base × perpendicular height
3 cm, 3 cm	2 cm, 3 cm	2 cm, 4 cm
$A = l^2$ $= 3\text{ cm} \times 3\text{ cm}$ $= 9\text{ cm}^2$	$A = l \times w$ $= 2\text{ cm} \times 3\text{ cm}$ $= 6\text{ cm}^2$	$A = b \times h$ $= 4\text{ cm} \times 2\text{ cm}$ $= 8\text{ cm}^2$

Word Bank

Perpendicular height

→ Perpendicular lines look like this:

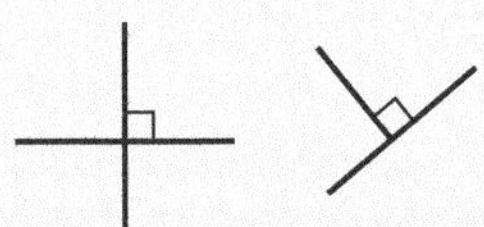

Perpendicular height is the distance to the opposite side when the line is drawn at right angles to the base.

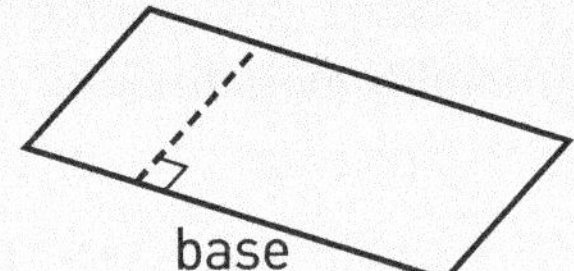

Hectare (ha)

→ A hectare is the area inside a square with length and width of 100 m.

1 Complete the following conversions.

Tip There are 100 mm squares in 1 square centimetre.

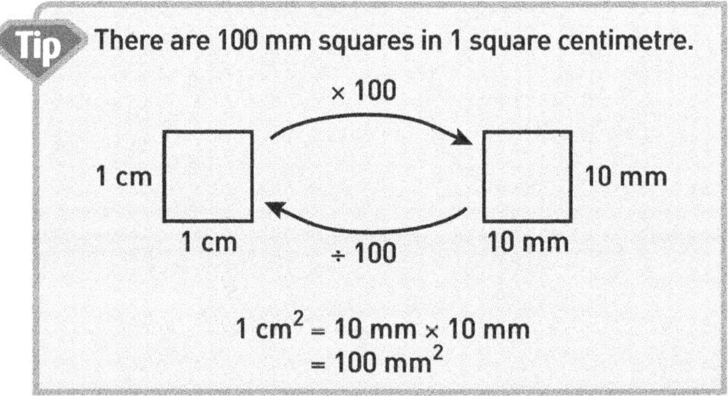

a $2\text{ cm}^2 =$ ______ mm^2

× 100

b $8.5\text{ cm}^2 =$ ______ mm^2

c $300\text{ mm}^2 =$ ____ cm^2

÷ 100

d $620\text{ mm}^2 =$ ______ cm^2

2 Complete the following conversions.

Tip There are 10 000 cm squares in 1 square metre.

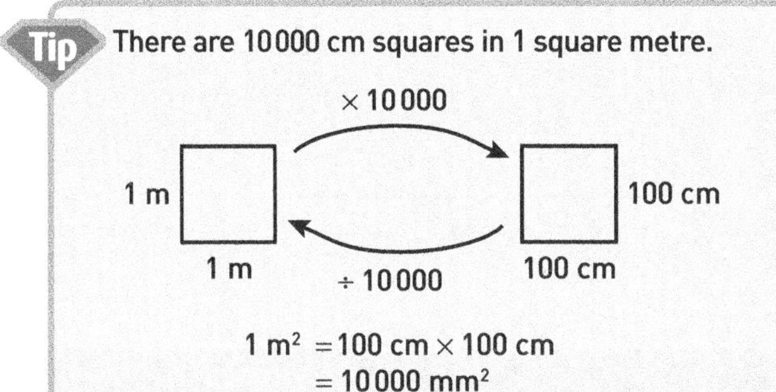

$1 \text{ m}^2 = 100 \text{ cm} \times 100 \text{ cm}$
$= 10\,000 \text{ mm}^2$

a $2 \text{ m}^2 =$ __________ cm^2

b $3.6 \text{ m}^2 =$ __________ cm^2

c $40\,000 \text{ cm}^2 =$ ______ m^2

d $16\,000 \text{ cm}^2 =$ ______ m^2

3 What is the area of these shapes?

a

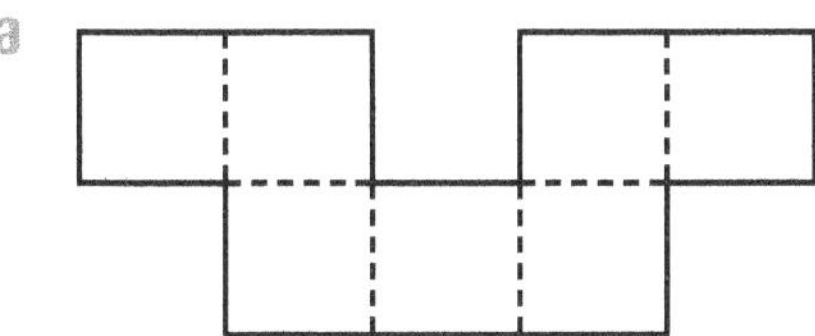

$A =$

b

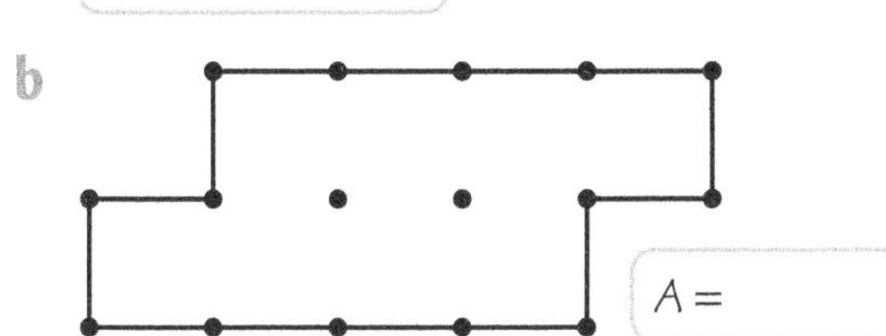

$A =$

c

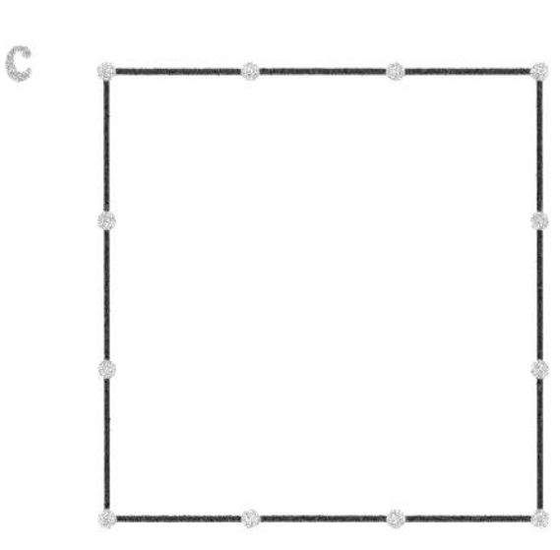

$A =$

4 Calculate the area.

a

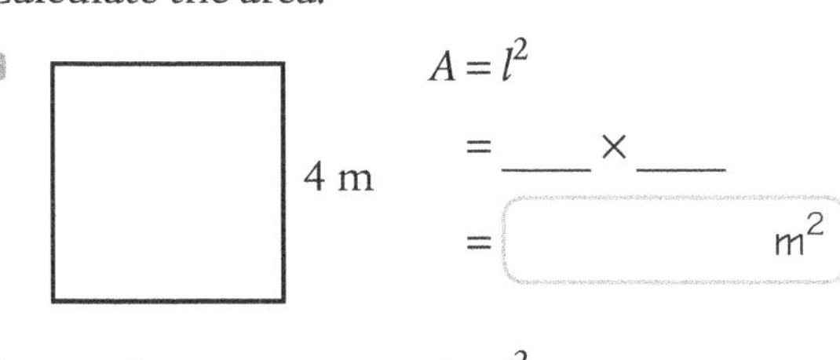

$A = l^2$

$=$ ____ × ____

$=$ m^2

b

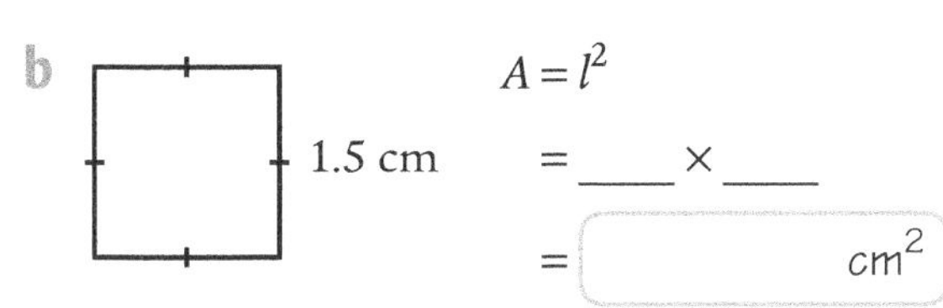

$A = l^2$

$=$ ____ × ____

$=$ cm^2

5 Calculate the area of the rectangles, using the formula $A = \textit{length} \times \textit{width}$.

a

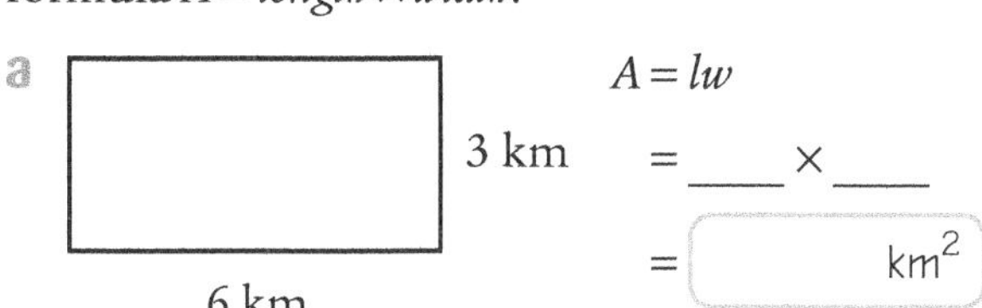

$A = lw$

$=$ ____ × ____

$=$ km^2

b

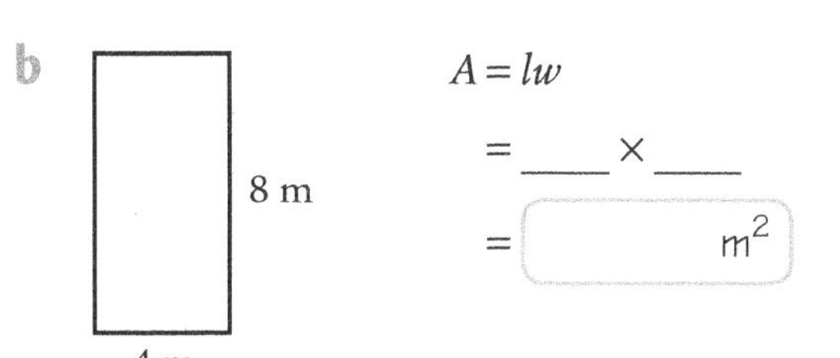

$A = lw$

$=$ ____ × ____

$=$ m^2

c

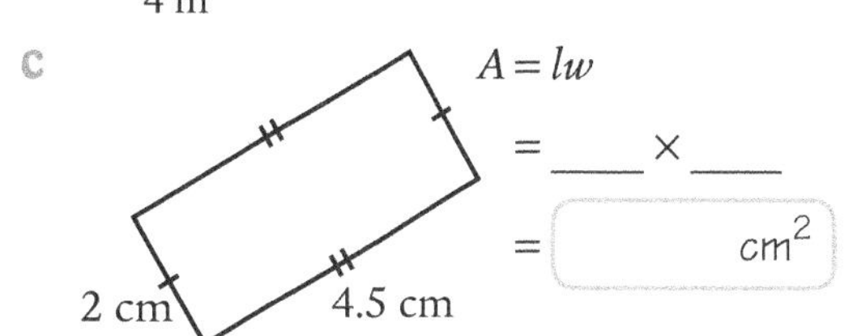

$A = lw$

$=$ ____ × ____

$=$ cm^2

6 Calculate the area of the parallelograms, using the formula $A = \textit{base} \times \textit{perpendicular height}$

a

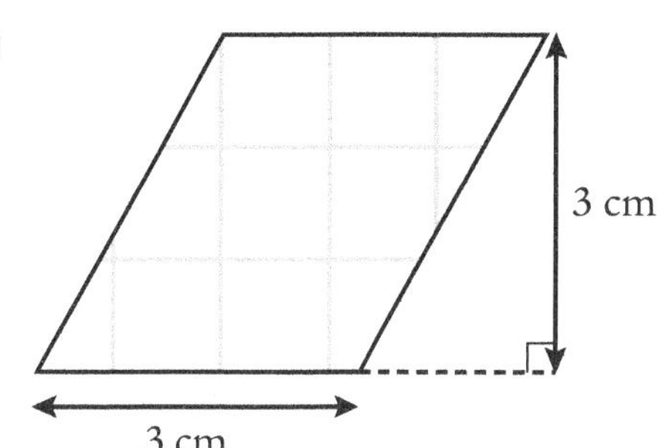

$A = bh$

$=$ ____ × ____

$=$ cm^2

b

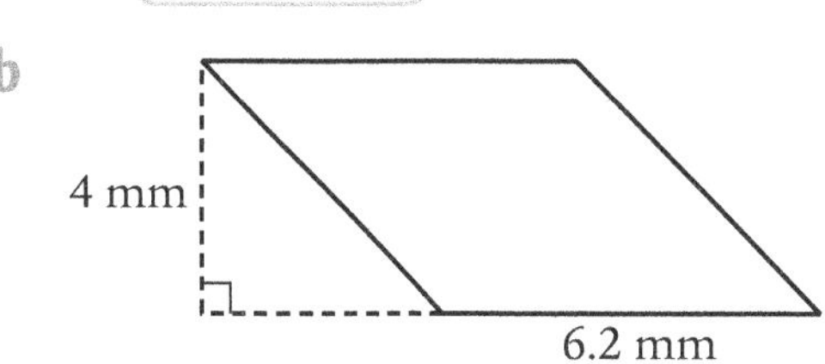

$A = bh$

$=$ ____ × ____

$=$ mm^2

5.4 Area B

The rectangle **on the right** has an area of 8 cm^2.

$A = 4 \times 2$
$= 8$ cm^2

The area of a **triangle**, **kite** and **rhombus** are all **half** the area of the rectangle with the same height and base.

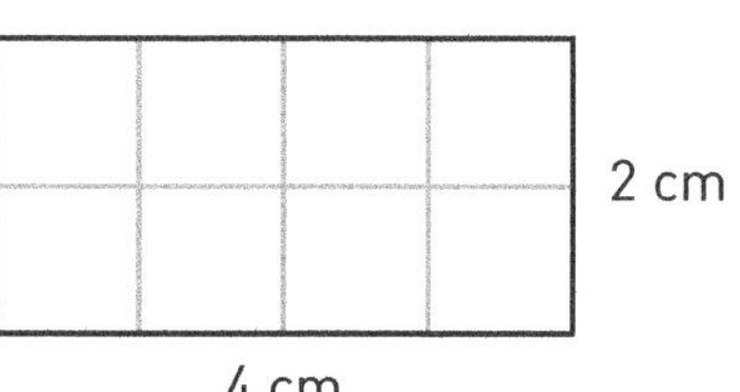

Area formulas

Triangle	Kite	Rhombus
$A = \dfrac{\text{base} \times \text{height}}{2}$	$A = \dfrac{x \times y}{2}$	$A = \dfrac{x \times y}{2}$
$A = \dfrac{bh}{2}$ $= \dfrac{4 \times 2}{2}$ $= 4$ cm^2	x and y are the lengths of the diagonals. $A = \dfrac{xy}{2}$ $= \dfrac{4 \times 2}{2}$ $= 4$ cm^2	x and y are the lengths of the diagonals. $A = \dfrac{xy}{2}$ $= \dfrac{4 \times 2}{2}$ $= 4$ cm^2

Area of a trapezium

$$A = \frac{(a+b) \times h}{2}$$

- Add the two parallel sides together, multiply this by the height, and then halve the result.

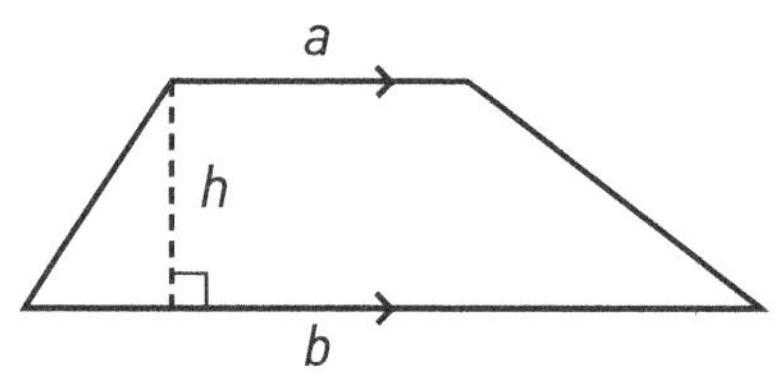

1 What is the area of the rectangle?

a

$A = lw$

$= \_\_\_\_ \times \_\_\_\_$

$A =$

b What is the area of the triangle?

Tip Base b and height h are used for triangles, instead of length l and width w.

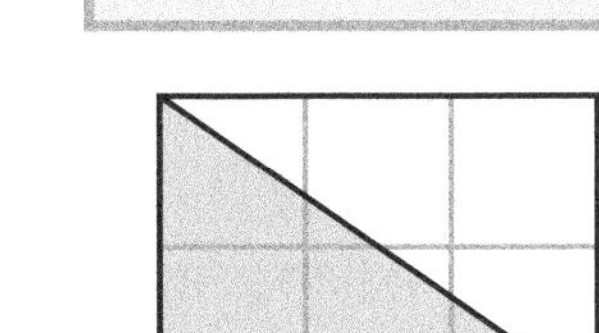

Area of the rectangle = ____ cm^2

Area of triangle = ____ cm^2 ($\div 2$)

2 What is the area of the triangle?

6 m

10 m

$A = \dfrac{b \times h}{2}$

$= (\_\_\_\_ \times \_\_\_\_) \div 2$

$=$ ____ m^2

3 a Measure the lengths of the diagonals in the kite.

Tip The diagonals are called x and y. It does not matter which is x and which is y.

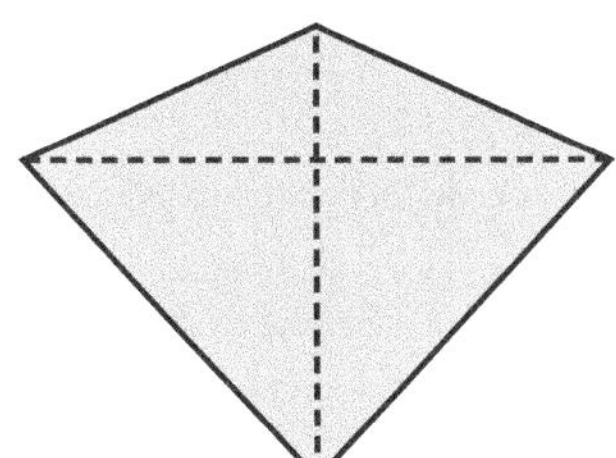

$x=$

$y=$

b Find the area of the above kite.

$A=\frac{x \times y}{2}$

$=(\_\_\_\_ \times \_\_\_\_) \div 2$

$=$ cm²

4 The area of the kite is stated. Show the working.

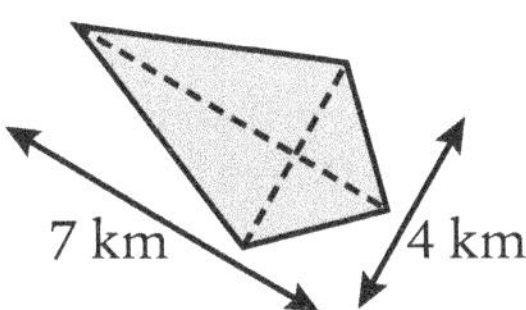

$A=\frac{x \times y}{2}$

$=(\_\_\_\_ \times \_\_\_\_) \div 2$

$=$ 14 km²

5 a Measure the lengths of the diagonals.

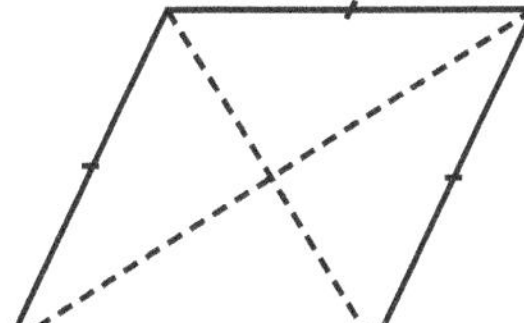

$x=$

$y=$

b Find the area of the above rhombus.

$A=\frac{x \times y}{2}$

$=(\_\_\_\_ \times \_\_\_\_) \div 2$

$=$

6 What is the area of the rhombus below?

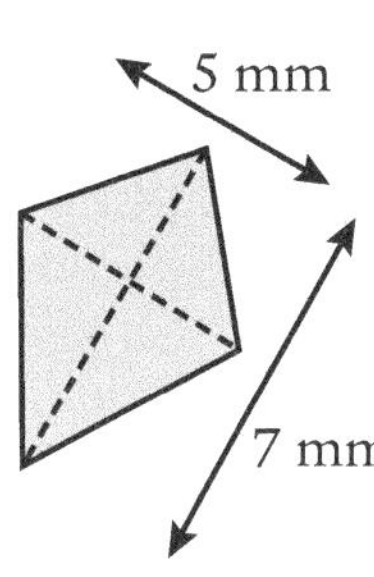

$A=\frac{x \times y}{2}$

$=(\_\_\_\_ \times \_\_\_\_) \div 2$

$=$ mm²

7 Complete the working to find the area of each trapezium below.

a

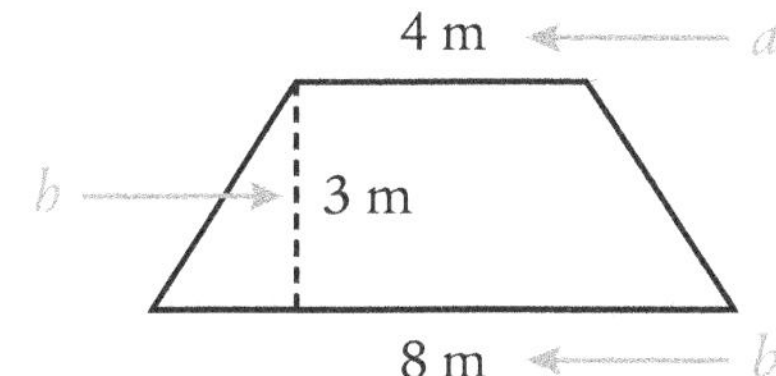

$A=\frac{(a+b) \times h}{2}$

$=\frac{(\_\_+\_\_) \times \_\_}{2}$

$=\frac{\_\_}{2}$

$=$ 18 m²

b

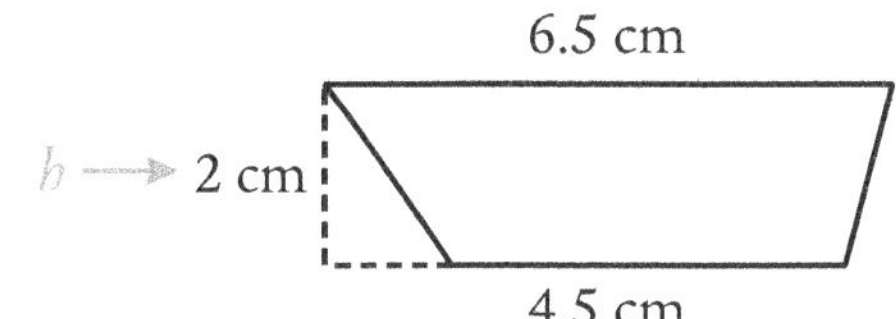

$A=\frac{(a+b) \times h}{2}$

$=\frac{(\_\_+\_\_) \times \_\_}{\_\_}$

$=$ 11 cm²

NAPLAN-ready

Shade the box beneath the correct answer.

A tangram is an ancient Chinese puzzle with seven pieces cut from a square.

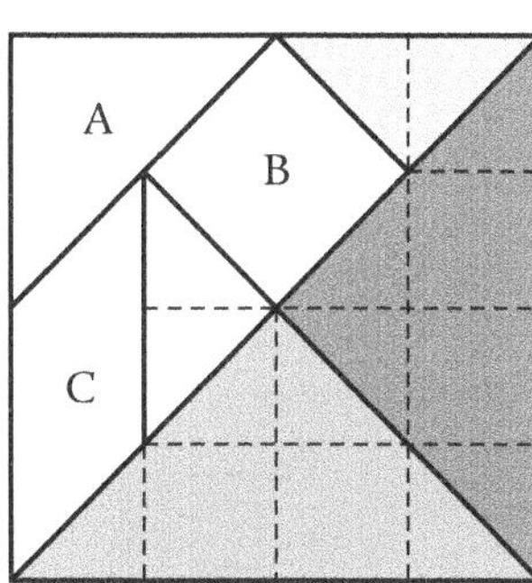

The puzzle pieces A, B and C have the same area. The area of each of these pieces is:

1 cm²	2 cm²	3 cm²	4 cm²
☐	☐	☐	☐

Tip Complete the grid and then count the squares.

5.5 Area of a circle

Approximately how many squares are in this circle?

(count the whole squares and then combine part squares to estimate)

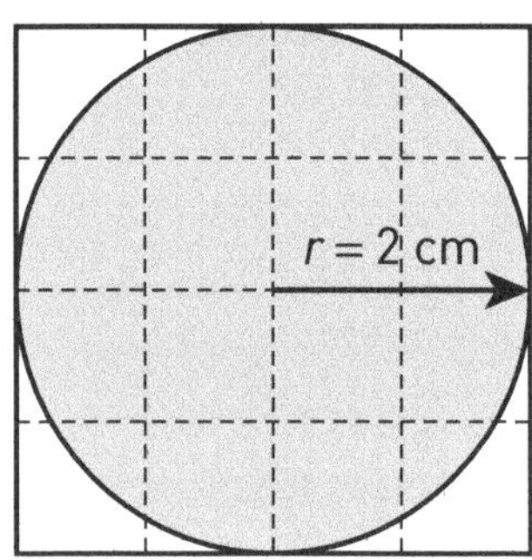

Estimate:

cm^2

Calculating the area of a circle

The area of a circle can be calculated using the formula:

$A = \pi \times r^2$

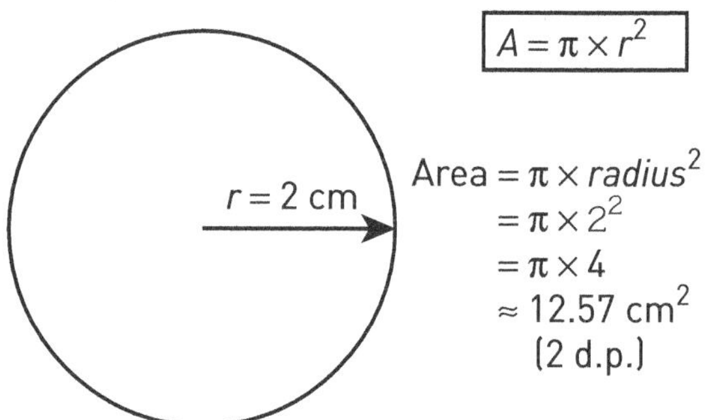

Area $= \pi \times radius^2$
$= \pi \times 2^2$
$= \pi \times 4$
≈ 12.57 cm^2
(2 d.p.)

π is an irrational number, so its decimal places go on forever, without a repeating pattern. The symbol $\approx$ is used to show it is an approximate answer.

1 Answer the following.

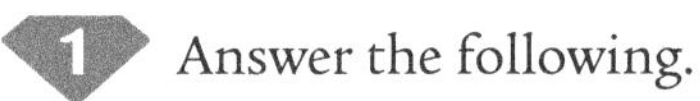

Tip To square a number is to multiply it by itself (e.g. $3^2 = 3 \times 3 = 9$).

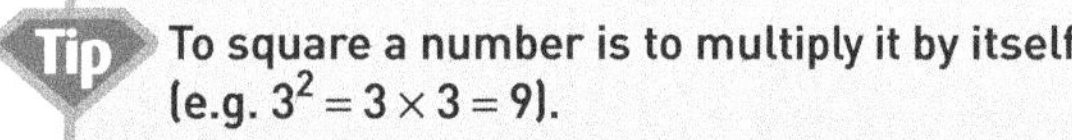

a $4^2 =$ ____ $\times$ ____ $=$ ____

b $6^2 =$ ____ $\times$ ____ $=$ ____

c $10^2 =$ ____ $\times$ ____ $=$ ____

d $12^2 =$ ____ $\times$ ____ $=$ ____

2 A circle has been drawn on cm square paper.

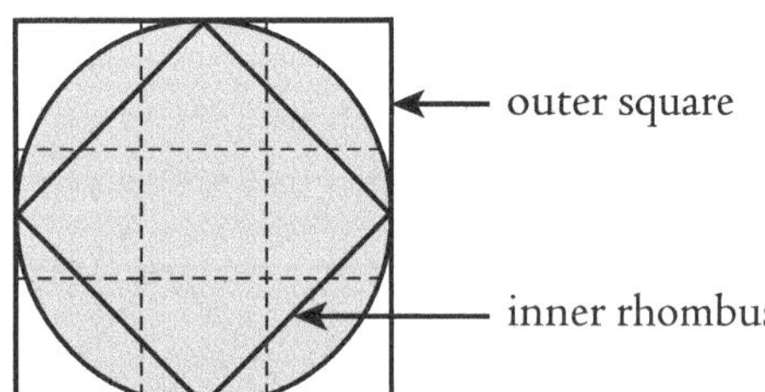

a What is the area of the *outer* square?

$A = l^2$

$=$ ____ $\times$ ____

$=$ ____ cm^2

b What is the area of the *inner* rhombus?

Tip The diagonals of the inner rhombus are the length of the diameter of the circle.

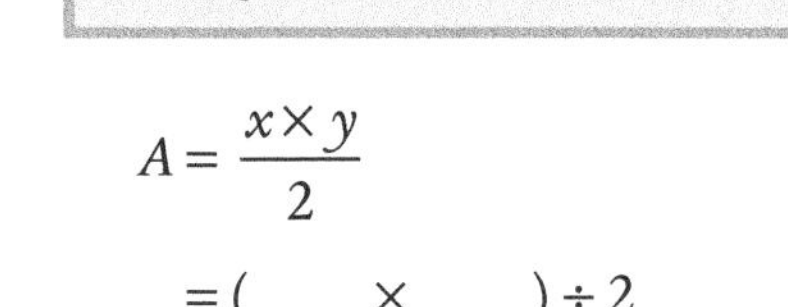

$A = \frac{x \times y}{2}$

$= ($____ $\times$ ____$) \div 2$

$=$ ____ cm^2

c Refer to part **a** and **b** to estimate the area of the circle.

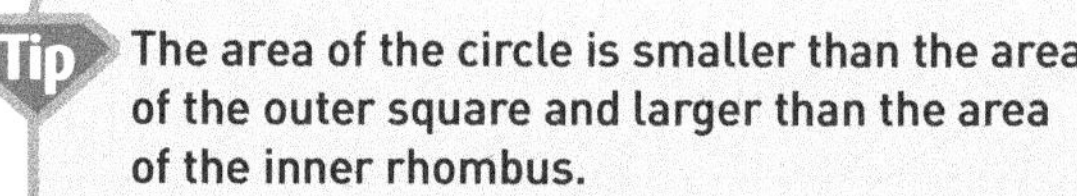

Tip The area of the circle is smaller than the area of the outer square and larger than the area of the inner rhombus.

$A \approx$ cm^2

In Questions 3–6, round answers to two decimal places.

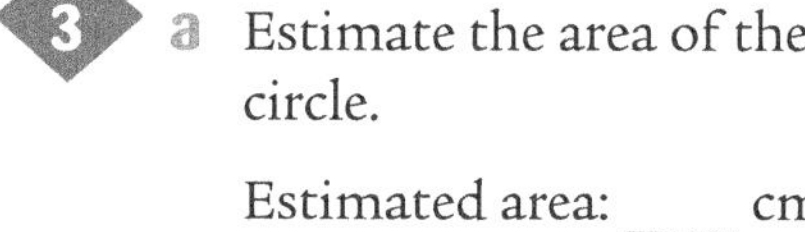

3 a Estimate the area of the circle.

Estimated area: ____ cm^2

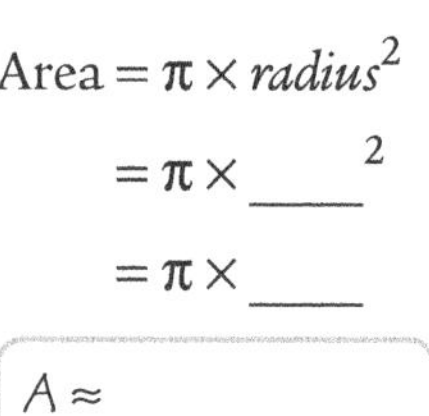

b Calculate the area of the circle.

Area $= \pi \times radius^2$

$= \pi \times$ ____^{2}

$= \pi \times$ ____

$A \approx$

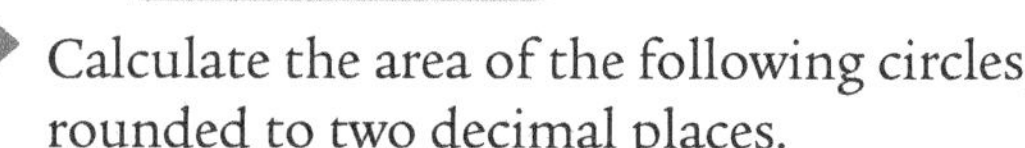

4 Calculate the area of the following circles, rounded to two decimal places.

a

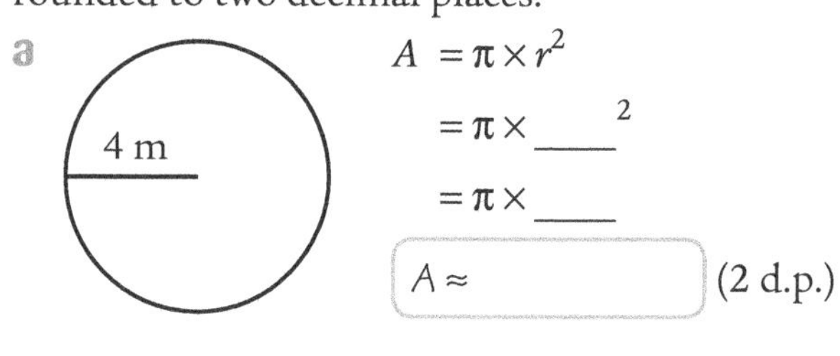

$A = \pi \times r^2$

$= \pi \times$ ____^{2}

$= \pi \times$ ____

$A \approx$ (2 d.p.)

b

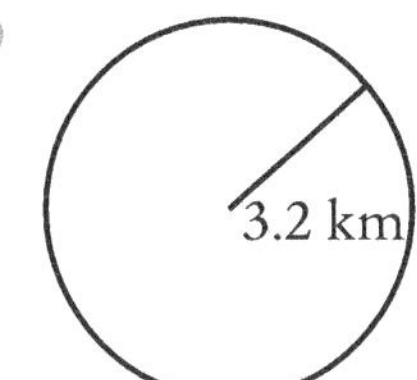

$A = \pi \times r^2$

$= \pi \times \_\_\_^2$

$A \approx$ (2 d.p.)

5 Calculate the area of the following circles.

Tip The radius (r) is half the length of the diameter.

a

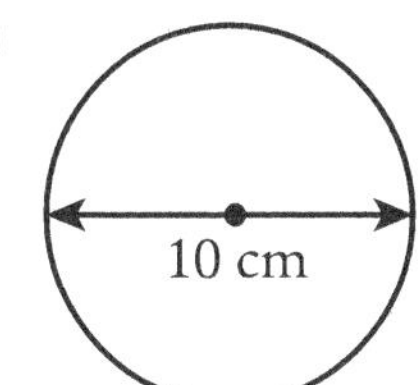

$A = \pi \times r^2$

$= \pi \times \_\_\_^2$

$A \approx$

b

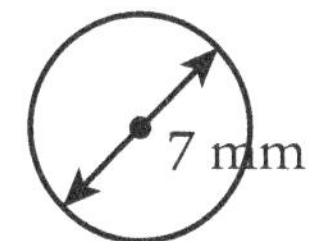

$A = \pi \times r^2$

$= \pi \times \_\_\_^2$

$A \approx$

c

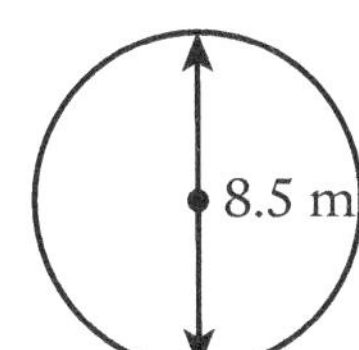

$A = \pi \times r^2$

$= \pi \times \_\_\_^2$

$A \approx$

6 **a** What is the area of the circle below?

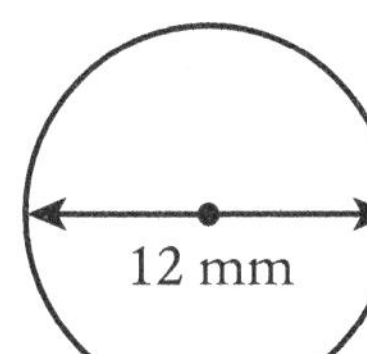

$A = \pi \times r^2$

$= \pi \times \_\_\_^2$

$A \approx$

b The above circle is cut in half. What is the area of one-half of the circle?

Tip Remember, **area is the number of squares** *inside* **a shape. The length of the straight side is not added on.**

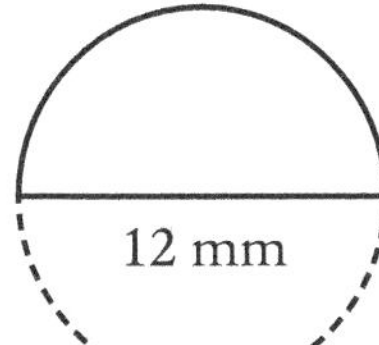

Area of whole circle ≈ ________ mm^2 ÷ 2

Area of half the circle = mm^2

7 What is the area of the shaded semicircle, correct to one decimal place?

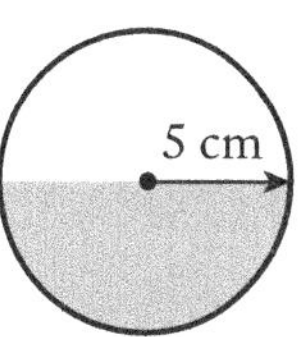

Area of the whole circle

$A = \pi \times r^2$

$= \pi \times \_\_\_^2$

$= \_\_\_\_\_\_ cm^2$ ÷ 2

Area of the half circle

8 **a** What is the area of the circle below?

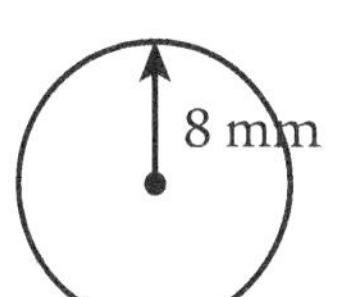

$A = \pi \times r^2$

$= \pi \times \_\_\_^2$

$A \approx$

b The above circle is cut into quarters. What is the area of one-quarter?

Area of whole circle ≈ ________ mm^2 ÷ 4

Area of quarter a circle = mm^2

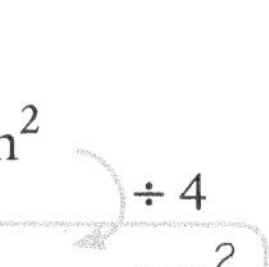

NAPLAN-ready

Shade the box beneath the correct answer.

The design below is drawn to scale.

Shade the statement that most accurately describes the area of the circle.

between 2 cm^2 and 3 cm^2	between 4 cm^2 and 9 cm^2
☐	☐
between 8 cm^2 and 9 cm^2	between 8 cm^2 and 12 cm^2
☐	☐

Tip What is the area of the outer square? What is the area of the inner rhombus?

5.6 Finding the area of composite shapes

What is a 'composite shape'?

A shape made up of simpler shapes is said to be **composite**. Composite shapes can be divided into shapes where the area formulas are known—such as circles, triangles and squares.

The area of the composite shape is written as A_{total}, which means total area.

The total area of a composite shape can be found by adding the area of each individual shape.

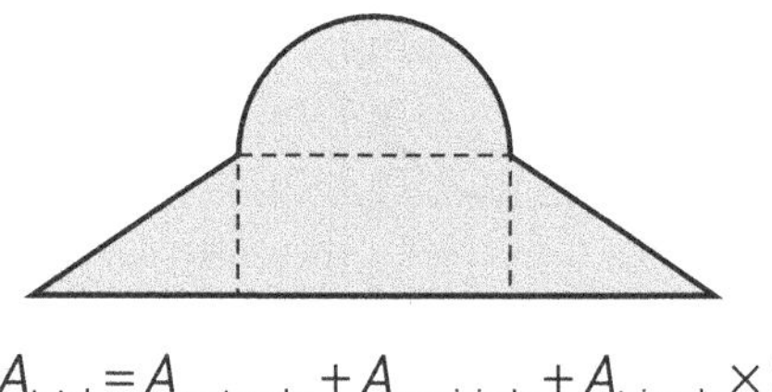

$A_{\text{total}} = A_{\text{rectangle}} + A_{\text{semicircle}} + A_{\text{triangle}} \times 2$

e.g. Find the area of the shape below.

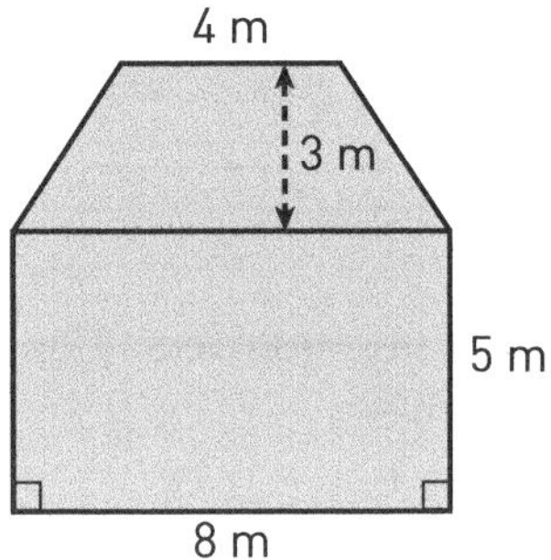

Step 1: Break the composite shape into known shapes and calculate the area of each shape.

$$A_{\text{rectangle}} = lw = 8 \times 5 = 40 \text{ m}^2$$

$$A_{\text{trapezium}} = \frac{(a+b) \times h}{2} = \frac{(4+8) \times 2}{2} = \frac{24}{2} = 12 \text{ m}^2$$

Step 2: Add together the area of each individual shape.

$$A_{\text{total}} = A_{\text{rectangle}} + A_{\text{trapezium}} = 40 \text{ m}^2 + 12 \text{ m}^2 = 52 \text{ m}^2$$

1 Divide the following shapes into known shapes.

a

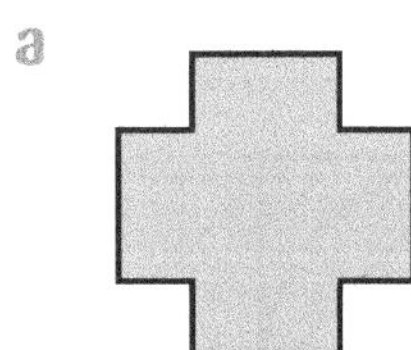

b

2 Here is a composite shape:

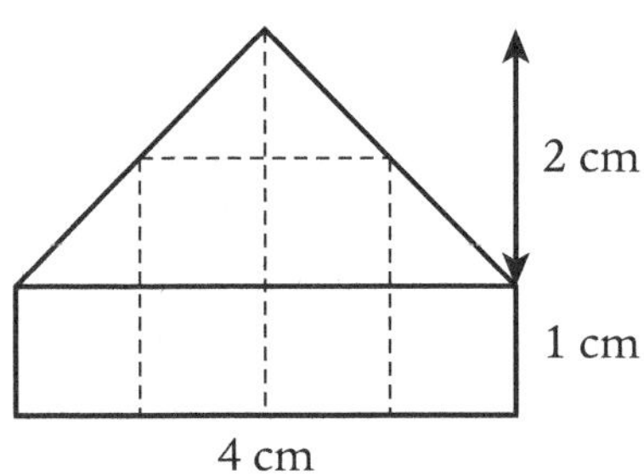

a Find the area of the above triangle and rectangle.

$A_{\text{triangle}} =$ ______ cm^2

$A_{\text{rectangle}} =$ ______ cm^2

b Add the areas above to find the total area of the composite shape.

$A_{\text{total}} = A_{\text{triangle}} + A_{\text{rectangle}}$

$=$ ____ $\text{cm}^2 +$ ____ cm^2

$=$ ______ cm^2

3 **a** Divide the shape into a semicircle and a trapezium and state the required measurements.

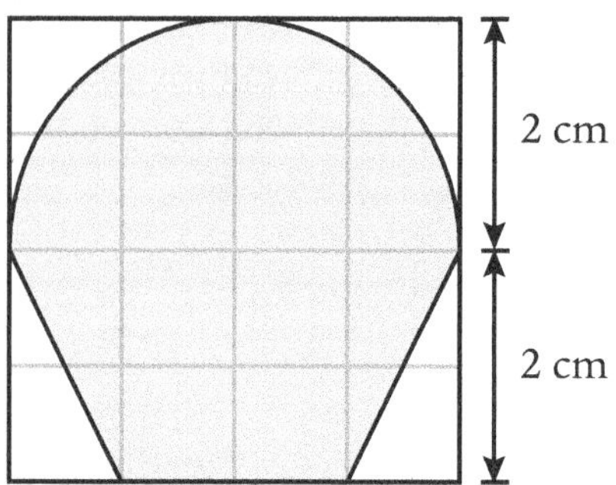

Semicircle: $r =$ ______

Trapezium: $a =$ ______

$b =$ ______

$h =$ ______

b Calculate the areas of each individual shape.

$A_{semicircle} = (\pi \times r^2) \div 2$

$= (\pi \times \_\_\_\_^2) \div 2$

$\approx$ [cm^2]

$A_{trapezium} = \dfrac{(a+b)\times h}{2}$

$= \dfrac{(\_\_+\_\_)\times\_\_}{2}$

$\approx$ [cm^2]

c What is the total area of the composite shape?

Tip Estimate the area first by counting the squares to make sure your answer is reasonable.

$A_{total} = A_{semicircle} + A_{trapezium}$

$\approx \_\_\_\_ \text{ cm}^2 + \_\_\_\_ \text{ cm}^2$

$\approx$ [cm^2]

4 **a** Divide the below hexagon into two trapeziums. Measure the required dimensions with a ruler.

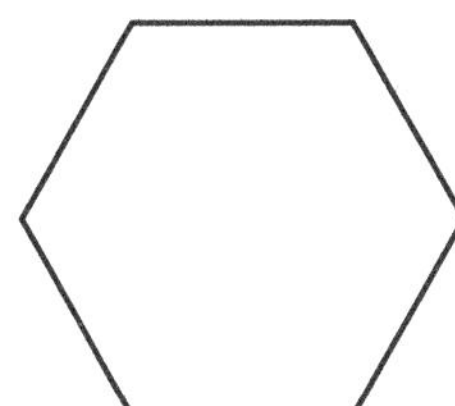

b What is the area of the above hexagon?

5 The total area of the shape below is approximately 257.08 m^2. Show the workings.

Tip Two semicircles make one whole circle.

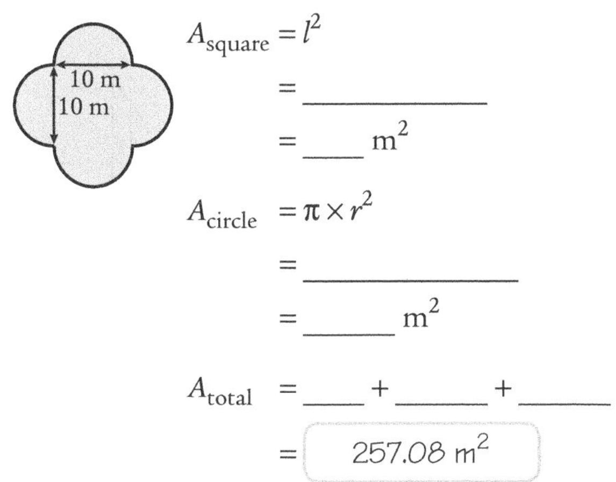

$A_{square} = l^2$

$= \_\_\_\_\_\_\_\_\_\_$

$= \_\_\_\_ \text{ m}^2$

$A_{circle} = \pi \times r^2$

$= \_\_\_\_\_\_\_\_\_\_$

$= \_\_\_\_ \text{ m}^2$

$A_{total} = \_\_\_\_ + \_\_\_\_ + \_\_\_\_$

$=$ [257.08 m^2]

6 Calculate the shaded area.

Tip Calculate the area of the outer shape and then subtract the area of the inner shape.

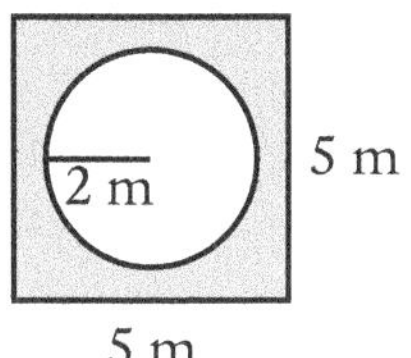

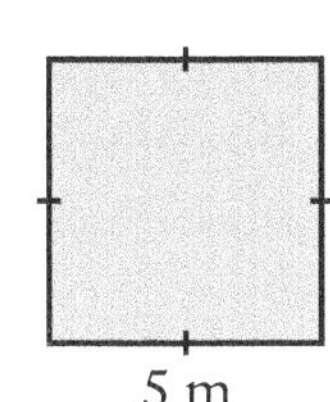

$A_{square} = l^2$

$= \_\_\_\_ \times \_\_\_\_$

$= \_\_\_\_ \text{ m}^2$

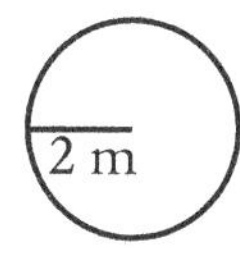

$A_{circle} = \pi \times r^2$

$= \pi \times \_\_\_\_^2$

$\approx \_\_\_\_ \text{ m}^2$

$A_{total} = A_{square} - A_{circle}$

$= \_\_\_\_ \text{ m}^2 - \_\_\_\_ \text{ m}^2$

$\approx$ [m^2]

NAPLAN-ready

Shade the box beneath the correct answer.

A kite is to be packaged to post overseas. It is placed in a rectangular box, as shown below.

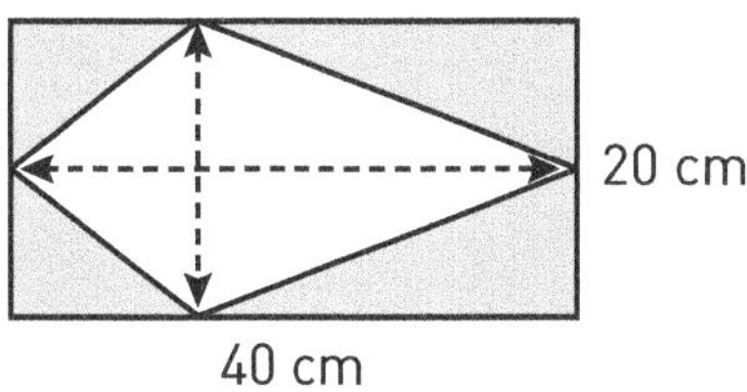

The shaded area represents the packaging cardboard, which fits around the kite so that it does not move in transit. What is the area of the packaging cardboard required?

60 cm^2	240 cm^2	400 cm^2	680 cm^2
☐	☐	☐	☐

Tip Subtract the area of the kite from the total area of the box.

5.7 Volume and capacity A

A three-dimensional solid takes up space. The amount of space it takes up is its **volume**. Volume is measured in cubes—mm^3, cm^3, m^3 and km^3.

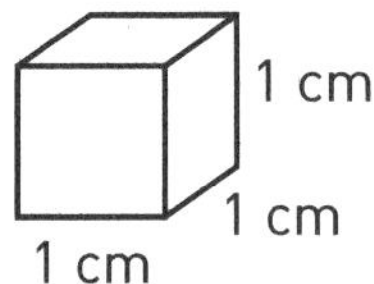

One cubic centimetre
$1\ cm^3$

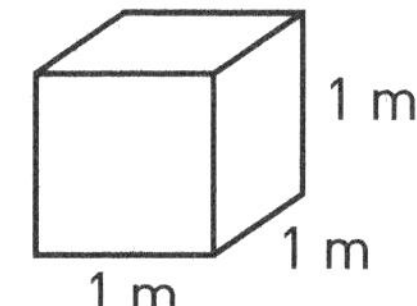

One cubic metre
$1\ m^3$

Volume of a rectangular prism

A rectangular prism can be viewed as *layers* of cubes. The formula to calculate the volume of a rectangular prism is:

$V = \text{length} \times \text{width} \times \text{Height}$
$V = l \times w \times H$
$= 4 \times 2 \times 3$
$= 24\ cm^3$

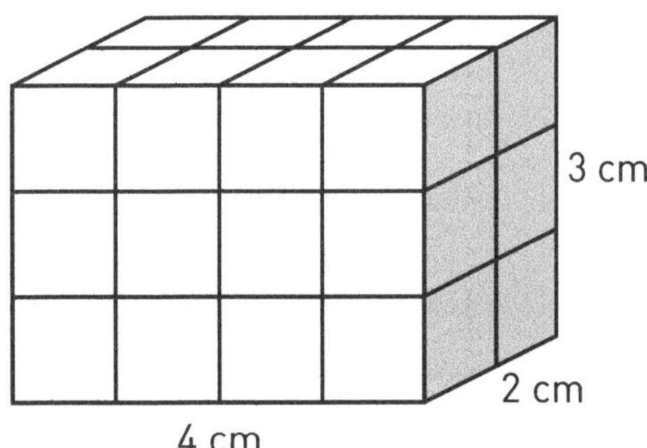

The volume of a shape with a **uniform cross-section** is calculated by multiplying the area of the base by the height.

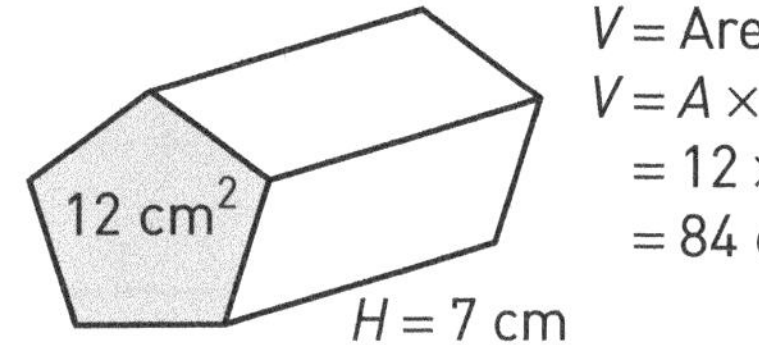

$V = \text{Area of base} \times \text{Height}$
$V = A \times H$
$= 12 \times 7$
$= 84\ cm^3$

If the area of the base is not stated, use the formulas in Exercise 5.4 and Exercise 5.5 to calculate the area of the base, and then multiply it by the height to find the volume.

Word Bank

Cross-section

→ When a 3D shape is cut, a 2D face is exposed. This face is its cross-section.

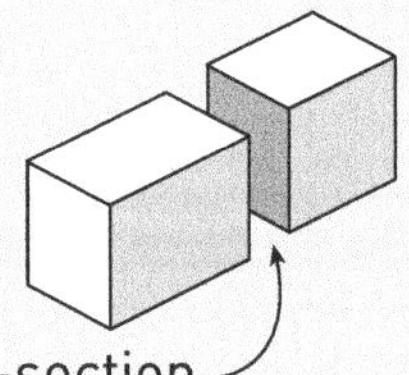

A shape with constant cross-sections is said to have a uniform cross-section.

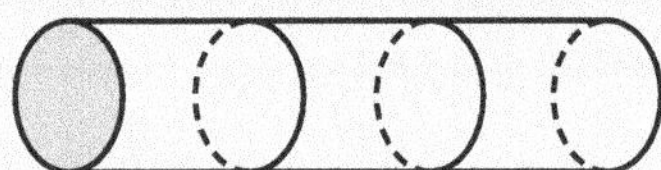

The cross-section of the cylinder above is the same wherever it is cut parallel to the base.

1 Find the volume of the following rectangular prisms. Each cube represents $1\ cm^3$.

a

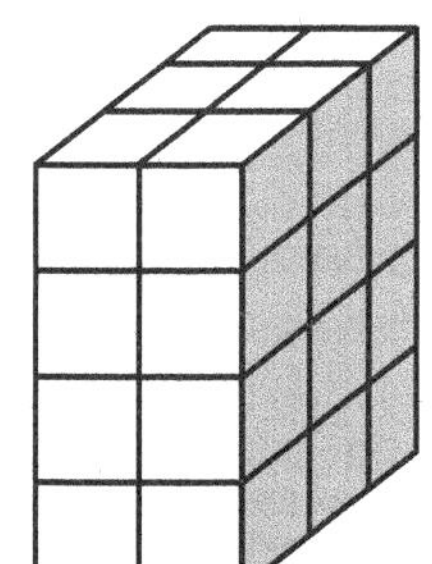

$V =$ ______ cm^3

b

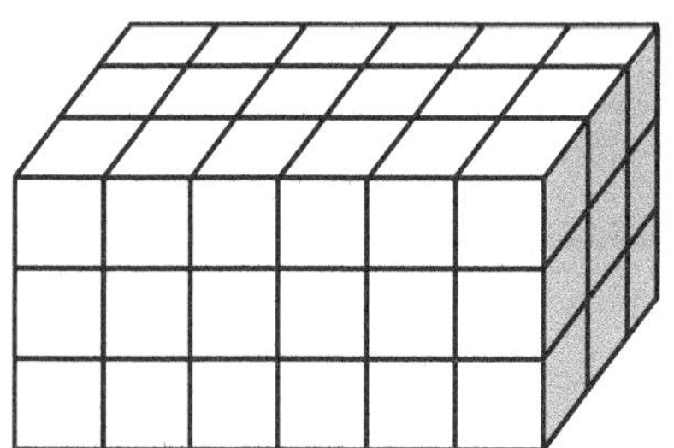

$V =$ ______ cm^3

2 Find the volumes of these rectangular prisms. Write the correct unit with your answer.

a

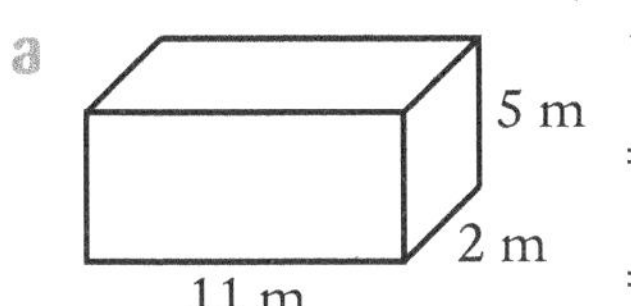

$V = l \times w \times H$

= ____ × ____ × ____

= [ ]

b

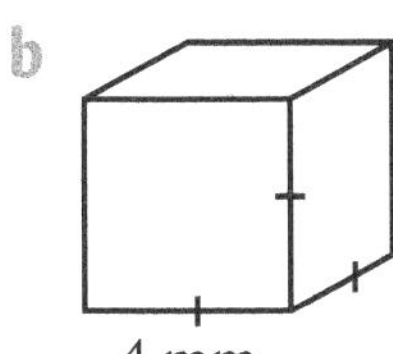

$V = l \times w \times H$

= ____ × ____ × ____

= [ ]

3 The area of each base is stated. Calculate the volumes using the formula $V = A \times H$.

a

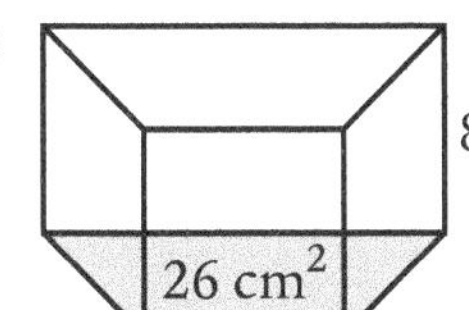

$V = A \times H$

= ____ × ____

= [cm³]

b

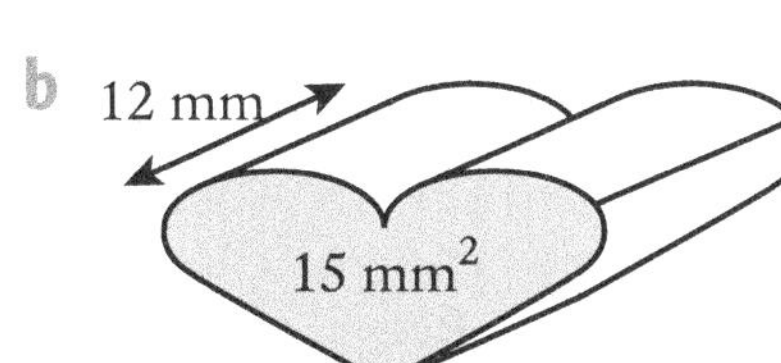

$V = A \times H$

= ____ × ____

= [ ]

4 **a** Shade in the base of the shape below.

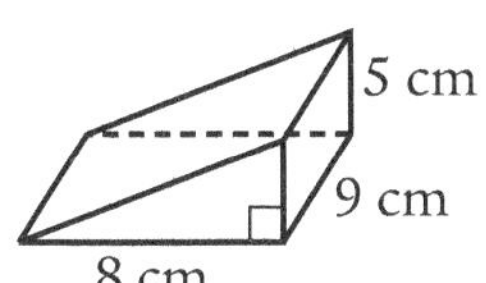

b What is the shape of the base?

____

c Calculate the area of the base.

A = __________ ← (write area formula here)

= __________ ← (substitute measurements from diagram)

= __________

d Find the volume of the shape.

Tip **Multiply the area of the base (part c) by the height of the 3D shape.**

$V = A \times H$

= ____ × ____

= [ ]

5 Calculate the volume of the triangular prism by first finding the area of the shaded triangle.

Tip **There are two heights in the formula. *h* is the height of the triangle. *H* is the height of the prism.**

a

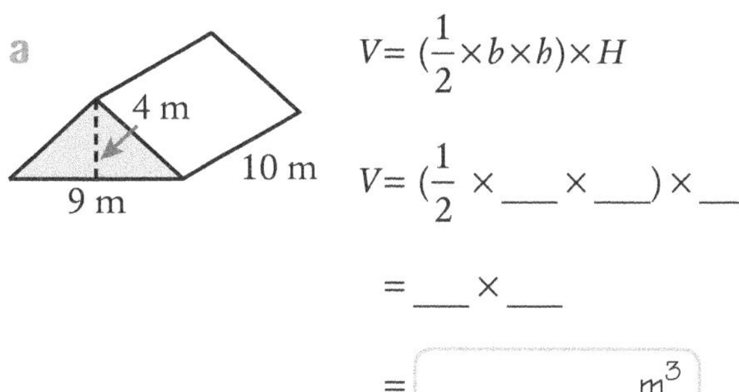

$V = (\frac{1}{2} \times b \times h) \times H$

$V = (\frac{1}{2} \times$ ____ $\times$ ____ $) \times$ ____

= ____ × ____

= [m³]

b

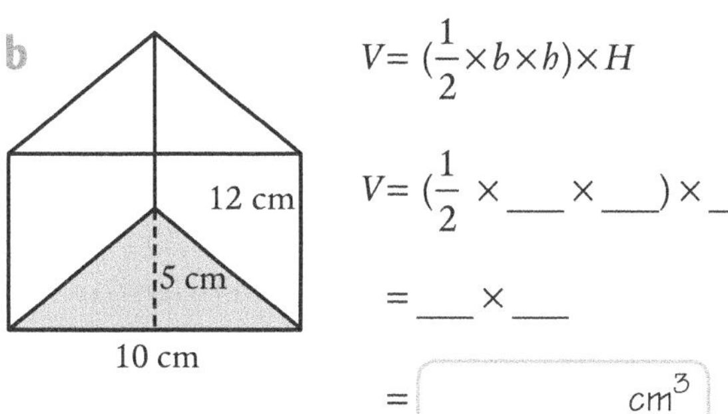

$V = (\frac{1}{2} \times b \times h) \times H$

$V = (\frac{1}{2} \times$ ____ $\times$ ____ $) \times$ ____

= ____ × ____

= [cm³]

6 Calculate the volume of each cylinder. Round answers to one decimal place.

Tip **Volume of a cylinder**

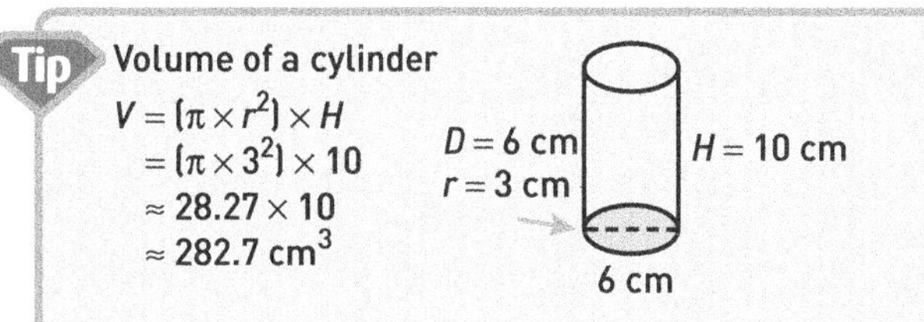

$V = (\pi \times r^2) \times H$
$= (\pi \times 3^2) \times 10$
$\approx 28.27 \times 10$
≈ 282.7 cm³

a $V = (\pi \times r^2) \times H$

$= (\pi \times$ ____$^2) \times$ ____

≈ ____ × ____

≈ [ ] (1 d.p.)

b $V = (\pi \times r^2) \times H$

= __________

≈ [ ] (1 d.p.)

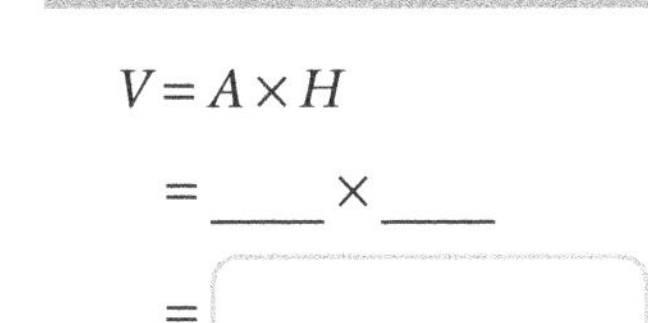

5.7 Volume and capacity B

Some 3D objects can hold liquids, such as containers. **Capacity** is the maximum amount of liquid a hollow 3D object can hold. Capacity is measured in millilitres (mL), litres (L) and kilolitres (kL).

The capacity of a container with side lengths of 10 cm can be found by first calculating the volume, $V = l \times w \times h$.

$V = 10 \times 10 \times 10$
$\quad = 1000 \text{ cm}^3$

Now change cm^3 to mL.

$1000 \text{ cm}^3 = 1000 \text{ mL}$
$\qquad\qquad = 1 \text{ L}$

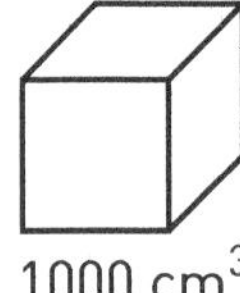

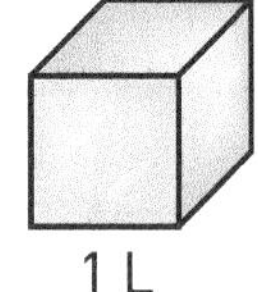

Calculating capacity

To determine the capacity of a container, calculate the *volume* it can hold and then convert to *capacity*.

Step 1: Calculate volume

$V = \text{Area of base} \times \text{height}$
$\quad = (\pi \times r^2) \times H$
$\quad = \pi \times 3^2 \times 15$
$\quad \approx 424.12 \text{ cm}^3 \text{ (2 d.p.)}$

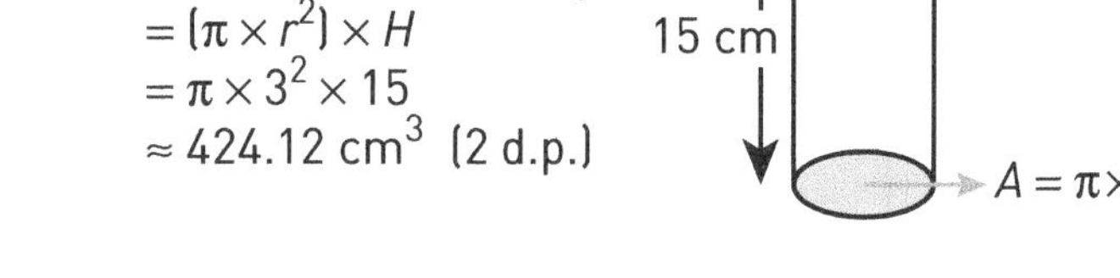

Step 2: Convert to mL

$424.12 \text{ cm}^3 = 424.12 \text{ mL}$

The cylinder can hold approximately 424 mL, or 0.424 L.

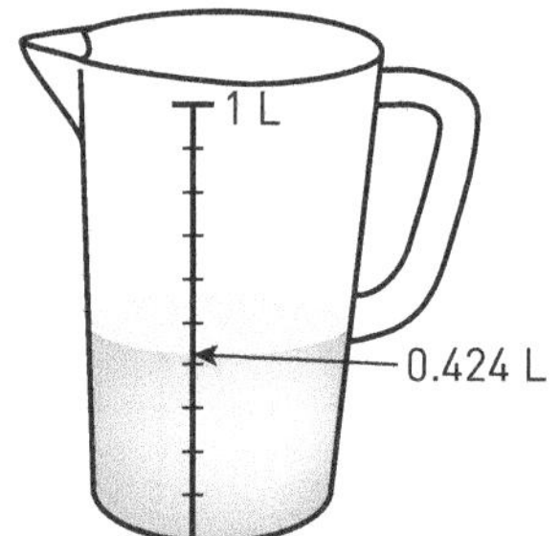

1 Convert the following volumes to capacity.

a $5 \text{ cm}^3 =$ ______ mL

b $12 \text{ cm}^3 =$ ______ mL

c $1000 \text{ cm}^3 =$ ______ mL = ______ L

2 How much liquid can the containers hold?

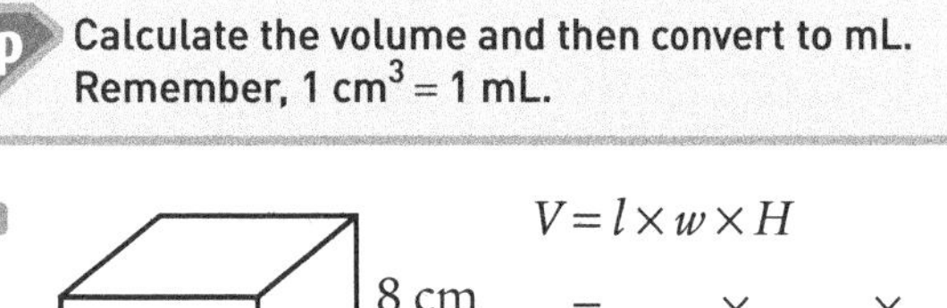

Tip Calculate the volume and then convert to mL. Remember, $1 \text{ cm}^3 = 1 \text{ mL}$.

a

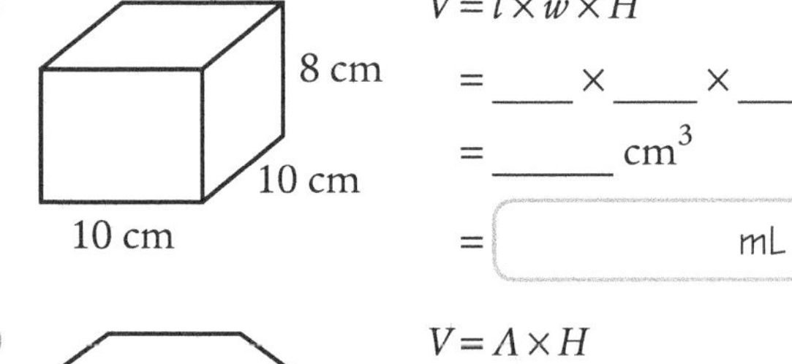

$V = l \times w \times H$
$= \_\_\_ \times \_\_\_ \times \_\_\_$
$= \_\_\_\_\_\_ \text{ cm}^3$
$=$ ______ mL

b

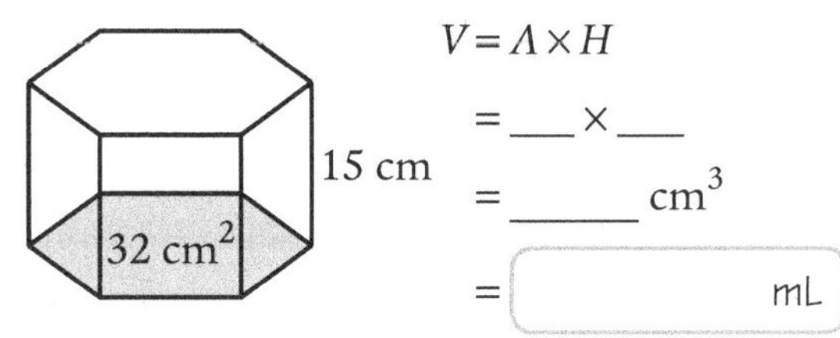

$V = A \times H$
$= \_\_\_ \times \_\_\_$
$= \_\_\_\_\_\_ \text{ cm}^3$
$=$ ______ mL

3 Find the capacity, in mL. Round to two decimal places where necessary.

a

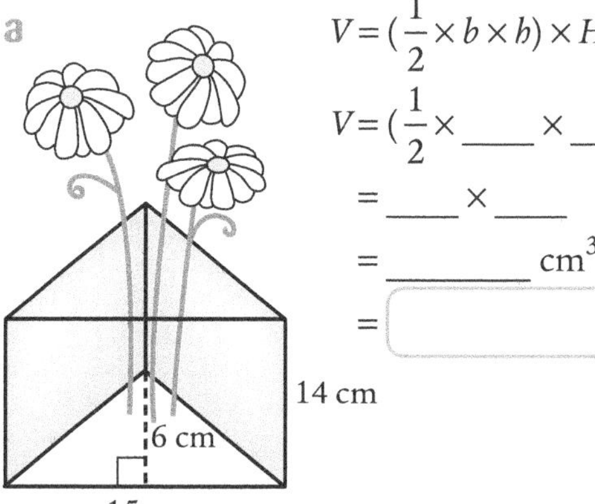

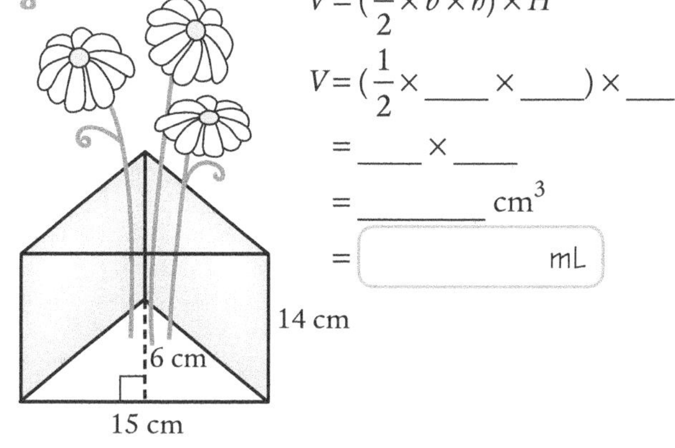

$V = (\frac{1}{2} \times b \times h) \times H$

$V = (\frac{1}{2} \times \_\_\_\_ \times \_\_\_\_) \times \_\_\_\_$
$= \_\_\_\_ \times \_\_\_\_$
$= \_\_\_\_\_\_\_\_ \text{ cm}^3$
$=$ ______ mL

b

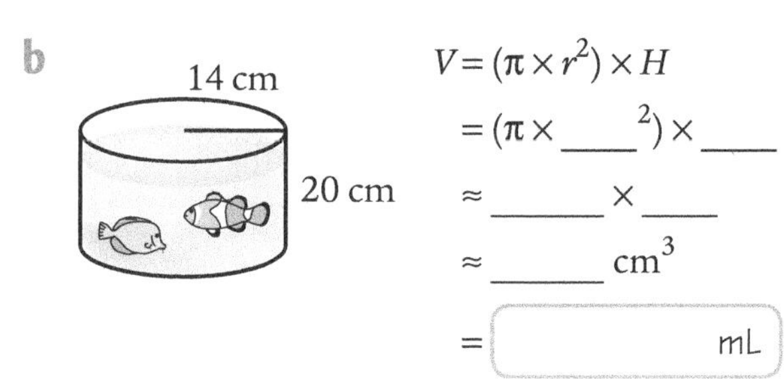

$V = (\pi \times r^2) \times H$
$= (\pi \times \_\_\_\_^2) \times \_\_\_\_$
$\approx \_\_\_\_\_\_ \times \_\_\_\_$
$\approx \_\_\_\_\_\_ \text{ cm}^3$
$=$ ______ mL

4 Convert the following measurements.

> **Tip** There are 1000 mL in 1 L.
>
> L $\xrightarrow{\times 1000}$ mL
>
> mL $\xrightarrow{\div 1000}$ L

a

300 mL = ____ L

÷ 1000

b

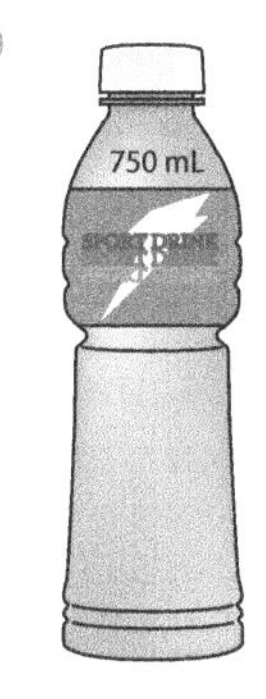

750 mL = ______ L

c

1.25 L = ______ mL

× 1000

d

3.2 L = ______ mL

5 What is the capacity of this petrol drum, to the nearest litre?

> **Tip** $1000 \text{ cm}^3 = 1000 \text{ mL} = 1 \text{ L}$

$D =$ ____ cm

$r =$ ____ cm

$V = (\pi \times r^2) \times H$

$= (\pi \times$ ____$^2) \times$ ____

$\approx$ ______ × ____

$\approx$ ______ cm^3

$=$ ______ mL

$=$ ____ L

÷ 1000

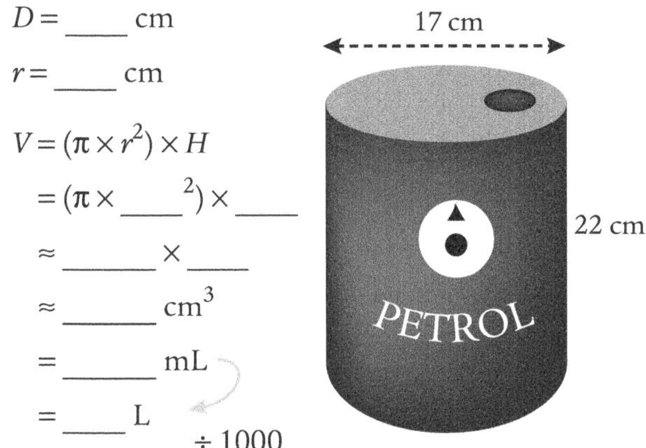

6 Convert from volume to capacity.

> **Tip** 1 m^3 has the capacity of 1 kL (kilolitre), which is 1000 L.

a $4 \text{ m}^3 =$ ____ kL

b $14.5 \text{ m}^3 =$ ____ kL

c $8 \text{ kL} =$ ____ m^3

d $0.5 \text{ kL} =$ ____ m^3

7 The dimensions of a small pool are shown. How many litres of water will be needed to fill it?

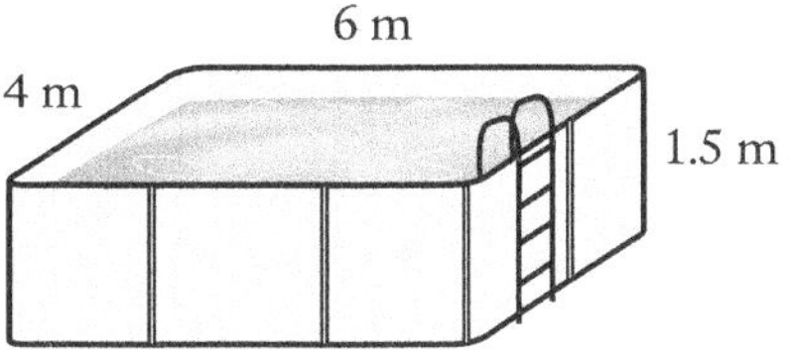

$V = l \times w \times H$

$=$ ____ × ____ × ____

$=$ ____ m^3

$=$ ____ kL → [   ] L

× 1000

NAPLAN-ready

Shade the box beneath the correct answer.

A shape was cut from a thin piece of flexible plastic and folded into a rectangular container.

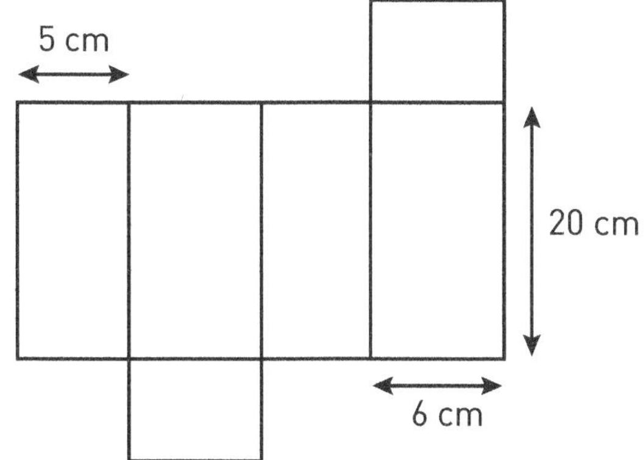

What is the capacity of the container?

6 mL	60 mL	600 mL	6 L
☐	☐	☐	☐

> **Tip** What are the length, width and height of the container? Calculate its volume and then convert to mL.

5.8 Time

24-hour time

Most commonly, the 24 hours in a day are divided into two 12-hour blocks, a.m. and p.m. On occasions, time is shown using 24-hour time, which is expressed as a four-digit number.

a.m. and p.m. time		24-hour time
12 a.m.		0000 (midnight)
2.30 a.m.	↔	0230
10.15 a.m.	↔	1015
12 p.m.	↔	1200 (noon)
2.50 p.m.	↔	1450
11.45 p.m.	↔	2345

It is not necessary to state a.m. or p.m. when using 24-hour time.

Calculating elapsed time

Time passed is known as **elapsed time**.

How much time passes between 11.20 a.m. and 2.35 p.m?

11.20 a.m.
→ 40 min (to the next hour)
12.00 p.m.
→ 2 hours (number of whole hours)
2.00 p.m.
→ 35 minutes (extra after last hour)
2.35 p.m.

Total: 2 hours and 75 minutes
= 3 hours and 15 minutes

Australian time zones

Australia is divided into three time zones.

At 2 p.m. in WA, it is 3.30 p.m. in SA and the NT, and 4 p.m. in the eastern states and ACT.

During **daylight savings**, Vic, NSW, SA, ACT and Tasmania move their clocks forward by 1 hour.

WA	NT and SA	Eastern states
2.00 p.m.	3.30 p.m.	4.00 p.m.

$+1\frac{1}{2}$ hours $\quad + \frac{1}{2}$ hour

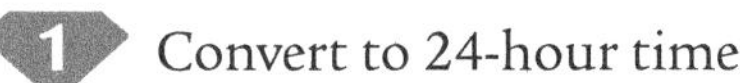

1 Convert to 24-hour time.

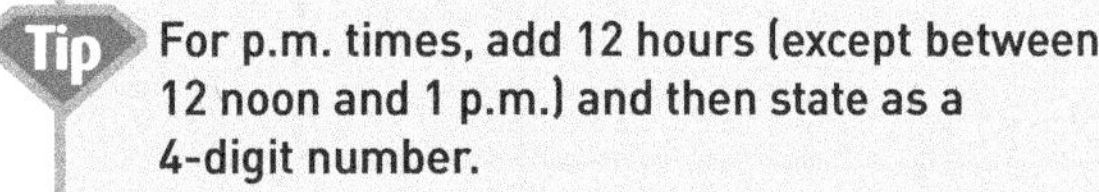

Tip For p.m. times, add 12 hours (except between 12 noon and 1 p.m.) and then state as a 4-digit number.

e.g. 3.20 p.m.
320 + 1200 (p.m. so add 12 hours)
1520

a 9.30 a.m. **b** 1.45 p.m. **c** 10.08 p.m.

2 Convert to a.m. and p.m. times.

a 0725 **b** 1105

c 1650 **d** 2130

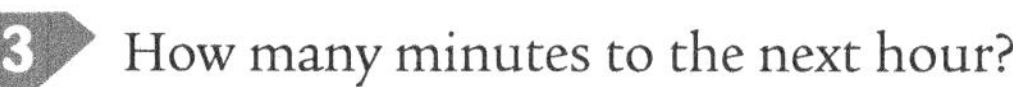

3 How many minutes to the next hour?

a 5.10 a.m. 6.00 a.m.
60 − 10
= ____ min

b

4.32 p.m. __.00 p.m.
60 − 32
= ____ min

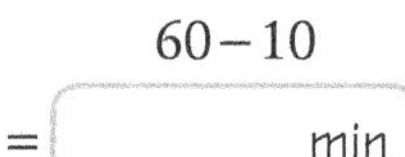

c 3.43 a.m to 4.00 a.m.
= ____ min

d 11.18 a.m. to 12.00 p.m.
= ____ min

4 How many hours have elapsed between:

a 4.00 a.m. and 11.00 a.m.
= ____ hours

b 9.00 p.m. and 2 p.m. the next day?
= ____ hours

5 How much time has elapsed?

a 2.30 a.m. to 5.15 a.m.

2.30 a.m.
→ 30 min
3.00 a.m.
→ ____ h
5.00 a.m.
→ ____ min
5.15 a.m.

Total: = ____h ____min

b 10.45 a.m. to 7.10 p.m.

10.45 a.m.
→ ____ min
11.00 a.m.
→ 1 h
noon
→ ____ h
7.00 p.m.
→ ____ min
7.10 p.m.

Total: = ____h ____min

6 What will the time be in 40 minutes?

Tip Move the minute hand clockwise, counting 5 minutes at a time.

a 

b 

7 What is the time:

Tip Add and subtract hours and minutes in separate steps. If the minutes total 60 or more, go up to the next hour.

a 5 hours after 3.15 p.m.?

```
   3   15
+  5 h
________
________  ←  [        p.m.]
```

b $6\frac{1}{2}$ hours after 1530?

```
  15    30
+  6 h  30
__________
     60 min  ←  [        p.m.]
__________
```

c $2\frac{1}{2}$ hours before 0315

```
   3    15
-  2 h  30
__________
     45 min  ←  [        ]
__________
```

8 The map below shows Australian time zones.

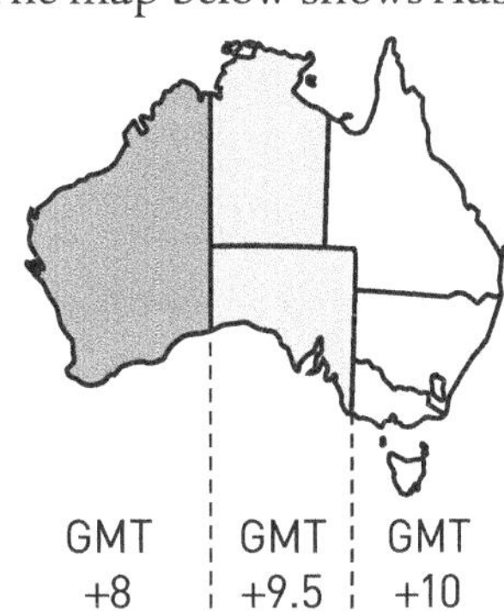

Show the time on the clocks below.

Perth　　Alice Springs　　Hobart

9 The opening ceremony of the 2000 Olympic Games held in Sydney was broadcast live around Australia. It started at 7.30 p.m. in Sydney (GMT + 10). Find the time of broadcast in the following locations.

a Melbourne (GMT + 10)

At 7.30 p.m. in Sydney, it is ______ in Melbourne.

b Broome (GMT + 8)

At 7.30pm in Sydney, it is ______ in Broome.

c Darwin (GMT + 9.5)

At 7.30pm in Sydney, it is ______ in Darwin.

NAPLAN-ready

Shade the box beneath the correct answer.

When it is 3.00 p.m. in WA, it is 4.30 p.m. in SA and 5.00 p.m. in NSW.

At 11.00 a.m. in NSW, what is the time in SA?

9.00 a.m.	9.30 a.m.	10.30 a.m.	12.30. p.m.
☐	☐	☐	☐

Tip What is the time difference between SA and NSW?

6.1 Interpreting line graphs

A **line graph** can be used to show how one variable changes with respect to another. An example of a line graph is a travel graph, a graph with *time* on the horizontal axis and *distance* on the vertical axis.

The travel graph on the right describes Lucinda's hike. She began at the ski town of Thredbo, NSW.

The graph shows:

- Lucinda started and ended at Thredbo.
- Two stops were made (B and D).
- The first stop (B) was shorter than the second stop (D).
- Lucinda travelled faster returning to Thredbo (E).
- The total distance travelled was 8 km (4 km away from Thredbo and 4 km returning to Thredbo).

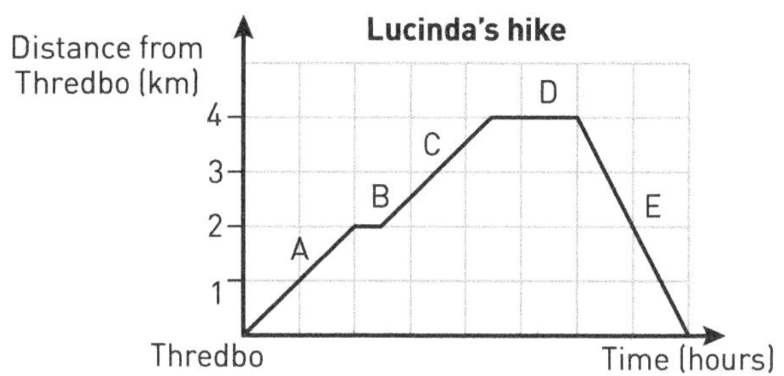

Word Bank

Variables

→ Variables are quantities that can change (vary). A graph shows the relationship between two variables.

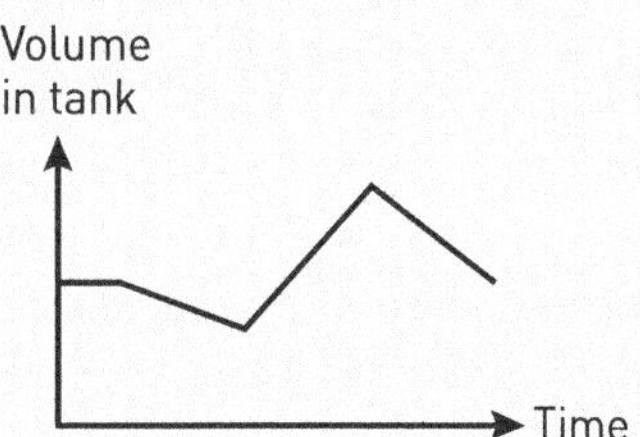

Here the two variables are time and volume. Other examples of variables are distance, speed and temperature.

1 Evie travels to work by train.

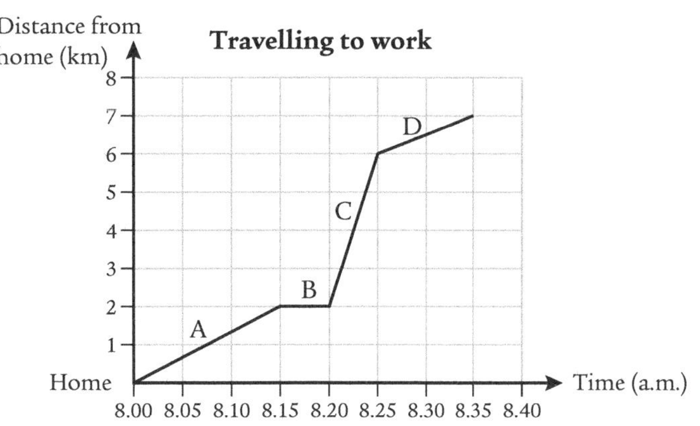

a Refer to the graph to complete the following travel story.

Evie left from ______ at ______ and walked to the train station. She waited for ______ minutes for the train. She travelled ______ kilometres on the train. She exited the train and walked ______ kilometres to work. It took Evie a total of ______ minutes to travel from home to work. Evie lives ______ kilometres from work.

b In which section is Evie not moving?

c In which section is Evie travelling the fastest?

2 Which graph could match the statement?

a Olivia walked quickly to school.

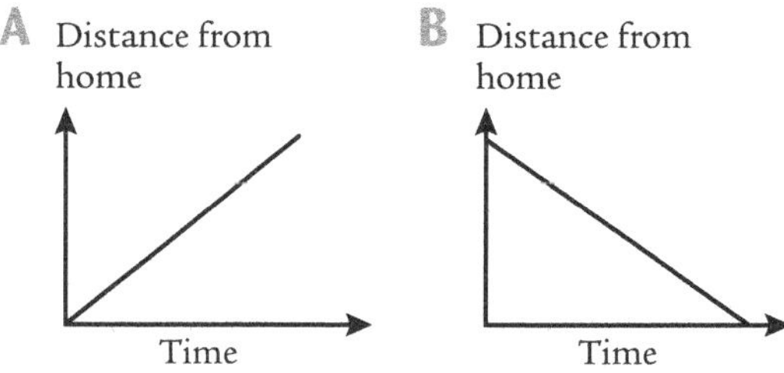

b The full tank was emptied by a leaking tap.

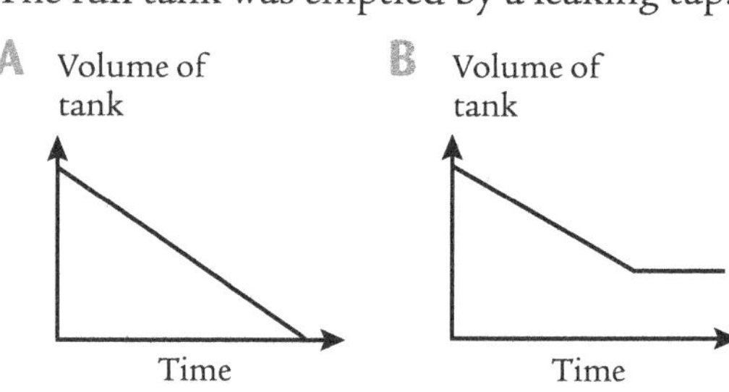

c Govi stopped at a friend's house on the way home from tennis.

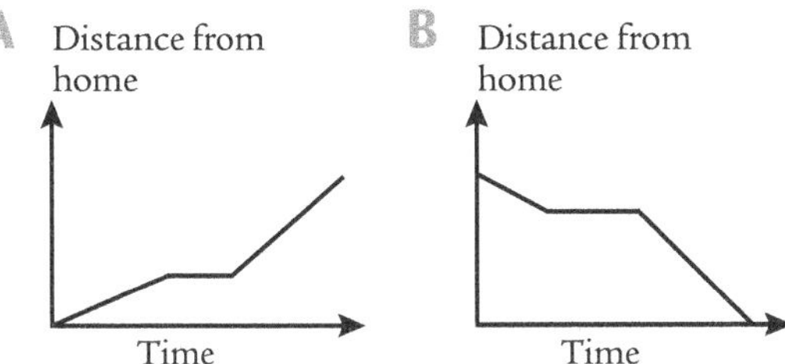

3 The graph shows Rihbi's heart rate before, during and after exercise.

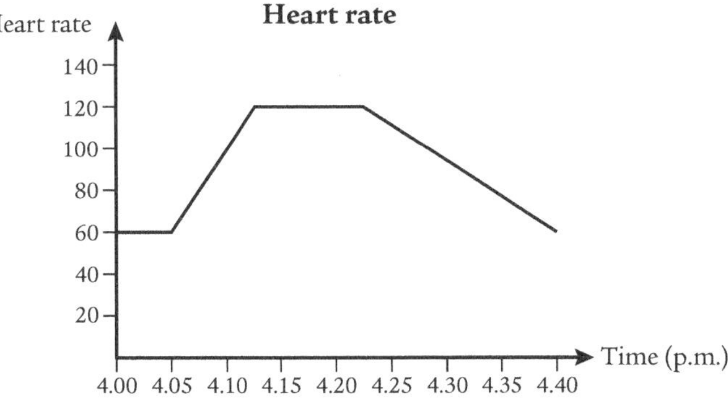

a Label each section of the graph from left to right as *A*, *B*, *C* and *D*.

b Describe what is happening in:

i Section *A*

______

ii Section *B*

______

iii Section *C*

______

iv Section *D*

______

c In which section was Rihbi's heart rate *changing* the fastest?

4 The graph below shows the height above sea level of an aeroplane from takeoff to landing.

Tip A line graph can tell a story without the need for numbers on the axes.

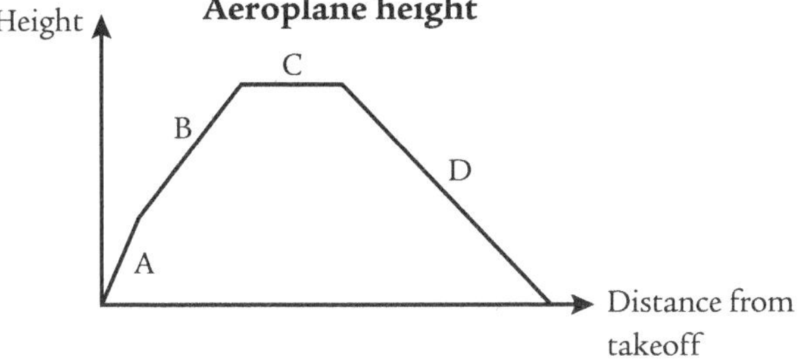

a Which speed was the fastest—the take off or the landing?

b In which sections did the aeroplane maintain a stable height?

c Does this graph show a short flight or a long flight? Short / Long

Explain

______

______

d Did the aeroplane land at the same airport as it took off from?

Yes / No

Explain.

______

______

______

NAPLAN-ready

Shade the box next to the correct answer.

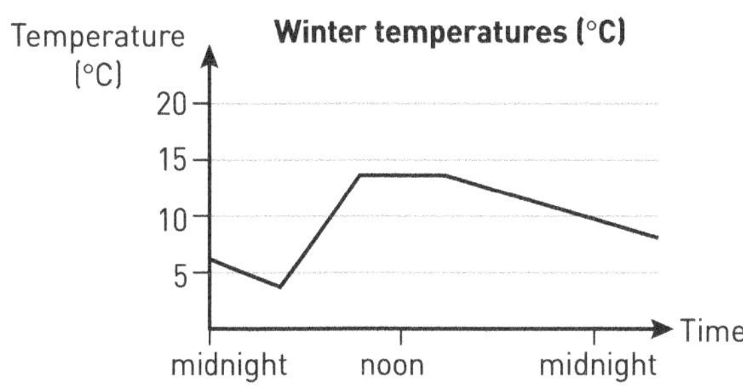

Which of the following statements is true?

- ☐ The temperature was coldest at midnight
- ☐ The temperature remained steady for a few hours at the day's maximum
- ☐ The temperature remained steady at the day's minimum
- ☐ The temperature dropped quickly at the end of the day

Tip What are the minimum and maximum temperatures? How steep is the graph to and from these points?

6.2 Linear relationships A

Linear equations

Here is an equation:

$$y = x + 2$$

This equation tells us that the y-value is always two more than the x-value. If we substitute $x = 1$ into the equation:

$$y = 1 + 2$$
$$y = 3$$

This tells us that when $x = 1$, $y = 3$, making the ordered pair (1, 3).

x-value y-value

Table of values

Ordered pairs can be recorded in a table of values.

Rule: $y = x + 2$

x	-3	-2	-1	0	1	2
y	-1	0	1	2	3	4
(x, y)	(-3, -1)	(-2, 0)	(-1, 1)	(0, 2)	(1, 3)	(2, 4)

Notice that the y-value is always two more than the x-value.

Linear graphs

The ordered pairs can be graphed to show how the points are related.

The graph of $y = x + 2$ is shown on the right

The graph is a straight line. Because of this we say that the points have a **linear** relationship.

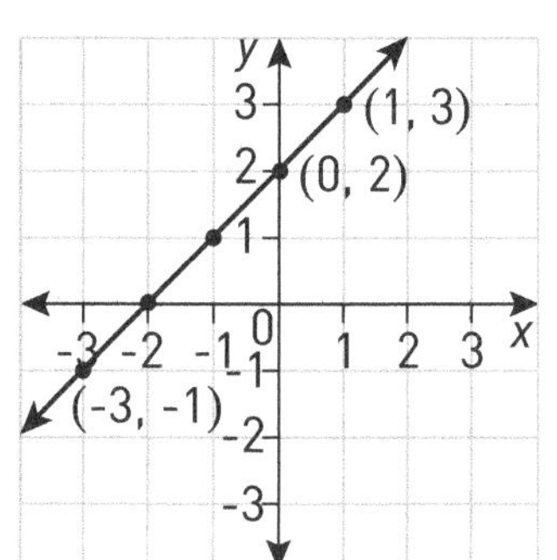

Word Bank

Cartesian plane

→ A Cartesian plane is a grid made with a horizontal line (x-axis) and a vertical line (y-axis), which intersect at the point (0, 0), the origin.

Coordinate

→ A coordinate (or **ordered pair**) is used to locate an exact position on a Cartesian plane. The x-value is stated first and then the y-value.

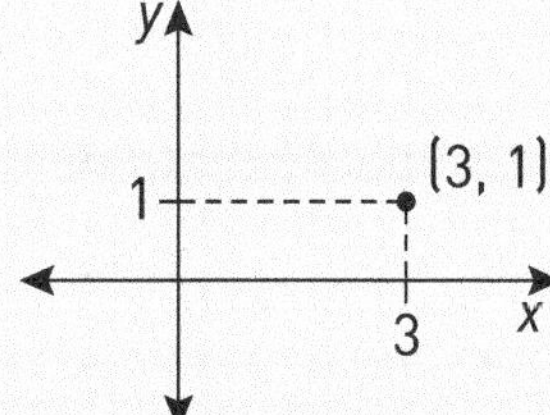

1 Write the following equations in words.

(e.g. $y = 2x$: To find y, multiply x by 2)

a $y = x - 6$

To find y, ________________________.

b $y = 3x + 1$

To find y, multiply ______ and then ______.

2 **a** For the equation $y = x + 4$, find the y-values when:

i $x = 0$ $y = x + 4$

$y =$ ____ $+ 4$

$y =$ ☐

ii $x = 1$ $y = x + 4$

$y =$ ____ $+ 4$

$y =$ ☐

iii $x = 2$ $y = x + 4$

$y =$ ____ $+ 4$

$y =$ ☐

iv $x = 3$ $y = x + 4$

$y =$ ____ $+ 4$

$y =$ ☐

b Use the answers in part **a** to complete the table of values and write the ordered pairs.

x	0	1	2	3
y				
(x, y)	(0, 4)			

c Graph the four ordered pairs in part **b**.

Tip The x-value is written first. Start at (0, 0) and '*walk*' across to the x-value, then '*jump*' up or down to the y-value.

$y = x + 4$

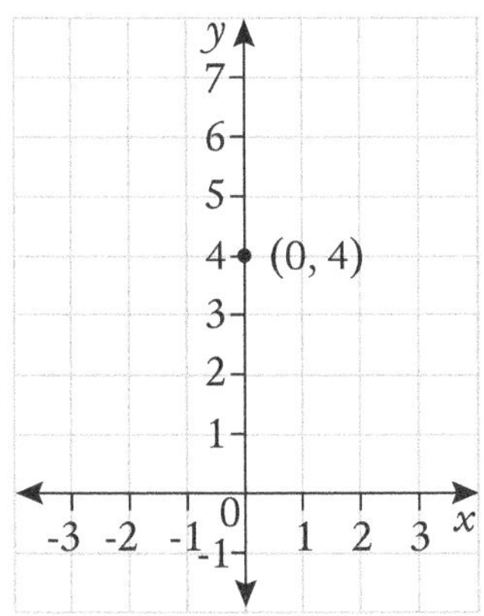

d With a ruler, join the ordered pairs in part **c** with a straight line, extending to the edge of the Cartesian plane. Draw in arrows at each end of the line.

3 **a** Fill in the table of values for the equation $y = x - 2$ and state the ordered pairs.

Tip In the equation $y = x - 2$, the y-value is always 2 less than the x-value.

x	0	1	2	3
y	-2			
(x, y)	(0, -2)			

-2

b Graph $y = x - 2$ using the ordered pairs in the table of values above.

Tip Graphing an equation from a table of values:

1. Plot the ordered pairs on a Cartesian plane.
2. Rule a straight line through the points.
3. Write the equation next to the graph.

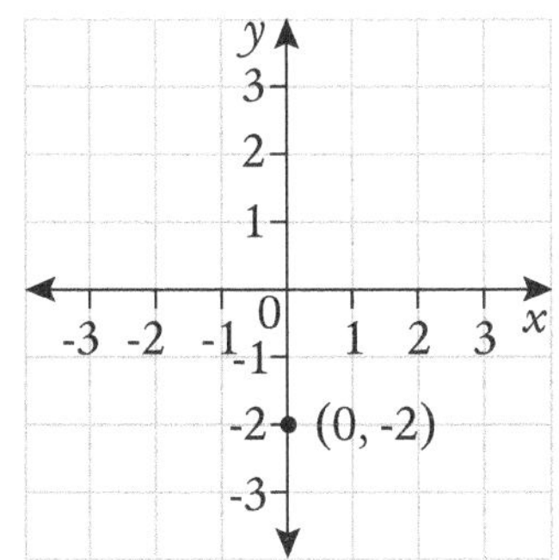

c Which of the following points lie on the graph of $y = x - 2$? (There is more than one)

Tip For $y = x - 2$, the y-value must be two less than the x-value. Refer to your graph in part **b**.

A (3, 5) **B** (4, 2)

C (0, -2) **D** (-1, 1)

d Write two more ordered pairs that lie on the graph of $y = x - 2$.

(2, ____) (____, ____)

4 **a** Write the equations $y = 2x - 3$ in words.

To find y, ________________________

____

b Complete the following ordered pairs for $y = 2x - 3$

(4, ____) (1, ____) (-2, ____)

5 **a** List three ordered pairs that lie on the graph of $y = 3x$.

Tip For $y = 3x$ the y-value is three times the x-value. If $x = 2$, $y = 6$ or (2, 6).

(____, ____) (____, ____) (____, ____)

b Complete a table of values for the equation $y = 3x$.

x	-1	0	1	2
y				
(x, y)	(-1,)			

$\times 3$

c Draw the graph of $y = 3x$.

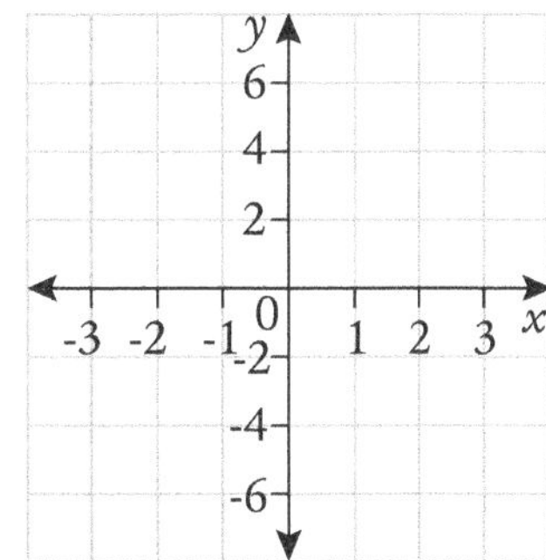

d How steep is the graph of $y = 3x$?

Tip The steepness of a graph is known as its gradient.

____

6.2 Linear relationships B

The slope of a graph shows the relationship between the x- and the y-values. **Gradient** is another word for slope.
The graph of $y = -x + 2$ slopes downwards as the line moves from left to right, which means it has a *negative gradient*.

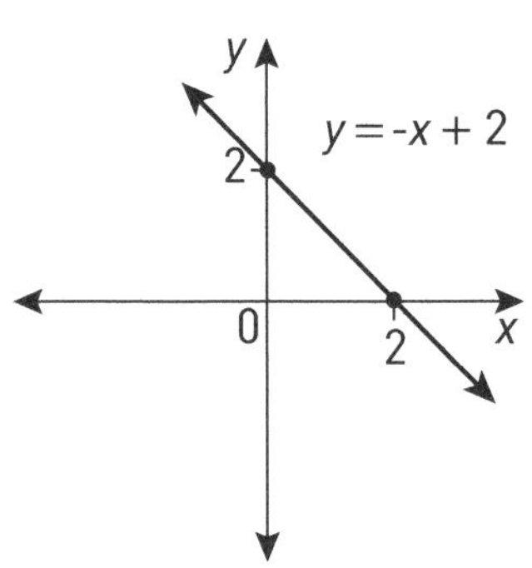

Types of linear gradients

- A **positive gradient** shows that as the x-values increase, so do the y-values. The line slopes UP from left to right.

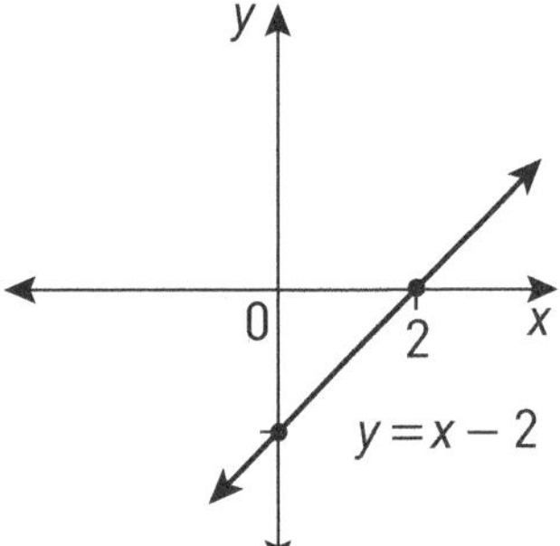

- A **negative gradient** shows that as the x-values increase, the y-values decrease. The line slopes DOWN from left to right.

$y = -\frac{x}{2} + 1$

- A **zero gradient** shows that as the x-values increase, the y-values do not change. The graph is a horizontal line.

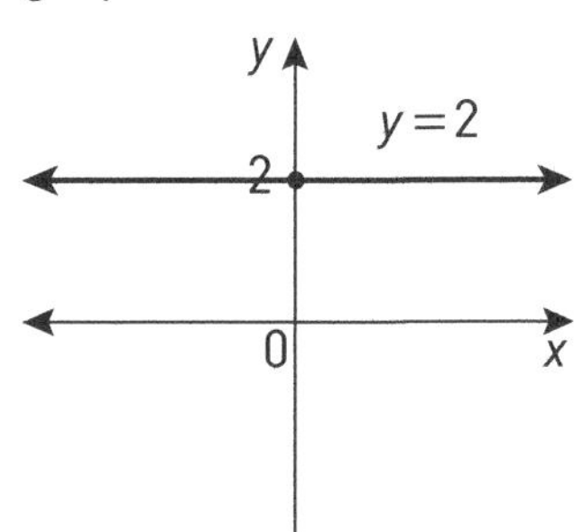

- An **undefined gradient** shows that the x-values do not change. The graph is a vertical line.

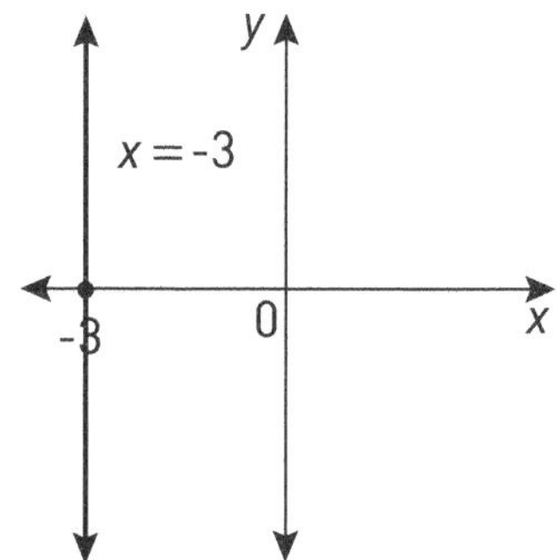

Word Bank

Intercepts

→ Intercepts are points where a graph crosses an axis.

The **x-intercept** is the point where the line crosses the x-axis. It is the x-value when $y = 0$.

The **y-intercept** is the point where the line crosses the y-axis. It is the y-value when $x = 0$.

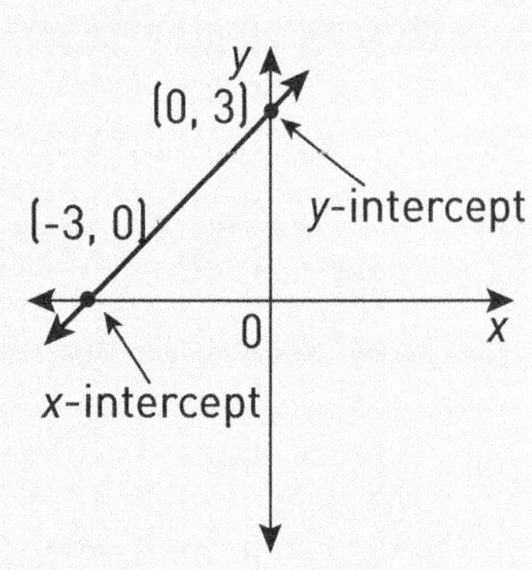

Gradient

→ The gradient is the slope of the line on a graph.

1 Here is a graph of $y = 3x + 3$.

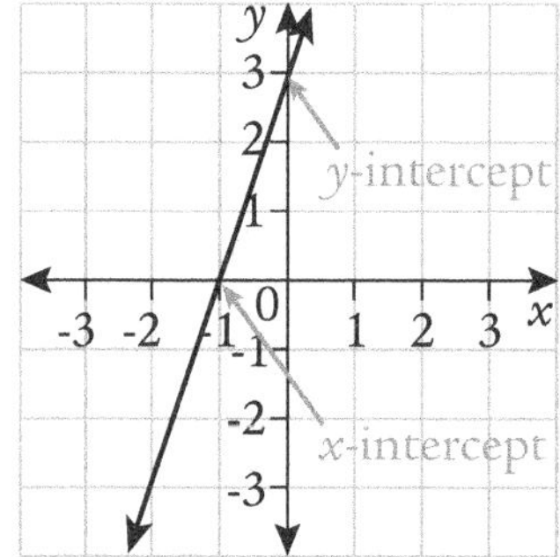

a Write the coordinates of the x-intercept.

(______, 0)

b Write the coordinates of the y-intercept.

(0, ______)

c Does the graph have a positive or negative gradient?

____

d When $x = -2$, what is the value of y?

Tip The value of y can be found in two ways: by looking at the graph or by substituting $x = -2$ into the equation.

Graphically (look at the graph on the previous page)

When $x = -2$, $y =$ ☐

Substitute $x = -2$ into the equation:

$y = 3x + 3$ $(x = -2)$

$= 3 \times$ ____ $+ 3$

$=$ ________

So, when $x = -2$, $y =$ ☐

2 For $y = 1 - x$:

a Complete a table of values.

Tip Substitute each x-value into the equation to find the y-value.
e.g. $y = 1 - x$
$= 1 - -2$ $(x = -2)$
$= 1 + 2$
$= 3$

x	-2	-1	0	1	2
y					
(x, y)			(0, 1)		

b Draw a graph using the ordered pairs in part **a**.

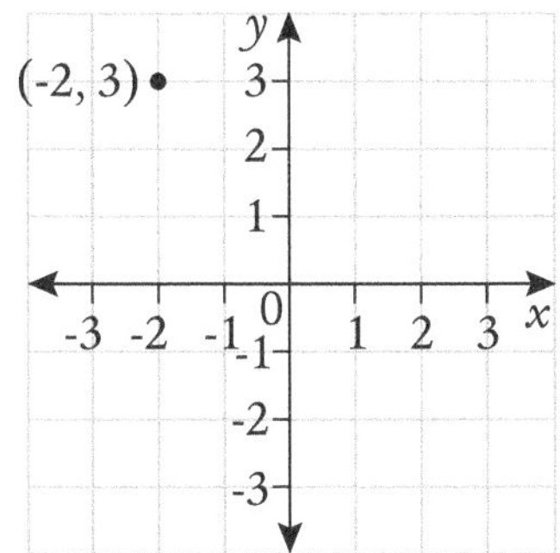

c State the coordinates of the intercepts.

x-intercept (____, ____)

y-intercept (____, ____)

3 State whether the gradients of the following graphs are positive, negative, zero or undefined.

a

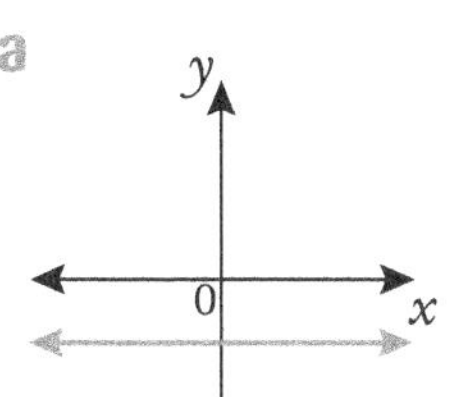

________ gradient

b

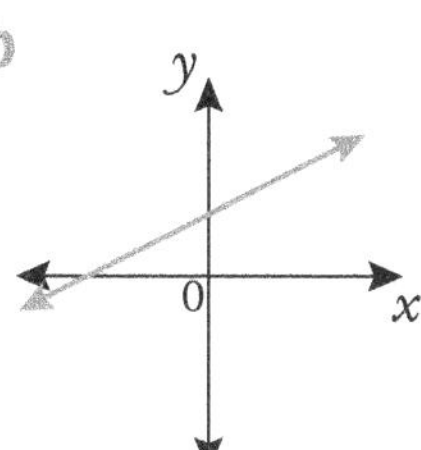

________ gradient

c

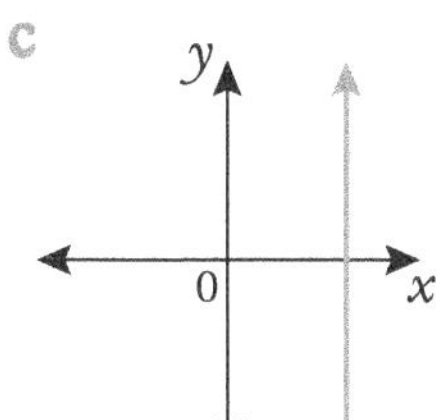

________ gradient

d

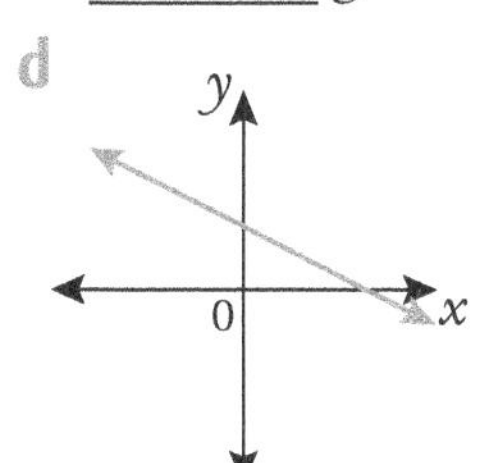

________ gradient

4 Two points on a linear graph are (-1, 3) and (2, 3).

a Use these two points to draw the graph.

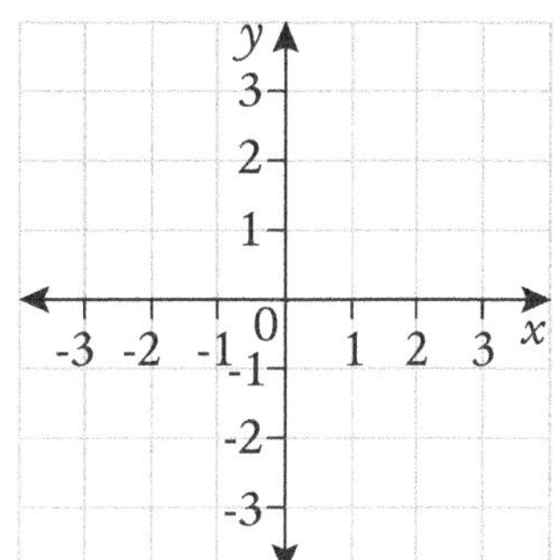

b State the coordinates of the y-intercept.

(____, ____)

c Describe the gradient. ____________________

NAPLAN-ready

Shade the box beneath the correct answer.

$y = 2x - 5$

x	-4	-2	0	2
y	-13	-9	-5	-1

When $x = 5$, y is equal to:

3 ☐ 5 ☐ 7 ☐ 9 ☐

Tip Look for a pattern in the table of values. Check your answer by substituting into the equation.

6.3 Finding the rule

An ordered pair has an x- and y-value. These two values are linked by a rule.

- For the ordered pair (4, 6), y is two more than x, so a rule that links these values is $y = x + 2$. When the x- and y-values are substituted into the rule, both sides are equal. If they are equal, it is said that they *satisfy the rule.*

(4, 6) → $y = x + 2$
$6 = 4 + 2$
$6 = 6$ ✓

All ordered pairs in a set must satisfy the rule.

Finding a rule

To find a rule from a set of ordered pairs, follow these steps:

Step 1: Find the pattern.

(0, -3), (1, -1), (2, 1), (3, 3)

+1 +2

As x increases by 1, y is increasing by 2.

change in y → 2
change in x → 1

$\frac{2}{1} = 2$

Step 2: Write this as the coefficient of x.

$y = 2x +$ ____

Step 3: What else needs to be added or subtracted to make both sides equal?

Substitute the x- and y-values from one of the ordered pairs into the equation in step 2.

(2, 1) → $1 = 2 \times 2 +$ ____
$1 = 4 + -3$

Subtracting 3 makes both sides equal

Add or subtract from the right-hand side to make both sides equal.

$1 = 4 - 3$
$1 = 1$ ✓

Step 4: Write the equation.

$y = 2x - 3$

1 Show that the ordered pairs satisfy the rule $y = x - 4$.

Tip Substitute the x- and y-values into the equation. The rule is satisfied if both sides are equal.

a (3, -1) $y = x - 4$

___ = ___ -4

___ = ___

b (0, -4) $y = x - 4$

___ = ___ -4

___ = ___

c (8, 4) $y = x - 4$

___ = ______

___ = ___

d (-3, -7) $y = x - 4$

___ = ______

___ = ___

2 Here is a set of ordered pairs.

(1, -2), (2, -1), (3, 0)

a What operation has been performed to the x-value to obtain the y-value?

x	1	2	3
y	-2	-1	0

____

b Write the rule for the ordered pairs.

'To find y, subtract 3 from x'

$y = x$ ________

3 Find the rule for the following sets of ordered pairs.

a x y
(0, 0), (1, 4), (2, 8)
+ 1 + 4

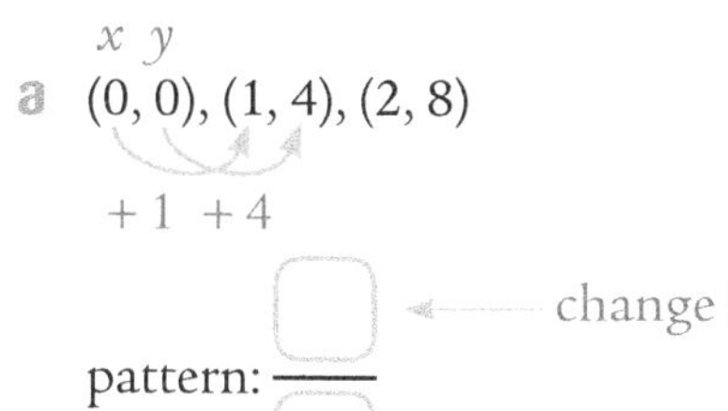

pattern: $\frac{\square}{\square}$ ← change in y / ← change in x

$y =$ ____ x

b x y
(-1, -2), (0, 1), (1, 4)

pattern: $\frac{\square}{\square}$ ← change in y / ← change in x

What else needs to be added or subtracted to satisfy the rule?

$y =$ ____ $x +$ ____

4 Find the rule for the table of values.

x	-2	0	2	4
y	-4	2	8	14

pattern: $\frac{\square}{\square}$ ← What is y increasing by? / ← What is x increasing by?

What else needs to be added or subtracted to satisfy the rule?

$y =$ ____ x ________

5 a Write the ordered pairs next to each point on the linear graph.

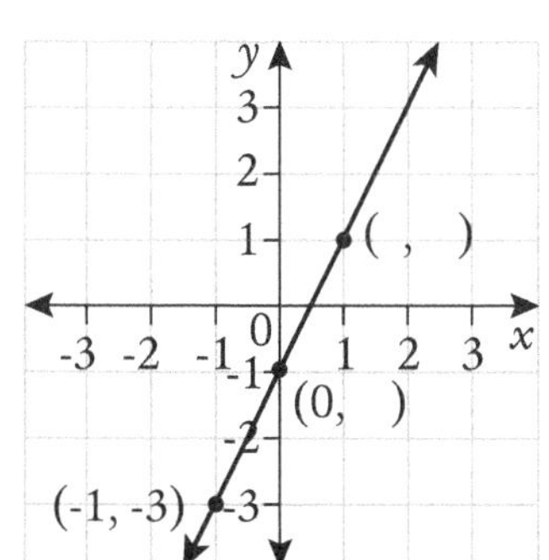

b Write the three ordered pairs below from the graph in part **a**.

(____, ____), (____, ____), (____, ____)

c Find the rule:

pattern: As x increases by ____,
y increases by ____.

What else needs to be added or subtracted to satisfy the rule?

Tip The y-intercept tells us what needs to be added or subtracted.

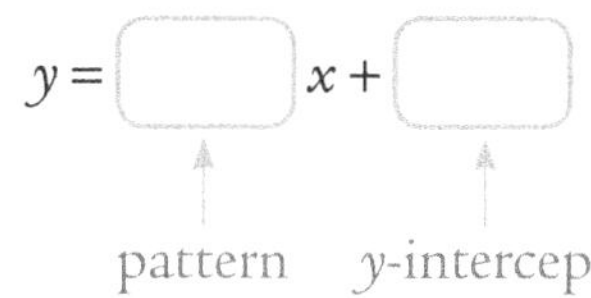

$y = \square x + \square$

↑ pattern ↑ y-intercept

d Check that each ordered pair satisfies the rule.

e.g. (-1, -3) $y = 2x - 1$
$\underline{-3} = 2 \times \underline{-1} - 1$
$-3 = -3$ ✓

i (0, -1) $y = 2x - 1$
____ $= 2 \times$ ____ $- 1$
____ $=$ ____

ii (1, 1) $y = 2x - 1$
__ = ________
__ = ____

NAPLAN-ready

Shade the box beneath the correct answer.

The graph of $y = 4x$ is drawn below.

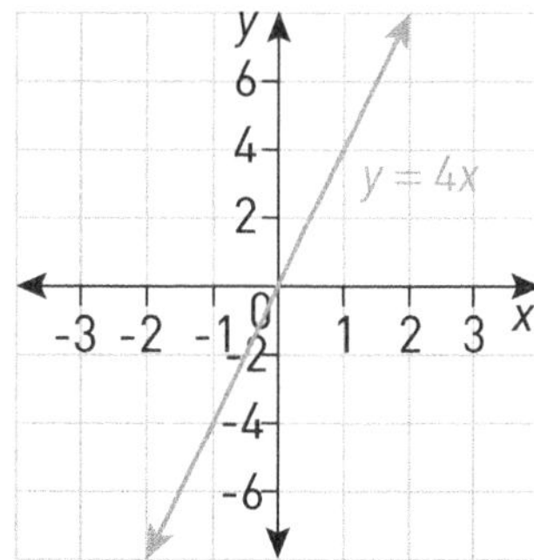

Which of the following ordered pairs does not satisfy the rule?

(0, 4)	(2, 8)	(-3, -12)	(-1, -4)
☐	☐	☐	☐

Tip Which ordered pair does not lie on the line of $y = 4x$?

6.4 Using linear relationships

Many real-life situations can be described as linear relationships. When graphed, a linear relationship between two variables gives a straight line. Linear graphs display a relationship between values and allow detailed information to be read from the graph.

Using linear graphs

Students baked, decorated and then sold cupcakes for a charity fundraiser. The ingredients cost \$30. The cupcakes were sold for \$3 each.

- Defining the variables

Let C be the number of cupcakes sold.

Let P be the profit made.

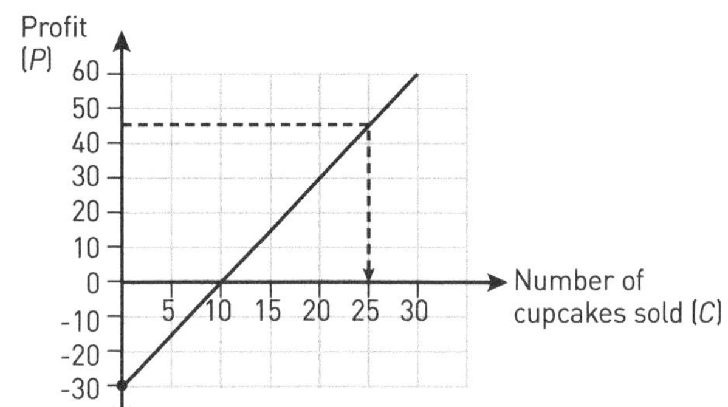

This relationship can be described by the equation:

$$P = 3C - 30$$

The equation shows us:

The gradient is \$3. (for each cupcake sold, \$3 is made)

When $C = 0$, $P =$ -\$30 (the class spent \$30 and have not sold a cupcake yet)

The graph shows us:

If 10 cupcakes are sold, the class get back the money spent on ingredients.

To make \$45 profit, 25 cupcakes need to be sold.

1 Which graphs are linear?

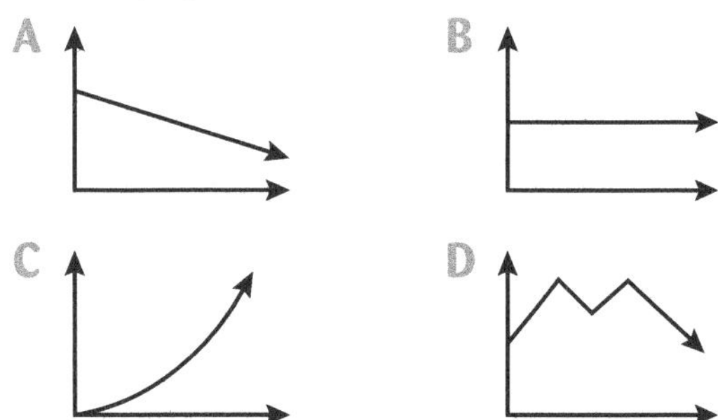

2 On average 8 L of water are used every minute in the shower.

a Define the variables.

Tip Defining a variable means giving it a letter or symbol to represent it.

____ = the amount of water used (dependent variable)

$T =$ ________________ (independent variable)

b Complete a table of values.

Length of shower (minutes)	0	1	2	3
Water used (litres)				

c Write a rule that describes the relationship between the amount of water used and time.

Tip How much water is used per minute?

____ = ____ ____

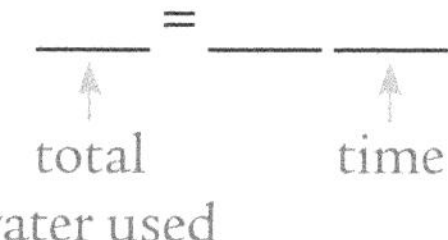

d How much water is used in a 4-minute shower?

Tip Substitute the length of time, $T = 4$, into the equation.

3 The graph below shows the charges for voice calls from a mobile phone.

Total cost of call (\$)

3.00
2.50
2.00
1.50
1.00
0.50
0
1 2 3 4 5
Time (minutes)

a Use the graph to estimate:

i the cost of a $3\frac{1}{2}$-minute phone call.______

ii the length of a call with a cost of $1.______

b Define the two variables.

Tip The variables can be found on the axes on the graph.

Let ____ be the ______________________________.

Let ____ be the ______________________________.

c Use the graph to complete a table of values.

Length of call (minutes)	0	1	2	3	4	5
Total cost of call ($)	$0.30	$0.80				

d Refer to the table to answer the following.

How much is:

i the connection cost for a call? ______

ii the cost per minute? ______

e Write a rule to describe the relationship between the length of a call and the total cost.

____ = ____ ____ + ____

total

f Use the rule written in part **e** to determine the cost of a $4\frac{1}{2}$-minute call.

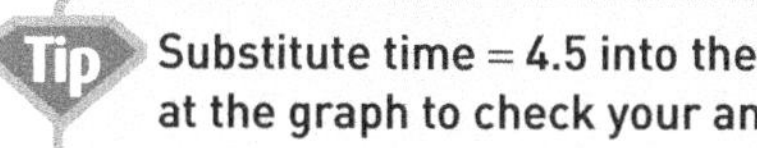

Tip Substitute time = 4.5 into the equation. Look at the graph to check your answer.

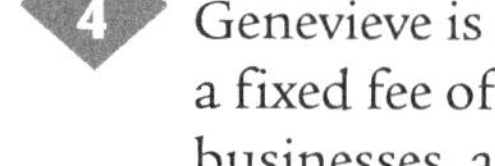

4 Genevieve is a computer technician. She charges a fixed fee of $45 to travel to homes and businesses, and $30 for each hour of work.

a Complete a table of values.

Time worked (hours)	1	2	3	4	5	6
Total fee charged ($)	75					

b Plot the points from the table onto a graph and join with a straight line.

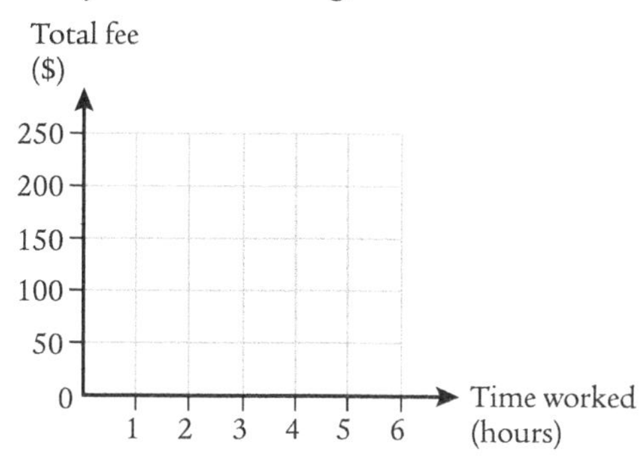

c Is this graph linear?

d Write a rule that shows the relationship between the hours worked and the total fee charged.

$T =$ ____ $H +$ ____

e How much does Genevieve charge for a 3-hour job?

f Genevieve charged $180 for a job. How many hours did she work?

NAPLAN-ready

Shade the box beneath the correct answer.

The graph shows the distance travelled when driving at an average speed of 100 km/h.

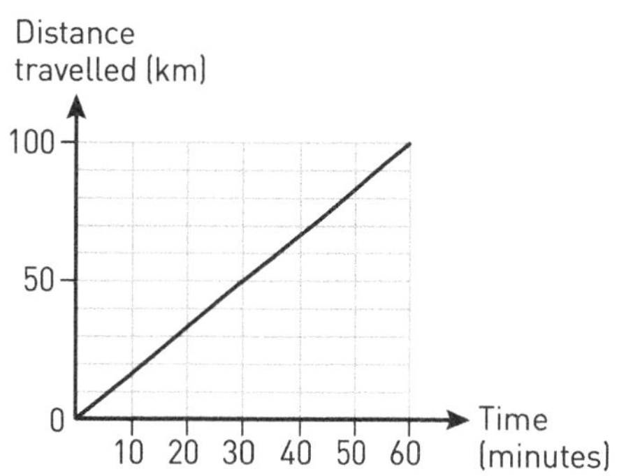

Travelling at an average speed of 100 km/h, approximately how many minutes will it take to travel 70 km?

36 ☐ 38 ☐ 42 ☐ 48 ☐

Tip When distance travelled is 70 km, what is the value on the time axis?

7.1 The language of equations

What is an equation?

An equation is a number sentence containing one or more variables and an equal sign.

$$x + 9 = 17$$

The **variable** in the above equation is the x.

To *solve* an equation is to find the value of the variable (unknown), which will make the equation true.

e.g.'9 is added to a number, x, to give the result of 19'

This statement can be written as an equation and solved.

$x + 9 = 17$

$\underline{8} + 9 = 17$ ← The solution is $x = 8$

Equation key points:

- The correct solution will make the equation true, meaning values on both sides of the equal sign will be equal.
- $\times$ and $\div$ are not written in equations:

  $4k$ means $4 \times k$

  $3(a + 7)$ means $3 \times (a + 7)$

  $\frac{a}{6}$ means $a \div 6$
- Words used to describe mathematical operations:

  + sum – difference

  × product ÷ quotient

Word Bank

Variable

→ A variable is an unknown amount. The word 'pronumeral' can refer to the letter or symbol used to represent the variable in equations.

$4k = 28$

variable

1 Simplify each of the following.

a $6 \times w = 42$ ________

b $y \times 11 - 5 = 28$ ________

c $h \div 8 = 2$ ________

d $f \div 10 + 6 = 56$ ________

2 Which equation describes this sentence?

'Twelve is subtracted from a number (b) to give a result of seven.'

A $12 - b = 7$

B $12 - 7 = b$

C $b - 7 = 12$

D $b - 12 = 7$

3 Write an equation to describe the following sentences. Simplify where necessary.

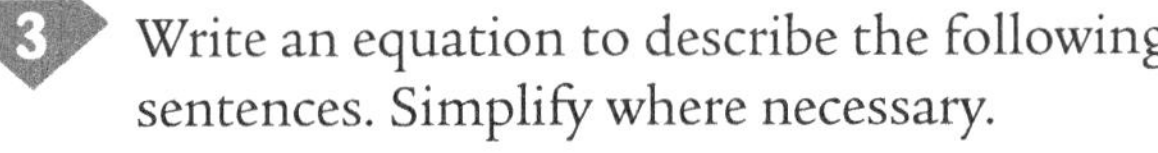

Tip Use the pronumeral (letter) stated to represent the unknown. When writing equations, any number or symbol can be chosen as the unknown.

a The sum of a number (g) and six is seventeen.

☐ + ☐ = ☐

b A number (x) is subtracted from twenty-three to give a result of eleven.

☐ – ☐ = ☐

c A number (m) is divided by two to give a result of nine.

☐ ÷ ☐ = ☐

________ = ____

d Ten is multiplied by a number (t) and then eight is added to make sixty-eight.

☐ × ☐ + 8 = ☐

________ = ____

4 Find the solution.

Tip Write the sentence as an equation and then find the value of the variable that makes the equation true.

a A number (d) divided by twelve is five.

b A number (v) is multiplied by three and then seven is subtracted to give a result of fourteen.

5 Write the following equations in words.

a $s + 9 = 15$

____

____

b $6m = 18$

____

____

6 Does the value in the brackets make the equation true?

Tip Substitute the number in the brackets into the equation.

a $m - 7 = 9$ ($m = 16$)

16 $- 7 = 9$

____ $= 9$ ✓ ✗

Is $m = 16$ the solution? Yes / No

b $7n = 21$ ($n = 4$)

$7 \times$ ____ $= 21$

____ $= 21$ ✓ ✗

Is $n = 4$ the solution? Yes / No

c $\frac{p}{3} = 6$ ($p = 18$)

$\frac{\_\_}{3} = 6$

____ $= 6$ ✓ ✗

Is $p = 18$ the solution? Yes / No

d $4q - 12 = 20$ ($q = 8$)

$4 \times$ ____ $- 12 = 20$

____ $- 12 = 20$

____ $= 20$ ✓ ✗

Is $q = 8$ the solution? Yes / No

7 What value of y will make the equations true?

a $y + 15 = 23$

____ $+ 15 = 23$

Therefore, $y =$ ____

b $12y = 84$

$12 \times$ ____ $= 84$

Therefore, $y =$ ____

8 In a game of *Indian Dice*, Alby rolled five dice. His total score was 24. The numbers on three dice are shown.

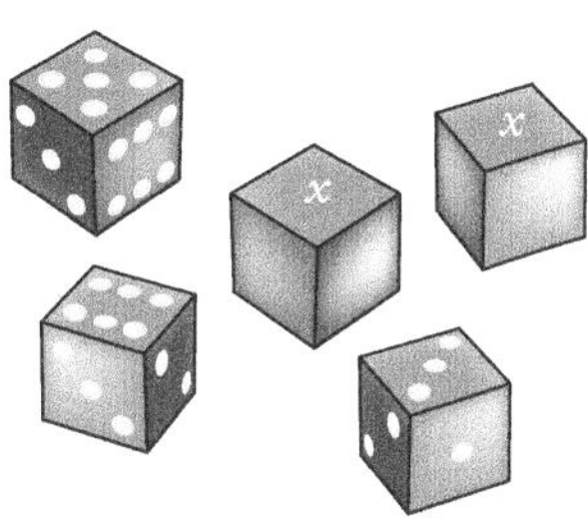

a Write an equation to describe this situation.

Tip Values represented with the same pronumeral are the same.

____ + ____ + ____ + ____ + ____ = ____

____ + ____ = ____

b What is the value on the other two dice?

Tip Values represented with the same pronumeral are the same (each x represents the same number).

NAPLAN-ready

Shade the box beneath the correct answer.

☺ + ☺ + 10 = ✧

✧ ÷ 4 = ☺

What is the value of ☺?

1	4	5	6
☐	☐	☐	☐

Tip Substitute the possible values of ☺ into the equation. Which value makes the equations true?

7.2 Solving linear equations A

To solve an equation is to determine the value of the *variable* that makes the equation true.

Simpler equations can be **solved by inspection** (this means by just looking at it). Here is an equation with one unknown, x.

$$x + 8 = 20$$

This means:

$$\square + 8 = 20$$

By looking at the equation, we can see that we add 12 to 8 to get 20.

$$\boxed{12} + 8 = 20$$

The solution, therefore, is $x = 12$.

Solving equations using algebra

The value of an unknown can be calculated by 'undoing' each operation in an equation.

In the equation below the variable is g.

$$4g - 7 = 13$$

g has been multiplied by 4 and then 7 has been subtracted to get 13.

An equation is solved by performing the **inverse operations** in the reverse order.

To solve the equation:

- add 7 → $4g - 7 + 7 = 13 + 7$
- divide by 4 → $\frac{4g}{4} = \frac{20}{4}$

$$g = 5$$

Word Bank

Inverse operation

→ The inverse is the *opposite* operation.

+ and − are inverse operations. $+4 \leftrightarrow -4$

× and ÷ are inverse operations. $\times 5 \leftrightarrow \div 5$

1 Fill in the box to make true number sentences.

a $20 - \square = 7$ b $3 \times \square = 36$

c $\square + 17 = 23$ d $48 \div \square = 12$

2 What is the value of x?

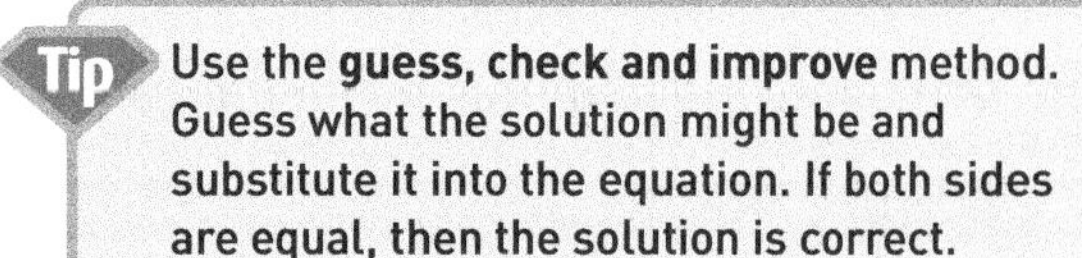
Tip: Use the **guess, check and improve** method. Guess what the solution might be and substitute it into the equation. If both sides are equal, then the solution is correct.

a $5x = 45$

$5 \times \square = 45$

Therefore, $x = \square$

b $2x + 7 = 23$

$2 \times \square + 7 = 23$

$\_\_\_\_ + 7 = 23$

Therefore, $x = \square$

c $\frac{x}{4} - 9 = -5$

$x \div 4 - 9 = -5$

$\_\_\_\_ - 9 = -5$

Therefore, $x = \square$

3 Show that the solution for each equation is $x = 6$.

a $17 - x = 11$

$17 - 6 = 11$

$11 = 11$

b $\frac{x}{2} = 3$

c $3x + 5 = 23$

d $13 - \frac{x}{6} = 12$

4 Write the inverse operations.

a $+9 \leftrightarrow \_\_\_\_$ b $-5 \leftrightarrow \_\_\_\_$

c $\times 10 \leftrightarrow \_\_\_\_$ d $\div 3 \leftrightarrow \_\_\_\_$

5 Find the value of x.

Tip The equation needs to stay balanced, so what you do to one side, you must do to the other side.

a $x+8=19$

$x+8-8=19-8$

$x=$ ____

b $x+13=21$

c $x-3=25$

$x-3+3=25+3$

$x=$ ____

d $x-7=-4$

6 Find the value of x.

a $6x=54$

$\frac{6x}{6}=\frac{54}{6}$ $54 \div 6$

$x=$ ____

b $3x=-21$

c $\frac{x}{11}=8$

$\frac{x}{11}\times 11=8\times 11$

$x=$ ____

d $\frac{x}{4}=12$

7 The equation $\frac{x}{5}+9=13$ is shown in the following flowchart.

Tip A flowchart shows operations that were used to 'build up' the equation. Going backwards, the flowchart shows the inverse operations needed to solve the equation.

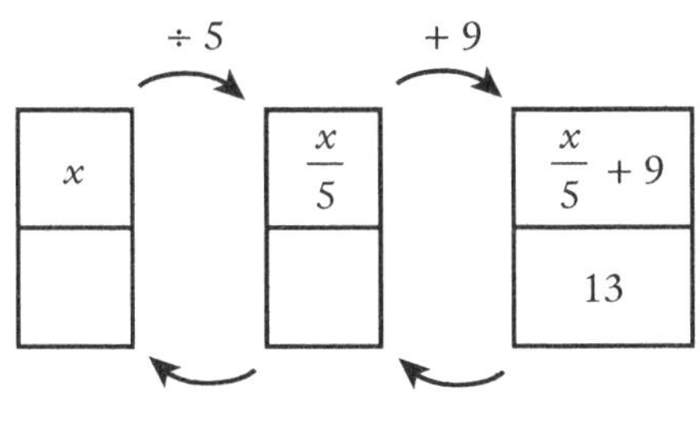

a Write the inverse operations on the flowchart.

b Find the value of x by completing the flowchart.

$x=$ ☐

c Check the solution by substituting the value of x into the equation.

$\frac{\_\_}{5}+9$

____ $+9$

$=13$

8 Solve the following equations.

Tip The order you 'undo' the equation is important. The inverse operations are performed in the reverse order.

a $3x-8=1$ + ____

____ = ____ ÷ ____

____ = ____

b $\frac{x}{6}+4=11$ − ____

____ = ____ × ____

____ = ____

9 Check your answers to Question **8** by substituting the value for x back into the equation.

a $(x=3)$ $3\times$ ____ $-8=1$

____ $-8=1$

____ $=1$ ✓ ✗

b $(x=$ ____ $)$ $\frac{\_\_}{6}+4=11$

____ $=11$

____ $=11$ ✓ ✗

10 Sari cooked six trays of muffins and left them on the bench to cool. Her little brother and his friend ate one tray of muffins when Sari wasn't looking. How many muffins were on each tray if Sari had 20 muffins left?

7.2 Solving linear equations B

Linear equations can be solved by reading values from a graph. All points on a graph give a solution to an equation.

Solving equations graphically

Here is the graph of $y = 3x - 2$.

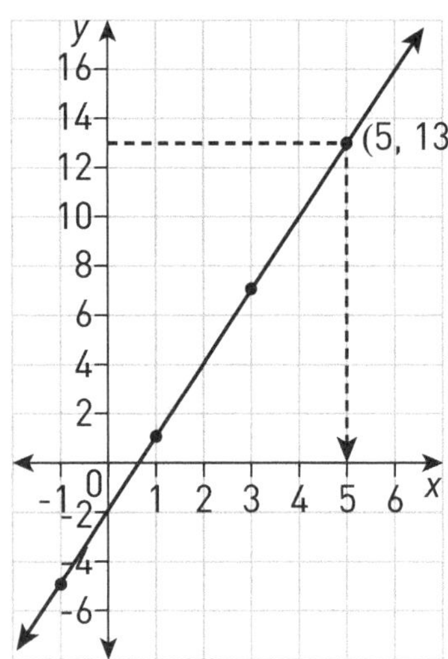

To solve the equation $3x - 2 = 13$:

Find $y = 13$ on the graph. What does x equal?

When $y = 13$, the value of x is 5.

The graph can be used to solve equations.

$3x - 2 = \underline{1}$	When $y = \underline{1}$, $x = 1$	$(1, \underline{1})$
$3x - 2 = \underline{7}$	When $y = \underline{7}$, $x = 3$	$(3, \underline{7})$
$3x - 2 = \underline{-5}$	When $y = \underline{-5}$, $x = -1$	$(-1, \underline{-5})$

1 Here is a graph of $y = x + 3$.

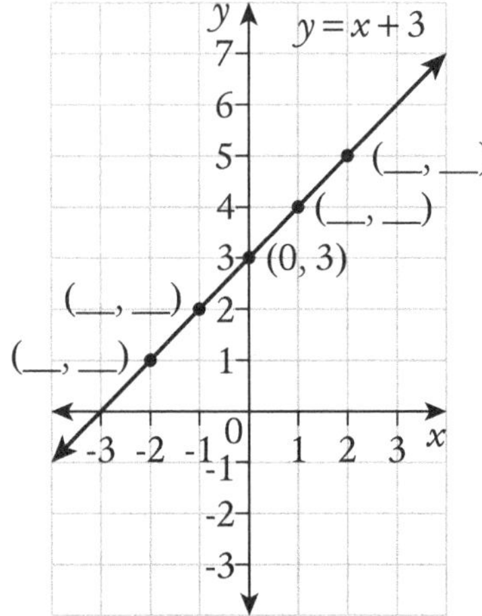

a Write the coordinates next to each point on the graph.

b Copy the coordinates from the graph and fill in the spaces below.

(-2, 1) → When $y = 1$, $x = -2$

(____, ____) → When $y =$ ____, $x =$ ____

(____, ____) → When $y =$ ____, $x =$ ____

(____, ____) → When $y =$ ____, $x =$ ____

(____, ____) → When $y =$ ____, $x =$ ____

2 Use the graph of $y = 2x - 4$ to answer the following.

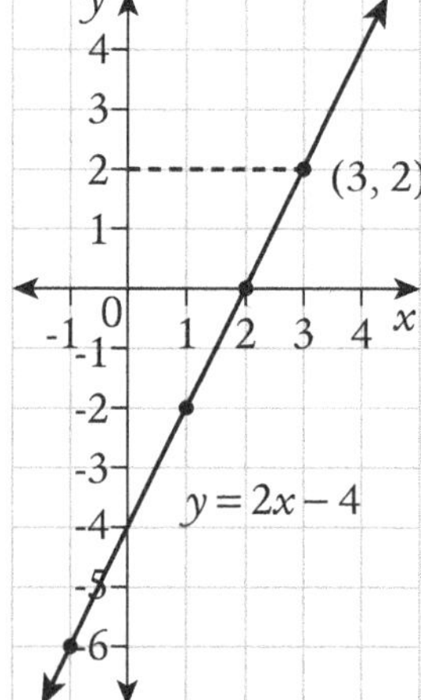

What is the value of x when:

e.g. $y = 2 \rightarrow (\underline{3}, 2) \rightarrow x =$ 3

a $y = -2 \rightarrow$ (____, -2) $\rightarrow x =$

b $y = 0 \rightarrow$ (____, ____) $\rightarrow x =$

c $y = -4 \rightarrow$ (____, ____) $\rightarrow x =$

3 a Solve $2x-5=3$ using the graph below.

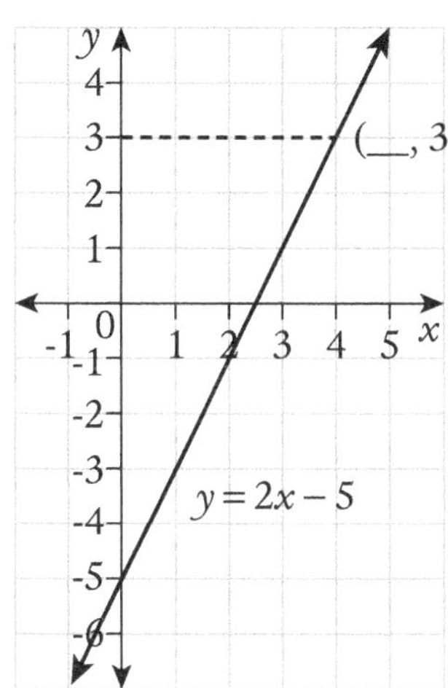

When $y=3, x=$ ☐

b Check the solution in part **a**.

Tip Substitute the answer into the equation to make sure it is a true number sentence.

$2x-5=3$

$2\times$ ____ $-5=3$

____ = ____

4 Refer to the graph of $y=\frac{x}{2}$ below to solve the following equations.

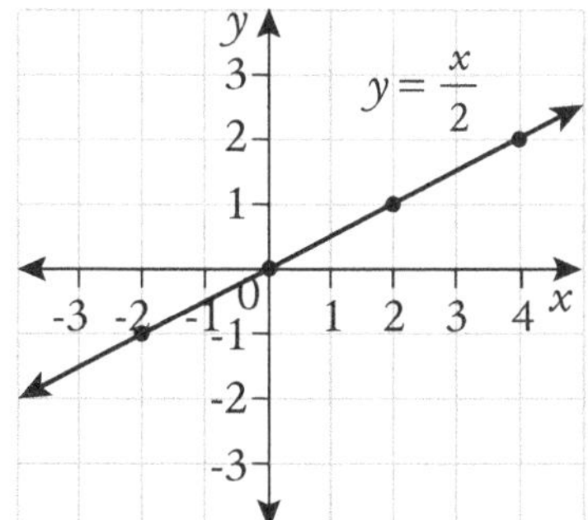

Tip The number on the right side of the equal sign is the y-value. Find the matching value of x on the graph.

a $\frac{x}{2}=1$ when $y=1, x=$ ☐

b $\frac{x}{2}=2$ when $y=$ ____, $x=$ ☐

c $\frac{x}{2}=-1$ when $y=$ ____, $x=$ ☐

5 a To find the solution to $4x-1=15$ graphically, what graph should we draw?

____ = ______________

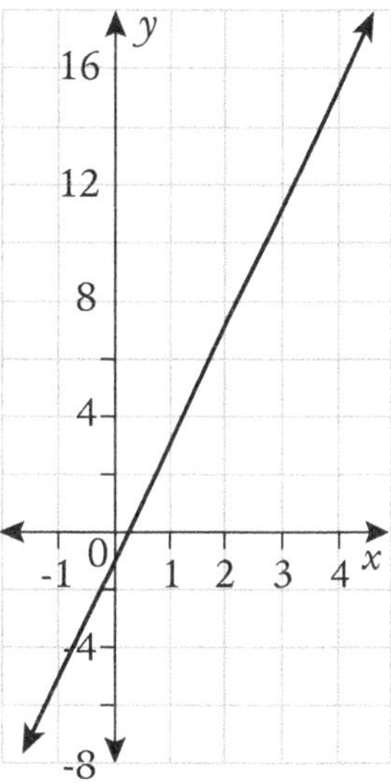

b Refer to the above graph. What is the solution to the equation in part **a**?

$4x-1=15$

c What is the solution to $4x-1=-5$?

NAPLAN-ready

Shade the box beneath the correct answer.

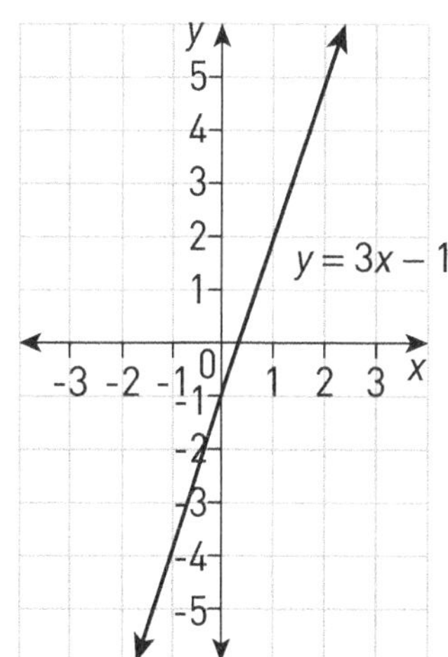

In the equation $3x-1=-4$, the value of x is:

-4	-2	-1	3
☐	☐	☐	☐

Tip Use the graph to find the solution. What is the value of x when $y=-4$?

7.3 Solving more complex equations

Solving equations using inverse operations

Let's look at the equation $\frac{x}{5} - 2 = 4$.

To *solve* this equation (find the value of x):

Step 1: Determine what operations have been performed on the unknown and in what order.

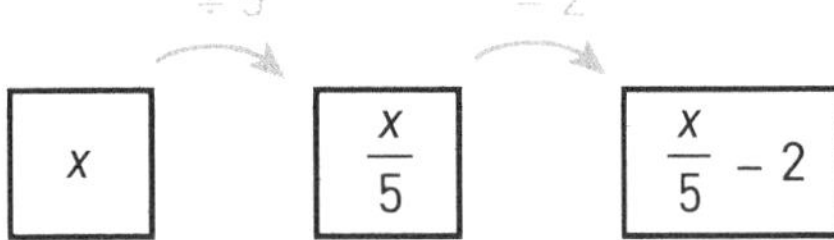

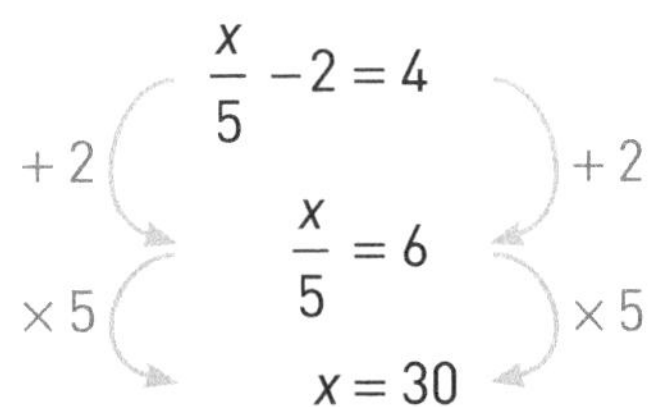

x has been divided by 5 and then 2 has been subtracted.

Step 2: Now, perform the **inverse** operations in the reverse order to both sides of the equal sign.

$$\frac{x}{5} - 2 = 4 \quad (+2)$$
$$\frac{x}{5} = 6 \quad (\times 5)$$
$$x = 30$$

The solution to the above equation is $x = 30$.

Check the solution:

Check that the solution is correct by substituting the value for x back into the equation.

$$\frac{30}{5} - 4 = 2$$
$$\frac{30}{5} - 4 = 2 \quad (x = 30)$$
$$6 - 4 = 2$$
$$2 = 2 \quad ✓$$

Both sides are equal, so the value of x is correct.

Word Bank

Solving an equation

➜ To solve an equation is to find the value of the variable (unknown) that makes the equation true.

1 Here is the flowchart for $\frac{g+8}{3} = 5$.

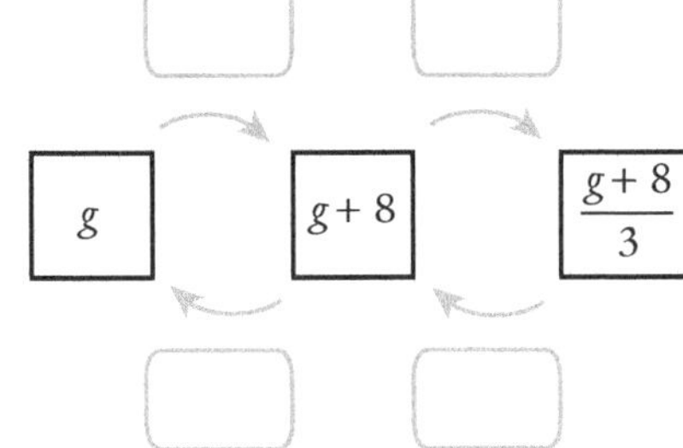

a State the operations, in order, that have been performed on g in the equation $\frac{g+8}{3} = 5$.

b Write the *inverse* operations of the operations stated in part **a**.

c Use the inverse operations in part **b** to solve for g.

$\frac{g+8}{3} = 5$ × ____

$g + 8 =$ ____   − ____

$g =$ ____

What is the value of g? ☐

d Check the value for g found in part **c** by substituting the value back into the equation.

2 Write the performed operations and inverse operations.

a

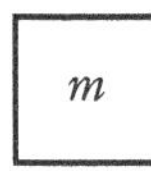

m → $\frac{m}{3}$ → $\frac{m}{3}+11$

b

p → $p-6$ → $\frac{p-6}{4}$

3 Use the inverse operations stated in Question **2** to solve the following equations.

a $\frac{m}{3}+11=12$

$\frac{m}{3}=$ ____

$m=$ ____

b $\frac{p-6}{4}=7$

$p-6=$ ____

$p=$ ____

4 Solve:

a $\frac{y}{10}-6=2$

+6 +6

$\frac{y}{10}=$ ____

×10

$y=$ ____

b $\frac{k+9}{3}=7$

×3

$k+9=$ ____

$k=$ ____

5 The following equations have been solved. State the inverse operations that were performed.

Tip 5(x − 9) means 5 × (x − 9). The inverse of × 5 is ÷ 5. 'Undo' operations that are outside the brackets first.

a

÷ ____ ÷ ____

− ____ − ____

$3(x+8)=36$

$x+8=12$

$x=4$

b

÷ ____ ÷ ____

+ ____ + ____

$7(x-10)=14$

$x-10=2$

$x=12$

6 Solve $6(x+5)=54$.

÷ ____ ÷ ____

− ____ − ____

$6(x+5)=54$

________ = ____

$x=$ ____

7 The operations and their order performed on x in the equation $\frac{4x+1}{7}=3$ is shown below.

x → ×4 +1 ÷7 → $\frac{4x+1}{7}$

Tip Remember to do the inverse operations in the reverse order.

Solve for x.

$\frac{4x+1}{7}=3$

________ = ____

________ = ____

____ = ____

8 In the equation $\frac{3h}{4}-2=4$, h has been multiplied by 3, and then divided by 4 and then 2 has been subtracted. Solve for h.

$\frac{3h}{4}-2=4$

________ = ____

________ = ____

____ = ____

NAPLAN-ready

Shade the box beneath the correct answer.

$$\frac{2(x+5)}{3}=4$$

What value for x is the solution to the equation?

1	2	3	4
☐	☐	☐	☐

Tip Substitute each of the answers into the equation. Which value makes the equation true?

7.4 Solving equations where the unknown appears on both sides A

Sometimes, equations have the variable on both sides of the equal sign, such as $2x + 1 = x + 3$.

Equations like this can be solved using algebra or by drawing linear graphs (see the following section 7.4B).

An equation is like a set of balanced scales—the same operation can be performed to *both* sides of the equal sign to simplify it.

Solving equations using algebra

The scales show the equation:

$$2x + 1 = x + 3$$

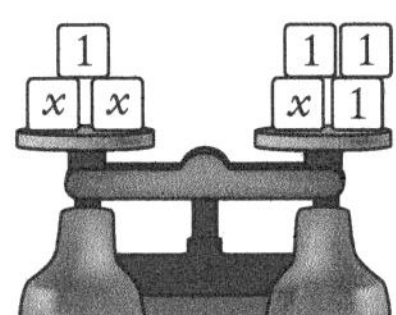

Step 1: Remove (subtract) x from both sides, and the equation simplifies to:

$$2x - x + 1 = x - x + 3$$
$$x + 1 = 3$$

Step 2: Now, solve for x by using *inverse* operations to both sides.

$$x + 1 - 1 = 3 - 1$$
$$x = 2$$

Check the solution:

Substituting $x = 2$ into the equation.

$$2x + 1 = x + 3$$
$$2 \times \underline{2} + 1 = \underline{2} + 3$$
$$5 = 5 \quad ✓$$

Word Bank

Lowest common denominator (LCD)

→ In the equation below, the two denominators are 3 and 5.

$$\frac{2x - 6}{3} = \frac{x + 11}{5}$$

The lowest common denominator is the smallest number that is a multiple of two or more denominators.

LCD of 3 and 5:

3: 3, 6, 9, 12, <u>15</u>, 18

5: 5, 10, <u>15</u>, 20, 25

The LCD of the fractions is 15.

1 An equation can be seen as a set of balanced scales.

a Write values on the blocks below to represent the equation $3x + 1 = x + 5$.

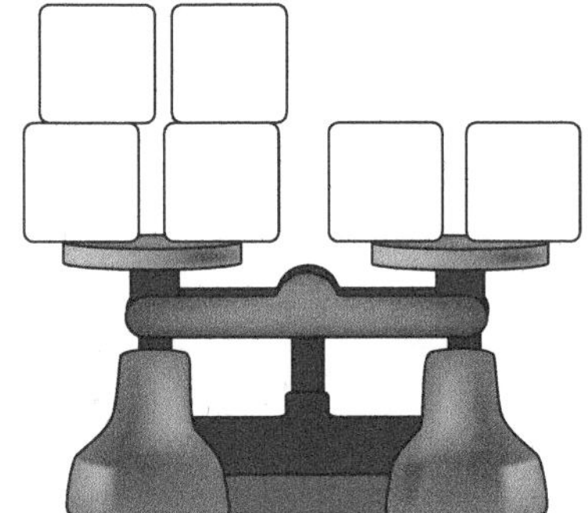

b Write an equation to describe the scales after one x block has been removed from each side.

________ = ________

2 What is the value of x?

Tip How many xs are on the right-hand side? Remove this number of xs from both sides (to keep it balanced) and then solve the equation that results.

a

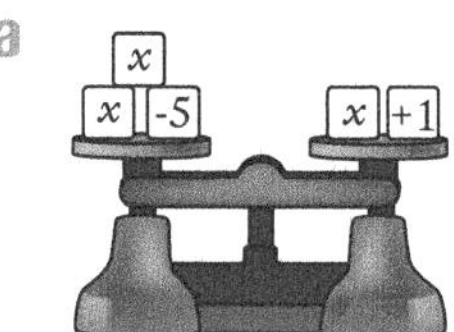

$$2x - 5 = x + 1$$

________ = ________ ($-x$ from both sides)

____ = ____

b

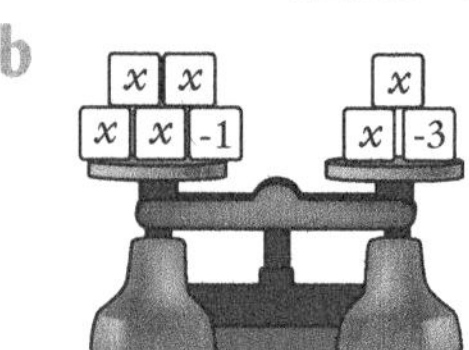

$$4x - 1 = 2x - 3$$

________ = ________ ($-2x$ from both sides)

________ = ____

____ = ____

3 Expand the brackets in the following equations.

> **Tip** Each term inside the bracket is multiplied by the number outside the bracket.
> e.g. $3(b-4)$
> $= 3 \times b - 3 \times 4$
> $= 3b - 12$

a $6(y+2)$

$=$ ___ $y+$ ___

b $5(2k-4)$

$=$ ________

c $4(m-9)$

$=$ ________

d $8(3+7w)$

$=$ ________

4 The solutions to the equations below are stated. Show the workings.

> **Tip** Expand the brackets before solving.

a $2(p-8) = p-6$

________ $= p-6$

________ $= -6$

$p = 10$

b $5(y-8) = y-4$

________ = ________

________ = ________

________ = ________

________ = ________

$y = 9$

c $2(3h-5) = 4(h-3)$

________ = ________

________ = ________

________ = ________

________ = ________

$h = -1$

5 Complete the following to solve $\frac{x+1}{3} = \frac{x+3}{4}$.

> **Tip** By multiplying both fractions by the lowest common multiple (LCM), the denominators cancel out.

a Find the LCM of the two denominators.

3: ____, ____, ____, ____, ____

4: ____, ____, ____, ____, ____

∴ the LCD of ____ and ____ is ____

b Multiply both sides by the LCD and cancel down.

$\_\left(\frac{x+1}{3}\right) = \_\left(\frac{x+3}{4}\right)$

Write LCD here.

$\_(x+1) = \_(x+3)$

c Once cancelled down, the equation can be written as $4(x+1) = 3(x+3)$. Expand and solve.

________ = ________

________ = ________

____ = ____

d Check your solution in part **c** by substituting the value for x into the original equation.

$\frac{x+1}{3} = \frac{x+3}{4}$

$\frac{\_+1}{3} = \frac{\_+3}{4}$

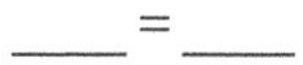

____ = ____

✓ ✗

6

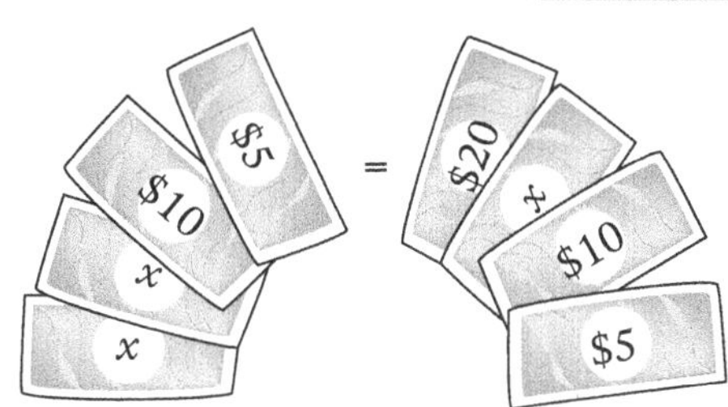

a Write an equation to describe the situation.

____

b What is the value of the unknown note, x?

> **Tip** Solve the equation you wrote in part **a**.

________ = ________

________ = ________

$x =$ ____

The value of the unknown notes is ____.

c Substitute your answer to part **b** into the equation in part **a**. Are the left-hand and right-hand sides equal?

7.4 Solving equations where the unknown appears on both sides B

Solving equations graphically

Equations with an unknown on both sides can be solved by drawing linear graphs. Each side of the equation is graphed as a separate equation on the same Cartesian plane. The solution is the x-value of the position where the two lines intersect.

e.g. Solve $3x - 4 = x + 2$.

This equation can be solved graphically by drawing the graphs of:

$y = 3x - 4$
$y = x + 2$

From the graph, we can see that the **point of intersection** is at (3, 5). The x-value is 3.

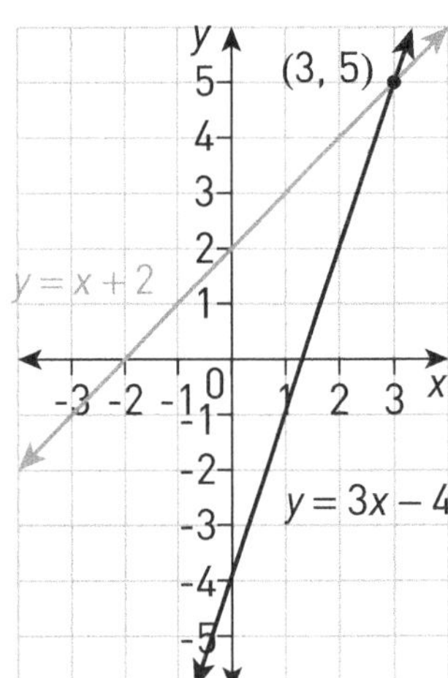

Therefore, the solution is $x = 3$.

Check the solution:

Substitute $x = 3$ into the equation.

$3x - 4 = x + 2$
$3 \times \underline{3} - 4 = \underline{3} + 2$
$5 = 5$ ✓

Not all equations will have a solution. Linear graphs that are parallel never cross and therefore, have no solution for x.

Word Bank

Point of intersection

➜ The point where two or more lines cross is called the point of intersection.

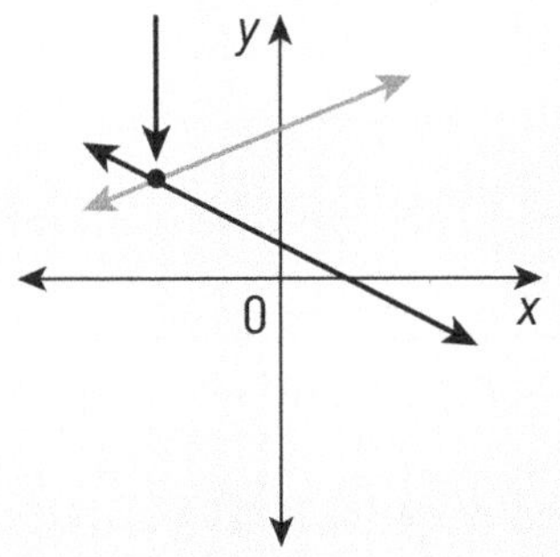

1 To solve the equation $-3x - 4 = x + 4$, two graphs have been sketched below.

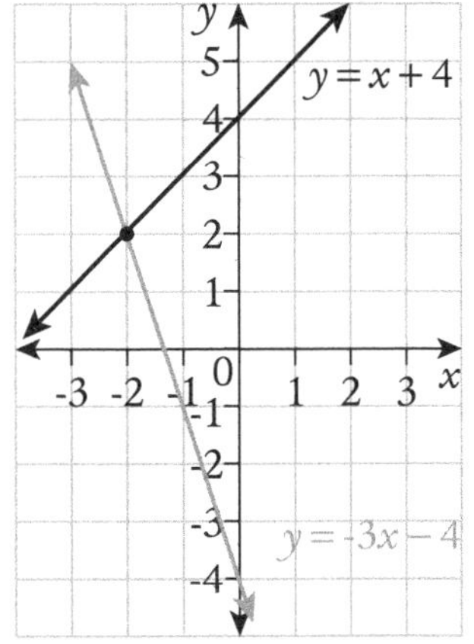

a State the coordinates of the *point of intersection* on the graph.

(,)

b What is the x-value in the coordinate in part **a**?

$x =$

c Check your solution from part **b** by substituting the x-value into the equation.

$-3x - 4 = x + 4$

$-3 \times \_\_\_\_ - 4 = \_\_\_\_ + 4$

$\_\_\_\_ = \_\_\_\_$ ✓ ✗

2 a Solve $3x + 1 = x - 1$ using the graph below.

Tip The solution to the equation is the x-value where the two lines intersect.

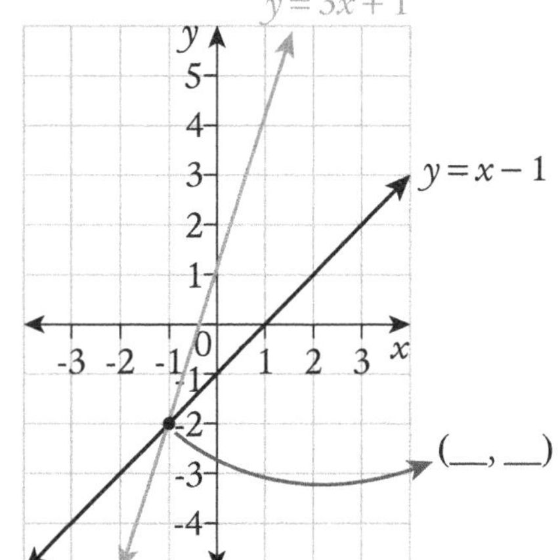

The solution to the equation $3x + 1 = x - 1$ is:

x =

b Check your solution to part **a** by substituting the value of x into the equation.

$3x+1 = x - 1$

$3 \times$ ____ $+1 =$ ____ $- 1$

____ = ____ ✓ ✗

3 To solve the equation $x + 3 = -x + 5$ graphically, the intersection of which two graphs is needed?

$y =$ __________ and $y =$ __________

4 a Plot the two graphs stated in Question **3** on the Cartesian plane below.

Tip Linear graphs can be drawn from three points. Use a ruler to draw each line, extending past the points.

$y =$ _____

x	0	1	2
y			

$y =$ _____

x	0	1	2
y			

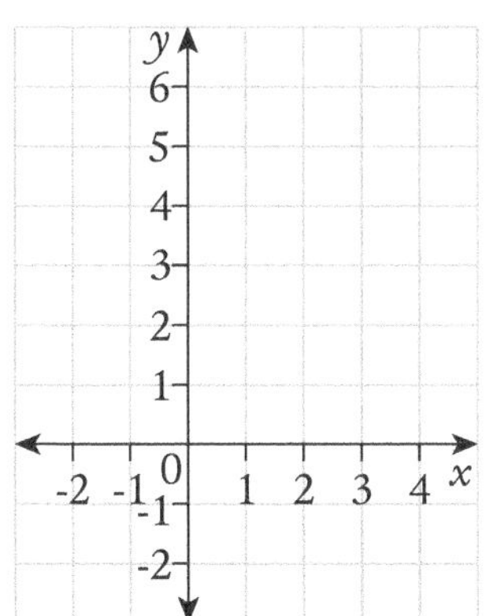

b At what point do the graphs intersect?

(,)

c Use parts **a** and **b** to solve the equation $x + 3 = -x + 5$.

x =

5 The graph of $y = 5$ is shown below.

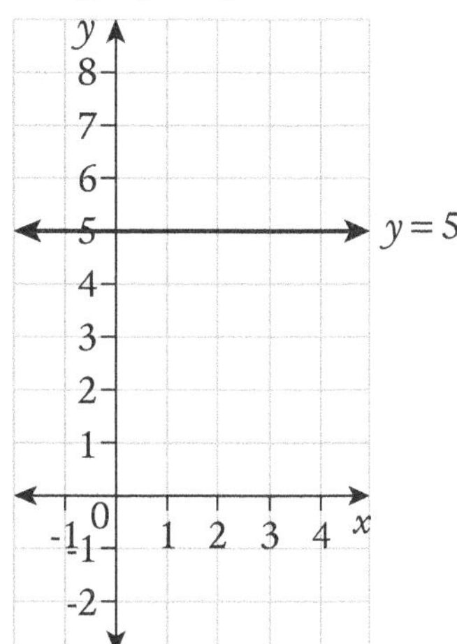

a Plot the graph $x = y + 2$ on the above axis by first completing a table of values

$x = y + 2$

x	-1	0	1	2	3	4
y						

b State the coordinate of the point of intersection. (____ , ____)

c Use the answer in part **b** to solve $x + 2 = 5$.

$x =$ ___

NAPLAN-ready

Shade the box beneath the correct answer.

$y = 2x + 5$

x	-2	-1	0	1	2
y	1	3	5	7	9

$y = 2 - x$

x	-2	-1	0	1	2
y	4	3	2	1	0

What is the solution to the equation $2x + 5 = 2 - x$?

$x = 2$ ☐ $y = 3$ ☐ $x = -2$ ☐ $x = -1$ ☐

Tip Look at the tables of values. For what value of x would the graphs of the two lines intersect?

7.5 Solving problems using equations

A real life problem:

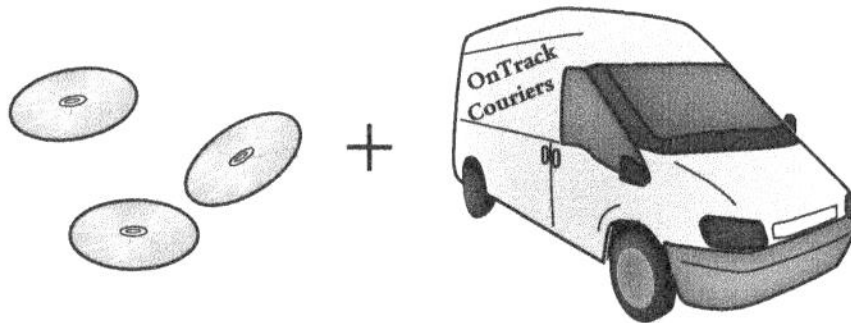

After buying CDs online, Lacie forgot how many CDs she had just purchased. She knew she had spent a total of $110.95. The delivery charge was $14.95. All CDs were on sale for $16. How many CDs did Lacie purchase?

Problems in real life, like the one Lacie encountered, can be solved using equations.

Step 1: Define variables

Let n = number of CDs

Step 2: Write an equation

$16 \times n + 14.95 = 110.95$

(cost of a CD; delivery fee; total cost)

Step 3: Solve the equation

Use *inverse operations* to solve for n.

$$16n + 14.95 = 110.95$$
$$16n + 14.95 - 14.95 = 110.95 - 14.95$$
$$\frac{16n}{16} = \frac{96}{16}$$
$$n = 6$$

Step 4: State the answer in words

Lacie purchased 6 CDs.

Word Bank

Pronumeral

→ A pronumeral (or variable) is a letter used to represent a variable in an expression or equation.

1 The diagram below can be represented with the equation $6c = 4.20$, where c is the cost of a banana in dollars.

What is the cost of 1 banana?

$6c = 4.2$ ÷ ____

$c =$ ____

∴ the cost of a banana is $________.

2 Ricky Ponting and Michael Clarke achieved a 386-run partnership in a Cricket Test. Ponting scored 221 of these runs.

a Write an equation to represent the situation.

Let d = the number of runs made by Clarke.

______ + ______ = 386

b How many runs in this partnership did Clarke make?

$d =$ ______

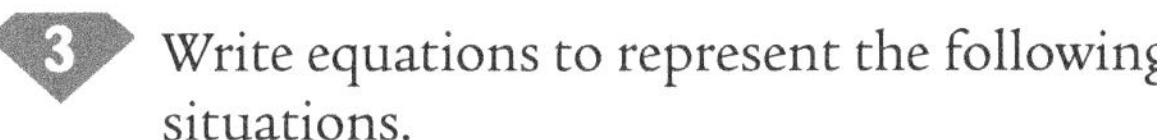

3 Write equations to represent the following situations.

a 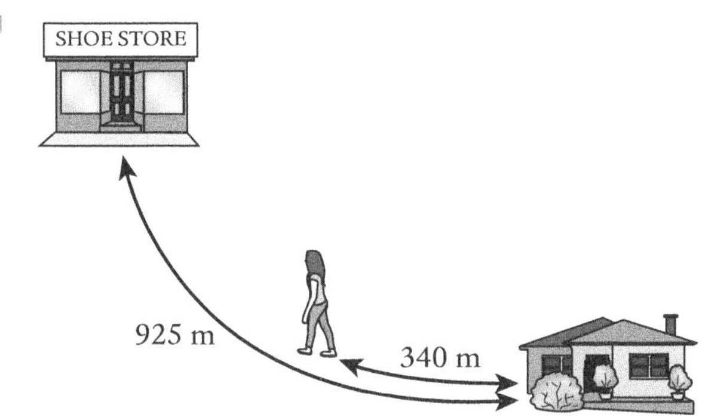

Let ____ = the distance from the girl to the store in metres.

____ + ____ = ____

b 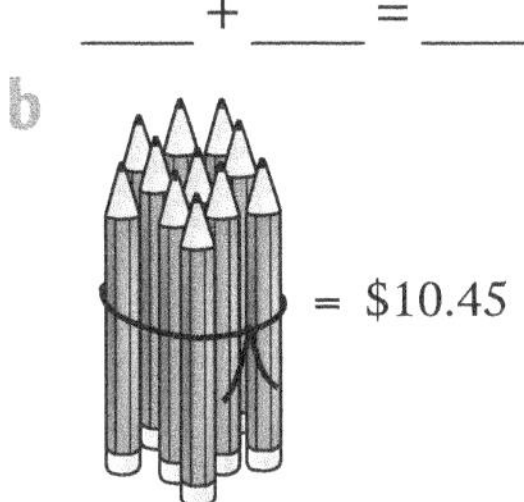

Let ____ = cost of a pencil in dollars

____ ____ = ____

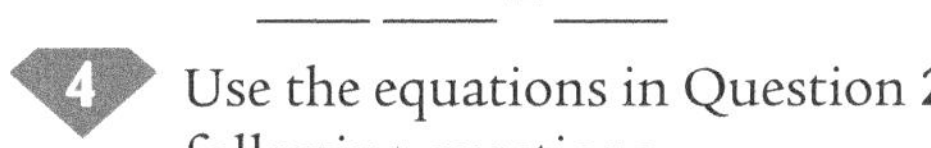

4 Use the equations in Question **2** to answer the following questions.

a How far is the girl from the store?

____ = ____

b What is the cost of 1 pencil?

____ = ____

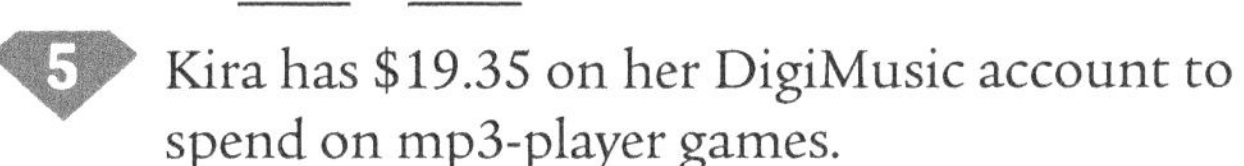

5 Kira has $19.35 on her DigiMusic account to spend on mp3-player games.

The games cost $1.29 each. How many games can she download?

a Define the variable.

Let ____ = the number of games.

b Write an equation to find the number of games that can be downloaded.

________ ________ = ________

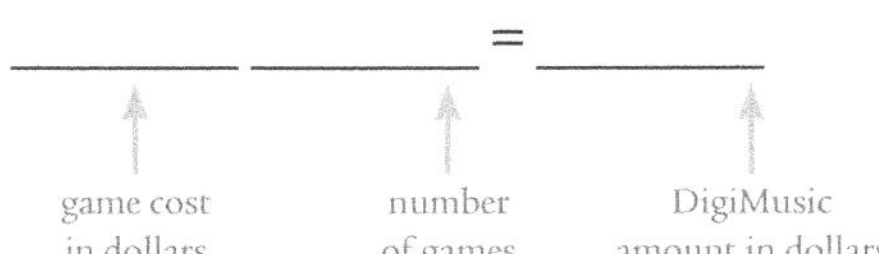

c Use *inverse operations* to solve the equation.

Therefore, the number of games Kira can download is ______.

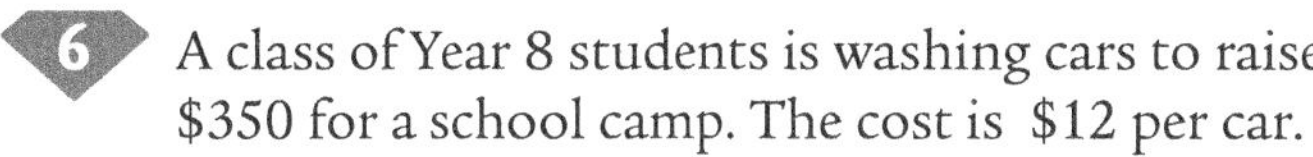

6 A class of Year 8 students is washing cars to raise $350 for a school camp. The cost is $12 per car.

a Write an equation to find out how many cars they have to wash to reach their target.

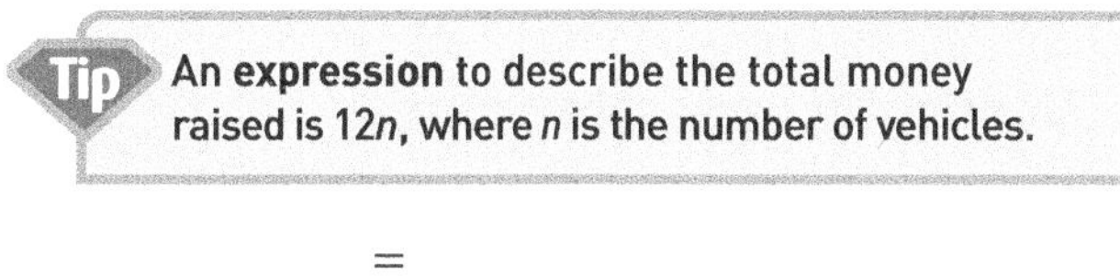

Tip An **expression** to describe the total money raised is $12n$, where n is the number of vehicles.

____ ____ = ____

b Solve the equation using inverse operations.

Therefore, the class needs to wash ____ cars to reach their target.

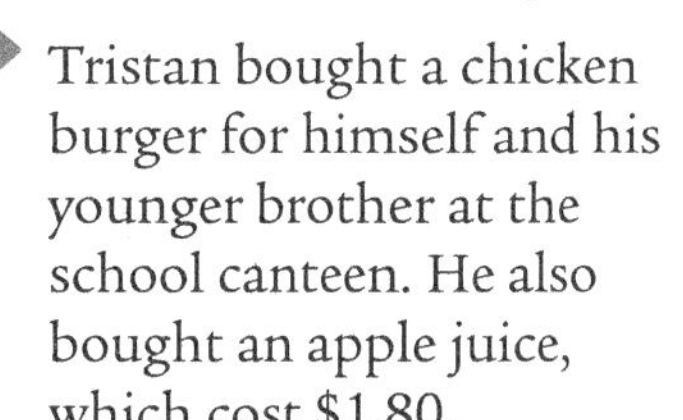

7 Tristan bought a chicken burger for himself and his younger brother at the school canteen. He also bought an apple juice, which cost $1.80.

a Write an expression for the total cost of their lunch in dollars.

Let ____ be the cost of a chicken burger in dollars.

____ ____ + ____

b If the total cost of lunch was $10.20, how much does a chicken burger cost?

NAPLAN-ready

Shade the box beneath the correct answer.

In the 2012 Australian Open Men's singles final, Djokovic won 5 more games than Nadal to win the Grand Slam 3 sets to 2. Fifty-five games were played in total.

How many games did Djokovic win?

20	22	25	30
☐	☐	☐	☐

Tip Write the problem as an equation. Let x represent the number of games Nadal won, so Djokovic won $x + 5$.

8.1 Angles review

Angles are formed when two lines meet or intersect at a point.

- **Complementary** angles are pairs or groups of angles that add to 90°.
- **Supplementary** angles are pairs or groups of angles that add to 180°.

Vertically opposite angles

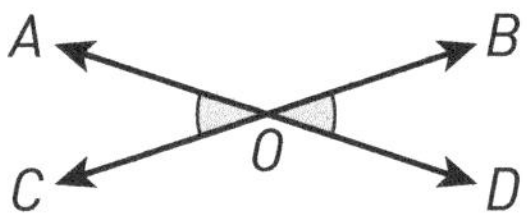

∠*AOC* and ∠*BOD* are a pair of **vertically opposite angles**. They are the same size.

Adjacent angles

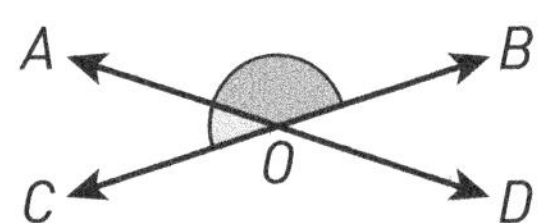

∠*AOB* and ∠*AOC* are a pair of **adjacent angles**. They are supplementary angles; they add to 180°.

Angles on parallel lines

Pairs of angles, formed when a line (called a **transversal**) intersects **parallel lines**, have special names and special properties.

Corresponding angles	Alternate angles	Co-interior angles
Corresponding angles on parallel lines are equal.	Alternate angles on parallel lines are equal.	Co-interior angles inside parallel lines add to 180°.

Understanding the relationships between the pairs of angles, as outlined above, can help to calculate unknown angles on diagrams with two or more lines.

Word Bank

Angle

→ An **angle** is the amount of turn between two angle *arms*. Angles are measured in degrees (°). There is 360° in one full turn.

Transversal

→ A line that intersects *parallel lines* is called a transversal.

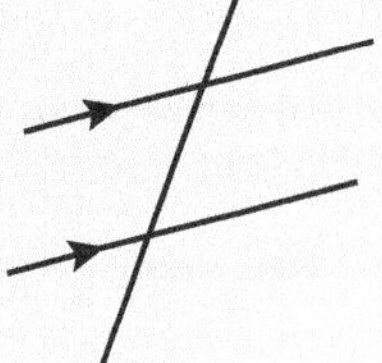

1 State the size of the following angles.

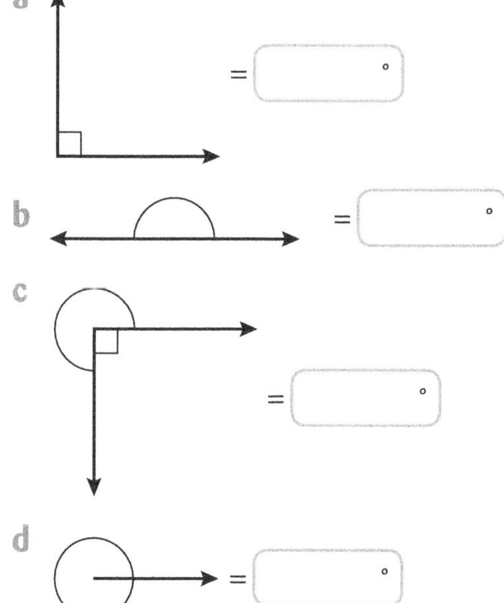

2 Estimate the size of the angles below.

a

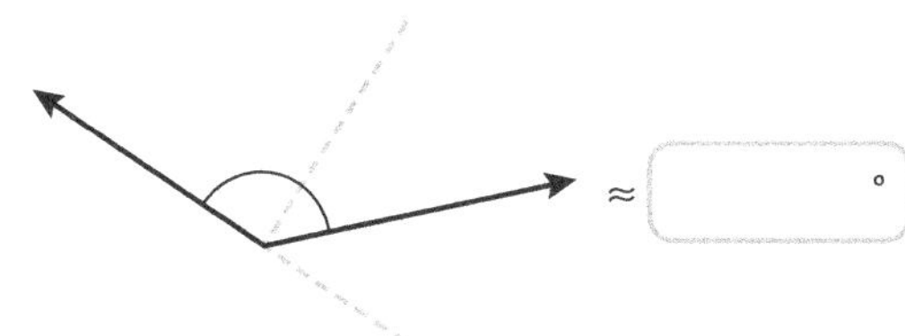

$\approx$ ☐ °

b

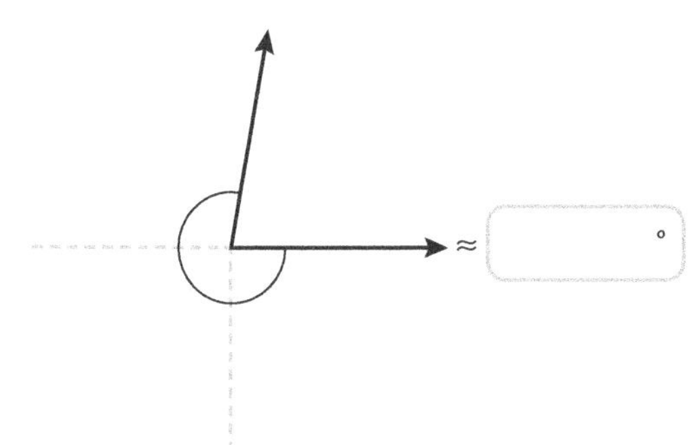

$\approx$ ☐ °

3 What is the complement of 23°?

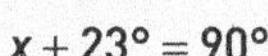

Tip Complementary angles add to 90°, a right angle.

$x + 23° = 90°$

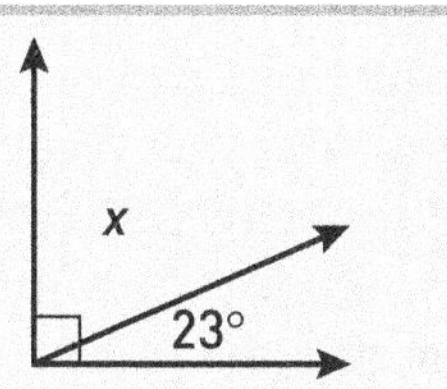

The complement of 23° is ☐.

4 What is the supplement of 65°?

Tip Supplementary angles add to 180°, a straight angle.

$y + 65° = 180°$

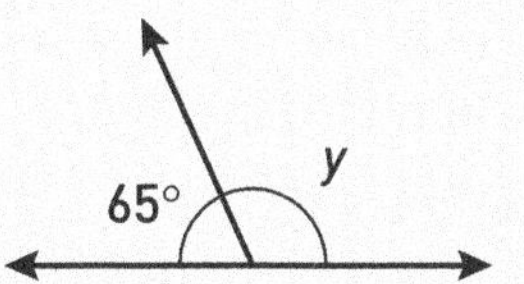

The supplement of 65° is ☐.

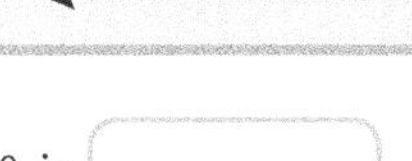

5 What is the value of the unknown angles?

Tip If two or more angles are identified with the same pronumeral (letter), they are the same size.

a $w +$ ____ $= 360°$

$w =$ ______

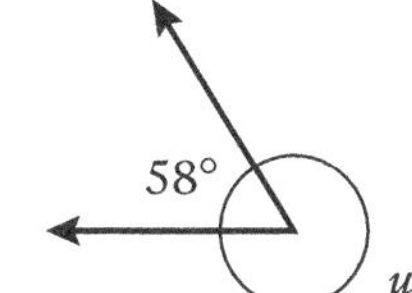

b $x + x + 116° =$ ____

________ $=$ ____

$2x =$ ____

$x =$ ____

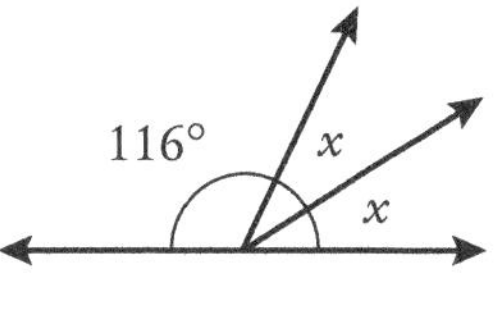

6 In the diagram below:

a mark the parallel lines with arrows

b use two different colours to identify equal angles.

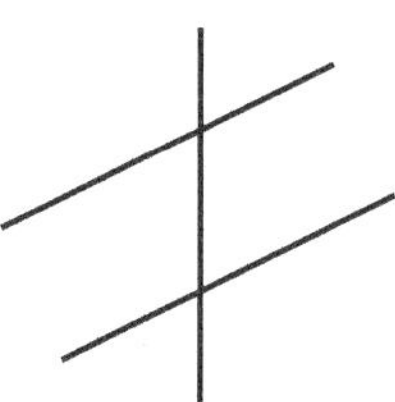

Tip Eight angles are formed, creating two sets of four equal angles.

7 Find the value of the pronumerals below, stating the special property of the pair of angles.

Tip Firstly, look for parallel lines and identify equal angles.

a $f =$ ☐ °

f and 58° are __________ angles.

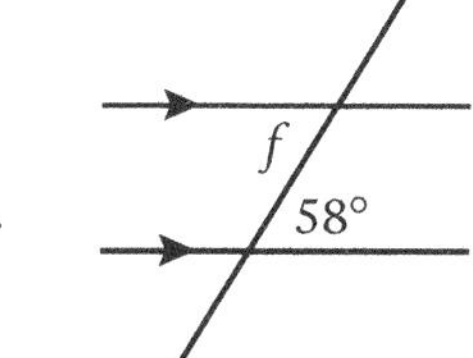

b $m =$ ☐ °

m and 105° are __________ angles.

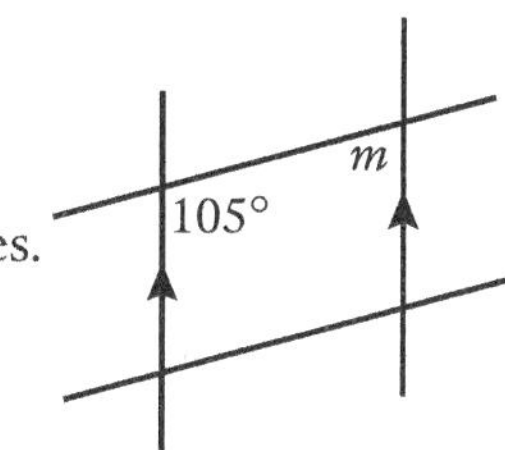

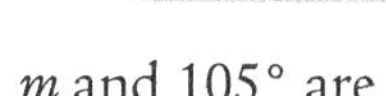

NAPLAN-ready

Shade the box beneath the correct answer.

The diagram below shows the design of a large, wooden table.

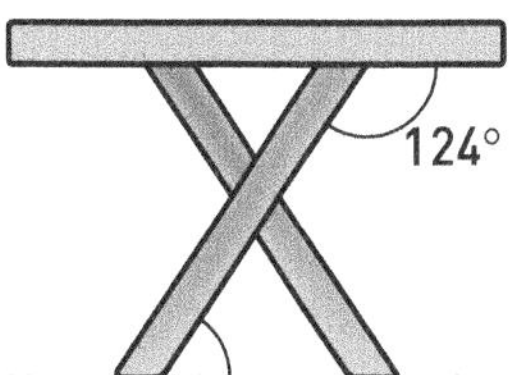

What angle do the table legs make with the ground?

56°	62°	66°	76°
☐	☐	☐	☐

Tip Look for parallel lines. What special property do the pair of angles have?

8.2 Shapes review

Angle sums of polygons

Polygons are two-dimensional (2D), closed shapes with straight sides. The number of triangles a polygon can be divided into determines the sum of its interior angles.

Triangle	Quadrilateral	Pentagon
$a + b + c = 180°$	$a + b + c + d = 360°$	$a + b + c + d + e = 540°$
	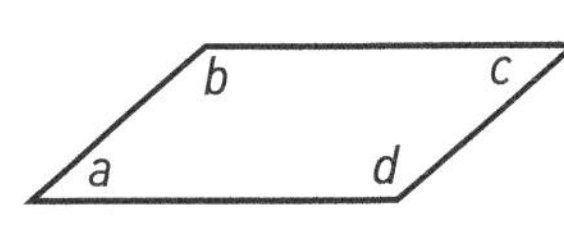	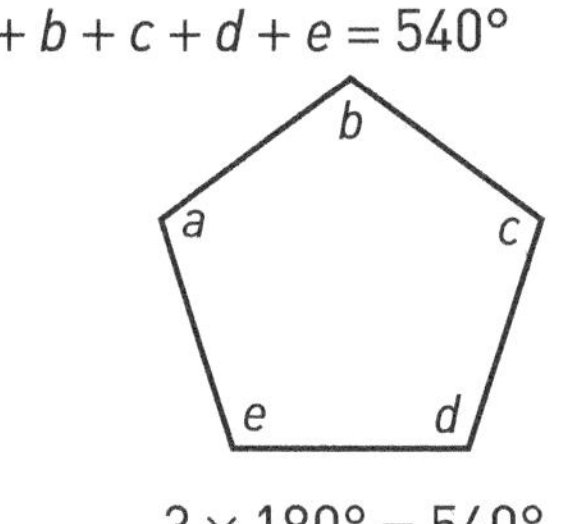
	$2 \times 180° = 360°$	$3 \times 180° = 540°$
The interior angles of a triangle add up to 180°.	The interior angles of a quadrilateral add up to 360°.	The interior angles of a pentagon add up to 540°.

Calculating interior angles

Unknown angles can be calculated using the angle sums for polynomials.

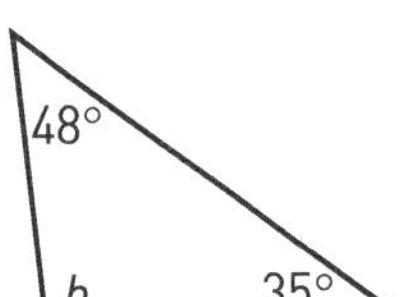

$h + \underline{48 + 35} = 180$

$h + 83 = 180$

$h + 83 - 83 = 180 - 83$

$h = 97°$

Check: $97° + 48° + 35° = 180°$ ✓

Calculating exterior angles

An exterior angle is formed when one side of a polygon extends past a vertex. It makes a straight angle (180°) with the interior angle next to it.

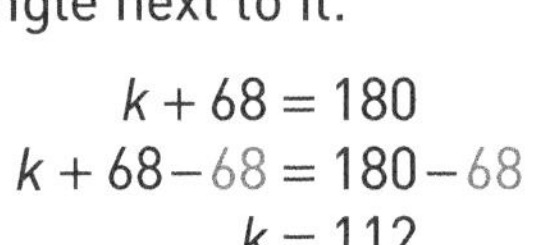

$k + 68 = 180$

$k + 68 - 68 = 180 - 68$

$k = 112$

The exterior angle k is 112°.

The exterior angle of a triangle is also equal to the sum of the two opposite interior angles.

$42 + 70 = 112$

Therefore, $k = 112°$.

Word Bank

Quadrilateral

→ Quadrilaterals are four-sided polygons. Types of quadrilaterals include parallelograms, kites and trapeziums.

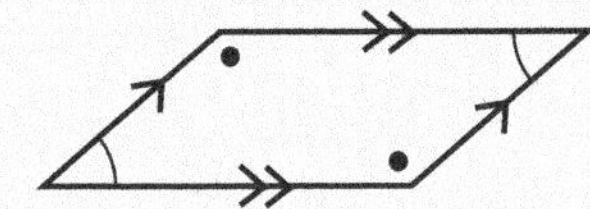

1 What is the value of the variable?

a

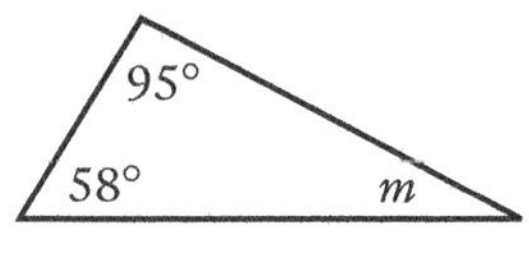

$m +$ ____ $+$ ____ $= 180$

$m +$ ________ $= 180$

$m =$ ____ °

b

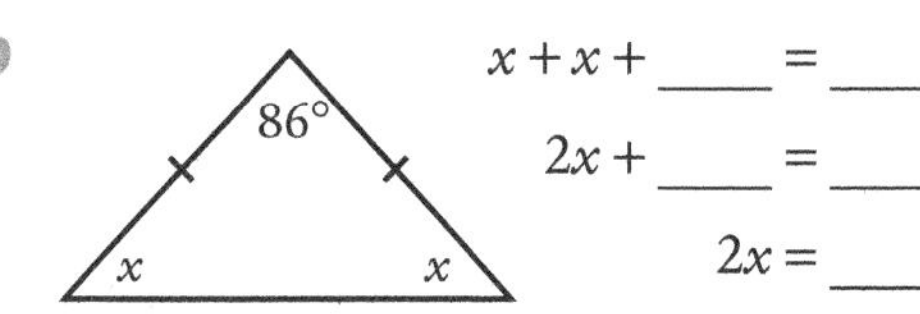

$x + x +$ ____ $=$ ____

$2x +$ ____ $=$ ____

$2x =$ ____

$x =$ ____ °

2 Find the value of the unknown angle.

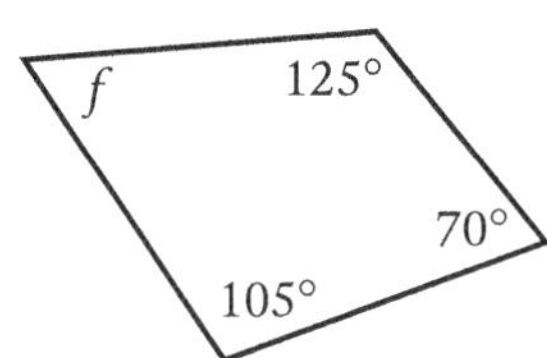

$f+$ ____ $+$ ____ $+$ ____ $=360$

$f+$ ____________ $=360$

$f=$ [ ]°

3 What are the values of the three unknowns in the rhombus below?

Tip A rhombus is a type of parallelogram. Opposite angles in a rhombus are equal. All interior angles add to 360°.

b is opposite 95°.

$\therefore b=$ ____

a is adjacent to 95°.

$a+95=180$

$\therefore a=$ ____

c is ______________ a.

$\therefore c=$ _____

4 What is the value of t?

Tip t is an exterior angle.

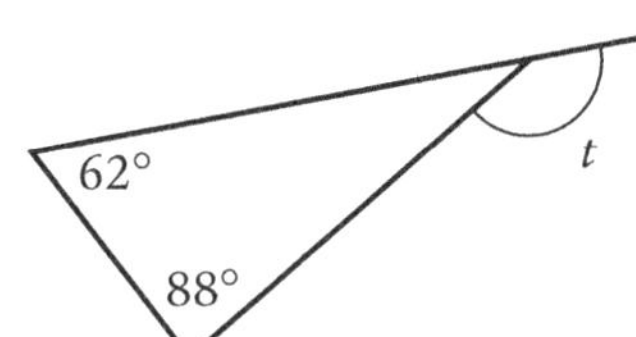

$t=$ ____ $+$ ____

[ ]°

5 On the shapes below, mark equal side lengths (dashes) and angles, and parallel sides (arrows). Name and describe the shape.

Tip Use mathematical symbols to identify equal angles and parallel sides:
$\angle ABC = \angle CDA$ (equal angles)
$AB \parallel CD$ (parallel sides)

a

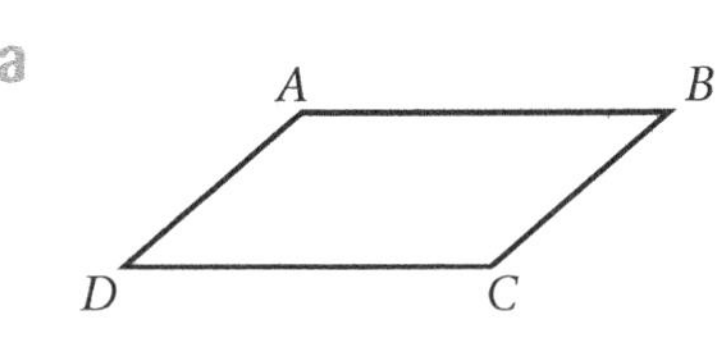

Name of shape: [ ]

Description: ____________________

____

____

____

b

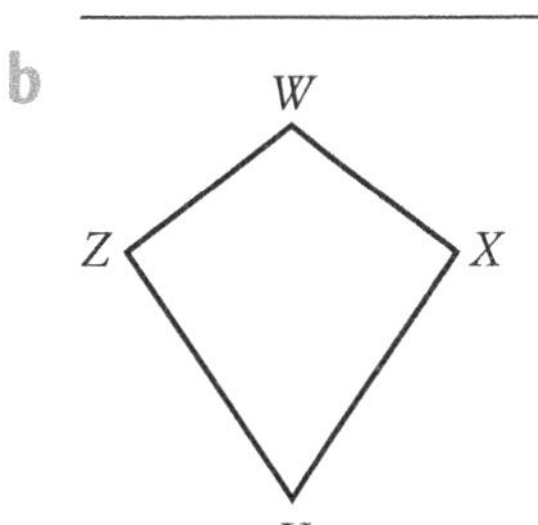

Name of shape: [ ]

Description: ____________________

____

____

____

6 An octagon is shown below.

a How many triangles is the octagon divided into?

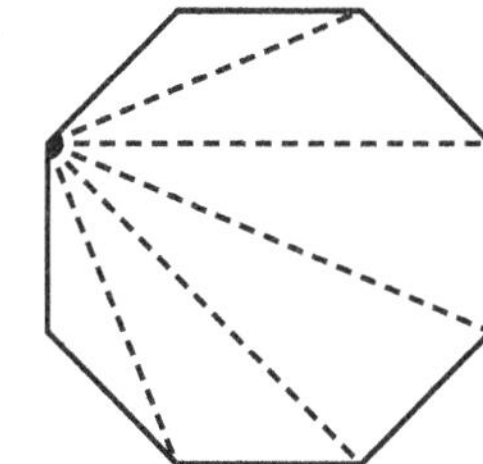

[ ]

b What is the sum of the angles in an octagon?

Tip The angle sum of a polygon can be found by multiplying the number of triangles by 180°.

____ $\times 180° =$ ________

NAPLAN-ready

Shade the box beneath the correct answer.

What is the value of x?

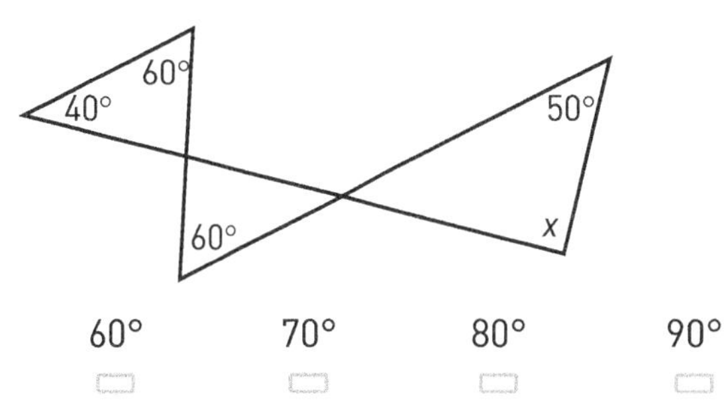

60°	70°	80°	90°
☐	☐	☐	☐

Tip The angles inside a triangle add to 180°. Vertically opposite angles are equal.

8.3 Congruence and transformation

Transformations include *translation* (a slide), *reflection* (a flip) and *rotation* (a turn). Each of these transformations creates a **congruent** figure, which is the same size and shape as the original. We call this figure the *image* of the original.

Writing a congruence statement

The Cartesian plane on the right shows the figure *ABCD translated* 5 units left and 2 units up. This translation can be described as [-5, 2].

[-5, 2] $\rightarrow$ 5 left, 2 up

The figures *ABCD* and *A′B′C′D′* are congruent, therefore a **congruence statement** can be written:

$ABCD \cong A'B'C'D'$

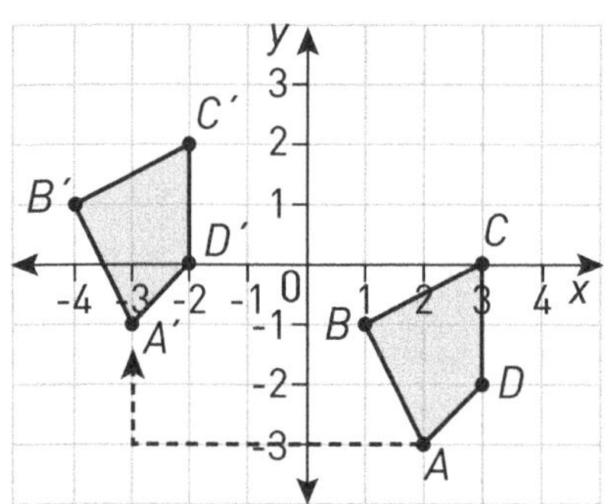

Word Bank

Congruent

➜ Figures that are the same shape and same size are congruent. The orientation and position of a shape does not affect congruence.

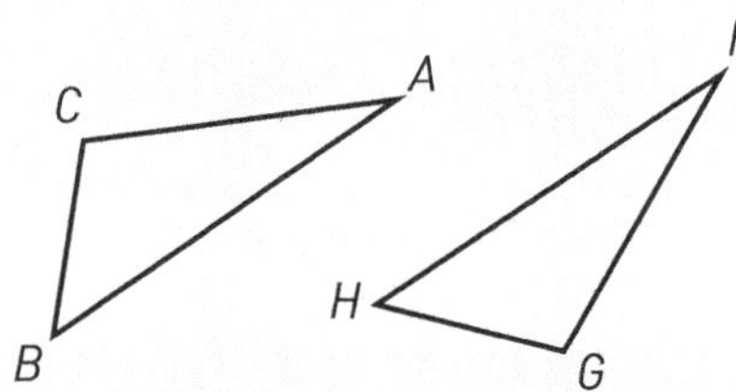

$\Delta ABC \cong \Delta HFG$

The symbol ≅ means 'is congruent to'.

1 What has triangle *ABC* been translated by to produce triangle *A′B′C′*?

Tip Look at one vertex. What translation has happened from *A* to *A′*?

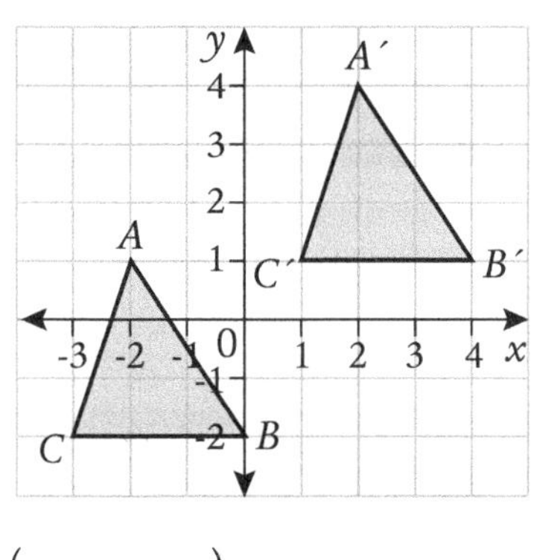

(____, ____)

2 a Translate the shape [3, -1]. Label each vertex of the image with a dash (i.e. $A \rightarrow A'$).

Tip Move one vertex at a time and then join the points with straight lines.

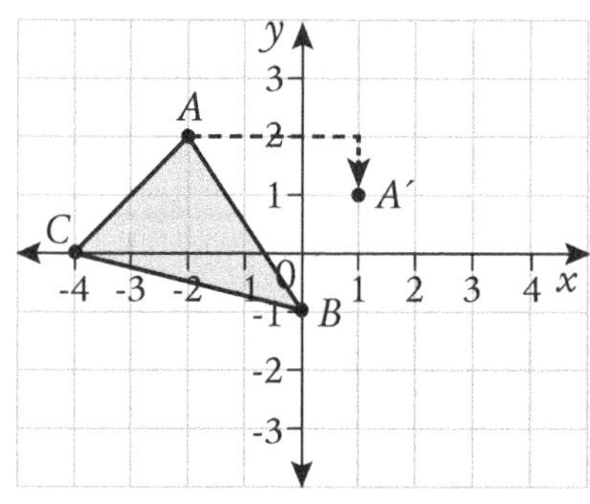

b Write the coordinates of the vertices of the new shape.

A′ (____, ____)

B′ (____, ____)

C′ (____, ____)

3 a Plot the points (2, 2), (0, 0), (-2, 2) and (1, 3). Join with straight lines in order to form a trapezium. Label the vertices in order *W*, *X*, *Y* and *Z*.

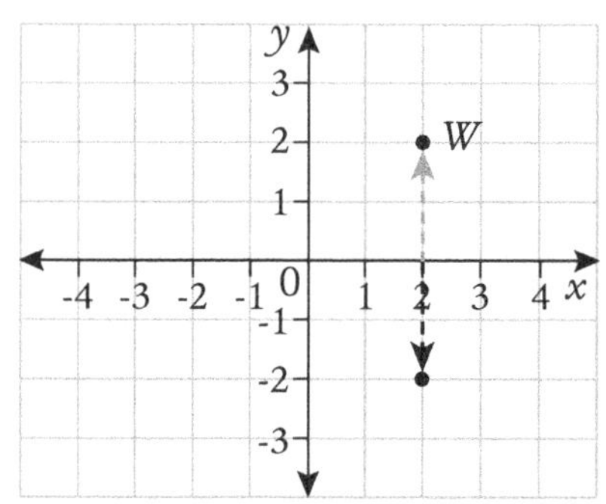

b Reflect the shape drawn in part **a** in the x-axis.

Tip Each vertex in the image must be the same distance from the x-axis as in the original figure.

c Write the coordinates of the vertices of the new shape.

W' (____, ____)

X' (____, ____)

Y' (____, ____)

Z' (____, ____)

4 Rotate ΔRST 90° clockwise about the origin (0, 0).

Tip Draw a line from each vertex to the point of rotation (in this case, (0, 0)). This is the baseline of the 90° angle.

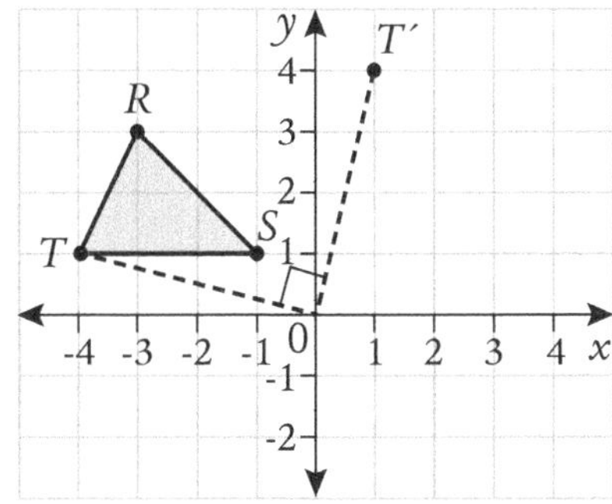

5 **a** On the diagram below, label the matching vertices on the transformed figure using 'dash' notation ($M \leftrightarrow M'$, etc.).

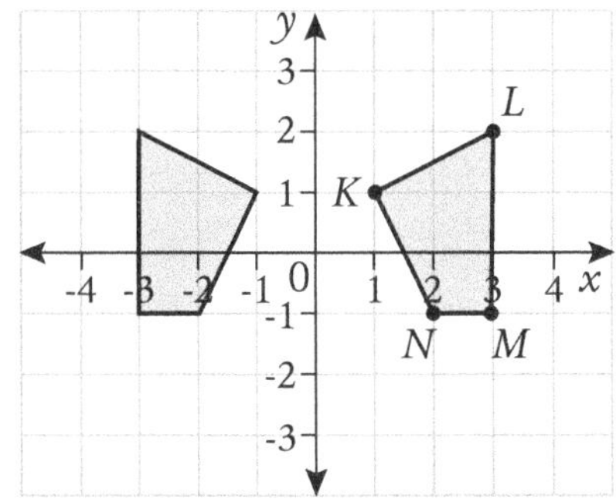

b Circle the transformation that has been applied to the original figure to produce the image.

translation   reflection   rotation

6 The two figures below are congruent.

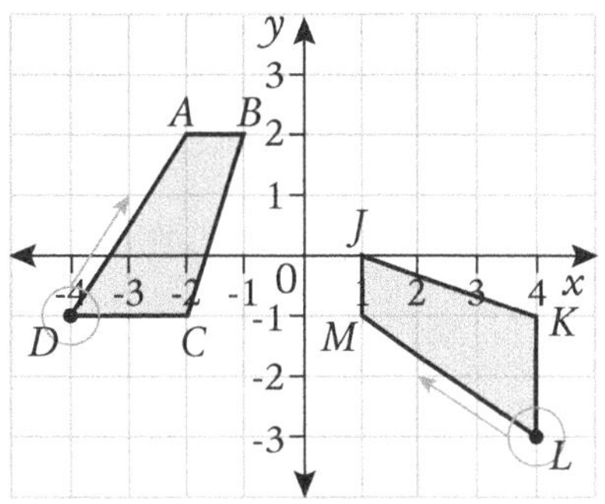

a Pair the matching vertices.

$D \leftrightarrow L$ ____ $\leftrightarrow$ ____

____ $\leftrightarrow$ ____   ____ $\leftrightarrow$ ____

b Which side matches CD?

$CD \leftrightarrow$ ____

c Which angle matches $\angle JKL$?

$\angle JKL \leftrightarrow$ ________

d Write a congruence statement.

Tip When naming congruent figures, the vertices of both figures must be written in the same order.

≅

NAPLAN-ready

Shade the box beneath the correct answer.

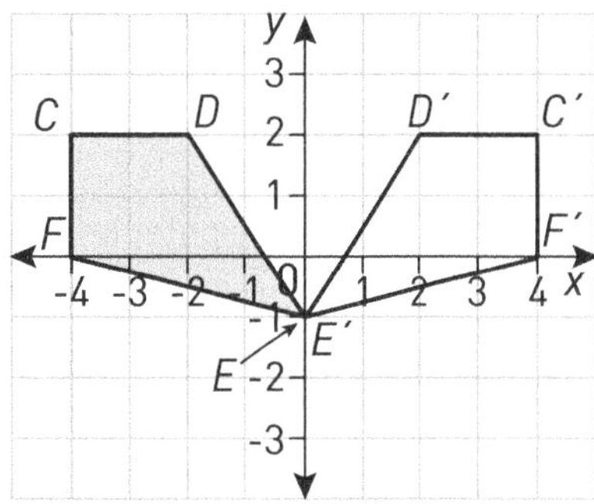

What transformation has been applied to produce the congruent image?

translation ☐   reflection ☐

rotation ☐   reflection and rotation ☐

Tip Look at the position of the matching vertices.

8.4 Congruent triangles

Triangles are congruent if one triangle can be placed on top of the other, with all sides and angles matching up.

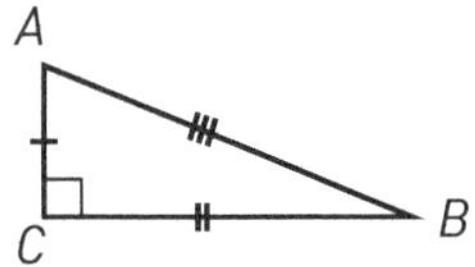

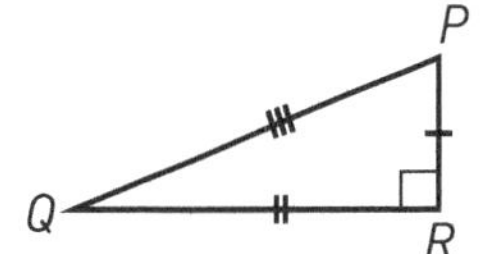

As the two triangles on the left are congruent, a congruency statement can be written.

$\Delta ABC \cong \Delta PQR$

The matching vertices, sides and angles can be determined by the congruency statement.

$A \leftrightarrow P$	vertex *A* matches vertex *P*
$BC \leftrightarrow QR$	side *BC* matches side *QR*
$\angle CAB \leftrightarrow \angle PQR$	angle *CAB* matches angle *PQR*

Congruency tests

There are four tests that can be applied to see if triangles are congruent.

Two triangles are congruent if:

- Side, Side, Side (SSS) — Each pair of matching sides has the same length.
- Side, Angle, Side (SAS) — Two pairs of sides and the included angle are equal.
- Angle, Angle, Side (AAS) — Any two pairs of angles and a pair of matching sides are equal.
- Right angle, Hypotenuse, Side (RHS) — In a right-angled triangle the hypotenuse and one other side are equal.

Example:

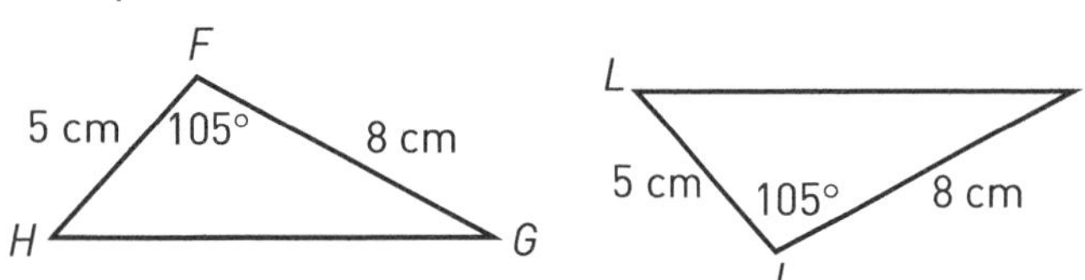

These two triangles are congruent because:

$FG = LK$	(**S**ide)
$\angle JKL = \angle HFG$	(included **A**ngle)
$FH = JL$	(**S**ide)
So, $\Delta FGH \cong \Delta KJL$	(SAS)

Word Bank

Hypotenuse

→ The hypotenuse is the name given to the longest side of a triangle.

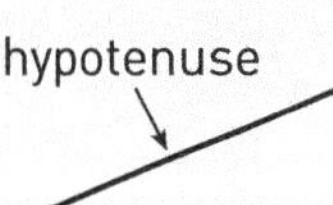

Included angle

→ The included angle is the angle between two known sides.

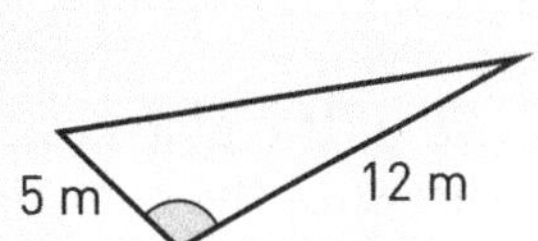

1 The two triangles below are congruent.

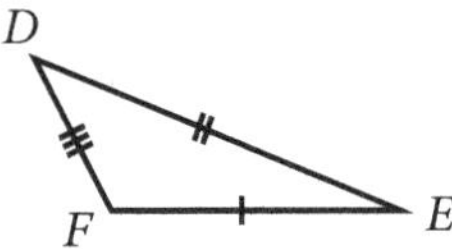

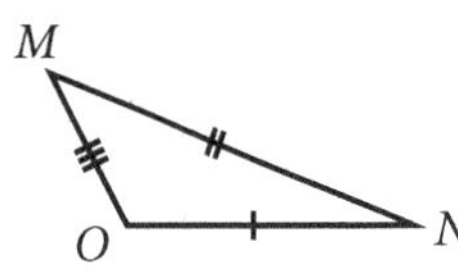

a Match the vertices.

$D \leftrightarrow$ ___ ___ $\leftrightarrow$ ___ ___ $\leftrightarrow$ ___

b Match the sides.

$DE \leftrightarrow$ ___

___ $\leftrightarrow$ ___

___ $\leftrightarrow$ ___

c Write a congruency statement.

Tip Look at the matching vertices. They must be in the same positions in the congruency statement.

Δ ______ $\cong \Delta$ ______

2 Three pieces of information are shown on the triangles below.

> **Tip** Not all sides and angles have to be known to determine if triangles are congruent.

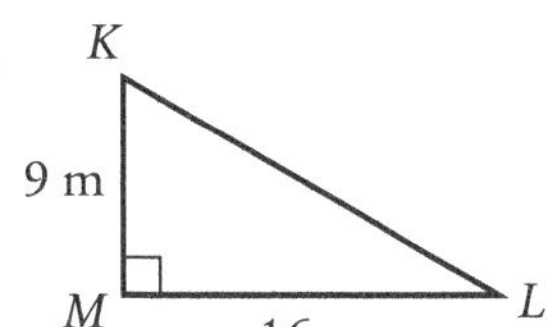

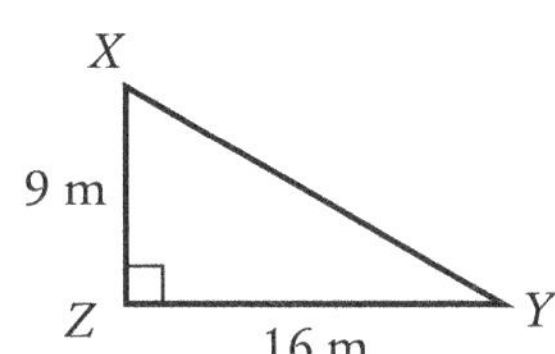

a Complete the following:

$KM \leftrightarrow$ ______ (side)

$\angle KML \leftrightarrow$ ______ (included angle)

$LM \leftrightarrow$ ______ (side)

b Which of the congruency tests does the matching information in part **a** satisfy?

SSS SAS AAS RHS

3 Look at the triangles below.

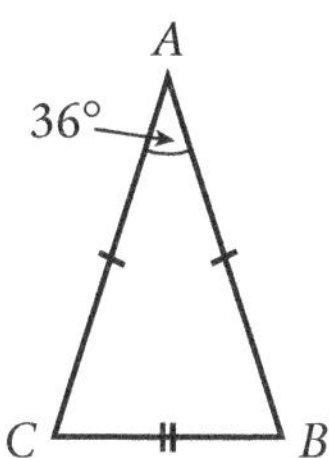

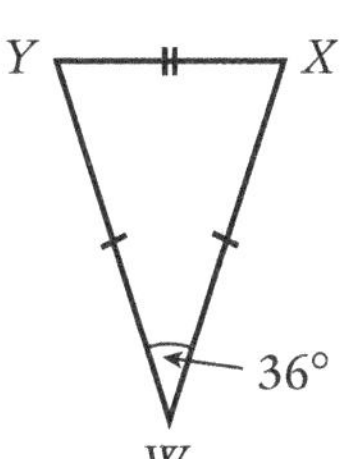

a State the three matching sides to prove congruency using SSS.

______ = ______

______ = ______

______ = ______

b State two matching sides and the included angle to prove congruency using SAS.

______ = ______

______ = ______

______ = ______

c Write a congruency statement for the two triangles, stating one of the tests used to prove it.

Δ ______ $\cong \Delta$ ______ (______)

4 Prove that $\Delta EFG \cong \Delta TUV$

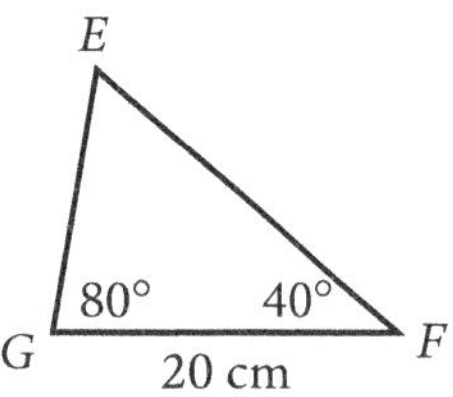

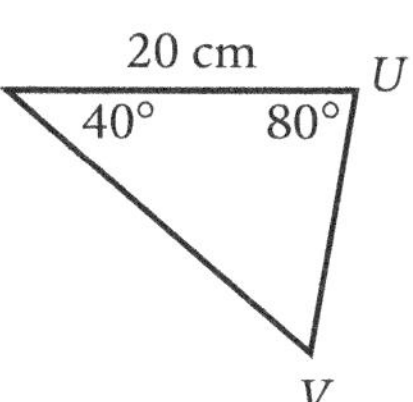

______ = ______ (angle)

______ = ______ (angle)

______ = ______ (side)

$\therefore \Delta$______ $\cong \Delta$______ (___ ___ ___)

5 $\Delta ABC \cong \Delta JKL$. Complete the missing information on each triangle so that all vertices, sides and angles are labelled.

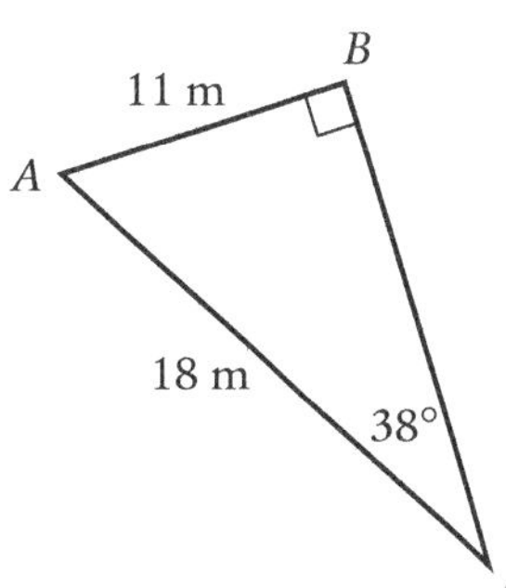

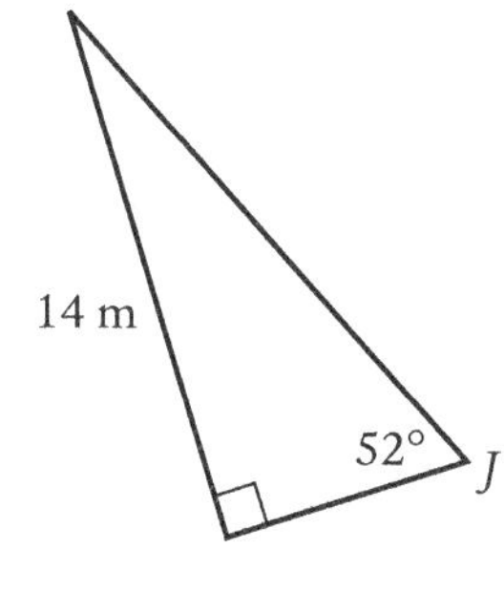

NAPLAN-ready

Shade the box beneath the correct answer.

A parallelogram can be divided into two congruent triangles.

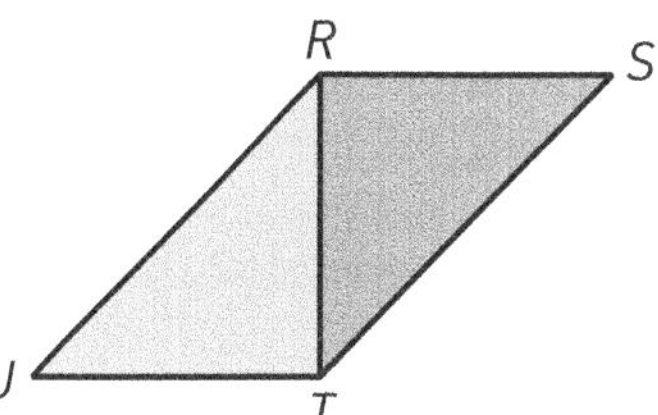

Which of the following congruency statements is correct?

$\Delta RST \cong \Delta RTU$ ☐	$\Delta RST \cong \Delta RUT$ ☐
$\Delta TRS \cong \Delta URT$ ☐	$\Delta RUT \cong \Delta TSR$ ☐

> **Tip** Mark the equal sides and equal angles.

8.5 Congruence and quadrilaterals

A quadrilateral is a four-sided polygon. Some quadrilaterals have special properties.

rectangle	parallelogram	rhombus	kite

Proving special properties

Properties of quadrilaterals, such as equal angles and side lengths, can be proven using knowledge of congruent triangles, angle sums and angles on parallel lines.

All quadrilaterals can be divided into two triangles. To prove a property of a quadrilateral it is useful to first prove that the two triangles are congruent.

e.g. Given that opposite sides of a parallelogram are parallel, prove that opposite sides are equal.

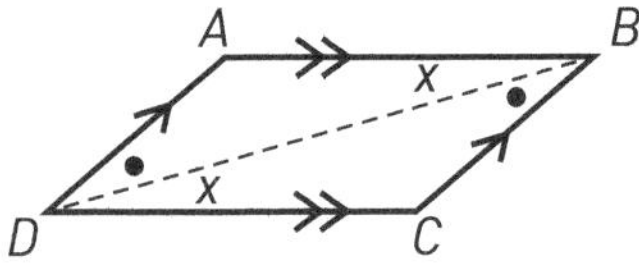

Step 1: Divide the parallelogram into two triangles and prove that the triangles are congruent.

$\angle ADB = \angle CBD$ (alternate **A**ngles)

$\angle ABD = \angle CDB$ (alternate **A**ngles)

$DB = BD$ (common **S**ide)

$\Delta ABD \cong \Delta CDB$ (AAS)

Step 2: Use facts about congruent triangles to prove the special property of the shape.

Matching sides of congruent triangles are equal in length.

$AB = CD$ $AD = CB$

So, opposite sides of a parallelogram are equal.

Word Bank

Alternate angles

→ Alternate angles are on opposite sides of a transversal, between parallel lines. Alternate angles are equal.

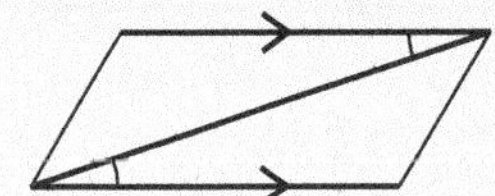

Bisect

→ To bisect is to divide in half.

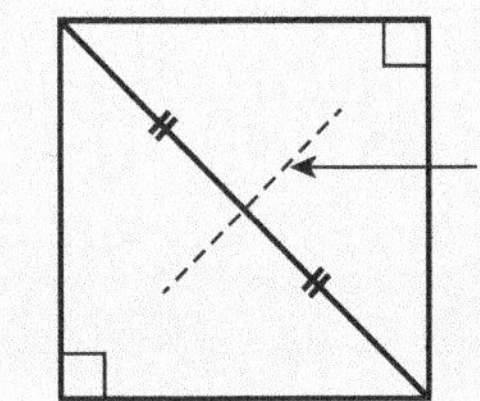

This line is bisecting the diagonal line.

1 Use a single line to divide the following quadrilaterals into two congruent triangles. Mark the shape to show the equal angles and equal lengths, and the parallel sides.

a rectangle

b kite

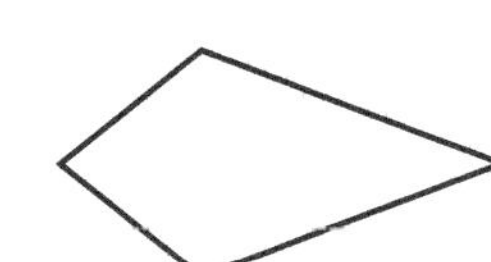

c rhombus **d** parallelogram

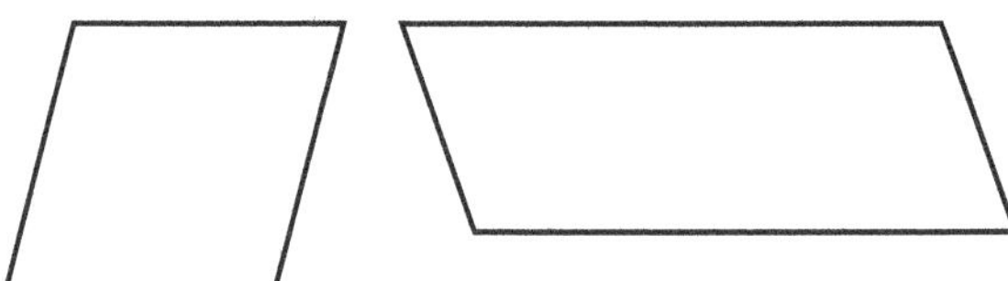

2 A parallelogram is divided into two triangles below.

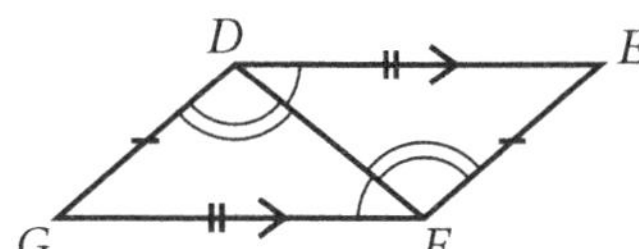

a State three equal side lengths and/or angles of the two triangles that could satisfy one of the congruency tests: SSS, SAS, AAS or RHS

_____ = _____ (   )

_____ = _____ (   )

_____ = _____ (   )

b Write a *congruency statement* for the two triangles, stating the congruency test used.

Δ_____ ≅ Δ_____ (_ _ _)

3 Complete the following to prove that one diagonal will bisect (cut in half) the other diagonal in a rhombus.

a Divide the rhombus below into four triangles using two diagonals and mark equal lengths and angles.

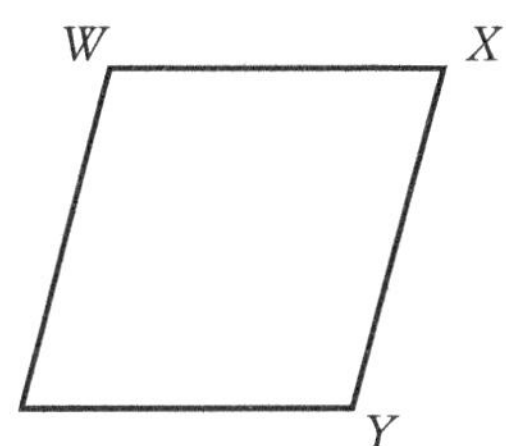

b Prove that the two large triangles formed in a rhombus are congruent.

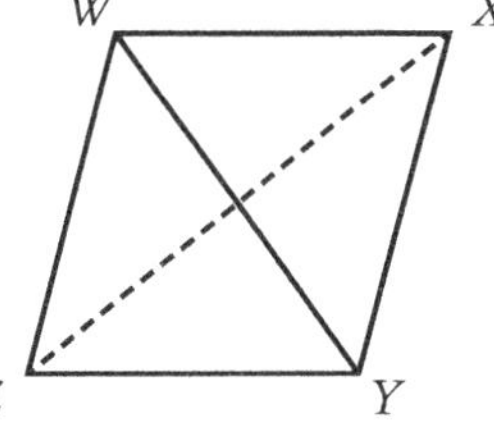

_____ = _____

_____ = _____

_____ = _____

Δ_____ ≅ Δ_____ (_ _ _)

c Prove that the small opposite triangles are congruent.

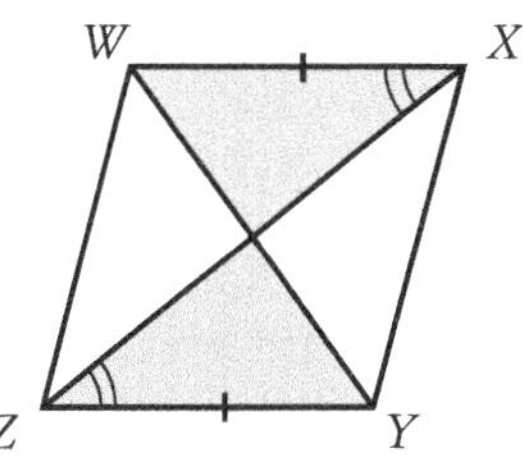

_____ = _____ (side)

_____ = _____ (vertically opposite angles)

_____ = _____ (alternate angles)

Δ_____ ≅ Δ_____ (AAS)

d Prove that one diagonal line will bisect (cut in half) the other diagonal line in a rhombus.

All matching sides of a congruent triangle are equal, so:

XW and XZ are

∴ One diagonal line __________ the other diagonal line.

4 Find the value of the pronumerals.

Tip Look at the special properties of each shape. What have you just proven about a rhombus in Question 3?

a

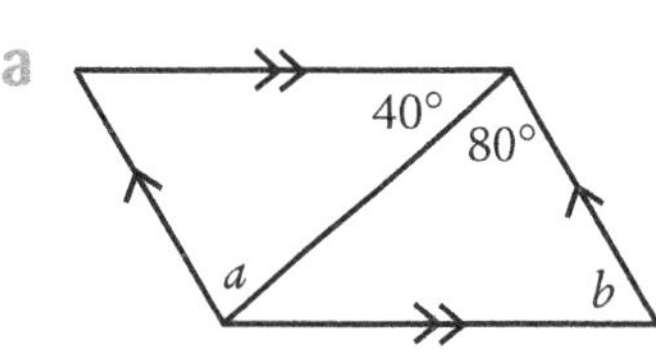

$a =$ _____

$b =$ _____

b

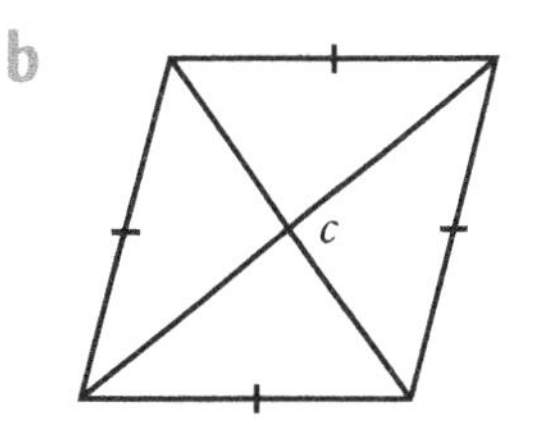

$c =$ _____

c

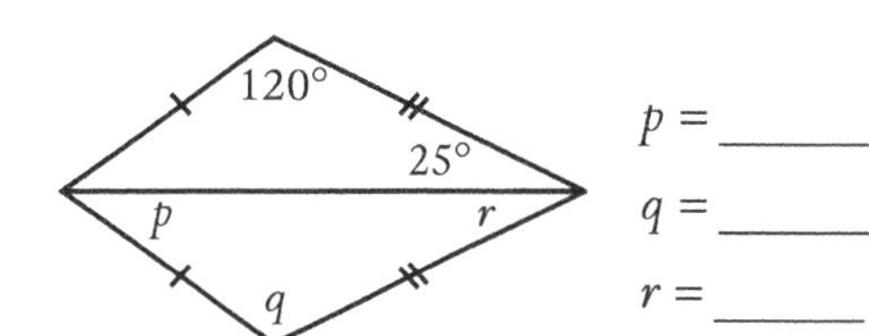

$p =$ _____

$q =$ _____

$r =$ _____

NAPLAN-ready

Shade the box beneath the correct answer.

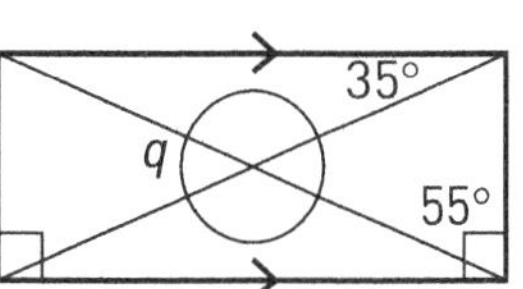

What is the value of q?

35°	55°	70°	110°
☐	☐	☐	☐

Tip Alternate angles are equal. The angles in a triangle add to 180°.

9.1 Population sampling

A **population** is the *entire* group of something such as people, animals, plants, or objects. A **sample** is a portion of the population, which can be used to predict information about the whole population.

e.g. How many students at Overton College have seen all of the Harry Potter movies?

A survey of 16 students can be used to predict the number of students at the school who have seen all of the Harry Potter movies. Of the 16 students, 9 have seen all of the movies.

Yes: $\frac{9}{16} \times 240 = 135$ students

Overton College: 240 students
Sample: 16 students

It is highly unlikely that *exactly* 135 students have seen all of the movies, so a **range** of values is calculated. This could be 5% either side of 135.

5% of $135 = 6.75$
≈ 7

$135 - 7 = 128$
$135 + 7 = 142$

5% 5%
120 130 140 150 160
135

Therefore, we can estimate that between 128 and 142 students have seen all the movies.

Word Bank

Sampling bias

➜ A selected sample that favours or excludes a section of the population can be classed as 'biased' (e.g. a survey conducted at a Farmers' Market on people's daily intake of fruit and vegetables).

Tag and release

➜ A method of estimating the size of a population is known as 'tag and release'. A known number of animals are captured, tagged and released on two separate occasions.

The population can be calculated with the following formula:

$$P = \frac{\text{total in 2nd sample}}{\text{no. of tagged in 2nd sample}} \times \text{tagged animals}$$

1 A ball room at an activity centre contains 600 white, red and black plastic balls.

Population = 600

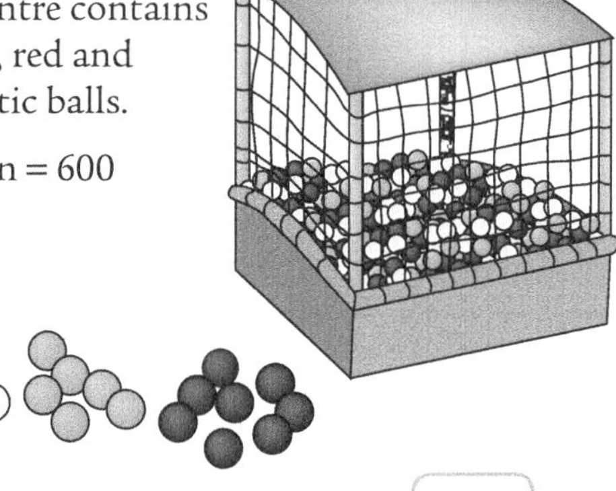

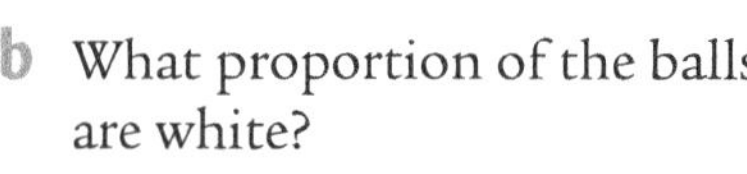

a What is the size of the sample? ☐

b What proportion of the balls are white? $\frac{\square}{24}$

c Estimate the number of white balls in the ball room.

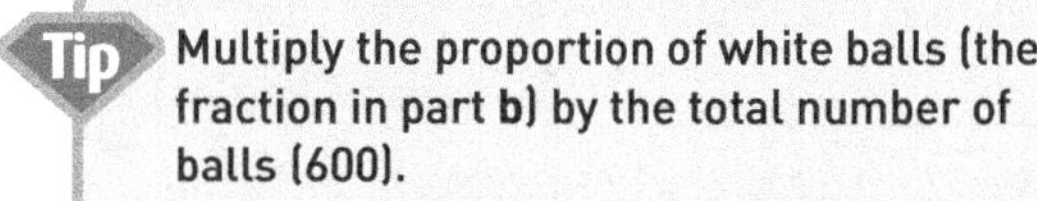

Tip Multiply the proportion of white balls (the fraction in part b) by the total number of balls (600).

☐ × ___ = ☐ white balls in the ball room.

2 A lolly bag contains 120 yellow, orange and green chocolate lollies. The bag is opened and 20 lollies are poured out.

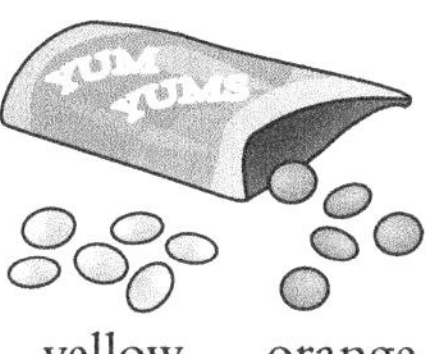

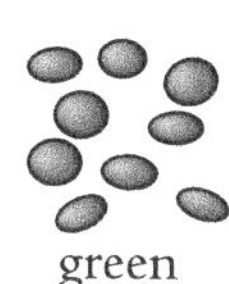

Fill in the table to estimate the number of each colour in the bag.

	Proportion of sample	Estimated number per bag
Yellow	$\frac{6}{20}$	$\frac{6}{20} \times 120 = 36$
Orange	$\frac{\_\_}{20}$	
Green	$\frac{\_\_}{20}$	
	Total	120

3 What is a reasonable range of values for the number of yellow chocolate lollies in the large bag in Question **2**?

Tip **Add and subtract 5% to the number calculated in Question 2. Round to the nearest whole number.**

5% of 36 = ______

36 − ______ = ______

36 + ______ = ______

Therefore, it is estimated that there are between ______ and ______ yellow chocolate lollies in the bag.

4 State if the following survey methods are *biased* or *fair*.

Tip **A survey is biased if people are excluded from the sampling process.**

a You want to know the distance people travel from home to work, so you randomly select people at a cafe during lunch hour.

biased / fair

b The owner of a canned fruit factory wants to know the proportion of flawed or faulty products that are being produced. He checks every 10th can on the conveyance belt.

biased / fair

5 A sample of 12 saltwater crocodiles was tagged in an area along the Nesbit River in Queensland. In a second sample of 20 crocodiles, caught 3 weeks later, 4 crocodiles had tags.

Complete the following.

a How many crocodiles were tagged? ______

b How many crocodiles were in the second sample? ____

c How many crocodiles had tags in the second sample? ______

d Estimate the population of crocodiles in that area.

Tip **Substitute the values calculated in part a–c into the formula.**

$$P = \frac{\text{total in 2nd sample}}{\text{no. of tagged in 2nd sample}} \times \text{tagged animals}$$

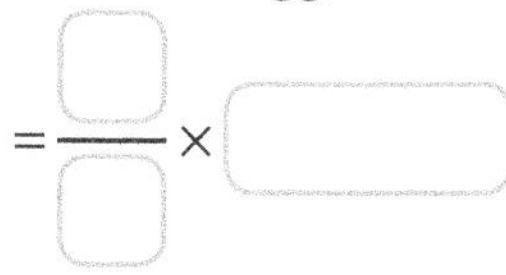

Therefore, an estimation of the number of crocodiles in that area of the Nesbit River is ______.

NAPLAN-ready

Shade the box beneath the correct answer.

A 4 kg bag of mixed nuts contains cashews, brazil nuts and almonds. The bag contains 800 nuts in total. A sample of 30 nuts is scooped from the bag.

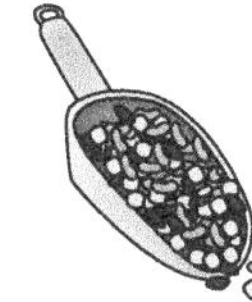

There were 12 brazil nuts in the sample. What is a good estimate of the number of brazil nuts in the 4 kg bag?

76 to 80	96 to 104
☐	☐
152 to 168	304 to 336
☐	☐

Tip **What fraction of the nuts in the sample were brazil nuts?**

9.2 Using sample measures of centre and spread

The data collected from a survey or census can be analysed to produce meaningful statistics. This includes finding **measures of centre** (mean, median and mode) and **measures of spread** (range).

e.g. The data values below show the number of hours of sleep school children had on a school night.

10 11 8 9 10 9 9 8

Calculate the following statistics.

- **Mean** is calculated by adding all the data values and then dividing the total by the number of data values.

$$\text{Mean} = \frac{\text{sum of all data values}}{\text{number of data values}}$$

$$= \frac{10+11+8+9+10+9+9+8}{8} = \frac{74}{8}$$

$= 9.25$ hours

- **Mode** is the most common value.

8 8 **9 9 9** 10 10 11

The modal hours of sleep is 9 hours.

- **Median** is the middle value, where half the values are lower and half the values are higher. The data must first be written in ascending order.

8 8 9 9 9 10 10 11

Median: $\frac{9+9}{2} = \frac{18}{2} = 9$ hours

- **Range** is calculated by subtracting the lowest value from the highest value.

$11 - 8 = 3$ hours

Word Bank

Outlier

➜ Outliers are data values that are outside the range of the rest of the data. They can be a lot less or a lot more than the other data values.

(4) 11 12 12 14 15

↑

outlier

1 The data set below shows the number of siblings that each member of a group of friends has.

2 0 0 1 2 4 1 1

a Calculate the mean.

$$\text{Mean} = \frac{\text{Sum of all data values}}{\text{Number of data values}}$$

$= \frac{\_+\_+\_+\_+\_+\_+\_+\_}{\_}$

$= \frac{\_\_}{\_\_}$

= ☐ siblings

b Find the median

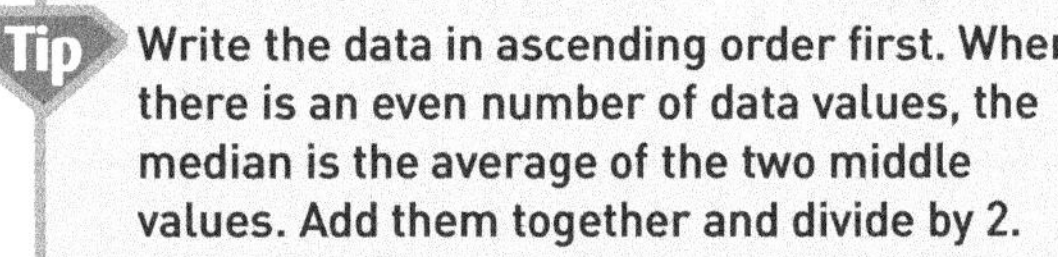
Tip Write the data in ascending order first. When there is an even number of data values, the median is the average of the two middle values. Add them together and divide by 2.

____, ____, ____, ____, ____, ____, ____, ____

Median = ☐ siblings

c What is the mode? ☐ siblings

d Calculate the range.

____ − ____ = ☐ siblings

2 The time (in minutes) taken for 10 students to travel to school are shown below.

12 15 8 3 10 23 5 12 11 16

a Calculate the mean

$\text{Mean} = \frac{☐}{☐}$

= ☐ minutes

b Calculate the median. [ ] minutes

c What is the mode of the data? [ ] minutes

3 One data value is different between Set 1 and Set 2 below.

Set 1: 2 2 3 4 4 4 6 7 9 15

Set 2: 2 2 3 4 4 4 6 7 9 10

a For each set of data, calculate:

i the mean

Set 1:

Set 2:

ii the median

Set 1:

Set 2:

iii the range

Set 1:

Set 2:

b Completing the following table using the statistics calculated in part **a**.

	Mean	Median	Mode	Range
Set 1				
Set 2				

What differences to the measure of centre and the range did one data value make?

____

____

4 Circle the outlier in each set of data.

a 9, 11, 12, 3, 15, 17, 12

b 23, 29, 36, 24, 41, 27, 27, 64, 41

5 The following data shows the amount of money ($) students brought to school to spend at the canteen.

5, 5, 5, 4, 6, 4, 5, 15, 6, 5

a Find the:

i mean = [ ] = [ ]

ii median = [ ]

iii mode = [ ]

iv range = [ ]

b Identify the outlier in the data.

Outlier = [ ]

c Remove the outlier from the data and then find the following.

i Mean = [ ] = [ ]

ii Median = [ ]

iii Mode = [ ]

iv Range = [ ]

d Complete the following table using the statistics calculated in part **a** and **c**.

	Mean	Median	Mode	Range
10 students (with outlier)				
10 students (with outlier)				

e Describe the effect the outlier had on the statistics.

____

____

NAPLAN-ready

Shade the box beneath the correct answer.

A mistake was noticed in a set of values after the statistics had been calculated. The incorrect value (11) was replaced with the correct value (17).

~~11~~ 17 18 18 20 21

Mean = 17.6 Median = 18

Mode = 18 Range = 21 - 11 = 10

The incorrect value will have the greatest effect on which statistic?

Mean	Median	Mode	Range
☐	☐	☐	☐

Tip Calculate the new statistics. Look at the changes.

9.3 Frequency tables and graphs

Data can be organised into a **frequency table**, a table that records the frequency of the different data values. This information can then be graphed to give a visual image of the data.

Number of tickets bought per customer at the cinema

2 2 3 2 2
1 4 3 2 2
2 2 5 1 2
3 2 2 3 2

→

Tickets purchased	Tally	Frequency
1	||	2
2	𝍸 𝍸 ||	12
3	||||	4
4	|	1
5	|	1
	Total:	20

Frequency column graph

A frequency column graph is used to visually represent **categorical** data.

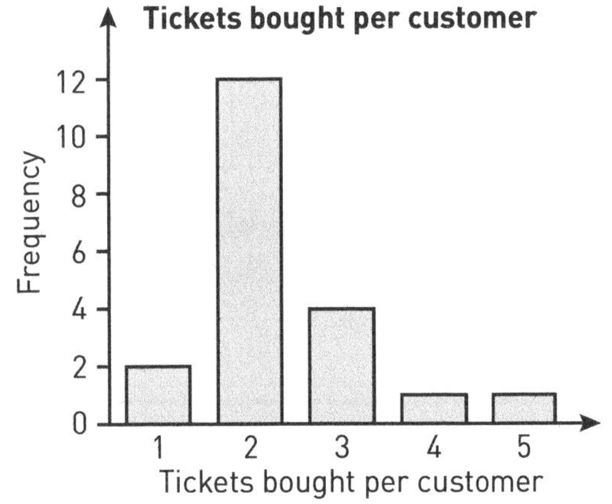

Histogram

A histogram is used to visually represent both single and grouped **numerical** data. A histogram shows the spread of the data.

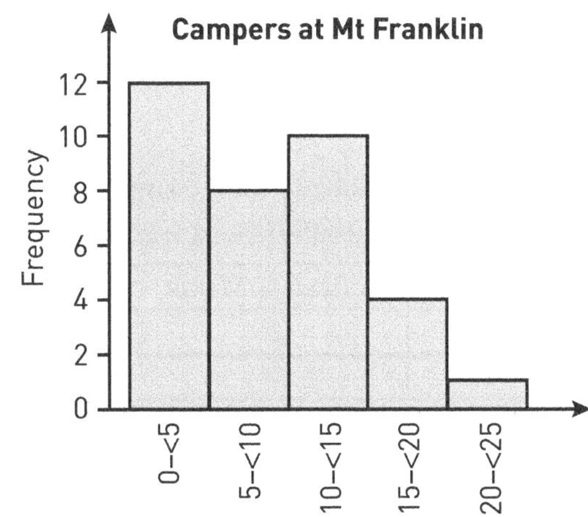

0–<5 means 'from 0 to less than 5'. A histogram does not have gaps between the columns.

Word Bank

Class interval

→ Large data sets can be grouped into class intervals such as groups of 5 or 10 (e.g. 15–<20 means data between 15 and less than 20).

Categorical data

→ Categorical data is data that is divided into categories such as favourite reading material (newspaper, magazines, novels, blogs etc.).

Numerical data

→ Numerical data can be counted or measured.

Discrete numerical data is counted (e.g. the number of participants in a fun run).

Continuous numerical data is measured (e.g. length, height, weight or time).

1 The number of slices of pizza eaten by customers ordering the 'all-you-can-eat' meal deal are shown below.

Slices of pizza	Frequency
3	5
4	18
5	14
6	8
7	3
8	2

a Draw a column frequency graph of the above data. Give the graph a title and label the axes.

Tip: To find a good scale for the vertical axis, look at the frequency values in the frequency table. Would a scale of 1, 2, 5 or 10 be best?

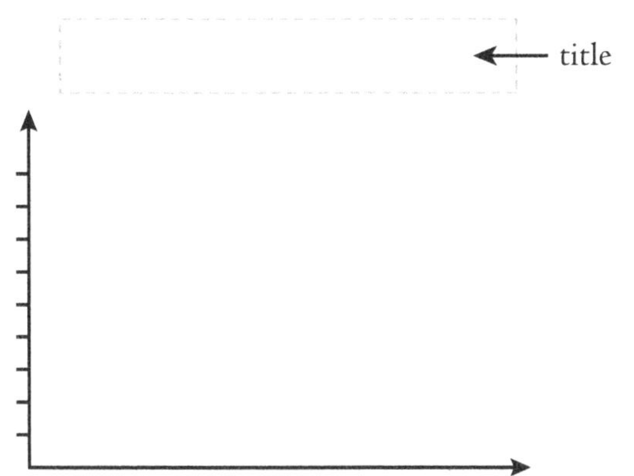

b How many people were in the sample? ______

2 Year 8 students with mobile phones were asked how many text messages they sent in a day. The results are as follows.

2	7	5	11	3	5	26	14	4	8
1	15	16	7	12	20	3	15	21	15
14	23	9	4	4	16	9	23	5	12

a Calculate the range.

Range = ____ − ____

= ☐

b Use the range to select a suitable class interval.

Tip Class intervals are most commonly a factor or multiple of 10 (1, 2, 5, 10, 20, etc.). Divide the range by each of these class intervals to see which will give between 5 and 10 groups?

e.g. Intervals of 1 → $\frac{\text{range}}{1} = \frac{25}{1} = 20$ groups (too many)

i Intervals of 2 →

ii Intervals of 5 →

iii Intervals of 10 →

The most suitable class interval is ________.

c Construct a frequency table.

Texts sent per day	Tally	Frequency
0 −<5		
	Total	

d Draw a histogram of the grouped data.

Tip All graphs must have:
- a title
- labelled axes
- evenly spaced scales on both axes.

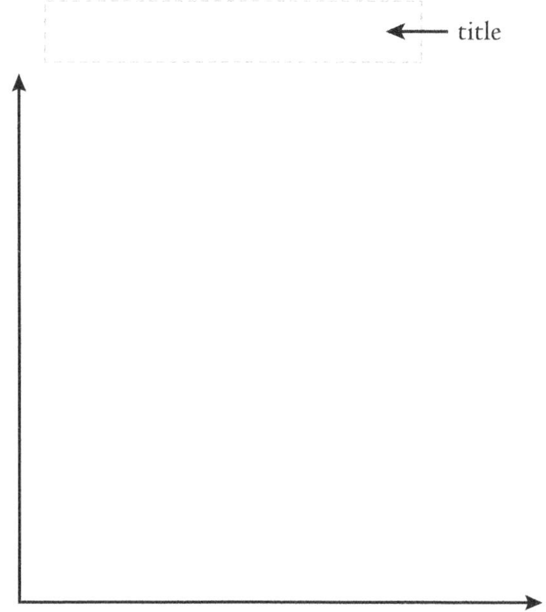

NAPLAN-ready

Shade the box beneath the correct answer.

The number of people in each car entering the Burnley tunnel was recorded over a 10-minute period. The results are shown below.

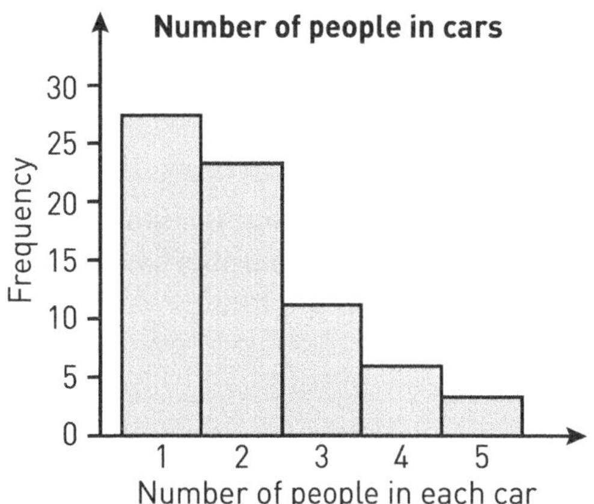

How many cars were in the sample?

5	28	68	134
☐	☐	☐	☐

Tip Add the frequencies.

9.4 Statistics from grouped data

From grouped data we can find statistics such as the mean, median class interval and modal class interval.

Year 8 students were asked to time their morning shower. Their results are shown on the right.

Length of shower (minutes)	Frequency
0–<5	6
5–<10	14
10–<15	8
15–<20	2

Mean

To find the mean, find the total of the frequency column and the total of the $f \times x$ (frequency × class centre) column.

Length of shower (minutes)	x	Frequency	$f \times x$
0–<5	2.5	6	15
5–<10	7.5	14	105
10–<15	12.5	8	100
15–<20	17.5	2	35
		$\Sigma f = 30$	$\Sigma fx = 255$

$$\text{Mean} = \frac{\Sigma fx}{\Sigma f}$$
$$= \frac{\text{sum of } fx}{\text{sum of } f}$$
$$= \frac{255}{30}$$
$$= 8.5$$

∴ The mean shower time was 8.5 minutes.

Median class interval

The median class interval is the class interval that contains the middle value. The sum of the frequency column, Σf, is the number of data values. It is referred to as n.

The middle value is the $\left(\frac{n+1}{2}\right)$th value.

$\frac{30+1}{2} = 15.5$ ← The middle value is half-way between the 15th and 16th value.

Find this value by looking at the frequency table in the frequency column.

∴ The median class interval is 5–<10 minutes.

Modal class interval

This is the most common class interval in the category with the highest frequency.

The modal class interval is 5–<10 minutes with 14 people.

Word Bank

Σ (sum)

➜ The Greek symbol, Σ (sigma), stands for 'sum'. It is used when all numbers have been added together to find the total.

Class centre

➜ The class centre is the midpoint (halfway) of a class interval. To find the class centre, add the two end points of the class interval and divide by 2.

The class centre of the interval 5–<10

$$= \frac{5+10}{2}$$
$$= 15 \div 2$$
$$= 7.5$$

1 Find the class centre of the following groups.

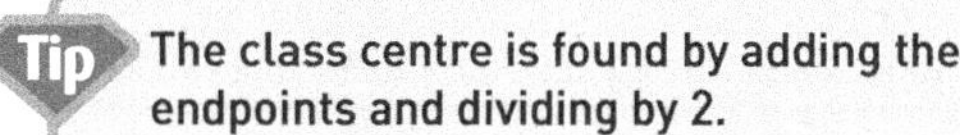

Tip The class centre is found by adding the endpoints and dividing by 2.

a 5–9 → $\frac{5+9}{2} = \frac{\_\_}{\_\_} =$ ☐

b 10–19 → $\frac{\_\_+\_\_}{\_\_} = \frac{\_\_}{\_\_}$ ☐

c 10–<20

d 25–<30

2 The number of rooms occupied each night at Eco Resort was recorded for the summer period.

a Complete the table.

Number of rooms occupied at Eco Resort	x	f	$f \times x$
0–9	4.5	12	
10–19		28	
20–29		40	980
30–39		10	
		$\Sigma f=$	$\Sigma fx=$

b Calculate the mean, rounded to two decimal places.

$$\text{Mean} = \frac{\Sigma fx}{\Sigma f}$$

=

= ☐ (2 d.p.)

c What is the median class interval? _________

Tip To find the middle value in the table, add 1 to the frequency total (Σf) and divide by 2.

d What is the modal class interval? _________

3 Des sells his honey at the local farmers' market. Weekly sales of jars are shown below.

36	23	40	42	33	38	48	27
32	45	46	32	14	43	49	36
31	45	25	21	26	34	39	41
44	26	23	42	46	29		

a Complete a frequency table.

Number of jars of honey sold	x	Tally	f	$f \times x$
10–<20	15			
20–<30				
30–<40				
40–<50				
			$\Sigma f=$	$\Sigma fx=$

b Calculate the mean and round to the nearest whole number.

$$\text{Mean} = \frac{\Sigma fx}{\Sigma f}$$

= __________

= __________

c What is the median class interval? _________

d What is the modal class interval? _________

e Draw a histogram for the data.

NAPLAN-ready

Shade the box beneath the correct answer.

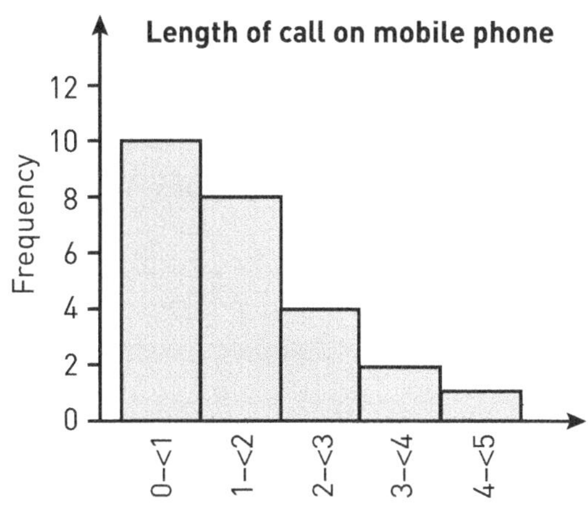

What is the median class interval?

0–<1 minutes ☐	1–<2 minutes ☐
2–<3 minutes ☐	3–<4 minutes ☐

Tip Find the middle value of the total number of values first. In which class interval is the middle value?

9.5 Understanding probability

Probability is a value between 0 and 1 given to the likelihood of a particular event happening, where 0 is impossible and 1 is certain to happen. Each trial of an experiment has **outcomes**. When rolling a die, the *possible outcomes* are 1, 2, 3, 4, 5 and 6. This is called the **sample space**.

Calculating probability

For a single roll of a die, the probability of rolling a 5 is $\frac{1}{6}$, where:

- 1 is the number of *successful* outcomes in the event (only one 5 on a die)
- 6 is the number of *possible* outcomes in the event 1, 2, 3, 4, 5, 6.

The formula for calculating probability is:

$$\text{Pr(event)} = \frac{\text{number of successful outcomes}}{\text{total number of outcomes}}$$

Complement

The results of an experiment can be divided into two complementary events—a particular outcome happens, or doesn't happen.

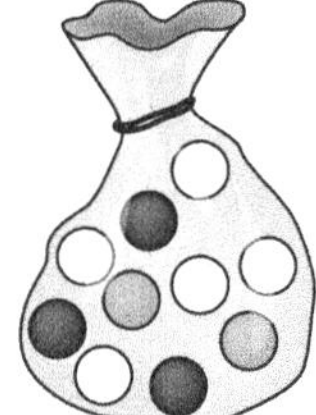

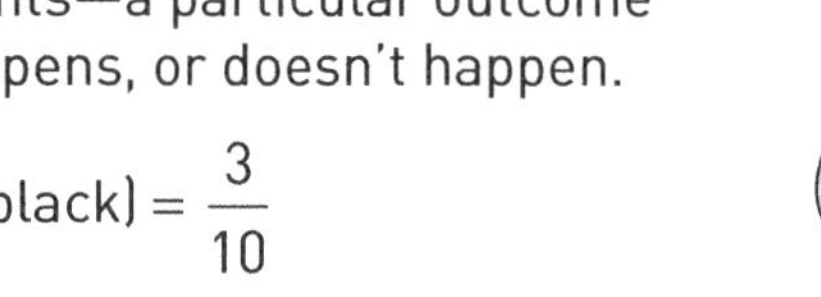

$\text{Pr(black)} = \frac{3}{10}$

$\text{Pr(not black)} = \frac{7}{10}$

The probability of an event and its **complement** always add up to 1.

1

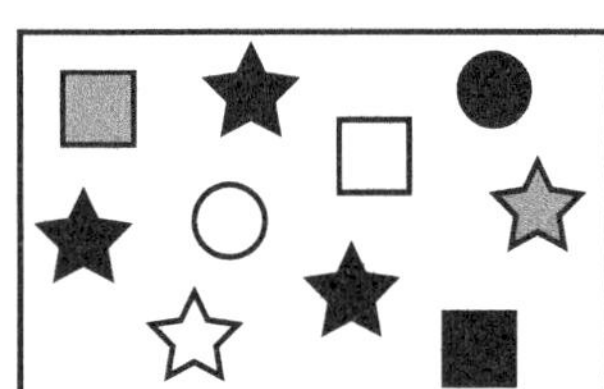

a How many shapes are there? ______

b A shape is picked from the box. What is the probability it will be:

i a square

Pr(square) = $\frac{\square}{\square}$

ii *not* a star

Pr(not a star) = $\frac{\square}{\square} = \frac{\_}{\_}$

iii grey

Pr(grey) = $\frac{\square}{\square} = \frac{\_}{\_}$

iv *not* white

Pr(not white) = $\frac{\square}{\square}$

2 In the school SRC, there are 6 students with blonde hair, 2 students with red hair, 5 students with brown hair and 3 students with black hair.

a Draw a diagram of the above information.

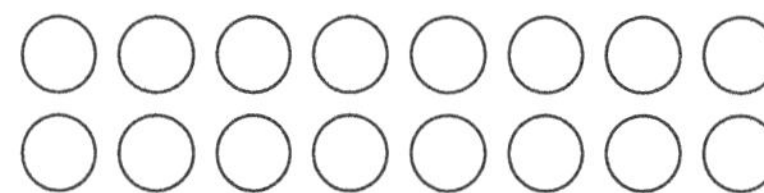

b One student was selected at random to be the spokesperson. What is the probability they will have:

i brown hair

Pr(brown) = $\frac{\square}{\square}$

ii *not* blonde hair

Pr(not blonde) = $\frac{\square}{\square} = \frac{\_}{\_}$

iii *not* brown or red hair

Pr(not brown or red) = $\frac{\square}{\square}$

3 a State the sample space for the following spinner.

> **Tip** The sample space is a list of all possible outcomes.

Sample space:

____, ____, ____, ____,

____, ____, ____, ____

b How many possible outcomes are there? ____

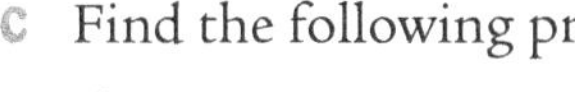

c Find the following probabilities.

i not spinning a 3

Pr(not 3) = $\frac{\square}{\square}$

ii spinning an odd number

Pr(odd number) = $\frac{\square}{\square} = \frac{\_}{\_}$

iii spinning a number less than 6

Pr(<6) = $\frac{\square}{\square}$

4 A pack of memory cards consists of 12 matching pairs. They are arranged face down.

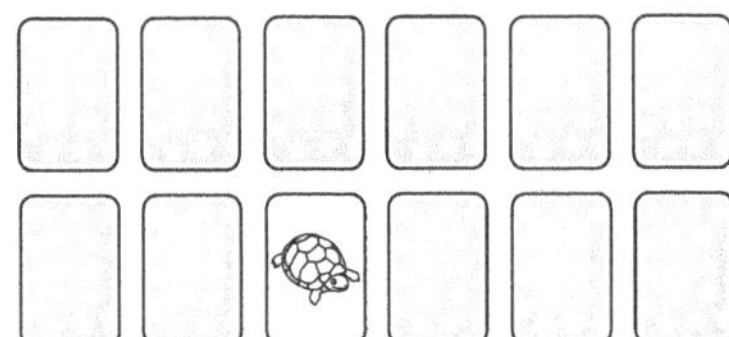

You turn over a turtle, as shown. What is the probability of turning over the matching turtle?

____

5 Mystery flights involve flying to unknown destination in Australia. A mystery flight is about to take off from Melbourne airport.

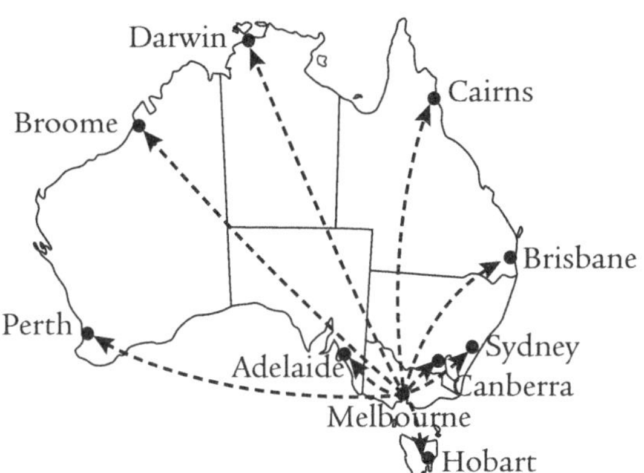

Find the probability of the flight arriving:

a in Hobart

Pr(Hobart) = $\frac{\square}{\square}$

b in an eastern state (Qld, NSW, ACT, Vic, Tas)

Pr(eastern state) = $\frac{\square}{\square}$

c not in Perth

Pr(not Perth) = $\frac{\square}{\square}$

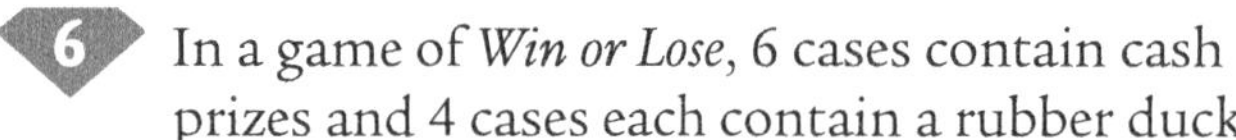

6 In a game of *Win or Lose*, 6 cases contain cash prizes and 4 cases each contain a rubber duck.

A contestant selects one case at a time to be opened. Once a case is opened, it stays open. They will win the amount in the last remaining case. Four cases have already been opened.

What is the probability of the contestant not opening a case containing a rubber duck on their next turn?

____

NAPLAN-ready

Shade the box beneath the correct answer.

On a school camp, students are organised into four activities: 8 students are rafting, 10 students are rock climbing, 15 students are hut building and 12 are bushwalking.

If one student is selected at random, what is the probability they will *not* be hut building?

$\frac{1}{3}$	$\frac{2}{5}$	$\frac{3}{5}$	$\frac{2}{3}$
☐	☐	☐	☐

> **Tip** How many students are hut building? How many students altogether?

9.6 Theoretical probability for single-step experiments

A single-step experiment is an act of doing something once such as throwing a die, spinning a spinner or pulling out a single card from a pack of cards.

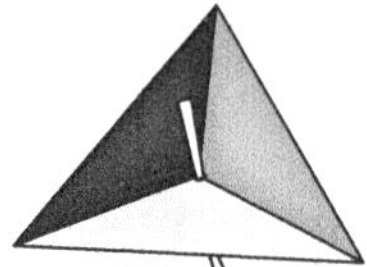

Sample space: 1, 2, 3, 4, 5, 6

Sample space: white, grey, black

Each possible outcome above has an equal chance of occurring. The probability of each outcome can be calculated **theoretically**, which means without performing an experiment.

Calculating theoretical probability

To calculate the probability of an outcome, two pieces of information need to be known:

- the number of *successful* outcomes
- the number of *possible* outcomes.

Probability can be calculated using the following formula:

$$\text{Pr(event)} = \frac{\text{number of successful outcomes}}{\text{total number of outcomes}}$$

e.g. A 6-sided die is rolled. What is the probability of rolling a number less than 5?

Sample space: 1, 2, 3, 4, 5, 6

∴ There are 6 *possible* outcomes

Successful outcomes (rolling a number less than 5): 1, 2, 3, 4

∴ There are 4 *successful* outcomes

$$\text{Pr}(<5) = \frac{4}{6} = \frac{2}{3}$$

Simplify if possible.

1 State the sample space of the following situations.

a Spinning the spinner once and noting the number on which it lands.

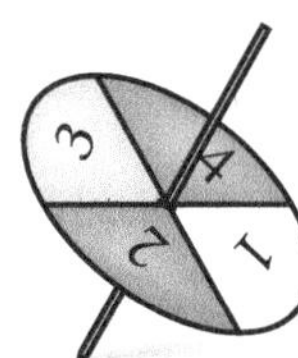

Sample space: ____, ____, ____, ____

b Tossing a coin and noting the face on which it lands.

Sample space: ________, ________

c Selecting one ball from the bag and noting its colour.

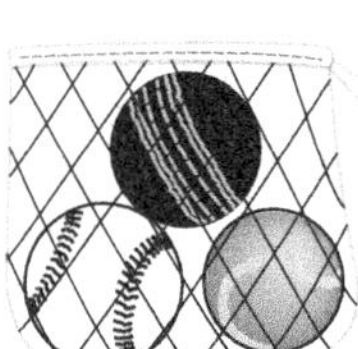

Sample space: ________, ________, ________

2 **a** For the spinner shown, list the sample space.

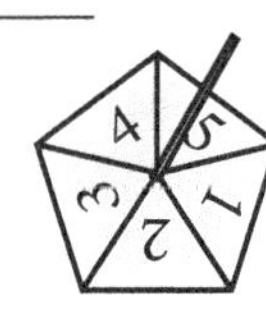

∴ the number of possible outcomes is ____.

b Calculate the following probabilities.

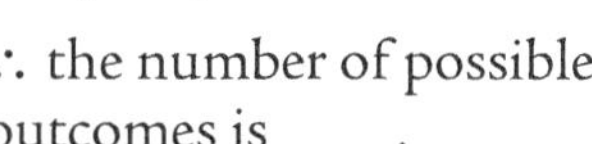

Tip The *successful* outcomes are shown in brackets.

i $\text{Pr}(4) = \frac{}{5}$

ii Pr(number greater than 2) =

iii Pr(not a 1) =

iv Pr(even number) =

3 A pack of cards consists of:

- 52 cards
- four suits (♠ and ♣ are black and ♥ and ♦ are red)
- 13 cards in each suit: Ace, 2, 3, 4, 5, 6, 7, 8, 9, 10, Jack, Queen and King.

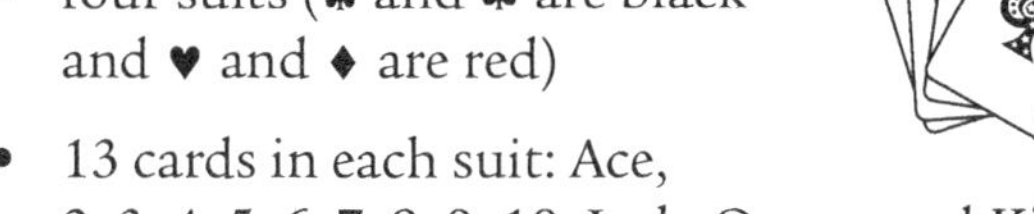

a What is the number of possible outcomes when drawing one card from a standard pack of cards? ______

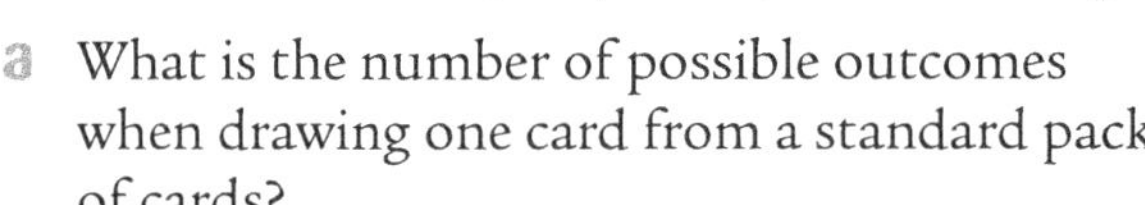

b For a magic trick, an audience member is asked to select one card from a standard pack of cards. What is the probability that the card is a:

i heart

$$\text{Pr(heart)} = \frac{\text{number of hearts}}{\text{total number of cards}}$$

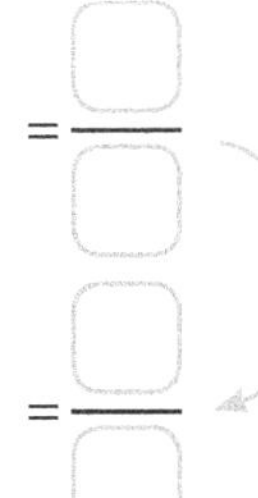

$= \frac{\square}{\square}$ Simplify the fraction

$= \frac{\square}{\square}$

ii 6

$$\text{Pr(6)} = \frac{\text{number of 6s}}{\text{total number of cards}}$$

$= \frac{\square}{\square}$

$= \frac{\square}{\square}$

iii not an ace

Pr(not an ace)

$$= \frac{\text{number of cards that are not an ace}}{\text{total number of cards}}$$

$= \frac{\square}{\square}$

$= \frac{\square}{\square}$

4 A pencil case is filled with pens, pencils and highlighters.

It is known that:

- Pr(pencil) = 0.5
- Pr(pen) = 0.1
- Pr(highlighter) = 0.4

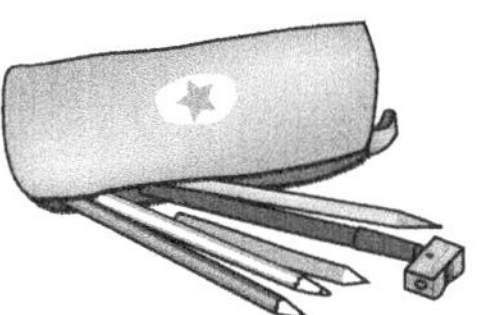

Tip Probabilities can be written as a fraction, decimal or percentage. The decimal number $0.3 = \frac{3}{10}$ is '3 out of 10'.

If one item was selected from the pencil case at random, find:

a Pr(not a pencil)

1 − ____ = $\square$

b Pr(pen or pencil)

____ + ____ = $\square$

c Pr(not a highlighter nor a pencil)

____ + ____ = $\square$

1 − ____ = $\square$

NAPLAN-ready

Shade the box beneath the correct answer.

A bag contains eighteen apples of three different varieties: Pink Lady, Royal Gala and Golden Delicious.

For an apple selected at random, the following probabilities are known:

$$\text{Pr(Pink Lady)} = \frac{1}{6}$$

$$\text{Pr(not a Golden Delicious)} = \frac{4}{9}$$

How many Royal Gala apples are in the bag?

5	7	8	11
☐	☐	☐	☐

Tip How many apples are Pink Lady? How many are Golden Delicious?

9.7 Venn diagrams and two-way tables A

A **Venn diagram** is a visual picture that is used to show how outcomes can be part of one or more different events.

Using a Venn diagram to find probabilities

Probabilities can be calculated from a Venn diagram.

e.g. A small school runs an after-school sports program, with cricket on Tuesdays and badminton on Thursdays.

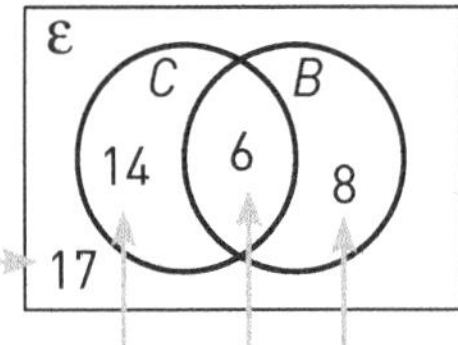

The Venn diagram shows the number of students participating in:

- cricket only (14)
- cricket and badminton (6)
- badminton (8)

It also shows that 17 students do not participate in cricket or badminton.

The number of students at the school is:

$n(\varepsilon) = 17 + 14 + 6 + 8 = 45$

If one student was selected at random, what is the probability that they participate in cricket?

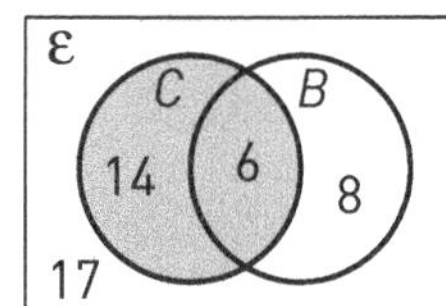

$$\Pr(\text{event}) = \frac{\text{number of successful outcomes}}{\text{total number of outcomes}}$$

$$\Pr(C) = \frac{n(C)}{n(\varepsilon)}$$ ← How many played cricket? ← How many students at the school?

$$= \frac{20}{45}$$

$$= \frac{4}{9}$$

Word Bank

Universal set (ε)

→ The Greek symbol ε (epsilon) stands for **universal set**, which refers to all possible outcomes.

ε: 1, 2, 3, 4, 5, 6

$n(\varepsilon)$ = number of outcomes
= 6

Union (or)

→ This Venn diagram has two sets. The union is all the outcomes in either A or B.

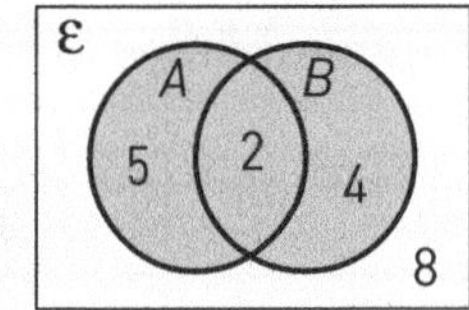

$n(A \text{ or } B) = 5 + 4 + 2 = 11$

Intersection (and)

→ Sometimes the sets in a Venn diagram overlap. The intersection includes the outcomes in both A and B.

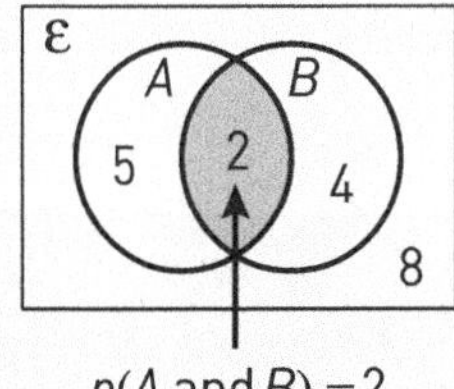

$n(A \text{ and } B) = 2$

1 This Venn diagram shows the number of people in Year 8 who walked to school or rode their bike.

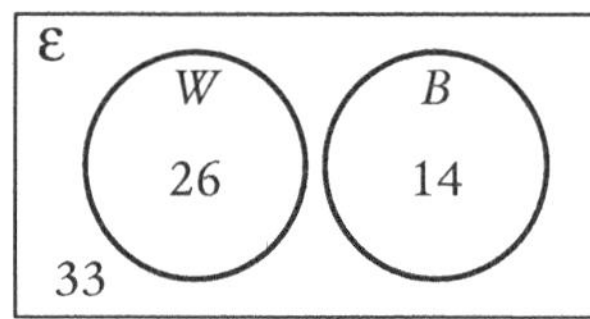

a How many students are in Year 8?

$n(\varepsilon) =$ ____ + ____ + ____

= ____

b How many students:

i walked to school?

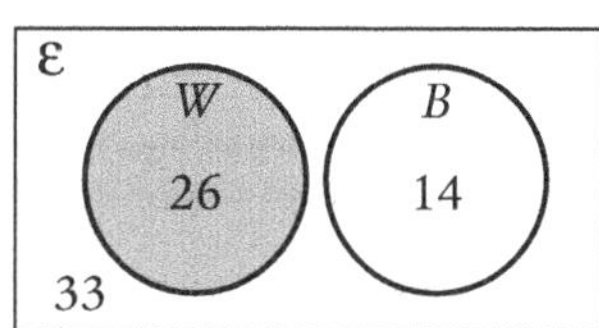

$n(W) =$ ☐

ii did not ride a bike to school?

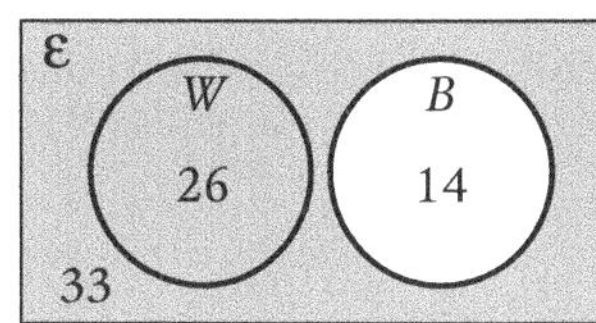

$n(\text{not } B) =$ ____ + ____

= ____

2 A class was asked if they liked apples (A).

The results are shown on the Venn diagram below.

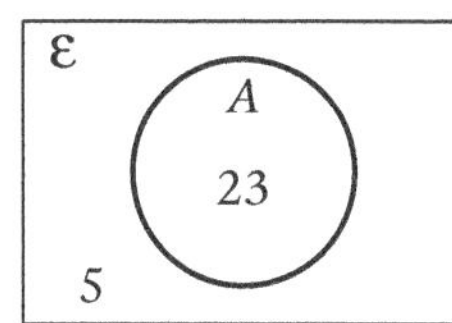

a How many people were in the class?

$n(\varepsilon) =$ ____ + ____

= ____

b If one person was selected at random, what is the probability that:

i they like apples

$\Pr(A) = \dfrac{\square}{\square}$

ii they do not like apples.

$\Pr(\text{not } A) = \dfrac{\square}{\square}$

3 Another class was asked if they liked apples, bananas, both fruits, or neither fruits.

The results are shown on the Venn diagram below.

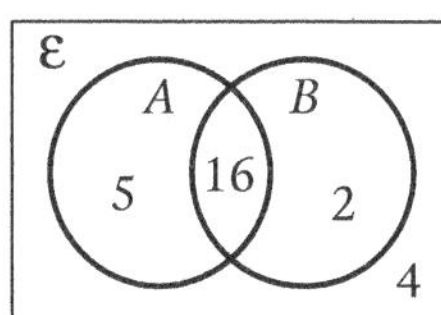

a How many people were in the class?

$n(\varepsilon) =$ ____ + ____ + ____ + ____

= ____

b If one person was selected at random, what is the probability that:

i They like both apples and bananas.

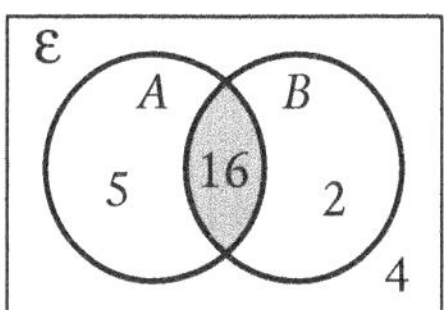

$\Pr(A \text{ and } B) =$ ____

ii They like apples, bananas or both.

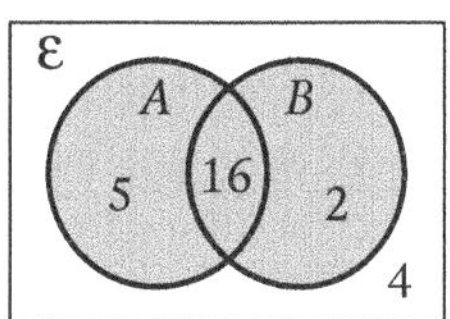

$\Pr(A \text{ or } B) =$ ____

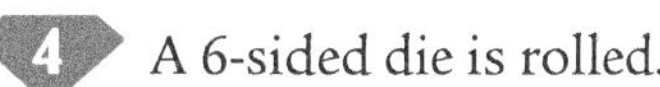

4 A 6-sided die is rolled.

Set A: even numbers

Set B: numbers more than 4

a List the outcomes in:

i Set A: { 2 , ____ , ____ }

Therefore, the number of outcomes in A is ____.

ii Set B: { ____ , ____ }

Therefore, $n(B) =$ ____

iii ε: { 1 , ____ , ____ , ____ , ____ , ____ }

Therefore, $n(\varepsilon) =$ ____

b Draw a Venn diagram to represent this information.

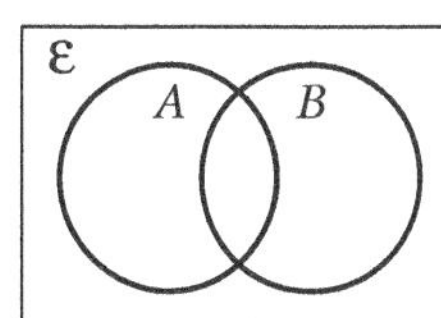

c Use the Venn diagram to calculate the following probabilities.

i $\Pr(A) = \dfrac{\;}{6} = \dfrac{\;}{\;}$

ii $\Pr(\text{not } B) =$

iii $\Pr(A \text{ and } B) =$

iv $\Pr(A \text{ or } B) =$

9.7 Venn diagrams and two-way tables B

A table can be used to display all of the equally likely outcomes (**sample space**) of two separate events. The outcomes of one event are written along the top. The outcomes of the other event are written down the left.

For example, all the outcomes from flipping two coins are listed in the table below.

	Heads	Tails
Heads	(H, H)	(T, H)
Tails	(H, T)	(T, T)

All *equally likely outcomes* are written within the table. There are four outcomes, so $n(\varepsilon) = 4$

Finding probabilities with tables

Probabilities are calculated using the formula:

$$\Pr(\text{event}) = \frac{\text{number of successful outcomes}}{\text{total number of outcomes}}$$

What is the probability of obtaining at least one tail?

Find the successful outcomes in the table—the outcomes with at least one tail.

(H, H)	(T, H)
(H, T)	(T, T)

← successful outcomes

$$\therefore \Pr(\text{at least one tail}) = \frac{n(\text{at least one tail})}{n(\varepsilon)} = \frac{3}{4}$$

1 Always check if probabilities that are in fraction form can be simplified. Simplify the following fractions.

Tip To simplify a fraction, divide both the numerator and denominator by their highest common factor.

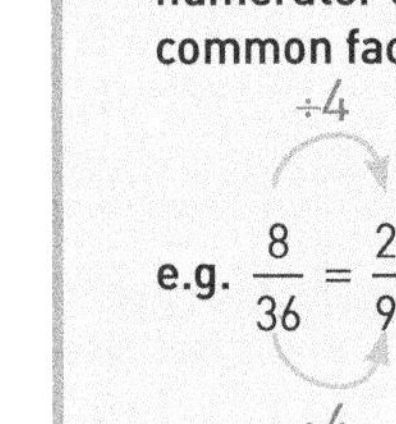

e.g. $\frac{8}{36} = \frac{2}{9}$ (÷4)

a $\frac{6}{8} =$

b $\frac{10}{12} =$

c $\frac{15}{36} =$

d $\frac{24}{36} =$

2 Two identical counters are flipped. They each have one white side and one black side.

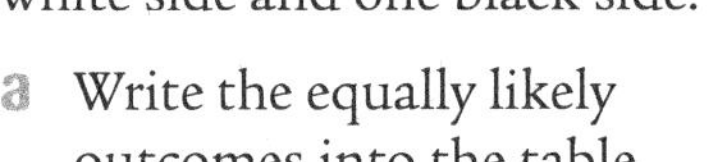

a Write the equally likely outcomes into the table.

	White	Black
White	WW	
Black		

b How many possible outcomes are there? _____

$\therefore n(\varepsilon) =$ ☐

c You win if both counters land with the same colour face up. What is your probability of winning?

____

3 A coin is flipped and a spinner is spun.

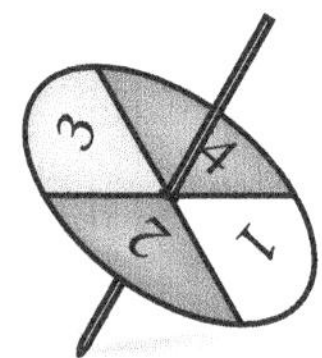

a Write the equally likely outcomes into the table.

	1	2	3	4
Heads				
Tails			(T, 3)	

b How many equally likely outcomes are there?

_____

$\therefore n(\varepsilon) =$ ☐

c What is the probability of:

i the coin landing on tails and the spinner landing on 3?

$$\Pr(\text{T}, 3) = \frac{n(\text{T}, 3)}{n(\varepsilon)}$$

$$= \frac{\square}{\square}$$

ii the coin landing on heads and the spinner landing on an even number?

$$\Pr(\text{H, even}) = \frac{n(\text{H, even})}{n(\varepsilon)}$$

$$= \frac{\square}{\square} = \frac{}{}$$

4 Two dice are rolled. The equally likely outcomes are shown in the table below.

	1	2	3	4	5	6
1	(1,1)	(2,1)	(3,1)	(4,1)	(5,1)	(6,1)
2	(1,2)	(2,2)	(3,2)	(4,2)	(5,2)	(6,2)
3	(1,3)	(2,3)	(3,3)	(4,3)	(5,3)	(6,3)
4	(1,4)	(2,4)	(3,4)	(4,4)	(5,4)	(6,4)
5	(1,5)	(2,5)	(3,5)	(4,5)	(5,5)	(6,5)
6	(1,6)	(2,6)	(3,6)	(4,6)	(5,6)	(6,6)

a How many equally likely outcomes are there?

______

$\therefore n(\varepsilon) = \square$

b Find the probability of the following outcomes.

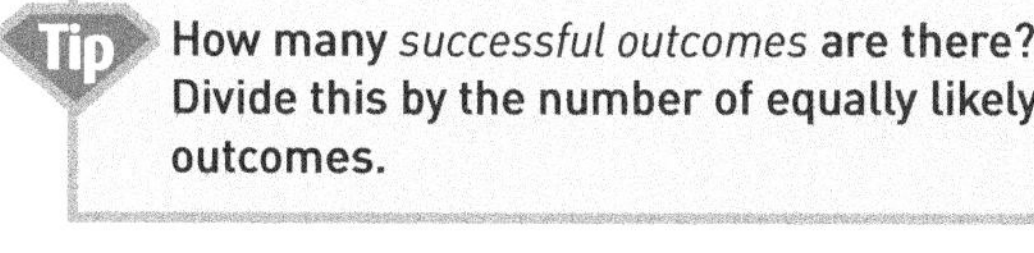

i $\Pr(\text{a double}) = \frac{\square}{\square} = \square$

ii $\Pr(\text{total of 6}) = \frac{\square}{\square}$

iii $\Pr(\text{total of less than 6}) = \frac{\square}{\square} = \square$

5 A game is played with two dice. The game can be played in two ways:

- You win if you score a total greater than 9.
- You win if you throw a double.

Which will you choose? Explain your answer.

Tip Look at the table in Question 4 and find the number of successful outcomes for each way to win.

____

____

____

____

6 Describe a dice game that is fair.

____

____

____

____

____

____

NAPLAN-ready

Shade the box beneath the correct answer.

The table below shows the participation in the lunchtime activities at the school swimming carnival.

	Boys	Girls
Participated in lunchtime activities	58	50
Did not participate in lunchtime activities	47	45

If one student was selected at random, what is the probability that they participated in the lunchtime activities?

$\frac{1}{2}$ ☐ $\frac{9}{10}$ ☐ $\frac{27}{50}$ ☐ $\frac{29}{100}$ ☐

Tip How many students participated? How many students altogether?

Answers

Chapter 1 Integers and indices

1.1 Integers review (p. 2)

1 a $6+2$ b $-5-3$ c $4-6$

2 a $2-4$ b $-2+6$ c $7+8$

3 a 7 b 10 c -9 d -8
e 11 f -11

4 a 7 b -2 c -3 d 3

5 a 3 b -10 c -3 d 3

6 a D b B

7 a -2 b -12 c 12 d 2

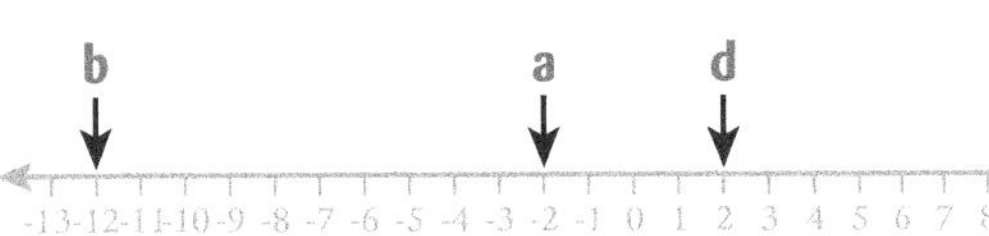

8 $-10 < -8 < -3 < +5$

9 Sample answers:
a $-12+8+4=0$ b $9-6-3=0$ c $-2+10-8=0$

1.1 NAPLAN-ready

490 m

1.2 Integer multiplication (p. 4)

1 a -14

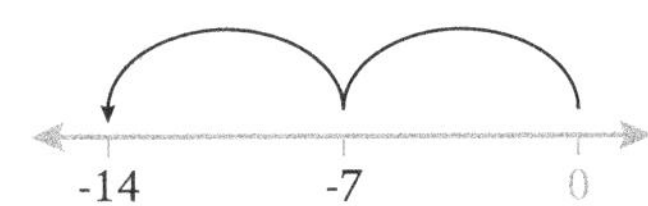

b -10

2 a 5 b -6 c -2 d -4
e 7 f -8

3 a -56 b -18 c 40 d 36

4 a T b T c F d T

5 a A b C

6 a C b D

7 a -40 b 18 c 40 d -210

8 a 36 b 9 c -81 d -1

9 a 50 b -160 c -300 d 36

1.2 NAPLAN-ready

-4

1.3 Integer division (p. 6)

1 $-2\times -9=18$ $-9\times -2=18$ $18\div -9=-2$ $18\div -2=-9$

2 a

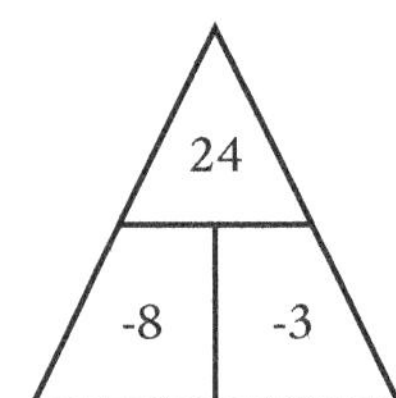

b

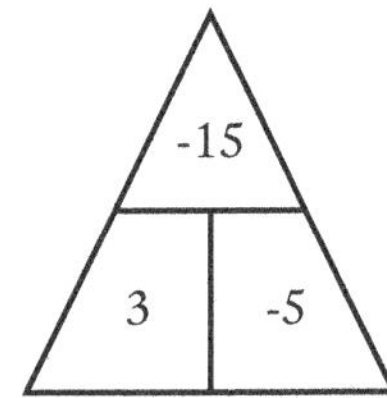

c

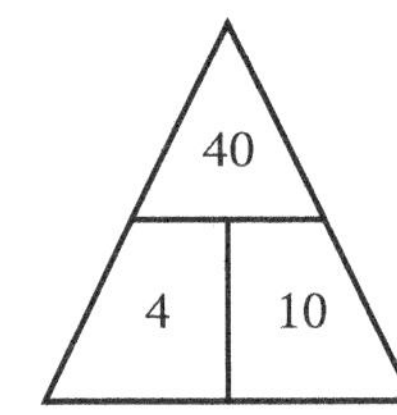

d

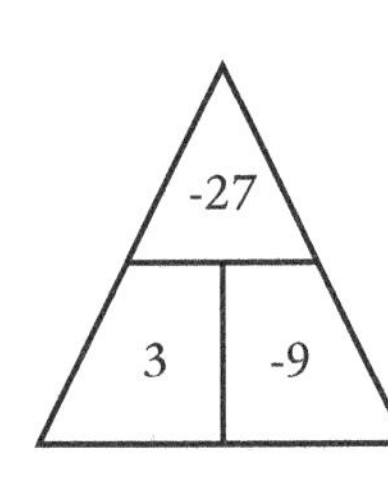

3 a F b T c T d T

4 a C b C

5 C

6 C

7 a

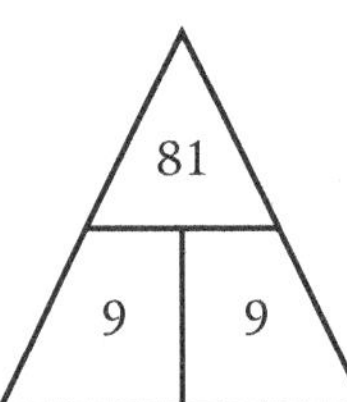

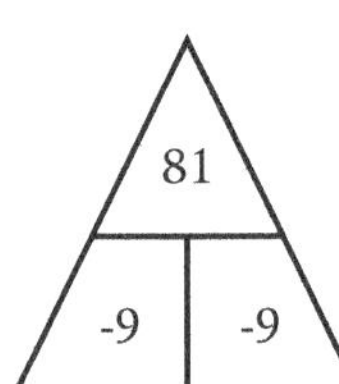

b

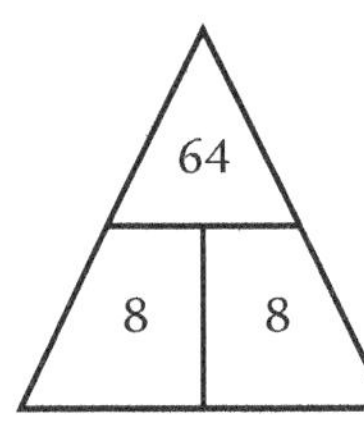

64
-8 -8

8 a 9 b -5 c -6 d 4

9 a 8 b -6 c -11 d 4

10 a -$330 b 12 months c 9 months

1.3 NAPLAN-ready

$360\div 10\times -6$

1.4 Combined operations with integers (p. 8)

1 a -8 b 3

2 a -36 b -4

3 a F b T c F

4 a $-2\times 15=-30$ b $-35--8=-27$
c $-6\times 2=-12$ d $9\div 3=3$
e $25-36=-11$ f $9-6\times 9=9-54=-45$

5 a $-7\times 4=-28$ b $\frac{18}{9}=2$
c $-36+49-5=8$

6 a -34 b -46 c -51

7 a $4-12\div 2=-2$ b $-5\times 4+2\times 12=4$
c $-12\times(2-4)=24$

1.4 NAPLAN-ready

$-8 + 10 \div (-2 \times 5)$

1.5 Multiplying and dividing numbers in index form (p. 10)

1 a $10 \times 10 \times 10$ b $4 \times 4 \times 4 \times 4 \times 4 \times 3 \times 3$

2 A

3 a $11 \times 11 \times 11 \times 11 \times 11 \times 11 \times 11 = 11^7$

b $\frac{5 \times 5 \times 5 \times 5 \times 5 \times 5 \times 5}{5 \times 5 \times 5 \times 5} = 5^3$

4 a 2^6 b 3^2 c 7^3

5 a F b T c T

6 a 16 b -27

7 a $3^5 \times 5^3$ b $10^3 \times 8^4$ c $5^3 = 125$

8 a $5^4 \times 4^2$ b $7^2 \times 3$

9 a $7^2 = 49$ b $4^3 = 64$ c $5^3 = 125$

1.5 NAPLAN-ready

1024 (2^{10})

1.6 Powers of powers, products and quotients (p. 12)

1 a $2^3 \times 5$ b $2^2 \times 3^2$

2 a 6^8 b 6^8

3 $3^3 \times 8^3$

4 $\frac{4^3}{7^3}$

5 a T b F c T

6 Sample answer: $14^5 = 7^5 \times 2^5$

7 $\frac{1}{6^2}$

8 a $20^3 = 8000$ b $\frac{6^2}{7^2} = \frac{36}{49}$

9 $\frac{9}{25}$

10 a $\frac{5^2 \times 3^8}{2^2}$ b $\frac{3}{4^5}$

1.6 NAPLAN-ready

10 000

Chapter 2 Fractions, decimals and percentages

2.1 Working with fractions and decimals A (p. 14)

1 a $\frac{4}{7}$ b $\frac{3}{4}$

2 a $\frac{25}{7}$ b $\frac{13}{2}$

3 a $5\frac{1}{3}$ b $1\frac{1}{7}$

4 a D b A

5 a 0.8 b 1.3

6 a $\frac{2}{10} = 0.2$ b $\frac{15}{20} = 0.75$

7 a 0.6 b 0.85

8 a D b C

9 $8 + \frac{4}{10} + \frac{5}{100} = 8\frac{45}{100}$

10 a $\frac{1}{20}$ b $\frac{3}{25}$ c $\frac{5}{4}$ d $\frac{11}{5}$

e $\frac{3}{500}$ f $\frac{3}{200}$

2.1 Working with fractions and decimals B (p. 16)

1

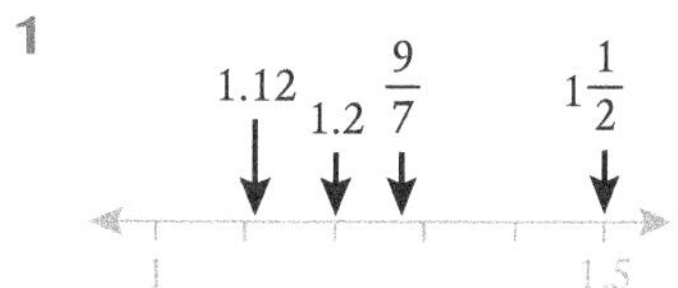

$1.12 < 1.2 < \frac{9}{7} < 1\frac{1}{2}$

2 a 4 pieces b 40 cm

3 a 56 glasses b 8400 mL c 100 mL

4 a C b D

5 $\frac{2}{5}$

6 10.001, $\frac{13}{4}$

7 $157.50

2.1 NAPLAN-ready

5 m

2.2 Types of decimals (p. 18)

1

$\sqrt{12}$ $\sqrt{43}$ $\sqrt{67}$ $\sqrt{80}$

0 5 10

2 $\sqrt{12} < \sqrt{43} < \sqrt{67} < \sqrt{80}$

3 a A b B

4 $\sqrt{8.6}$

5 a B b D

6 a $0.\dot{6}$ b $0.\overline{72}$ c $0.2\dot{7}$

d $1.1\dot{6}$ e $28.\overline{571428}$

7 a Y b Y

8 a 3.46 b 7.49

9 a 5.38 b 16.67 c 1.29

2.2 NAPLAN-ready

$5 \times \sqrt{1.04}$

2.3 Negative fractions and decimals A (p. 20)

1 a 

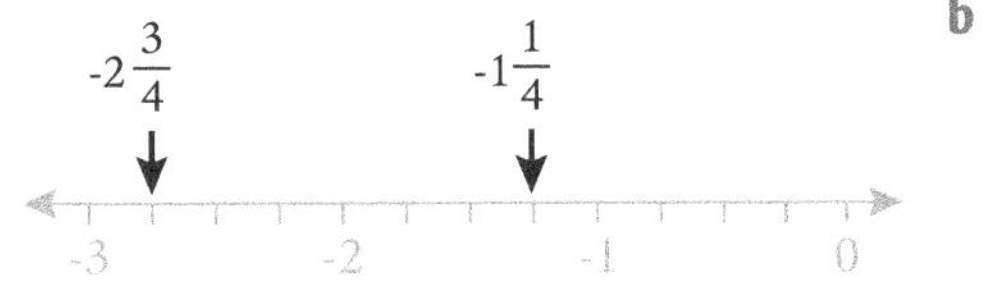

b $1\frac{1}{2}$

2 a C b A

3 a $\frac{-1}{4}$ b $\frac{3}{5}$ c $\frac{3}{8}$

4 a $\frac{-5}{6}$ b $\frac{-17}{24}$ c $-\frac{13}{35}$

5 8.13

6 a A good estimate: $-7 + 9 - 4 = -2$ b -2.1

2.3 Negative fractions and decimals B (p. 22)

1 C

2 a $\frac{-25}{42}$ b $1\frac{1}{5}$

3 a $\frac{-5}{18}$ b $-1\frac{11}{24}$

4 a -33.726 b 6240

5 a 2.7 b -0.07

6 $\frac{1}{15}$

2.3 NAPLAN-ready

$\frac{5}{4} \div -\frac{2}{3}$

2.4 Estimating percentages (p. 24)

1 a D b C c C

2 a

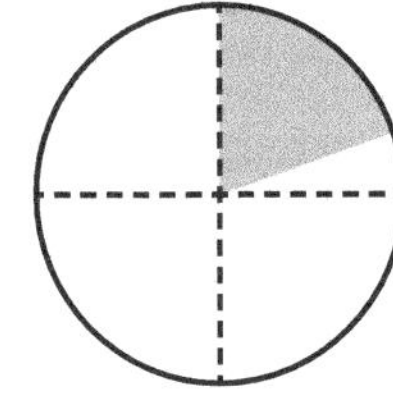

b

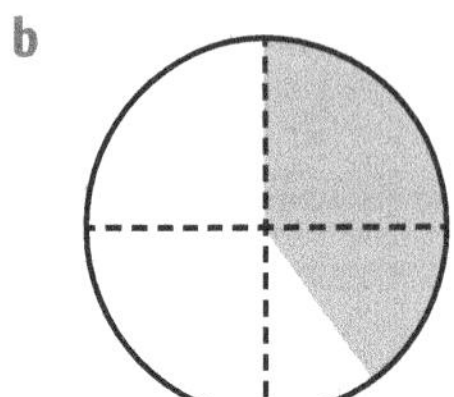

c

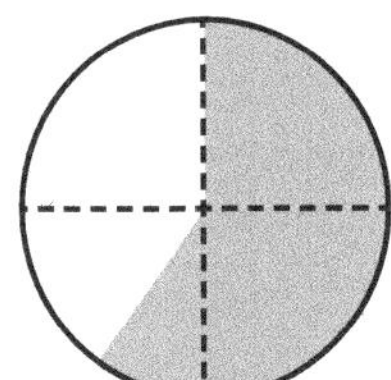

d

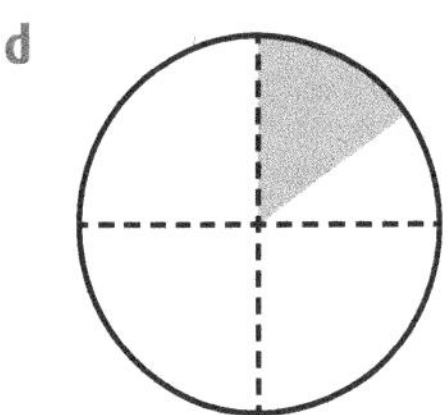

3

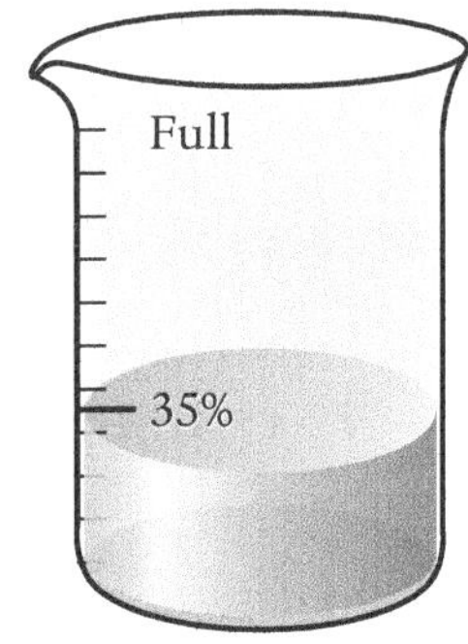

4 a

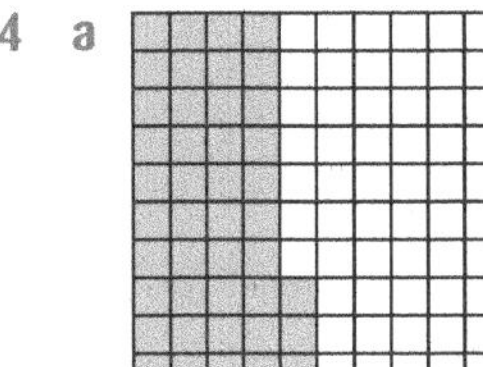

b

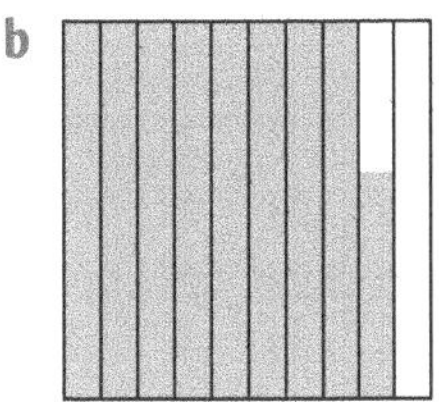

5 a 70 and 80% b 40 and 50% c 30 and 40%

2.4 NAPLAN-ready

15%

2.5 Writing fractions and decimals as percentages (p. 26)

1 a 6% b 59.01% c 180% d 0.4%

2 a 15% b 46%

3 A

4 a 150% b 270 %

5 a 66.7 % b 116.7 %

6 a $87\frac{1}{2}\%$ b $142\frac{6}{7}\%$

7

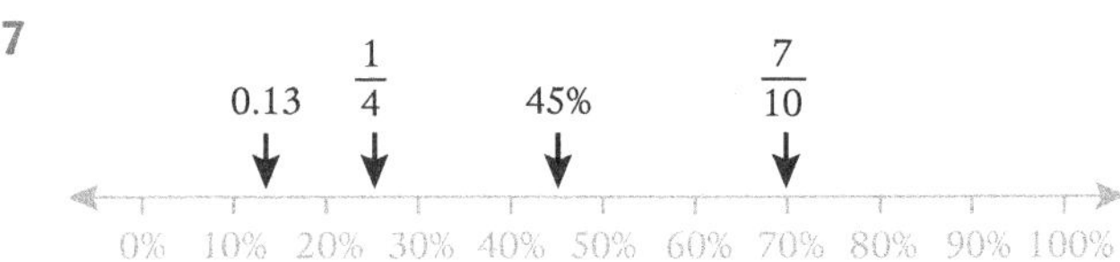

8 a F b T c T

9 a $\frac{5}{12} = 41.67\%$ b $\frac{7}{12} = 58.3\dot{3}$

2.5 NAPLAN-ready

German: 41 out of 50

2.6 Writing percentages as fractions and decimals (p. 28)

1 a 0.15 b 0.247 c 1.87 d 0.004

2 a 0.4525 b 0.675 c 0.094

3 a $\frac{3}{20}$ b $\frac{6}{25}$ c $\frac{4}{5}$

4 a $\frac{13}{200}$ b $\frac{33}{400}$ c $\frac{67}{300}$

5

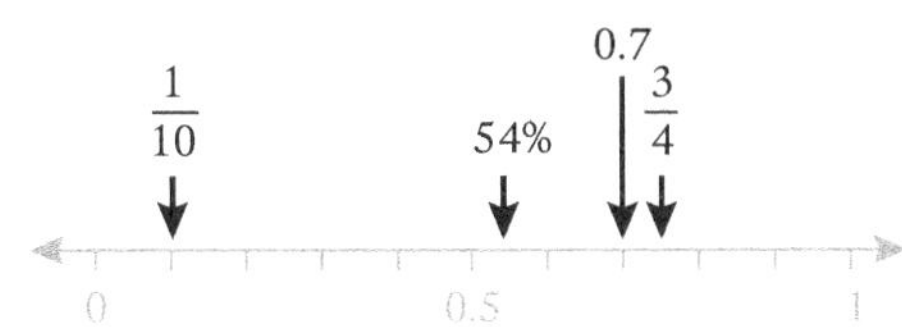

6 $\frac{1}{10} < 54\% < 0.7 < \frac{3}{4}$

7 **a** F **b** T **c** T

8 **a** $\frac{1}{400}$ **b** $\frac{1}{250}$

2.6 NAPLAN-ready

5 and 6

2.7 Writing one amount as a percentage of another (p. 30)

1 33.3%

2 **a** 70% **b** 142.9% **c** 16%

3 **a** 50% **b** 4% **c** 83.3% **d** 20% **e** 20%

4 D

5 50 out of 65 for Science

6 7.8%

2.7 NAPLAN-ready

89%

2.8 Finding a percentage of an amount (p. 32)

1 **a** \$9 **b** 22 kg **c** 11 mL

2 **a** 39 L **b** 10 cm

3 **a** F **b** T

4 \$4, \$0.70, \$0.03 (i.e. 400 cents, 70 cents, 3 cents)

5 **a** \$9.60 **b** \$7.50

6 **a** 3 L **b** 34 m

7 **a** \$26.19 **b** 20 mL

8 **a** 77 **b** 27 **c** 63 **d** 72

2.8 NAPLAN-ready

$(100 \div 25) \times 82$

2.9 Increasing or decreasing by a given percentage (p. 34)

1 **a** \$77 **b** \$350

2 **a** \$67.50 **b** \$306

3 3%

4 **a** C **b** A

5 **a** \$369.60 **b** \$87.98

6 **a** \$386.40 **b** \$39

7 **a** F **b** F

8 \$65.40

2.9 NAPLAN-ready

15%

2.10 Financial applications of percentages A (p. 36)

1 **a** \$1.40 per kg **b** \$2.50 per kg **c** \$1.10 per kg

2 **a** Loss, \$185 **b** Profit, \$13.80 **c** Profit, \$11.50

3 **a** 21% **b** 19% **c** 38%

4 \$577.50

5 \$26.25

6 D

7 B

8 D

2.10 Financial applications of percentages B (p. 38)

1 **a** $\div 1.1$ **b** $\div 1.52$ **c** $\div 0.75$

2 **a** \$3520 **b** \$17 050 **c** \$53.90 **d** \$27.50

3 \$385

4 \$450

5 \$560

6 \$350

7 \$37

8 \$240

9 D

10 B

2.10 NAPLAN-ready

\$729

Chapter 3 Algebra

3.1 Variables and expressions (p. 40)

1 **a** F **b** T **c** F **d** T

2 D

3 **a** x^2: 2; xy: 1; x: -5 **b** 3

4 **a** 2 **b** 3 **c** 1

5 **a** $9p$ **b** $\frac{k}{10}$ **c** $\frac{4d}{7}$ **d** $\frac{4}{ab}$ **e** $5x^2$ **f** $\frac{3y+x}{5}$

6 a $2k$ b $k-6$ c $\frac{k}{2}$ d $2k+5$

7 a The number of chips in 6 packets.

b The number of chips remaining after 30 chips have been eaten.

c The number of chips in half a packet.

3.1 NAPLAN-ready

$2x-5$

3.2 Substitution for variables (p. 42)

1 a -15 b 30

2 a 13 b 36 c -6 d 3

e 1 f -10

3 a 4 b 9 c -12 d 2

e 25

4 a $3\times\text{-}5$ b 2×9^3 c Correct d $(\text{-}7)^2$

5 a

x	-4	0	3
y	3	7	10

b

x	-2	0	5
y	4	0	-10

c

x	0	2	4
y	-5	1	7

3.2 NAPLAN-ready

$a=12, b=8$

3.3 Using formulas (p. 44)

1 a 11 b 21

2 a

Number of lawns mowed (*n*)	1	2	3	4	5
Money earned in dollars (*m*)	12	24	36	48	60

b $96 c 9 lawns

3 a 240 km b 100 km

4 a $9.30 b $27.30

5 $40

6 750 cm^2

7 a $E = 12$ b $E = 12$

8 a 50° b 95°

3.3 NAPLAN-ready

11.8 inches

3.4 Simplifying expressions (p. 46)

1 a $2x; 3x; x$ b $5ab; 6ab$

2 a B b D

3 A, B, D

4 a $10=25$ ✓ b $30+10=40$ ✓

c $10-2=5$ ✗ d $20+14=110$ ✗

5 $x+2x+1+3x-5=6x-4$

6 a $10e$ b $2f$ c $3y$ d $\text{-}3s$

e $14t^2$ f not possible g $10mn$ h $4a^2b$

7 a $15e+10xy$ b $\text{-}6f+9p$ c $y-3x$

d $\text{-}4s-8s^2t$ e $13t^2-10t^2$

8 a Both 105 b Both -225

9 a F b F c T d F

3.4 NAPLAN-ready

$170x$

3.5 Multiplying and dividing algebraic terms (p. 48)

1 a $10a$ b $32b$ c $21c$ d $60ae$

e $22st$ f $45mp$

2 a $\text{-}36q$ b $\text{-}15m$ c $30dn$ d $66dh$

e $\text{-}28gr$ f yz g $5a$

3 a $4f$ b $7ch$ c $6b$ d $4x$

e $\text{-}2b$ f $2k$

4 a $5b$ b $4q$ c -30

5 a B b D c A

6 a $12xy$ b $2xy$ c 6

3.5 NAPLAN-ready

$\frac{7abc}{2f}$

3.6 Expanding brackets A (p. 50)

1 a $240+32=272$ b $4200+21=4221$

c $43\,000+43=43\,043$

2 a $90+45=135$ b $4x+40$

3 a $6x+18$ b $14x+70$

4 a $18bc+45b$ b $16b+2b^2$

5 a $x+15$ b $5mp+21m$

c $2a^2+15a+12$

6 a $x+x+1+1=2x+2$ b $2(x+1)=2x+2$

7 a $2x(3x+5)$ b $6x^2+10x$

c $2(3x+5+2x)$ or $2(3x+5)+2\times 2x$ or $2(5x+5)$ or $10(x+1)$

d $10x+10$

3.6 Expanding brackets B (p. 52)

1 a $240 - 8 = 232$ b $770 - 28 = 742$
c $1600 - 8 = 1592$ d $2100 - 63 = 2037$

2 a $3a - 6$ b $8x - 4y$
c $m^2 - 7m$ d $4ab - b^2$

3 a $21mn - 7mr$ b $12f^2 - 15cf$

4 a $17m - 3$ b $43ps - 52s$
c $14ab - 21a$ d $-6agh$

5 $16p + 8$

6 a $-3a + 38$ b $b - 37$ c $-4mp - 12p - 9n$
d $-50hk + 9k$

3.6 NAPLAN-ready

$6x + 10$

3.7 Factorising (p. 54)

1 a 4 b $6p$

2 a $3(3 + b)$ b $2(5m - 4n)$ c $7(2d + 1)$

3 a $10g(2 + 3h)$ b $3p(5p - 6r)$

4 $-4k(4 - 3n)$

5 $P = 2(l + w)$

3.7 NAPLAN-ready

$2xy + 15z^2$

Chapter 4 Ratio and rate

4.1 Writing ratios (p. 56)

1 a 3:4 b 3:4 c 2:3

2 a 9:8 b 1:15 c 1:7 d 21:7:26

3 a 7:10 b 3:10 c 7:3 d 3:7

4 a 25% b 75%

5 a D b A c D

4.1 NAPLAN-ready

30%

4.2 Simplifying ratios (p. 58)

1 a 3:25 b 1:7 c 8:1 d 1:7:4

2 a 2:3 b 4:3 c 12:7 d 8:15

3 a 3:5 b 41:60 c 14:19

4 a D b D

5 a C b B

4.2 NAPLAN-ready

10:13

4.3 Unit ratios and scale factors (p. 60)

1 a 3:1 b 4:1

2 a 3 b 4

3 a 141 cm b 146 cm

4 a 43 seconds b 106 seconds

5 a 250 g b 700 g

6

Ratio of two quantities	Unit ratio	Scale factor	What it means
5:6	0.83:1	0.83	The first quantity is 0.83 of the second.
19:15	1.27:1	1.27	The first quantity is 1.27of the second.
20:3	6.67:1	6.67	The first quantity is 6.67 of the second.

4.3 NAPLAN-ready

85 mm

4.4 Using ratios to find amounts (p. 62)

1 a $a = 22$ b $b = 16$ c $c = 45$

2 a 128 drops b 40 lessons

3 a $a \approx 6.67$ b $b = 7.2$

4 1.3 kg

5 a F b T c T d F

4.4 NAPLAN-ready

1.35 m, 1.21 m

4.5 Scale drawings (p. 64)

1 a 1:200 b 1:1000 c 1:50 000

2 a 60 cm b 13.5 m

3 a 2.5 m b 17 m

4 a 48 mm b 700 mm

5 a 7 mm b 150 mm

6 a 350 m b 575 m

7 200

8	Scale ratio	Scale factor	Diagram distance	Real distance
a	1:4000	4000	5 m	20 km
b	1:500	500	12 cm	60 m
c	1:1 000 000	1 000 000	15 cm	150 km
d	1:50 000	50 000	4.2 cm	2.1 km

4.5 NAPLAN-ready

4150 km

4.6 Sharing an amount in a given ratio (p. 66)

1 a $4, $20 b $28, $8 c $40, $32 d $52, $13

2 a D b B

3 a 12 b 8

4 a $15, $12, $18 b $14, $7, $35 c $36, $36, $48

5

					Total
Parts	2	2	1	4	9
Amount	$18	$18	$9	$36	$81

6 a Total parts: 12 Leah 18, Lacie 42, Libby 12

b Lacie won by 24 hits.

7 12 chocolates

4.6 NAPLAN-ready

$\frac{5}{14}$

4.7 Rates A (p. 68)

1 a 80 km/h b 5 m/s c 900 km/h d 4 m/h

2 a $1.40/kg b $64/kg

3 a

Distance	Time
240 km	4 h
60 km	1 h
420 km	7 h

b

Cost	Mass
$48	1.5 kg
$32	1 kg
$102.40	3.2 kg

c

Beats	Time
20	15 seconds
80	1 minute
4800	1 hour

d

Amount	Time
12 mL	5 minutes
3.456 L	1 day
1.261 44 kL	1 year (365 days)

4 a T b T c F

5 $1.29 p/kg is better buy.

4.7 Rates B (p. 70)

1 a 8 cm b $20

2 a 2 cm/week b $5/week

3 12.5 cm per year

4 a 30 minutes b 75% c 25% per week

5 a 1200 b 2.7%

6 a 1.05 b 5% c 441 students

4.7 NAPLAN-ready>

14 500

Chapter 5 Measurement

5.1 Perimeter (p. 72)

1 14 cm

2 10.8 cm

3 a 32 cm b 10 km

4 126 mm

5 $P = 2 \times (6 + 11)$
$= 2 \times 17$
$= 34$ mm

6 15 m

7 a 2.4 cm b 3 m c 50 mm d 150 cm

e 1.2 km f 2500 m

8 12 cm

5.1 NAPLAN-ready

4000 mm

5.2 Circle relationships (p. 74)

1 b 4 cm c 2 cm

2 a 11 mm b 3.2 cm

3 a $r = 0.5$ cm, $d = 1$ cm b $C \approx 3.1$ cm

4 a $r = 1$ cm, $d = 2$ cm b $C \approx 6.3$ cm

5 a

	Radius	Diameter	Estimation of circumference
Button	0.5 cm	1 cm	3.1 cm
$2 coin	1 cm	2 cm	6.3 cm

b multiply by 3 and a bit

6 a $d = 1$ cm, $C \approx 3.14$ cm b $d = 2$ cm, $C \approx 6.28$ cm

c $d = 3$ cm, $C \approx 12.57$ cm

5.2 NAPLAN-ready

2.5 cm

5.3 Circumference (p. 76)

1 a 2 cm b $C \approx 6.28$ cm

2 a 3.141 592 654 b 3.14

3 3.14 cm

4 a 9.42 cm b 9.42 cm

5 a 62.83 cm b 51.42 cm

6 21.42 cm

5.3 NAPLAN-ready

24.85 cm

5.4 Area A (p. 78)

1 a 200 mm^2 b 850 mm^2
c 3 cm^2 d 6.2 cm^2

2 a 20 000 cm^2 b 36 000 cm^2
c 4 m^2 d 1.6 m^2

3 a 7 cm^2 b 8 cm^2 c 9 cm^2

4 a 16 m^2 b 2.25 cm^2

5 a 18 km^2 b 32 m^2 c 9 cm^2

6 a 9 cm^2 b 24.8 mm^2

5.4 Area B (p. 80)

1 a 6 cm^2 b 3 cm^2

2 30 m^2

3 a $x = 3$ cm, $y = 4$ cm b 6 cm^2

4 $(4 \times 7) \div 2 = 28 \div 2$
$= 14\ km^2$

5 a $x = 2.5$ cm, $y = 4.2$ cm b $(2.5 \times 4.2) \div 2 = 5.25\ cm^2$

6 17.5 mm^2

7 a $A = \dfrac{(4+8)\times 3}{2} = \dfrac{36}{2} = 18\ m^2$

b $A = \dfrac{(6.5+4.5)\times 2}{2} = 6.5 + 4.5 = 11\ cm^2$

5.4 NAPLAN-ready

2 cm^2

5.5 Area of a circle (p. 82)

1 a 16 b 36 c 100 d 144

2 a 9 cm^2 b 4.5 cm^2
c $\approx 6-7\ cm^2$. Student answers will vary.

3 a 3 cm^2 b $A \approx 3.14\ cm^2$

4 a 50.27 m^2 b 32.17 km^2

5 a 78.54 cm^2 b 38.48 mm^2 c 56.75 m^2

6 a 113.1 mm^2 b 56.55 mm^2

7 39.3 cm^2

8 a 201.06 mm^2 b 50.27 mm^2

5.5 NAPLAN-ready

Between 4 cm^2 and 9 cm^2

5.6 Finding the area of composite shapes (p. 84)

1 Students' own answers.

2 a $A_{triangle} = 4\ cm^2$ $A_{rectangle} = 4\ cm^2$ b 8 cm^2

3 a $r = 2$ cm $a = 4$ cm $b = 2$ cm $h = 2$ cm
b $A_{semicircle} \approx 6.28\ cm^2$ $A_{trapezium} = 6\ cm^2$
c $A_{total} \approx 12.28\ cm^2$

4 a

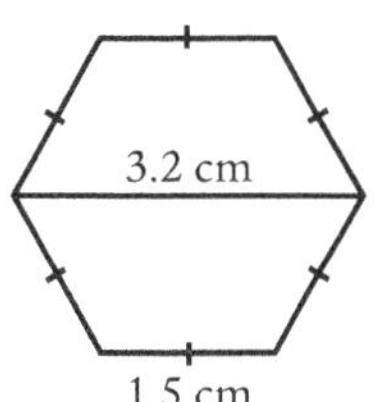

b $A_{hexagon} \approx 5.85\ cm^2$

5 $A_{square} = 10 \times 10 = 100\ m^2$ $A_{circle} = \pi \times 5^2 \approx 78.54\ m^2$

$A_{total} \approx 100 + 2 \times 78.54 \approx 257.08\ m^2$

6 $A_{square} = 25\ m^2$ $A_{circle} = 12.57\ m^2$
$A_{total} = 25\ m^2 - 12.57\ m^2 = 12.43\ m^2$

5.6 NAPLAN-ready

400 cm^2

5.7 Volume and capacity A (p. 86)

1 a 24 cm^3 b 54 cm^3

2 a 110 m^3 b 64 mm^3

3 a 208 cm^3 b 180 mm^3

4 a

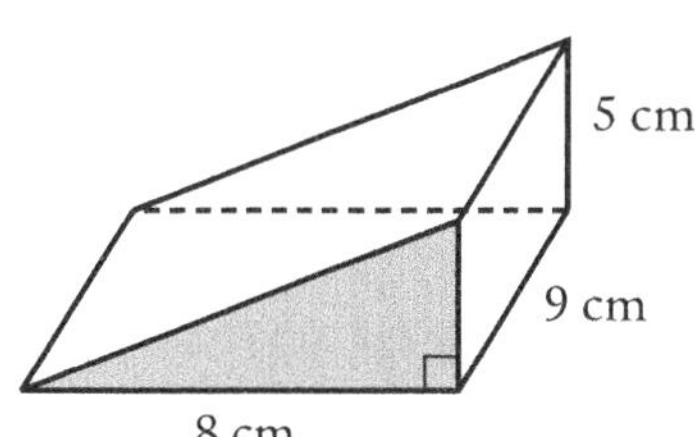

b triangle

c $A = \frac{1}{2}bh = 0.5 \times 8 \times 5 = 20\ cm^2$

d $V = 20 \times 9 = 180\ cm^3$

5 a $V = 180\ m^3$ b 300 cm^2

6 $r = 5$ m $H = 16$ m $V \approx 1256.64\ m^3$

5.7 Volume and capacity B (p. 88)

1 a 5 mL b 12 mL c 1000 mL = 1 L

2 a 800 mL b 480 mL

3 a 630 mL b 12 315.04 mL

4 a 0.3 L b 0.75 L c 1250 mL d 3200 mL

5 $D = 17$ cm, $r = 8.5$ cm, capacity = 5 L

6 a 4 kL b 14.5 kL c 8 m^3 d 0.5 m^3

7 36 000 L

5.7 NAPLAN-ready

600 mL

5.8 Time (p. 90)

1 a 0930 b 1345 c 2208

2 a 7.25 a.m. b 11.05 a.m.

c 4.50 p.m. d 9.30 p.m.

3 a 50 min b 28 min c 17 min d 42 min

4 a 7 hours b 17 hours

5 a 2 h 45 min b 8 h 25 min

6 a 1.10 b 9.25

7 a 8.15 p.m. b 2200 = 10 p.m.

c 0045 = 12.45 a.m.

8

Perth

6.00

Alice Springs

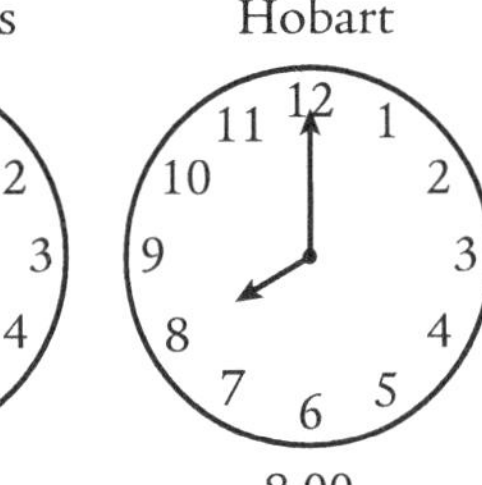

7.30

Hobart

8.00

9 a Melbourne 7.30 p.m. b Broome 5.30 p.m.

c Darwin 7.00 p.m.

5.8 NAPLAN-ready

10.30 a.m.

Chapter 6 Linear graphs

6.1 Interpreting line graphs (p. 92)

1 a Evie left from home at 8.00 a.m. and walked to the train station. She waited for 5 minutes for the train. She travelled 4 km on the train. She exited the train and walked 1 km to work. It took Evie a total of 35 minutes to travel from home to work. Evie lives 7 km from work.

b B c C

2 a A b A c B

3 a

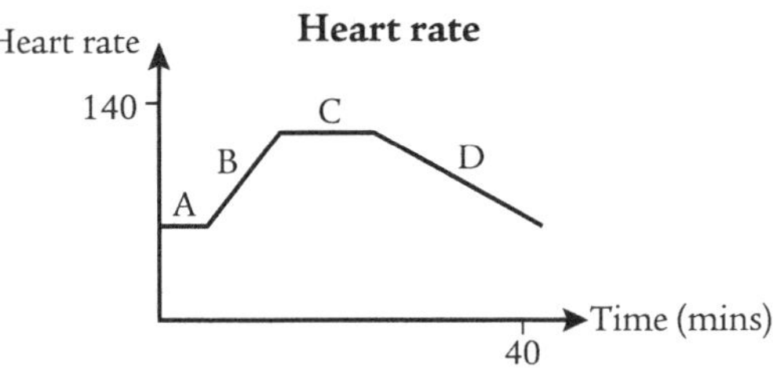

b i Section A: heart rate is low and steady

ii Section B: heart rate increasing quickly

iii Section C: heart rate is high and stable

iv Section D: heart rate decreasing slowly at a steady rate

c B

4 a Take off b C

c Short—This graph shows a short flight path as the length of time at a stable height in the air is shorter than the time taken to land.

d No—the horizontal axis shows the distance from takeoff. Take off and landing are not in the same position.

6.1 NAPLAN-ready

The temperature remained steady for a few hours at the day's maximum.

6.2 Linear relationships A (p. 94)

1 a To find y, subtract 6 from x.

b To find y, multiply x by 3 and then add 1.

2 a i $x = 0, y = 4$ ii $x = 1, y = 5$

iii $x = 2, y = 6$ iv $x = 3, y = 7$

b

x	0	1	2	3
y	4	5	6	7
(x, y)	(0, 4)	(1, 5)	(2, 6)	(3, 7)

c–d

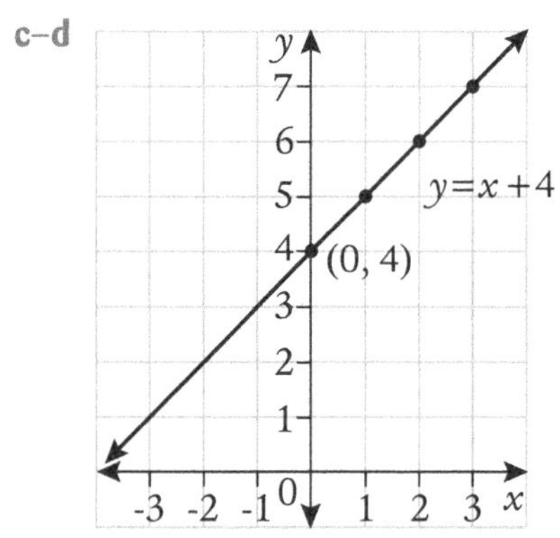

3 a $y = x - 2$

x	0	1	2	3
y	-2	-1	0	1
(x, y)	(0, -2)	(1, -1)	(2, 0)	(3, 1)

b

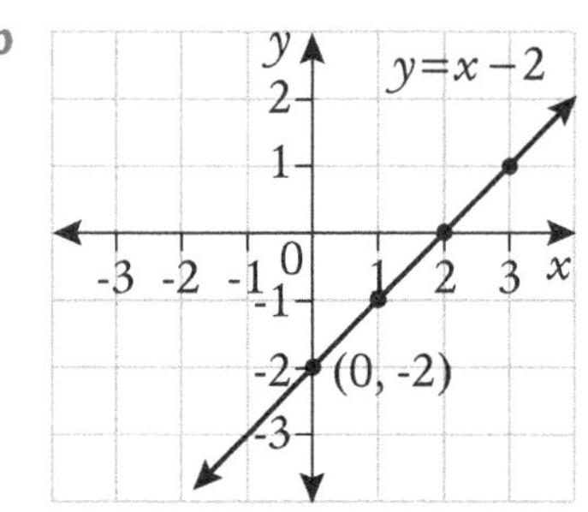

c B and C

d (2, 0), (1, -1) Students' answers will vary. The y-value must be 2 less than the x-value.

4 a To find y, multiply x by 2 and subtract 3.

b (4, 5) (1, -1) (-2, -1)

5 a Students' answers will vary. Examples include (1, 3) (-2, -6) (3, 9)

b $y = 3x$

x	-1	0	1	2
y	-3	0	3	6
(x, y)	(-1, -3)	(0, 0)	(1, 3)	(2, 6)

c

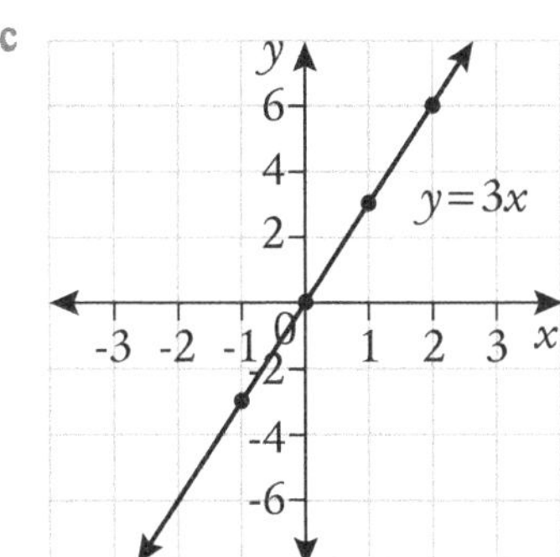

d The graph slopes upwards by 3 each x-value.

6.2 Linear relationships B (p. 96)

1 a (-1, 0) b (0, 3)

c positive d when $x = -2, y = -3$

2 a $y = 1 - x$

x	-2	-1	0	1	2
y	3	2	1	0	-1
(x, y)	(-2, 3)	(-1, 2)	(0, 1)	(1, 0)	(2, -1)

b

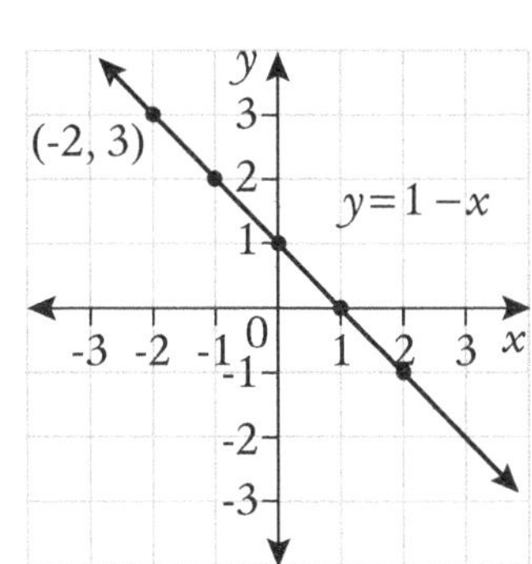

c x-intercept $\rightarrow$ (1, 0), y-intercept $\rightarrow$ (0, 1)

3 a zero b positive c undefined d negative

4 a

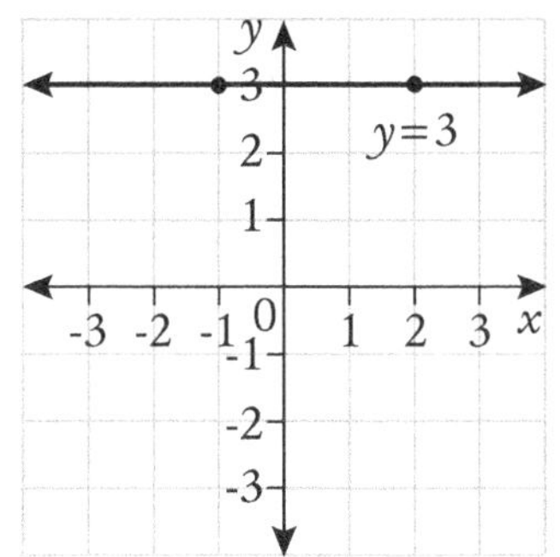

b (0, 3) c zero

6.2 NAPLAN-ready

5

6.3 Finding the rule (p. 98)

1 a $-1 = -1$ ✓ b $-4 = -4$ ✓ c $4 = 4$ d $-7 = -7$

2 a 3 is subtracted from x. b $y = x - 3$

3 a $y = 4x$ b $y = 3x + 1$

4 pattern: $\frac{6}{2} = 3; y = 3x + 2$

5 a

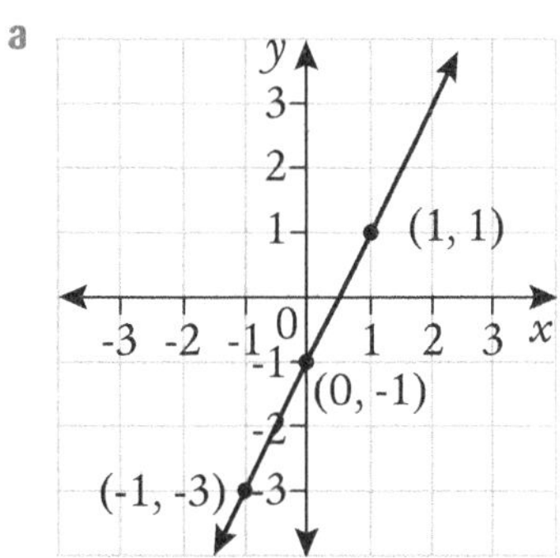

b (-1, -3), (0, -1), (1, 1) c $y = 2x - 1$

d i $-1 = -1$ ✓ ii $1 = 1$ ✓

6.3 NAPLAN-ready

(0, 4)

6.4 Using linear relationships (p. 100)

1 A and B

2 a w = amount of water in litres, T = length of time in minutes

b

Length of shower (minutes)	0	1	2	3
Water used (L)	0	8	16	24

c $w = 8T$ d 32 litres

3 a i $2.00

ii 1 minute and 30 seconds or 1.5 minutes

b Let t be the time in minutes. Let C be the total cost of a call in dollars.

c

Length of call (minutes)	0	1	2	3	4	5
Total cost of call	$0.30	$0.80	$1.30	$1.80	$2.30	$2.80

d i 30 cents = $0.30 ii 50 cents = $0.50

e $C = 0.5t + 0.3$ f $C = 0.5 \times 4.5 + 0.3 = \$2.55$

4 a

Hours worked	1	2	3	4	5	6
Total fee charged $	$75	$105	$135	$165	$195	$225

b

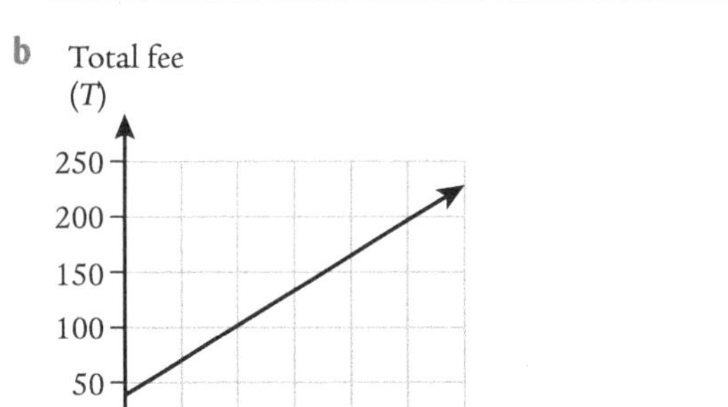

c Yes

d $T = 30H + 45$

e $135

f 4.5 hours

6.4 NAPLAN-ready

42

Chapter 7 Linear equations

7.1 The language of equations (p. 102)

1 a $6w = 42$ b $11y - 5 = 28$

c $\frac{h}{8} = 2$ d $\frac{f}{10} + 6 = 56$

2 D

3 a $g + 6 = 17$ b $23 - x = 11$

c $\frac{m}{2} = 9$ d $10t + 8 = 68$

4 a $\frac{d}{12} = 5, d = 60$ b $3v - 7 = 14, v = 7$

5 a Possible answers include: Nine is added to a number (s) to give fifteen, or The sum of a number (s) and nine is equal to fifteen.

b Six is multiplied by a number (m) to give a result of eighteen.

6 a $9 = 9$ ✓ Yes b $28 = 21$ ✗ No

c $6 = 6$ ✓ Yes d $20 = 20$ ✓ Yes

7 a $y = 8$ b $y = 7$

8 a $2x + 14 = 24$ b $x = 5$

7.1 NAPLAN-ready

5

7.2 Solving linear equations A (p. 104)

1 a $20 - \underline{13} = 7$ b $3 \times \underline{12} = 36$

c $\underline{6} + 17 = 23$ d $48 \div \underline{4} = 12$

2 a $x = 9$ b $x = 8$ c $x = 16$

3 a $11 = 11$ ✓ b $\frac{6}{2} = 3$ ✓

c $3 \times 6 + 5 = 23$ ✓ d $13 - \frac{6}{6} = 12$ ✓

4 a -9 b $+5$ c $\div 10$ d $\times 3$

5 a $x = 11$ b $x = 8$ c $x = 28$ d $x = 3$

6 a $x = 9$ b $x = -7$ c $x = 88$ d $x = 48$

7 a–b

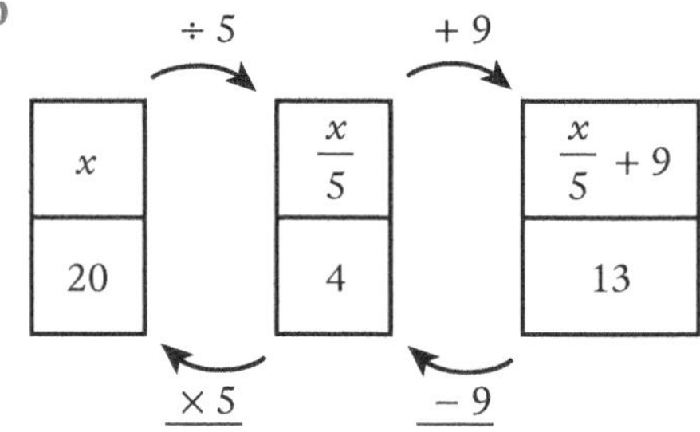

$x = 20$

c $\frac{20}{5} + 9 = 4 + 9$
$= 13$ ✓

8 a $x = 3$ b $x = 42$

9 a $3 \times 3 - 8 = 11$ b $\frac{42}{6} + 4 = 11$

10 4 muffins on each tray

7.2 Solving linear equations B (p. 106)

1 a

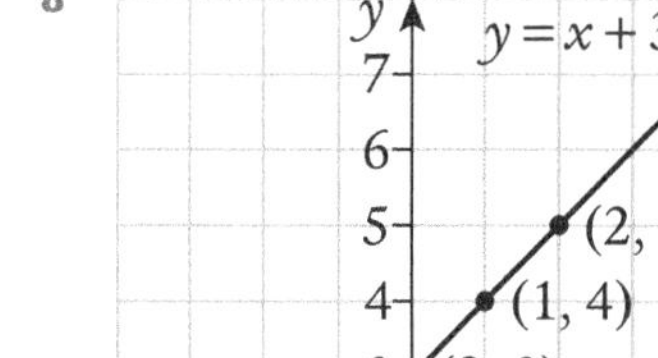

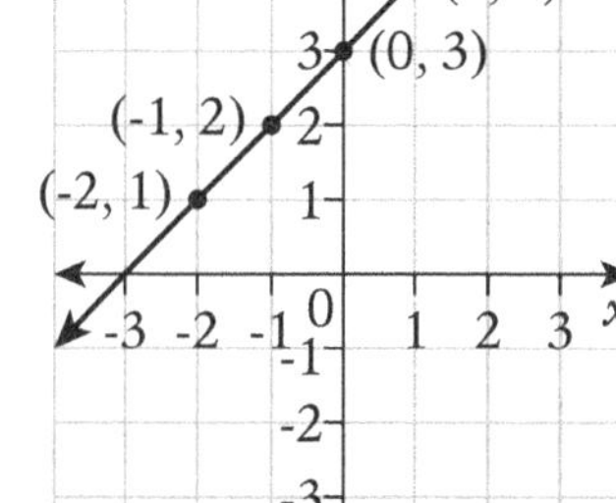

b $(-1, 2) \rightarrow$ When $y = 2, x = -1$

$(0, 3) \rightarrow$ When $y = 3, x = 0$

$(1, 4) \rightarrow$ When $y = 4, x = 1$

$(2, 5) \rightarrow$ When $y = 2, x = 5$

2 a $(1, -2) \rightarrow x = 1$ b $(2, 0) \rightarrow x = 2$ c $(0, -4) \rightarrow x = 0$

3 a $x = 4$ b $2 \times 4 - 5 = 3$ ✓

4 a $x = 2$ b $y = 2, x = 4$ c $y = -1, x = -2$

5 a $y = 4x - 1$ b $x = 4$ c $x = -1$

7.2 NAPLAN-ready

-1

7.3 Solving more complex equations (p. 108)

1 a–b

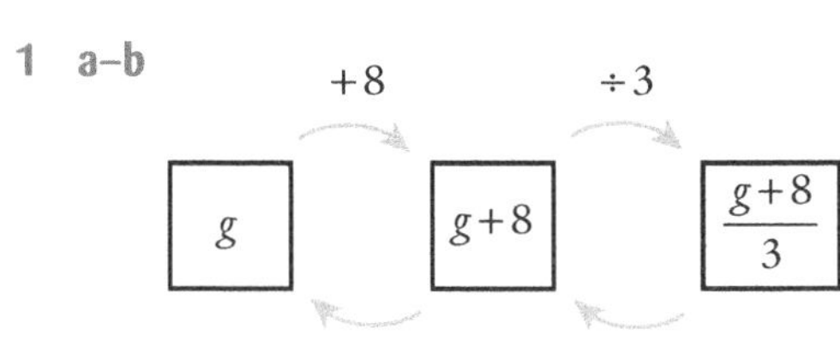

c $g = 7$ d $5 = 5$ ✓

2 a

÷ 3 + 11

m → $\frac{m}{3}$ → $\frac{m}{3} + 11$

× 3 − 11

b

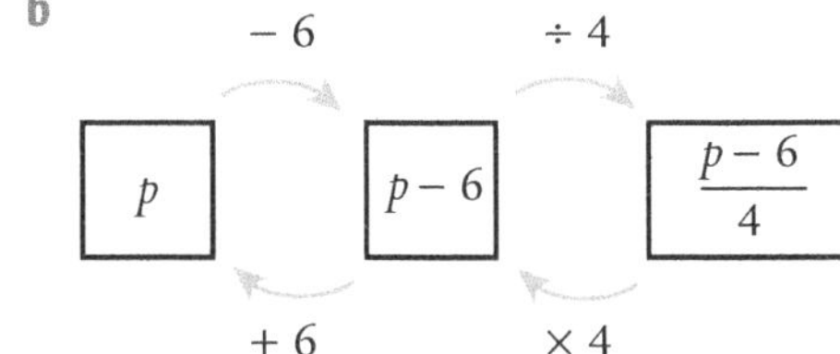

3 a $\frac{m}{3} = 1, m = 3$ b $p - 6 = 28, p = 34$

4 a $y = 80$ b $k = 12$

5 a $\div 3, -8$ b $\div 7, +10$

6 $6(x + 5) = 54$
$x + 5 = 9$
$x = 4$

7 $\frac{4x+1}{7} = 3$
$4x + 1 = 21$
$4x = 20$
$x = 5$

8 $\frac{3h}{4} - 2 = 4$
$\frac{3h}{4} = 6$
$3h = 24$
$h = 8$

7.3 NAPLAN-ready

1

7.4 Solving equations where the unknown appears on both sides A (p. 110)

1 a x $+1$ / x x | x $+5$ b $2x + 1 = 5$

2 a $2x - 5 = x + 1$
$x - 5 = 1$
$x = 6$

b $4x - 1 = 2x - 3$
$2x - 1 = -3$
$2x = -2$
$x = -1$

3 a $6y + 12$ b $10k - 20$
c $4m - 36$ d $24 + 56w$

4 a $2(p-8) = p - 6$
$2p - 16 = p - 6$
$p - 16 = -6$
$p = 10$

b $5(y-8) = y - 4$
$5y - 40 = y - 4$
$4y - 40 = -4$
$4y = 36$
$y = 9$

c $2(3h-5) = 4(h-3)$
$6h - 10 = 4h - 12$
$2h - 10 = -12$
$2h = -2$
$h = -1$

5 a 3: 3, 6, 9, 12, 15
4: 4, 8, 12, 16, 20
∴ the LCD of 3 and 4 is 12

b $4(x + 1) = 3(x + 3)$

c $4(x + 1) = 3(x + 3)$
$4x + 4 = 3x + 9$
$x + 4 = 9$
$x = 5$

d $\frac{5+1}{3} = \frac{5+3}{4}$
$2 = 2$ ✓

6 a $2x + 15 = x + 35$
b $2x + 15 = x + 35$
$x + 15 = 35$
$x = 20 \rightarrow \$20$
c $\underline{20} + \underline{20} + 10 + 5 = \underline{20} + 10 + 5 + 20$
$55 = \underline{55}$ ✓

7.4 Solving equations where the unknown appears on both sides B (p. 112)

1 a (-2, 2) b $x = -2$
c $-3 \times -2 - 4 = -2 + 4$
$+6 - 4 = 2$
$2 = 2$ ✓

2 a $(-1, -2) \rightarrow x = -1$ b $-2 = -2$ ✓

3 $y = x + 3$ and $y = -x + 5$

4 $y = x + 3$ $y = -x + 5$

x	0	1	2
y	3	4	5

x	0	1	2
y	5	4	3

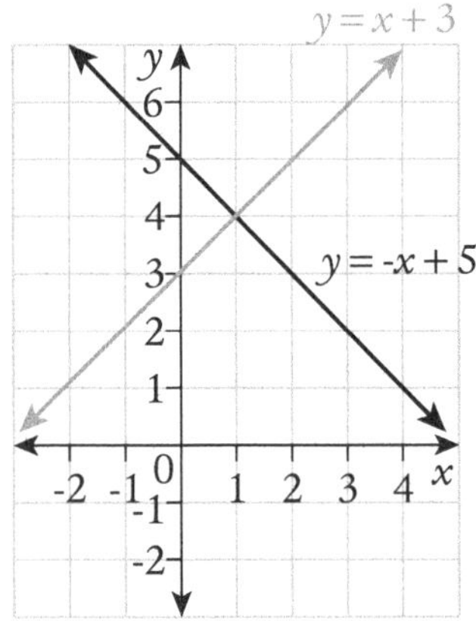

b (1, 4) c $x = 1$

5 a

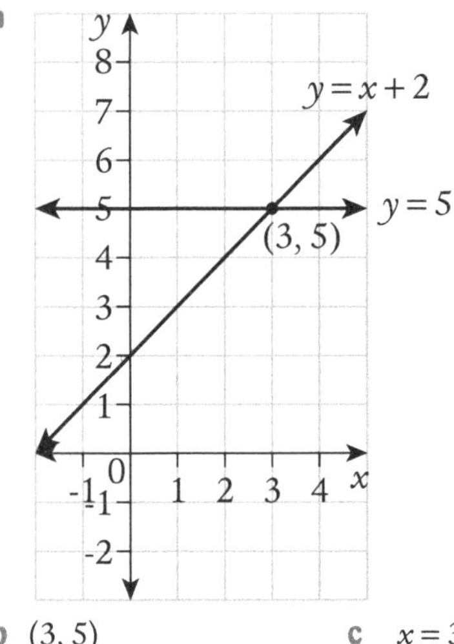

b (3, 5) c $x = 3$

7.4 NAPLAN-ready

$x = -1$

7.5 Solving problems using equations (p. 114)

1 $0.70

2 a $d + 221 = 386$ b $d = 165$

3 a Let x be the distance from the store in metres, $x + 340 = 925$

b Let c be the cost of a pencil in dollars, $11c = 10.45$

4 a $x = 585$ m b $c = \$0.95$

5 a Let n be the number of games

b $1.29n = 19.35$

c $n = 19.35 \div 1.29, n = 15$
$\therefore$ the number of games Kira can download is 15.

6 a $12n = 350$

b $n = 350 \div 12, n = 29.17$, so 30 vehicles

7 a Let x be the cost of a chicken burger in dollars, $2x + 1.80$.

b $2x + 1.80 = 10.20$
$2x = 8.40$
$x = 4.20$

Cost of a chicken burger is $4.20.

7.5 NAPLAN-ready

30

Chapter 8 Geometry

8.1 Angles review (p. 116)

1 a 90° b 180° c 270° d 360°

2 a 130 – 140° b 280 – 290°

3 67°

4 115°

5 a $w = 302°$ b $x = 32°$

6 a–b

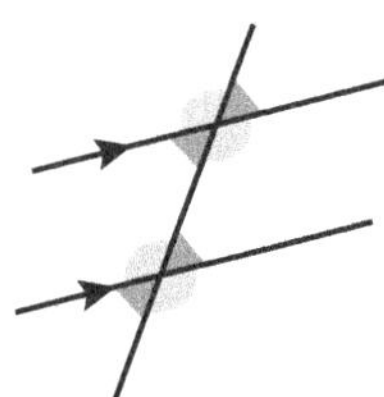

7 a $f = 58°$, f and 58° are alternate angles

b $m = 75°$, m and 105° are co-interior angles.

8.1 NAPLAN-ready

56°

8.2 Shapes review (p. 118)

1 a $m = 27°$ b $x = 47°$

2 $f = 60°$

3 $b = 95°, a = 85°, c = 85°$

4 $t = 150°$

5 a Parallelogram

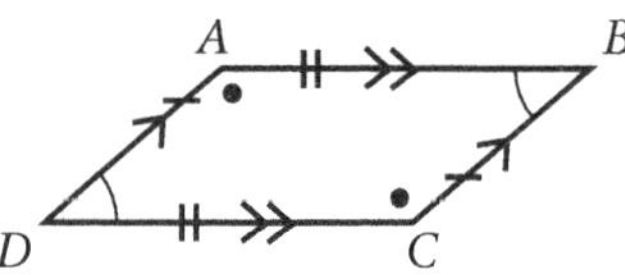

Opposite sides are of equal length $AB = CD$ $BC = AD$	Opposite sides are parallel $AB \parallel CD$ $BC \parallel AD$	Opposite angles are equal $\angle ABC = \angle ADC$ $\angle DAB = \angle BCD$

b Kite

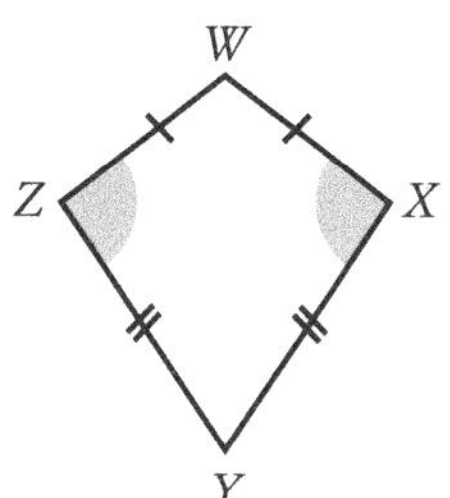

One pair of equal angles $\angle WZY = \angle WXY$

Two pairs of equal side lengths $WZ = WX$, $ZY = XY$

6 a 6 **b** $6 \times 180° = 1080°$

8.2 NAPLAN-ready

90°

8.3 Congruence and transformation (p. 120)

1 (4, 3)

2 a

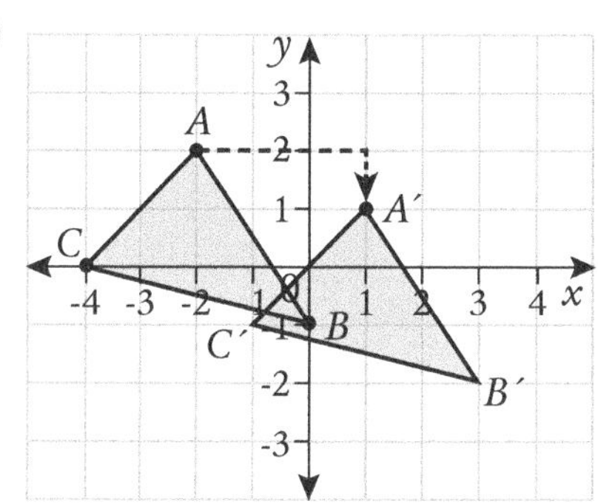

b $A'(1, 1)$ $B'(3, -2)$ $C'(-1, -1)$,

3 a–b

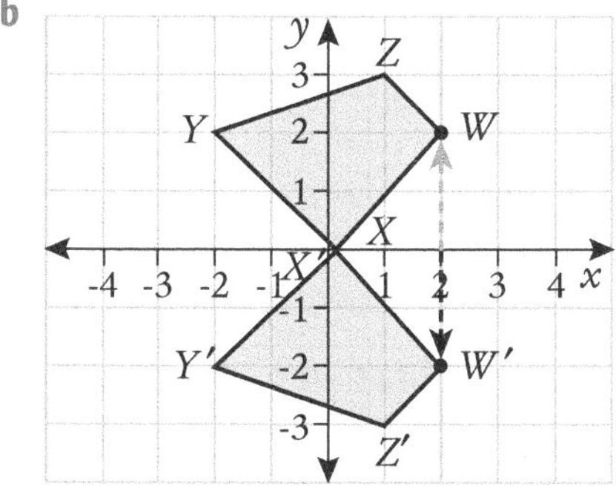

c $W'(2, -2)$ $X'(0, 0)$ $Y'(-2, -2)$ $Z'(1, -3)$

4

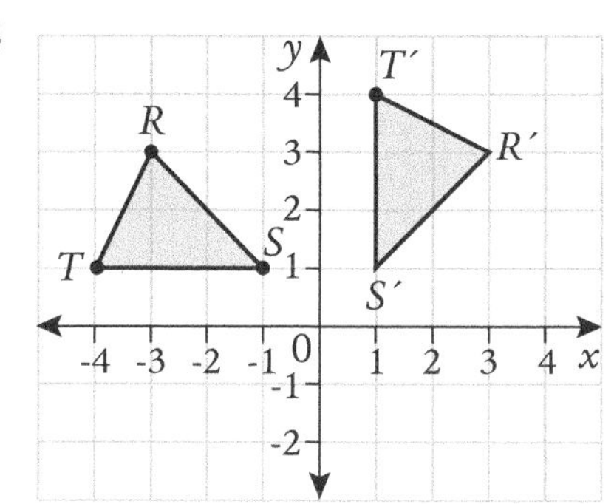

5 a

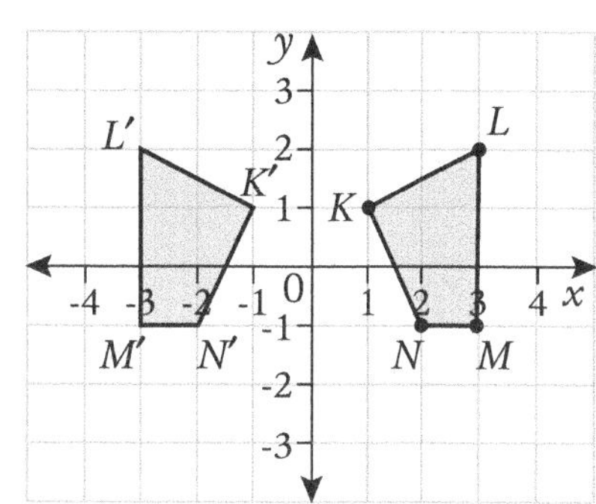

b reflection

6 a $A \leftrightarrow M$ $B \leftrightarrow J$ $C \leftrightarrow K$ **b** $CD \leftrightarrow KL$

c $\angle JKL \leftrightarrow \angle BCD$ **d** $ABCD \cong MJKL$

8.3 NAPLAN-ready

Reflection

8.4 Congruent triangles (p. 122)

1 a $D \leftrightarrow M$ $E \leftrightarrow N$ $F \leftrightarrow O$

b $DE \leftrightarrow MN$ $EF \leftrightarrow NO$ $FD \leftrightarrow OM$

c $\Delta DEF \cong \Delta MNO$

2 a $KM \leftrightarrow XZ$ $\angle KML \leftrightarrow \angle XZY$ $LM \leftrightarrow YZ$

b SAS

3 a $BC = YX$ (side)
$AC = WX$ (side)
$AB = WY$ (side)

b $AB = WY$ (side)
$\angle CAB = \angle XWY$ (angle)
$CA = XW$ (side)

c $\Delta ABC \cong \Delta WYX$ (SSS)

4 $\angle EFG = \angle VTU$ (angle) $\angle EGF = \angle VUT$ (angle)

$GF = UT$ (side) $\therefore \Delta EFG \cong \Delta VTU$ (AAS)

5

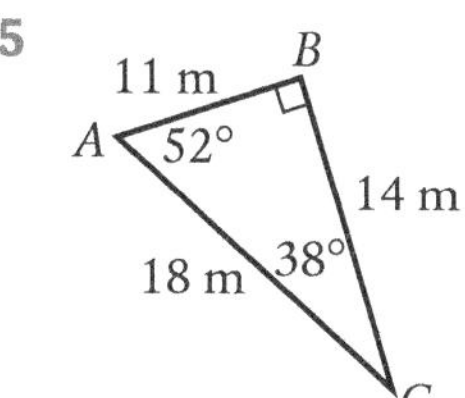

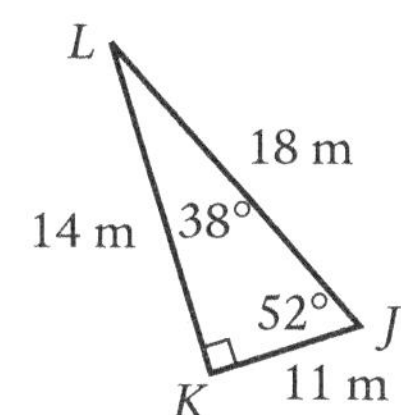

8.4 NAPLAN-ready

$\Delta RUT \cong \Delta TSR$

8.5 Congruence and quadrilaterals (p. 124)

1 a rectangle **b** kite

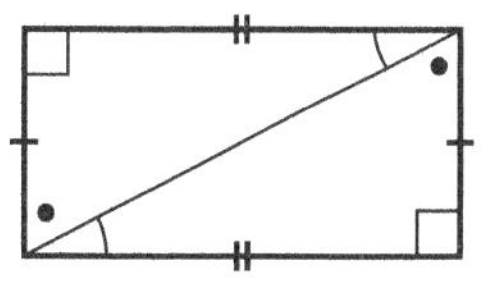

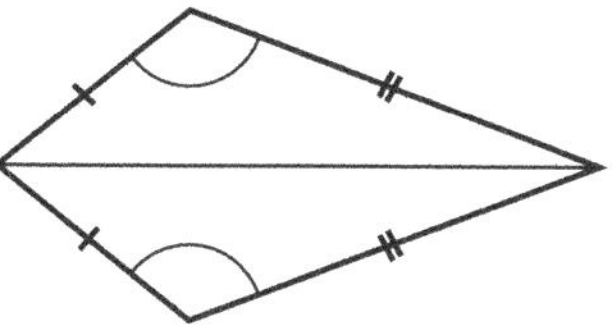

c rhombus **d** parallelogram

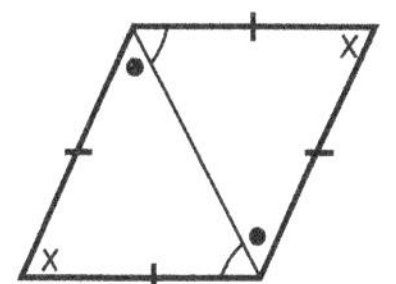

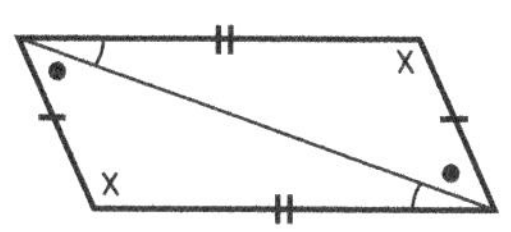

2 a Answers may vary. One possible answer is as follows:

$FG = DE$ (side) $DG = FE$ (side) DF (common side)

b $\Delta DEF \cong \Delta FGD$ (SSS)

3 a

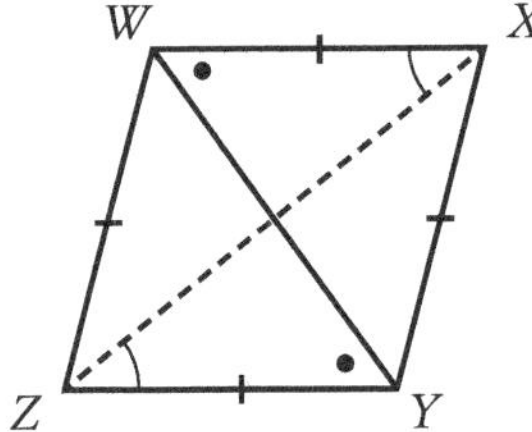

b $WX = YZ$ (side)
$WZ = YX$ (side)
WY (common side)
$\Delta WYZ \cong \Delta YWX$ (SSS)

c $UW = ZY$ (side)
$\angle UXW = \angle YXZ$ (vertically opposite angle)
$\angle UWX = \angle YZX$ (alternate angles)
$\Delta UWX \cong \Delta YZX$ (AAS)

d XW and XZ are equal
$\therefore$ one diagonal line bisects the other diagonal line.

4 a $a = 80°$ $b = 60°$ b $c = 90°$

c $p = 35°$ $q = 120°$ $r = 25°$

8.5 NAPLAN-ready

70°

Chapter 9 Statistics and probability

9.1 Population sampling (p. 126)

1 a Sample size = 24

b white: $\frac{10}{24}$

c $\frac{10}{24} \times 600 = 250$

2

	Proportion of sample	Estimated number per bag
Yellow	$\frac{6}{20}$	$\frac{6}{20} \times 120 = 36$
Orange	$\frac{5}{20}$	$\frac{5}{20} \times 120 = 30$
Green	$\frac{9}{20}$	$\frac{9}{20} \times 120 = 54$
	Total:	120

3 5% of 36 = 1.8
≈ 2

$36 - 2 = 34$

$36 + 2 = 38$

Therefore, it is estimated that there are between 34 and 38 yellow chocolate lollies in the bag.

4 a Biased – people who live close to work are more likely to travel home for lunch and therefore are less likely to be at a café.

b fair

5 a 12 b 20 c 4

d $\frac{20}{4} \times 12 = 60$

Therefore, an estimation of the number of crocodiles in that area of the Nesbit River is 60.

9.1 NAPLAN-ready

304 to 336

9.2 Using sample measures of centre and spread (p. 128)

1 a $\frac{2+0+0+1+2+4+1+1}{8} = \frac{11}{8} = 1.375$ siblings

b 0, 0, 1, 1, 1, 2, 2, 4
Median = 1 sibling

c Mode = 1 sibling

d Range = 4 − 0 = 4 siblings

2 a Mean = $\frac{115}{10} = 11.5$ minutes

b 3, 5, 8, 10, 11, 12, 12, 15, 16, 23

Median = 11.5 minutes

c Mode = 12 minutes

3 a i Set 1 mean: $\frac{56}{10} = 5.6$

Set 2 mean: $\frac{51}{10} = 5.1$

ii Set 1 median: 4

Set 2 median: 4

iii Set 1 range: 15 − 2 = 13

Set 2 range: 10 − 2 = 8

b

	Mean	Median	Mode	Range
Set 1	5.6	4	4	13
Set 2	5.1	4	4	8

The median and mode were unchanged by the different value. The mean was slightly changed. The range was significantly changed.

4 a 3 b 64

5 a i 6 ii 5 iii 5

b 15

c i 5 ii 5 iii 5 iv 6 − 4 = 2

d

	Mean	Median	Mode	Range
10 students (with outlier)	6	5	5	11
10 students (without outlier)	5	5	5	2

e The median and mode were unaffected by the outlier. The mean was slightly lower when the outlier was removed, making it the same (5) as the other measures of centre. The range was substantially lower when the outlier was removed.

9.2 NAPLAN-ready

Range

9.3 Frequency tables and graphs (p. 130)

1 a

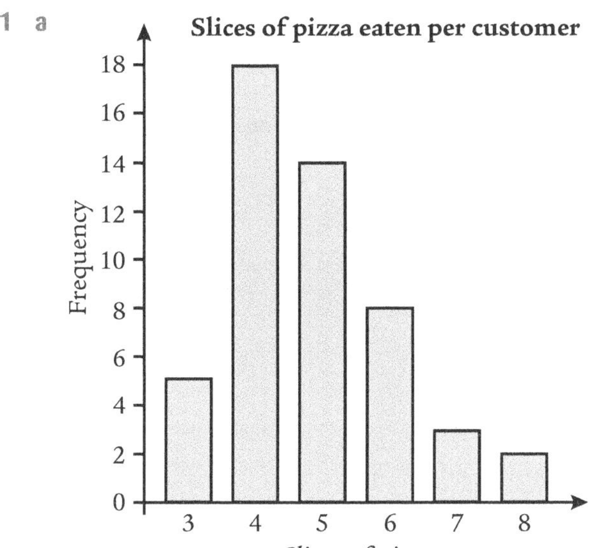

b 50

2 a Range = 26 − 1 = 25

b i Interval of 2 → $\frac{25}{2}$ = 12.5 groups (too many)

ii Interval of 5 → $\frac{25}{5}$ = 5 groups (good)

iii Interval of 10 → $\frac{25}{10}$ = 2.5 groups (not enough)

The most suitable class interval is 5.

c

Texts sent per day	Tally	Frequency
0–<5	𝍸 ||	7
5–<10	𝍸 |||	8
10–<15	𝍸	5
15–<20	𝍸	5
20–<25	||||	4
25–<30	|	1
	Total:	30

d

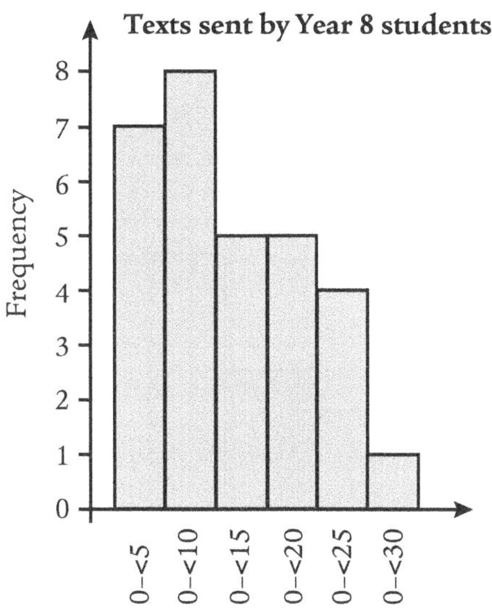

9.3 NAPLAN-ready

68

9.4 Statistics from grouped data (p. 132)

1 a 7 **b** 14.5 **c** 15 **d** 27.5

2 a

Number of rooms occupied at Eco Resort	x	frequency	$f \times x$
0–9	4.5	12	54
10–19	14.5	28	406
20–29	24.5	40	980
30–39	34.5	10	345
		$\Sigma f = 90$	$\Sigma fx = 1785$

b Mean: $\frac{1785}{90} = 19.83$

c Middle value is the $\frac{90+1}{2} = 45.5$, between the 45th and 46th number. Median class interval: 20–29

d Modal class interval: 20–29

3 a

Number of jars of honey sold	x	tally	frequency	$f \times x$
10–<20	15	|	1	15
20–<30	25	𝍸 |||	8	200
30–<40	35	𝍸 ||||	9	315
40–<50	45	𝍸 𝍸 ||	12	540
			$\Sigma f = 30$	$\Sigma fx = 1070$

b Mean: $\frac{1070}{30} \approx 36$

c The middle value is at $\frac{30+1}{2} = 15.5$, between the 15th and 16th value. Median class interval is 30–<40.

d Modal class interval is 40–<50.

e

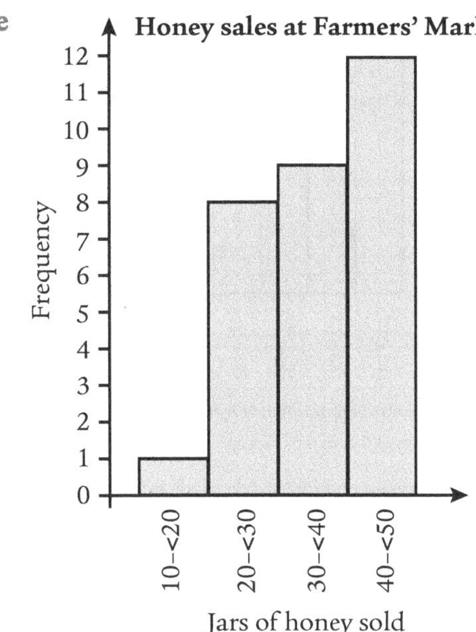

9.4 NAPLAN-ready

1–<2 minutes

9.5 Understanding probability (p. 134)

1 a 10

b i $\frac{3}{10}$ ii $\frac{5}{10}=\frac{1}{2}$

iii $\frac{2}{10}=\frac{1}{5}$ iv $\frac{7}{10}$

2 a

b i $\frac{5}{16}$ ii $\frac{10}{16}=\frac{5}{8}$ iii $\frac{7}{16}$

3 a 1, 2, 3, 4, 5, 6, 7, 8

b 8

c i $\frac{7}{8}$ ii $\frac{4}{8}=\frac{1}{2}$ iii $\frac{5}{8}$

4 $\frac{1}{11}$

5 a $\frac{1}{9}$ b $\frac{5}{9}$ c $\frac{8}{9}$

6 $\frac{3}{6}=\frac{1}{2}$

9.5 NAPLAN-ready

$\frac{2}{3}$

9.6 Theoretical probability for single-step experiments (p. 136)

1 a 1, 2, 3, 4 b heads, tails

c black, white, grey

2 a 1, 2, 3, 4, 5

$\therefore$ the number of possible outcomes is 5

b i $\frac{1}{5}$ ii $\frac{3}{5}$ iii $\frac{4}{5}$ iv $\frac{2}{5}$

3 a 52

b i $\frac{13}{52}=\frac{1}{4}$ ii $\frac{4}{52}=\frac{1}{13}$ iii $\frac{48}{52}=\frac{12}{13}$

4 a $1-0.5=0.5$ b $0.1+0.5=0.6$

c $0.4+0.5=0.9$, $1-0.9=0.1$

9.6 NAPLAN-ready

5

9.7 Venn diagrams and two-way tables A (p. 138)

1 a $n(\varepsilon)=33+26+14=73$

b i $n(W)=26$ ii $n(\text{not } B)=59$

2 a $n(\varepsilon)=5+23=28$

b i $\Pr(A)=\frac{23}{28}$ ii $\Pr(\text{not } A)=\frac{5}{28}$

3 a $n(\varepsilon)=27$

b i $\Pr(A \text{ and } B)=\frac{16}{27}$ ii $\Pr(A \text{ or } B)=\frac{23}{27}$

4 a i Set A: $\{2, 4, 6\}$ $n(A)=3$

ii Set B: $\{5, 6\} \rightarrow n(B)=2$

iii ε: $\{1, 2, 3, 4, 5, 6\} \rightarrow n(e)=6$

b

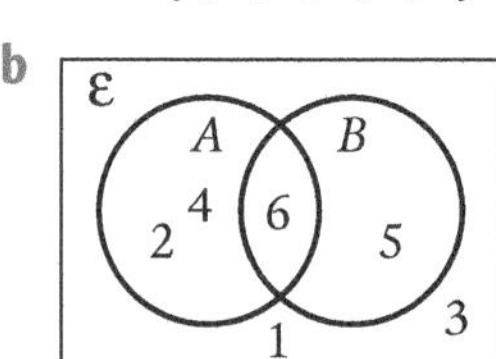

c i $\Pr(A)=\frac{3}{6}=\frac{1}{2}$ ii $\Pr(\text{not } B)=\frac{4}{6}=\frac{2}{3}$

iii $\Pr(A \text{ and } B)=\frac{1}{6}$ iv $\Pr(A \text{ or } B)=\frac{4}{6}=\frac{2}{3}$

9.7 Venn diagrams and two-way tables B (p. 140)

1 a $\frac{3}{4}$ b $\frac{5}{6}$ c $\frac{5}{12}$ d $\frac{2}{3}$

2 a

	White	Black
White	WW	BW
Black	WB	BB

b $n(\varepsilon) = 4$ c $\frac{2}{4} = \frac{1}{2}$

3 a

	1	2	3	4
Head	H, 1	H, 2	H, 3	H, 4
Tails	T, 1	T, 2	T, 3	T, 4

b $n(\varepsilon) = 8$

c i $\frac{1}{8}$ ii $\frac{2}{8} = \frac{1}{4}$

4 a $n(\varepsilon) = 36$

b i $\frac{6}{36} = \frac{1}{6}$ ii $\frac{5}{36}$ iii $\frac{10}{36} = \frac{5}{18}$

5 Pr(greater than 9) = $\frac{6}{36} = \frac{1}{6}$; Pr(a double) = $\frac{6}{36} = \frac{1}{6}$.

Both options have an equal probability, so either option can be selected.

6 Students' answers will vary.

9.7 NAPLAN-ready

$\frac{27}{50}$

Summary of important rules and formulas

Integer operations

Integer addition and subtraction

+	+	=	+	+	−	=	−
−	+	=	+	−	−	=	−

Integer multiplication and division

+	×	+	=	+	+	×	−	=	−
−	×	+	=	−	−	×	−	=	+
+	÷	+	=	+	+	÷	−	=	−
−	÷	+	=	−	−	÷	−	=	+

Measurement

Circumference of a circle

$C = \pi d$, d = diameter

$C = 2\pi r$, r = radius

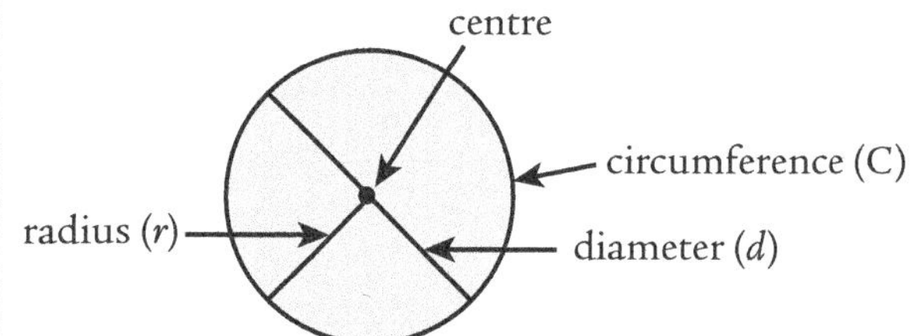

Area formulas

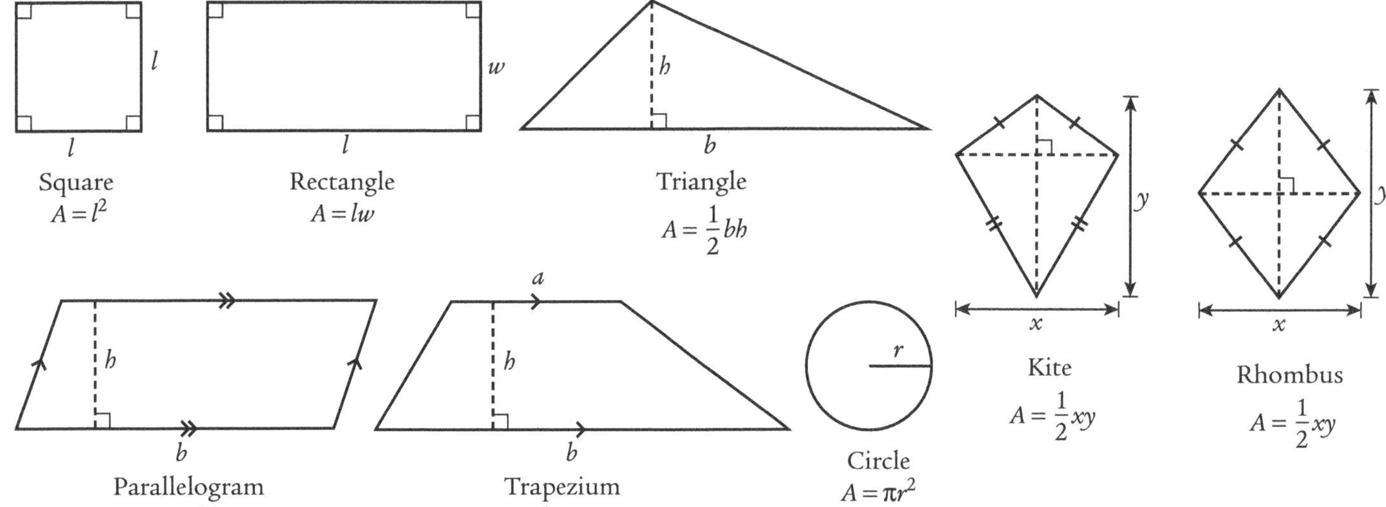

Square $A = l^2$

Rectangle $A = lw$

Triangle $A = \frac{1}{2}bh$

Kite $A = \frac{1}{2}xy$

Rhombus $A = \frac{1}{2}xy$

Parallelogram $A = bh$

Trapezium $A = \frac{1}{2}(a+b)h$

Circle $A = \pi r^2$

Converting units of length and area

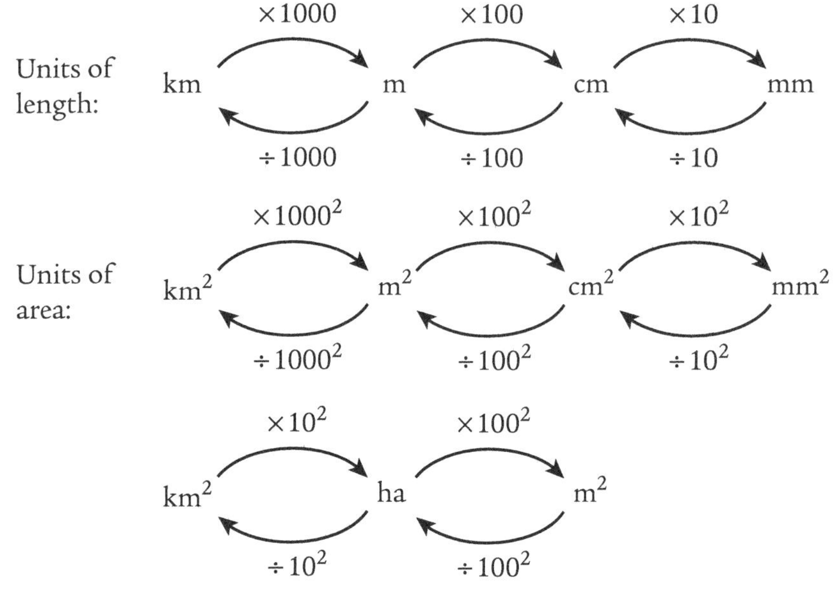

Volume formula

The formula for the volume of solids with a uniform cross-section:

$V = AH$

where A = area of the cross-section, H = height (H is perpendicular to A)

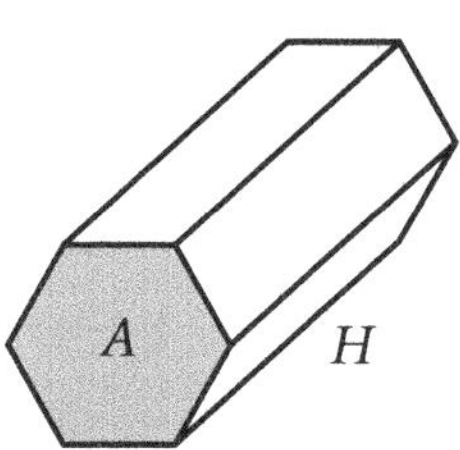

Converting units of volume and capacity

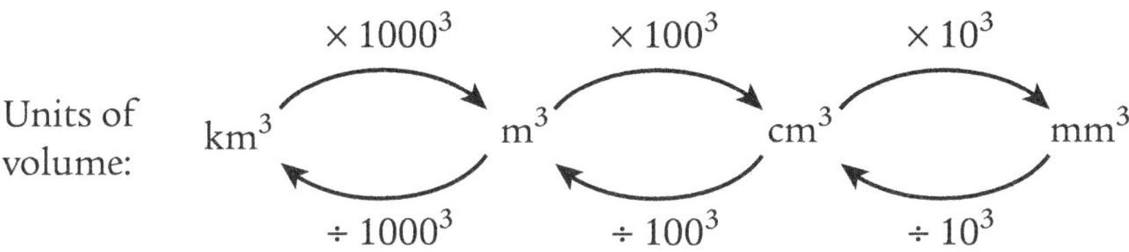

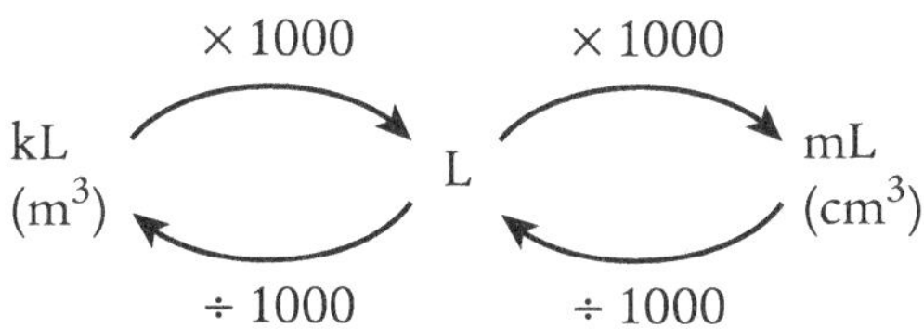

Angle properties

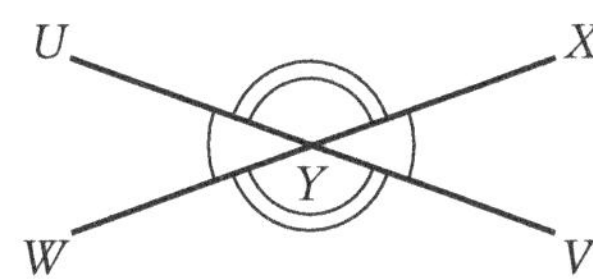

The lines UV and WX intersect at Y.

$\angle UYW = \angle XYV$ as they are a pair of vertically opposite angles.

$\angle UYX = \angle WYV$ as they are a pair of vertically opposite angles.

Vertically opposite angles are equal.

Complementary angles: a pair of angles that add to 90°

Supplementry angles: a pair of angles that add to 180°

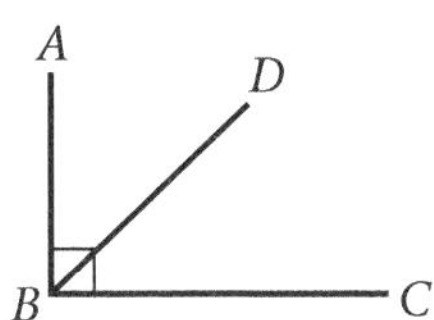

$\angle ABD + \angle DBC = 90°$

$\angle ABD$ and $\angle DBC$ are complementary angles.

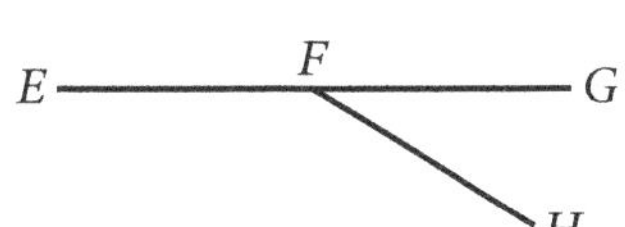

$\angle EFH + \angle GFH = 180°$

$\angle EFH$ and $\angle GFH$ are supplementary angles.

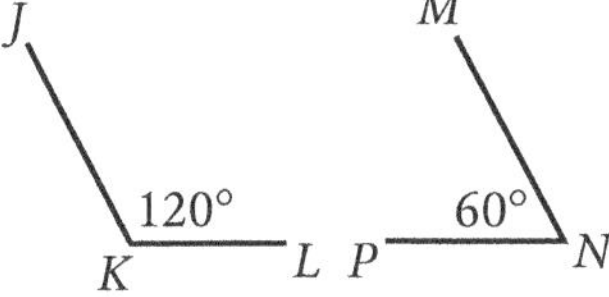

$\angle JKL + \angle MNP$ are supplementary angles.

Angles on parallel lines

A transversal is a line that intersects two or more other lines. When the lines that the transversal intersects are parallel:

- pairs of corresponding angles are equal
- pairs of alternate angles are equal
- pairs of co-interior angles are supplementary

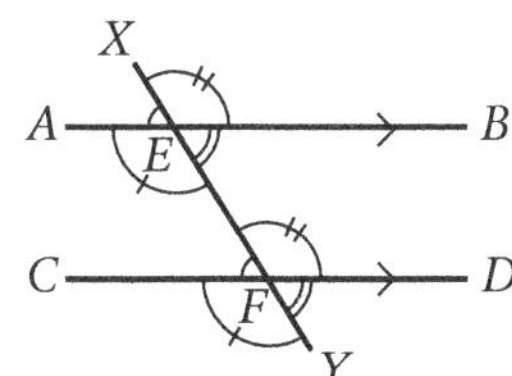

Four pairs of complementary angles
Two pairs of co-interior angles

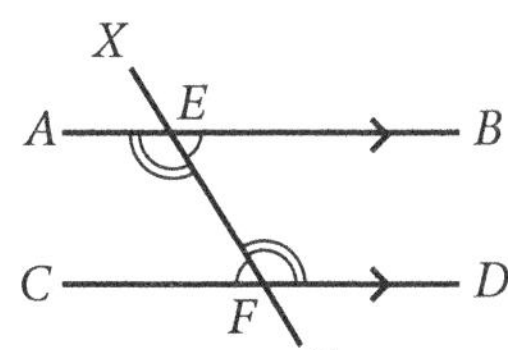

2 pairs of alternate angles

Angle sums

$a + b + c = 180°$

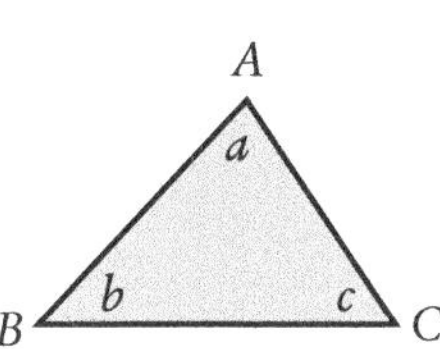

$z = x + y$

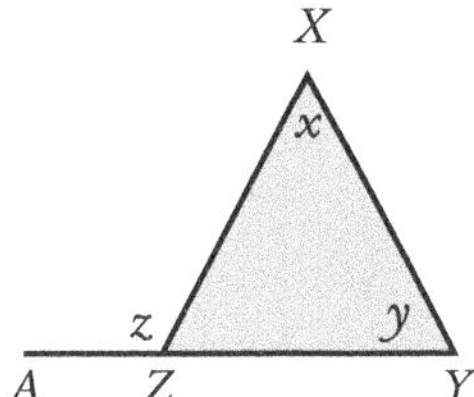

$a + b + c + d = 360°$

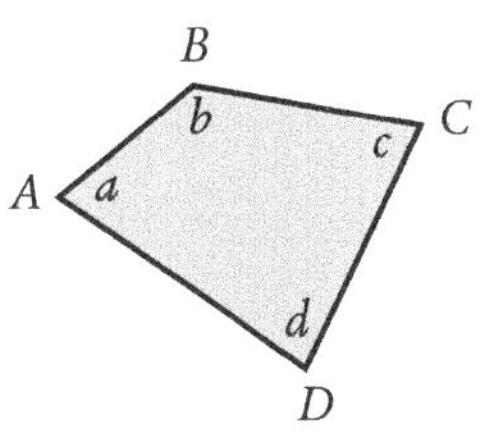